HOW TO
READ A BOOK

Mortimer J. Adler and Charles Van Doren

A Touchstone Book
Published by Simon & Schuster
New York   London   Toronto   Sydney   New Delhi

Touchstone
A Division of Simon & Schuster, Inc.
1230 Avenue of the Americas
New York, NY 10020

This Touchstone edition September 2014

TOUCHSTONE and colophon are registered trademarks of
Simon & Schuster, Inc.

For information about special discounts for bulk purchases,
please contact Simon & Schuster Special Sales at 1-866-506-1949
or business@simonandschuster.com.

The Simon & Schuster Speakers Bureau can bring authors to your
live event. For more information or to book an event contact the
Simon & Schuster Speakers Bureau at 1-866-248-3049 or visit our
website at www.simonspeakers.com.

Interior design by Lewelin Polanco
Cover design and illustration by Koppel & Scher

Manufactured in the United States of America

80 79 78 77 76 75 74 73 72 71

Library of Congress Catalog Card Number: 72-81451

ISBN 978-0-671-21209-4
ISBN 978-1-4391-4483-1 (ebook)

CONTENTS

Preface   ix

PART ONE
The Dimensions of Reading

1. *The Activity and Art of Reading*   3
   Active Reading 4 • The Goals of Reading: Reading for Information and Reading for Understanding 6 • Reading as Learning: The Difference Between Learning by Instruction and
   Learning by Discovery 11 • Present and Absent Teachers 14

2. *The Levels of Reading*   16

3. *The First Level of Reading: Elementary Reading*   21
   Stages of Learning to Read 24 • Stages and Levels 26 • Higher
   Levels of Reading and Higher Education 28 • Reading and the
   Democratic Ideal of Education 29

4. *The Second Level of Reading: Inspectional Reading*   31
   Inspectional Reading I: Systematic Skimming or Pre-reading
   32 • Inspectional Reading II: Superficial Reading 36 • On Reading Speeds 38 • Fixations and Regressions 40 • The Problem of
   Comprehension 41 • Summary of Inspectional Reading 42

5. *How to Be a Demanding Reader*   45
   The Essence of Active Reading: The Four Basic Questions a
   Reader Asks 46 • How to Make a Book Your Own 48 • The
   Three Kinds of Note-making 51 • Forming the Habit of
   Reading 52 • From Many Rules to One Habit 53

PART TWO

The Third Level of Reading: Analytical Reading

6. *Pigeonholing a Book*   59
   The Importance of Classifying Books 60 • What You Can
   Learn from the Title of a Book 61 • Practical vs. Theoretical
   Books 65 • Kinds of Theoretical Books 70

7. *X-raying a Book*   75
   Of Plots and Plans: Stating the Unity of a Book 78 • Mastering
   the Multiplicity: The Art of Outlining a Book 83 • The Reciprocal Arts of Reading and Writing 90 • Discovering the Author's Intentions 92 • The First Stage of Analytical Reading 94

8. *Coming to Terms with an Author*   96
   Words vs. Terms 96 • Finding the Key Words 100 • Technical
   Words and Special Vocabularies 103 • Finding the Meanings 106

9. *Determining an Author's Message*   113
   Sentences vs. Propositions 115 • Finding the Key Sentences
   119 • Finding the Propositions 123 • Finding the Arguments
   127 • Finding the Solutions 133 • The Second Stage of Analytical Reading 134

10. *Criticizing a Book Fairly*   136
    Teachability as a Virtue 138 • The Role of Rhetoric 139 • The
    Importance of Suspending Judgment 140 • The Importance
    of Avoiding Contentiousness 144 • On the Resolution of Dis-
    agreements 146

11. *Agreeing or Disagreeing with an Author*   150
    Prejudice and Judgment 152 • Judging the Author's Sound-
    ness 154 • Judging the Author's Completeness 158 • The
    Third Stage of Analytical Reading 161

12. *Aids to Reading*   166
    The Role of Relevant Experience 167 • Other Books as Ex-
    trinsic Aids to Reading 170 • How to Use Commentaries and
    Abstracts 171 • How to Use Reference Books 173 • How to
    Use a Dictionary 175 • How to Use an Encyclopedia 179

PART THREE
Approaches to Different Kinds of Reading Matter

13. *How to Read Practical Books*   187

The Two Kinds of Practical Books 189 • The Role of Persuasion 193 • What Does Agreement Entail in the Case of a Practical Book? 195

14. *How to Read Imaginative Literature*   198

How Not to Read Imaginative Literature 199 • General Rules for Reading Imaginative Literature 203

15. *Suggestions for Reading Stories, Plays, and Poems*   210

How to Read Stories 212 • A Note About Epics 217 • How to Read Plays 218 • A Note About Tragedy 220 • How to Read Lyric Poetry 222

16. *How to Read History*   229

The Elusiveness of Historical Facts 230 • Theories of History 232 • The Universal in History 234 • Questions to Ask of a Historical Book 236 • How to Read Biography and Autobiography 238 • How to Read About Current Events 243 • A Note on Digests 246

17. *How to Read Science and Mathematics*   249

Understanding the Scientific Enterprise 250 • Suggestions for Reading Classical Scientific Books 252 • Facing the Problem of Mathematics 254 • Handling the Mathematics in Scientific Books 258 • A Note on Popular Science 260

18. *How to Read Philosophy*   264

The Questions Philosophers Ask 265 • Modern Philosophy and the Great Tradition 269 • On Philosophical Method 271 • On Philosophical Styles 273 • Hints for Reading Philosophy 280 • On Making Up Your Own Mind 284 • A Note on Theology 285 • How to Read "Canonical" Books 287

19. *How to Read Social Science*   289

What Is Social Science? 290 • The Apparent Ease of Reading Social Science 292 • Difficulties of Reading Social Science 293 • Reading Social Science Literature 297

PART FOUR
The Ultimate Goals of Reading

20. *The Fourth Level of Reading: Syntopical Reading* 301
The Role of Inspection in Syntopical Reading 305 • The Five
Steps in Syntopical Reading 308 • The Need for Objectivity
314 • An Example of an Exercise in Syntopical Reading: The
Idea of Progress 317 • The Syntopicon and How to Use It 320
• On the Principles That Underlie Syntopical Reading 324 •
Summary of Syntopical Reading 326

21. *Reading and the Growth of the Mind* 328
What Good Books Can Do for Us 329 • The Pyramid of
Books 332 • The Life and Growth of the Mind 335

Appendix A. A Recommended Reading List 337

Appendix B. Exercises and Tests at the Four Levels
of Reading 355

Index 419

Preface

How to Read a Book was first published in the early months of 1940. To my surprise and, I confess, to my delight, it immediately became a best seller and remained at the top of the nationwide best-seller list for more than a year. Since 1940, it has continued to be widely circulated in numerous printings, both hardcover and paperback, and it has been translated into other languages—French, Swedish, German, Spanish, and Italian. Why, then, attempt to recast and rewrite the book for the present generation of readers?

The reasons for doing so lie in changes that have taken place both in our society in the last thirty years and in the subject itself. Today many more of the young men and women who complete high school enter and complete four years of college; a much larger proportion of the population has become literate in spite of or even because of the popularity of radio and television. There has been a shift of interest from the reading of fiction to the reading of nonfiction. The educators of the country have acknowledged that teaching the young to read, in the most elementary sense of that word, is our paramount educational problem. A recent Secretary of the Department of Health, Education, and Welfare, designating the seventies as the Decade of Reading, has dedicated federal funds in support of a wide variety of efforts to improve proficiency in this basic skill, and many of those efforts have scored some success at the level at which children are initiated into the art of reading. In addition, adults in large numbers have been captivated by the glittering promises made by speed-reading courses—promises to increase their comprehension of what they read as well as their speed in reading it.

However, certain things have not changed in the last thirty years. One constant is that, to achieve all the purposes of reading, the desideratum must be the ability to read different things at different—appropriate—speeds, not everything at the greatest possible speed. As Pascal observed three hundred years ago, "When we read too fast or too slowly, we understand nothing." Since speed-reading has become a national fad, this new edition of *How to Read a Book* deals with the problem and proposes variable-speed-reading as the solution, the aim being to read better, always better, but sometimes slower, sometimes faster.

Another thing that has not changed, unfortunately, is the failure to carry instruction in reading beyond the elementary level. Most of our educational ingenuity, money, and effort is spent on reading instruction in the first six grades. Beyond that, little formal training is provided to carry students to higher and quite distinct levels of skill. That was true in 1939 when Professor James Mursell of Columbia University's Teachers College wrote an article for the *Atlantic Monthly* entitled "The Failure of the Schools." What he said then, in two paragraphs that I am now going to quote, is still true.

Do pupils in school learn to read their mother tongue effectively? Yes and no. Up to the fifth and sixth grade, reading, on the whole, is effectively taught and well learned. To that level we find a steady and general improvement, but beyond it the curves flatten out to a dead level. This is not because a person arrives at his natural limit of efficiency when he reaches the sixth grade, for it has been shown again and again that with special tuition much older children, and also adults, can make enormous improvement. Nor does it mean that most sixth-graders read well enough for all practical purposes. A great many pupils do poorly in high school because of sheer ineptitude in getting meaning from the printed page. They can improve; they need to improve; but they don't.

The average high school graduate has done a great deal of reading, and if he goes on to college he will do a great deal more;

but he is likely to be a poor and incompetent reader. (Note that this holds true of the average student, not the person who is a subject for special remedial treatment.) He can follow a simple piece of fiction and enjoy it. But put him up against a closely written exposition, a carefully and economically stated argument, or a passage requiring critical consideration, and he is at a loss. It has been shown, for instance, that the average high school student is amazingly inept at indicating the central thought of a passage, or the levels of emphasis and subordination in an argument or exposition. To all intents and purposes he remains a sixth-grade reader till well along in college.

If there was a need for *How to Read a Book* thirty years ago, as the reception of the first edition of the book would certainly seem to indicate, the need is much greater today. But responding to that greater need is not the only, nor, for that matter, the main motive in rewriting the book. New insights into the problems of learning how to read; a much more comprehensive and better-ordered analysis of the complex art of reading; the flexible application of the basic rules to different types of reading, in fact to every variety of reading matter; the discovery and formulation of new rules of reading; and the conception of a pyramid of books to read, broad at the bottom and tapering at the top—all these things, not treated adequately or not treated at all in the book that I wrote thirty years ago, called for exposition and demanded the thorough rewriting that has now been done and is here being published.

The year after *How to Read a Book* was published, a parody of it appeared under the title *How to Read Two Books;* and Professor I. A. Richards wrote a serious treatise entitled *How to Read a Page.* I mention both these sequels in order to point out that the problems of reading suggested by both of these titles, the jocular as well as the serious one, are fully treated in this rewriting, especially the problem of how to read a number of related books in relation to one another and read them in such a way that the complementary and conflicting things they have to say about a common subject are clearly grasped.

Among the reasons for rewriting *How to Read a Book*, I have stressed the things to be said about the art of reading and the points to be made about the need for acquiring higher levels of skill in this art, which were not touched on or developed in the original version of the book. Anyone who wishes to discover how much has been added can do so quickly by comparing the present Table of Contents with that of the original version. Of the four parts, only Part Two, expounding the rules of Analytical Reading, closely parallels the content of the original, and even that has been largely recast. The introduction in Part One of the distinction of four levels of reading—elementary, inspectional, analytical, and syntopical—is the basic and controlling change in the book's organization and content. The exposition in Part Three of the different ways to approach different kinds of reading materials—practical and theoretical books, imaginative literature (lyric poetry, epics, novels, plays), history, science and mathematics, social science, and philosophy, as well as reference books, current journalism, and even advertising—is the most extensive addition that has been made. Finally, the discussion of Syntopical Reading in Part Four is wholly new.

In the work of updating, recasting, and rewriting this book, I have been joined by Charles Van Doren, who for many years now has been my associate at the Institute for Philosophical Research. We have worked together on other books, notably the twenty-volume *Annals of America,* published by Encyclopaedia Britannica, Inc., in 1969. What is, perhaps, more relevant to the present cooperative venture in which we have been engaged as co-authors is that during the last eight years Charles Van Doren and I have worked closely together in conducting discussion groups on great books and in moderating executive seminars in Chicago, San Francisco, and Aspen. In the course of these experiences, we acquired many of the new insights that have gone into the rewriting of this book.

I am grateful to Mr. Van Doren for the contribution he has made to our joint effort; and he and I together wish to express our deepest gratitude for all the constructive criticism, guidance, and help that we have received from our friend Arthur L. H. Rubin, who persuaded us to introduce many of the important changes that distinguish this book from its predecessor and make it, we hope, a better and more useful book.

MORTIMER J. ADLER
Boca Grande
March 26, 1972

PART 1

The Dimensions of Reading

1

The Activity and Art of Reading

This is a book for readers and for those who wish to become readers. Particularly, it is for readers of books. Even more particularly, it is for those whose main purpose in reading books is to gain increased understanding.

By "readers" we mean people who are still accustomed, as almost every literate and intelligent person used to be, to gain a large share of their information about and their understanding of the world from the written word. Not all of it, of course; even in the days before radio and television, a certain amount of information and understanding was acquired through spoken words and through observation. But for intelligent and curious people that was never enough. They knew that they had to read too, and they did read.

There is some feeling nowadays that reading is not as necessary as it once was. Radio and especially television have taken over many of the functions once served by print, just as photography has taken over functions once served by painting and other graphic arts. Admittedly, television serves some of these functions extremely well; the visual communication of news events, for example, has enormous impact. The ability of radio to give us information while we are engaged in doing other things—for instance, driving a car—is remarkable, and a great saving of time. But it may be seriously questioned whether the advent of modern communications media has much enhanced our understanding of the world in which we live.

Perhaps we know more about the world than we used to, and insofar as knowledge is prerequisite to understanding, that is all to the good. But knowledge is not as much a prerequisite to understanding as is commonly supposed. We do not have to *know* everything about something in order to *understand* it; too many facts are often as much of an obstacle to understanding as too few. There is a sense in which we moderns are inundated with facts to the detriment of understanding.

One of the reasons for this situation is that the very media we have mentioned are so designed as to make thinking seem unnecessary (though this is only an appearance). The packaging of intellectual positions and views is one of the most active enterprises of some of the best minds of our day. The viewer of television, the listener to radio, the reader of magazines, is presented with a whole complex of elements—all the way from ingenious rhetoric to carefully selected data and statistics—to make it easy for him to "make up his own mind" with the minimum of difficulty and effort. But the packaging is often done so effectively that the viewer, listener, or reader does not make up his own mind at all. Instead, he inserts a packaged opinion into his mind, somewhat like inserting a cassette into a cassette player. He then pushes a button and "plays back" the opinion whenever it seems appropriate to do so. He has performed acceptably without having had to think.

Active Reading

As we said at the beginning, we will be principally concerned in these pages with the development of skill in reading books; but the rules of reading that, if followed and practiced, develop such skill can be applied also to printed material in general, to any type of reading matter—to newspapers, magazines, pamphlets, articles, tracts, even advertisements.

Since reading of any sort is an activity, all reading must to some degree be active. Completely passive reading is impossible; we cannot read with our eyes immobilized and our minds asleep. Hence when we contrast active with passive reading, our purpose is, first, to call attention to the fact that reading can be *more* or *less* active, and second, to point out that the *more active* the reading the *better*. One reader is better than another in proportion as he is capable of a greater range of activity in reading and exerts more effort. He is better if he demands more of himself and of the text before him.

Though, strictly speaking, there can be no absolutely passive reading, many people think that, as compared with writing and speaking, which are obviously active undertakings, reading and listening are entirely passive. The writer or speaker must put out some effort, but no work need be done by the reader or listener. Reading and listening are thought of as *receiving* communication from someone who is actively engaged in *giving* or *sending* it. The mistake here is to suppose that receiving communication is like receiving a blow or a legacy or a judgment from the court. On the contrary, the reader or listener is much more like the catcher in a game of baseball.

Catching the ball is just as much an activity as pitching or hitting it. The pitcher or batter is the *sender* in the sense that his activity initiates the motion of the ball. The catcher or fielder is the *receiver* in the sense that his activity terminates it. Both are active, though the activities are different. If anything is passive, it is the ball. It is the inert thing that is put in motion or stopped, whereas the players are active, moving to pitch, hit, or catch. The analogy with writing and reading is almost perfect. The thing that is written and read, like the ball, is the passive object common to the two activities that begin and terminate the process.

We can take this analogy a step further. The art of catching is the skill of catching every kind of pitch—fast balls and curves, change-ups and knucklers. Similarly, the art of reading is the skill of catching every sort of communication as well as possible.

It is noteworthy that the pitcher and catcher are successful only to the extent that they cooperate. The relation of writer and reader is similar. The writer isn't trying *not* to be caught, although it sometimes seems so. Successful communication occurs in any case where what the writer wanted to have received finds its way into the reader's possession. The writer's skill and the reader's skill converge upon a common end.

Admittedly, writers vary, just as pitchers do. Some writers have excellent "control"; they know exactly what they want to convey, and they convey it precisely and accurately. Other things being equal, they are easier to "catch" than a "wild" writer without "control."

There is one respect in which the analogy breaks down. The ball is a simple unit. It is either *completely* caught or not. A piece of writing, however, is a complex object. It can be received more or less completely, all the way from very little of what the writer intended to the whole of it. The amount the reader "catches" will usually depend on the amount of activity he puts into the process, as well as upon the skill with which he executes the different mental acts involved.

What does active reading entail? We will return to this question many times in this book. For the moment, it suffices to say that, given the same thing to read, one person reads it better than another, first, by reading it more actively, and second, by performing each of the acts involved more skillfully. These two things are related. Reading is a complex activity, just as writing is. It consists of a large number of separate acts, all of which must be performed in a good reading. The person who can perform more of them is better able to read.

The Goals of Reading: Reading for Information and Reading for Understanding

You have a mind. Now let us suppose that you also have a book that you want to read. The book consists of language written by someone for the sake of communicating something to you. Your success in reading it is determined by the extent to which you receive everything the writer intended to communicate.

That, of course, is too simple. The reason is that there are two possible relations between your mind and the book, not just one. These two relations are exemplified by two different experiences that you can have in reading your book.

There is the book; and here is your mind. As you go through the pages, either you understand perfectly everything the author has to say or you do not. If you do, you may have gained information, but you could not have increased your understanding. If the book is completely intelligible to you from start to finish, then the author and you are as two minds in the same mold. The symbols on the page merely express the common understanding you had before you met.

Let us take our second alternative. You do not understand the book perfectly. Let us even assume—what unhappily is not always true—that you understand enough to know that you do not understand it all. You know the book has more to say than you understand and hence that it contains something that can increase your understanding.

What do you do then? You can take the book to someone else who, you think, can read better than you, and have him explain the parts that trouble you. ("He" may be a living person or another book—a commentary or textbook.) Or you may decide that what is over your head is not worth bothering about, that you understand enough. In either case, you are not doing the job of reading that the book requires.

That is done in only one way. Without external help of any sort, you go to work on the book. With nothing but the power of your own mind, you operate on the symbols before you in such a way that you gradually lift yourself from *a state of understanding less to one of understanding more*. Such elevation, accomplished by the mind working on a book, is highly skilled reading, the kind of reading that a book which challenges your understanding deserves.

Thus we can roughly define what we mean by the art of reading as follows: the process whereby a mind, with nothing to operate on but the symbols of the readable matter, and with no help from outside,* elevates itself by the power of its own operations. The mind passes from understanding less to understanding more. The skilled operations that cause this to happen are the various acts that constitute the art of reading.

To pass from understanding less to understanding more by your own intellectual effort in reading is something like pulling yourself up by your bootstraps. It certainly feels that way. It is a major exertion. Obviously, it is a more active kind of reading than you have done before, entailing not only more varied activity but also much more skill in the performance of the various acts required. Obviously, too, the things that are usually regarded as more difficult to read, and hence as only for the better reader, are those that are more likely to deserve and demand this kind of reading.

The distinction between reading for information and reading for understanding is deeper than this. Let us try to say more about it. We will have to consider both goals of reading because the line between what is readable in one way and what must be read in the other is often hazy. To the extent that we can keep these two goals of reading distinct, we can employ the word "reading" in two distinct senses.

The first sense is the one in which we speak of ourselves as reading newspapers, magazines, or anything else that, according to our skill and talents, is at once thoroughly intelligible to us. Such things may increase our store of information, but they cannot improve our understanding, for our understanding was equal to them before we started. Otherwise, we would have felt the shock of puzzlement and

---

* There is one kind of situation in which it is appropriate to ask for outside help in reading a difficult book. This exception is discussed in Chapter 18.

perplexity that comes from getting in over our depth—that is, if we were both alert and honest.

The second sense is the one in which a person tries to read something that at first he does not completely understand. Here the thing to be read is initially better or higher than the reader. The writer is communicating something that can increase the reader's understanding. Such communication between unequals must be possible, or else one person could never learn from another, either through speech or writing. Here by "learning" is meant understanding more, not remembering more information that has the same degree of intelligibility as other information you already possess.

There is clearly no difficulty of an intellectual sort about gaining new information in the course of reading if the new facts are of the same sort as those you already know. A person who knows some of the facts of American history and understands them in a certain light can readily acquire by reading, in the first sense, more such facts and understand them in the same light. But suppose he is reading a history that seeks not merely to give him some more facts but also to throw a new and perhaps more revealing light on *all* the facts he knows. Suppose there is greater understanding available here than he possessed before he started to read. If he can manage to acquire that greater understanding, he is reading in the second sense. He has indeed elevated himself by his activity, though indirectly, of course, the elevation was made possible by the writer who had something to teach him.

What are the conditions under which this kind of reading— reading for understanding—takes place? There are two. First, there is *initial inequality in understanding.* The writer must be "superior" to the reader in understanding, and his book must convey in readable form the insights he possesses and his potential readers lack. Second, *the reader must be able to overcome this inequality in some degree,* seldom perhaps fully, but always approaching equality with the writer. To the extent that equality is approached, clarity of communication is achieved.

In short, we can learn only from our "betters." We must know who they are and how to learn from them. The person who has this sort of knowledge possesses the art of reading in the sense with which we are especially concerned in this book. Everyone who can read at all probably has some ability to read in this way. But all of us, without exception, can learn to read better and gradually gain more by our efforts through applying them to more rewarding materials.

We do not want to give the impression that facts, leading to increased information, and insights, leading to increased understanding, are always easy to distinguish. And we would admit that sometimes a mere recital of facts can itself lead to greater understanding. The point we want to emphasize here is that this book is about the art of reading for the sake of increased understanding. Fortunately, if you learn to do that, reading for information will usually take care of itself.

Of course, there is still another goal of reading, besides gaining information and understanding, and that is entertainment. However, this book will not be much concerned with reading for entertainment. It is the least demanding kind of reading, and it requires the least amount of effort. Furthermore, there are no rules for it. Everyone who knows how to read at all can read for entertainment if he wants to.

In fact, any book that can be read for understanding or information can probably be read for entertainment as well, just as a book that is capable of increasing our understanding can also be read purely for the information it contains. (This proposition cannot be reversed: it is *not* true that *every* book that can be read for entertainment can also be read for understanding.) Nor do we wish to urge you never to read a good book for entertainment. The point is, if you wish to read a good book for understanding, we believe we can help you. Our subject, then, is the art of reading good books when understanding is the aim you have in view.

Reading as Learning: The Difference Between Learning by Instruction and Learning by Discovery

Getting more information is learning, and so is coming to understand what you did not understand before. But there is an important difference between these two kinds of learning.

To be informed is to know simply that something is the case. To be enlightened is to know, in addition, what it is all about: why it is the case, what its connections are with other facts, in what respects it is the same, in what respects it is different, and so forth.

This distinction is familiar in terms of the differences between being able to remember something and being able to explain it. If you remember what an author says, you have learned something from reading him. If what he says is true, you have even learned something about the world. But whether it is a fact about the book or a fact about the world that you have learned, you have gained nothing but information if you have exercised only your memory. You have not been enlightened. Enlightenment is achieved only when, in addition to knowing what an author says, you know what he means and why he says it.

It is true, of course, that you should be able to remember what the author said as well as know what he meant. Being informed is prerequisite to being enlightened. The point, however, is not to stop at being informed.

Montaigne speaks of "an abecedarian ignorance that precedes knowledge, and a doctoral ignorance that comes after it." The first is the ignorance of those who, not knowing their ABC's, cannot read at all. The second is the ignorance of those who have misread many books. They are, as Alexander Pope rightly calls them, bookful blockheads, ignorantly read. There have always been literate ignoramuses who have read too widely and not well. The Greeks had a name for such a mixture of learning and folly which might be applied to the bookish but poorly read of all ages. They are all *sophomores*.

To avoid this error—the error of assuming that to be widely read and to be well-read are the same thing—we must consider a certain distinction in types of learning. This distinction has a significant bearing on the whole business of reading and its relation to education generally.

In the history of education, men have often distinguished between learning by instruction and learning by discovery. Instruction occurs when one person teaches another through speech or writing. We can, however, gain knowledge without being taught. If this were not the case, and every teacher had to be taught what he in turn teaches others, there would be no beginning in the acquisition of knowledge. Hence, there must be discovery—the process of learning something by research, by investigation, or by reflection, without being taught.

Discovery stands to instruction as learning without a teacher stands to learning through the help of one. In both cases, the activity of learning goes on in the one who learns. It would be a mistake to suppose that discovery is active learning and instruction passive. There is no inactive learning, just as there is no inactive reading.

This is so true, in fact, that a better way to make the distinction clear is to call instruction "aided discovery." Without going into learning theory as psychologists conceive it, it is obvious that teaching is a very special art, sharing with only two other arts—agriculture and medicine—an exceptionally important characteristic. A doctor may do many things for his patient, but in the final analysis it is the patient himself who must get well—grow in health. The farmer does many things for his plants or animals, but in the final analysis it is they that must grow in size and excellence. Similarly, although the teacher may help his student in many ways, it is the student himself who must do the learning. Knowledge must grow in his mind if learning is to take place.

The difference between learning by instruction and learning by discovery—or, as we would prefer to say, between aided and unaided discovery—is primarily a difference in the materials on which the learner works. When he is being instructed—discovering with the help of a teacher—the learner acts on something communicated to him. He performs operations on discourse, written or oral. He learns by acts of reading or listening. Note here the close relation between reading and listening. If we ignore the minor differences between these two ways of receiving communication, we can say that reading and listening are the same art—the art of being taught. When, however, the learner proceeds without the help of any sort of teacher, the operations of learning are performed on nature or the world rather than on discourse. The rules of such learning constitute the art of unaided discovery. If we use the word "reading" loosely, we can say that discovery—strictly, unaided discovery—is the art of reading nature or the world, as instruction (being taught, or aided discovery) is the art of reading books or, to include listening, of learning from discourse.

What about thinking? If by "thinking" we mean the use of our minds to gain knowledge or understanding, and if learning by discovery and learning by instruction exhaust the ways of gaining knowledge, then thinking must take place during both of these two activities. We must think in the course of reading and listening, just as we must think in the course of research. Naturally, the kinds of thinking are different—as different as the two ways of learning are.

The reason why many people regard thinking as more closely associated with research and unaided discovery than with being taught is that they suppose reading and listening to be relatively effortless. It is probably true that one does less thinking when one reads for information or entertainment than when one is undertaking to discover something. Those are the less active sorts of reading. But it is not true of the more active reading—the effort to understand. No one who has done this sort of reading would say it can be done thoughtlessly.

Thinking is only one part of the activity of learning. One must also use one's senses and imagination. One must observe, and remember, and construct imaginatively what cannot be observed. There is, again, a tendency to stress the role of these activities in the process of unaided discovery and to forget or minimize their place in the process of being taught through reading or listening. For example, many people assume that though a poet must use his imagination in writing a poem, they do not have to use their imagination in reading it. The art of reading, in short, includes all of the same skills that are involved in the art of unaided discovery: keenness of observation, readily available memory, range of imagination, and, of course, an intellect trained in analysis and reflection. The reason for this is that reading in this sense is discovery, too—although with help instead of without it.

Present and Absent Teachers

We have been proceeding as if reading and listening could both be treated as learning from teachers. To some extent that is true. Both are ways of being instructed, and for both one must be skilled in the art of being taught. Listening to a course of lectures, for example, is in many respects like reading a book; and listening to a poem is like reading it. Many of the rules to be formulated in this book apply to such experiences. Yet there is good reason to place primary emphasis on reading, and let listening become a secondary concern. The reason is that listening is learning from a teacher who is present—a living teacher—while reading is learning from one who is absent.

If you ask a living teacher a question, he will probably answer you. If you are puzzled by what he says, you can save yourself the trouble of thinking by asking him what he means. If, however, you ask a book a question, *you must answer it yourself*. In this respect a book is like nature or the world. When you question it, it answers you only to the extent that you do the work of thinking and analysis yourself.

This does not mean, of course, that if the living teacher answers your question, you have no further work. That is so only if the question is simply one of fact. But if you are seeking an explanation, you have to understand it or nothing has been explained to you. Nevertheless, with the living teacher available to you, you are given a lift in the direction of understanding him, as you are not when the teacher's words in a book are all you have to go by.

Students in school often read difficult books with the help and guidance of teachers. But for those of us who are not in school, and indeed also for those of us who are when we try to read books that are not required or assigned, our continuing education depends mainly on books alone, read without a teacher's help. Therefore if we are disposed to go on learning and discovering, we must know how to make books teach us well. That, indeed, is the primary goal of this book.

2

The Levels of Reading

In the preceding chapter, we made some distinctions that will be important in what follows. The goal a reader seeks—be it entertainment, information or understanding—determines the way he reads. The effectiveness with which he reads is determined by the amount of effort and skill he puts into his reading. In general, the rule is: the more effort the better, at least in the case of books that are initially beyond our powers as readers and are therefore capable of raising us from a condition of understanding less to one of understanding more. Finally, the distinction between instruction and discovery (or between aided and unaided discovery) is important because most of us, most of the time, have to read without anyone to help us. Reading, like unaided discovery, is learning from an absent teacher. We can only do that successfully if we know how.

But important as these distinctions are, they are relatively insignificant compared to the points we are going to make in this chapter. These all have to do with the levels of reading. The differences between the levels must be understood before any effective improvement in reading skills can occur.

There are four levels of reading. They are here called levels rather than kinds because kinds, strictly speaking, are distinct from one another, whereas it is characteristic of levels that higher ones include lower ones. So it is with the levels of reading, which are cumulative. The first level is not lost in the second, the second in the third, the third in the fourth. In fact, the fourth and highest level of reading includes all the others. It simply goes beyond them.

The first level of reading we will call Elementary Reading. Other names might be rudimentary reading, basic reading or initial reading; any one of these terms serves to suggest that as one masters this level one passes from nonliteracy to at least beginning literacy. In mastering this level, one learns the rudiments of the art of reading, receives basic training in reading, and acquires initial reading skills. We prefer the name elementary reading, however, because this level of reading is ordinarily learned in elementary school.

The child's first encounter with reading is at this level. His problem then (and ours when we began to read) is to recognize the individual words on the page. The child sees a collection of black marks on a white ground (or perhaps white marks on a black ground, if he is reading from a blackboard); what the marks say is, "The cat sat on the hat." The first grader is not really concerned at this point with whether cats do sit on hats, or with what this implies about cats, hats, and the world. He is merely concerned with language as it is employed by the writer.

At this level of reading, the question asked of the reader is "What does the sentence say?" That could be conceived as a complex and difficult question, of course. We mean it here, however, in its simplest sense.

The attainment of the skills of elementary reading occurred some time ago for almost all who read this book. Nevertheless, we continue to experience the problems of this level of reading, no matter how capable we may be as readers. This happens, for example, whenever we come upon something we want to read that is written in a foreign language that we do not know very well. Then our first effort must be to identify the actual words. Only after recognizing them individually can we begin to try to understand them, to struggle with perceiving what they mean.

Even when they are reading material written in their own language, many readers continue to have various kinds of difficulties at this level of reading. Most of these difficulties are mechanical, and some of them can be traced back to early instruction in reading. Overcoming these difficulties usually allows us to read faster; hence, most speed reading courses concentrate on this level. We will have more to say about elementary reading in the next chapter; and in Chapter 4, we will discuss speed reading.

The second level of reading we will call Inspectional Reading. It is characterized by its special emphasis on time. When reading at this level, the student is allowed a set time to complete an assigned amount of reading. He might be allowed fifteen minutes to read this book, for instance—or even a book twice as long.

Hence, another way to describe this level of reading is to say that its aim is to get the most out of a book within a given time—usually a relatively short time, and always (by definition) too short a time to get out of the book everything that can be gotten.

Still another name for this level might be skimming or pre-reading. However, we do not mean the kind of skimming that is characterized by casual or random browsing through a book. Inspectional reading is the art of *skimming systematically*.

When reading at this level, your aim is to examine the surface of the book, to learn everything that the surface alone can teach you. That is often a good deal.

Whereas the question that is asked at the first level is "What does the sentence say?" the question typically asked at this level is "What is the book about?" That is a surface question; others of a similar nature are "What is the structure of the book?" or "What are its parts?"

Upon completing an inspectional reading of a book, no matter how short the time you had to do it in, you should also be able to answer the question, "What kind of book is it—a novel, a history, a scientific treatise?"

Chapter 4 is devoted to an account of this level of reading, so we will not discuss it further here. We do want to stress, however, that most people, even many quite good readers, are unaware of the value of inspectional reading. They start a book on page one and plow steadily through it, without even reading the table of contents. They are thus faced with the task of achieving a superficial knowledge of the book *at the same time that they are trying to understand it*. That compounds the difficulty.

The third level of reading we will call Analytical Reading. It is both a more complex and a more systematic activity than either of the two levels of reading discussed so far. Depending on the difficulty of the text to be read, it makes more or less heavy demands on the reader.

Analytical reading is thorough reading, complete reading, or good reading—the best reading you can do. If inspectional reading is the best and most complete reading that is possible given a limited time, then analytical reading is the best and most complete reading that is possible given unlimited time.

The analytical reader must ask many, and organized, questions of what he is reading. We do not want to state these questions here, since this book is mainly about reading at this level: Part Two gives its rules and tells you how to do it. We do want to emphasize here that analytical reading is always intensely active. On this level of reading, the reader grasps a book—the metaphor is apt—and works at it until the book becomes his own. Francis Bacon once remarked that "some books are to be tasted, others to be swallowed, and some few to be chewed and digested." Reading a book analytically is chewing and digesting it.

We also want to stress that analytical reading is hardly ever necessary if your goal in reading is simply information or entertainment. *Analytical reading is preeminently for the sake of understanding.* Conversely, bringing your mind with the aid of a book from a condition of understanding less to one of understanding more is almost impossible unless you have at least some skill in analytical reading.

The fourth and highest level of reading we will call Syntopical Reading. It is the most complex and systematic type of reading of all.

It makes very heavy demands on the reader, even if the materials he is reading are themselves relatively easy and unsophisticated.

Another name for this level might be comparative reading. When reading syntopically, the reader reads many books, not just one, and places them in relation to one another and to a subject about which they all revolve. But mere comparison of texts is not enough. Syntopical reading involves more. With the help of the books read, the syntopical reader is able to construct an analysis of the subject that *may not be in any of the books.* It is obvious, therefore, that syntopical reading is the most active and effortful kind of reading.

We will discuss syntopical reading in Part Four. Let it suffice for the moment to say that syntopical reading is not an easy art, and that the rules for it are not widely known. Nevertheless, syntopical reading is probably the most rewarding of all reading activities. The benefits are so great that it is well worth the trouble of learning how to do it.

3

The First Level of Reading: Elementary Reading

Ours is a time of great interest in and concern about reading. Public officials have declared that the 1970s will be "the decade of reading." Best-selling books tell us why Johnny can or can't read. Research and experimentation in all fields of initial reading instruction proceed at an ever-increasing pace.

Three historical trends or movements have converged upon our time to produce this ferment. The first is the continuing effort of the United States to educate all of its citizens, which means, of course, at a minimum, to make them all literate. This effort, which Americans have supported almost from the beginning of the national existence and which is one of the cornerstones of our democratic way of life, has had remarkable results. Near-universal literacy was obtained in the United States earlier than anywhere else, and this in turn has helped us to become the highly developed industrial society that we are at the present day. But there have been enormous problems, too. They can be summed up in the observation that teaching a small percentage of highly motivated children, most of them the children of literate parents, to read—as was the case a century ago—is a far cry from teaching every child to read, no matter how little motivated he may be, or how deprived his background.

The second historical trend is in the teaching of reading itself. As late as 1870, reading instruction was little changed from what it had been in Greek and Roman schools. In America, at least, the so-called ABC method was dominant throughout most of the nineteenth century. Children were taught to sound out the letters of the alphabet individually— hence the name of this method—and to combine them in syllables, first two letters at a time and then three and four, whether the syllables so constructed were meaningful or not. Thus, syllables such as *ab, ac, ad, ib, ic* were practiced for the sake of mastery of the language. When a child could name all of a determined number of combinations, he was said to know his ABC's.

This synthetic method of teaching reading came under heavy criticism around the middle of the last century, and two alternatives to it were proposed. One was a variant on the synthetic ABC method, known as the phonic method. Here the word was recognized by its sounds rather than by its letter-names. Complicated and ingenious systems of printing were evolved for the purpose of representing the different sounds made by a single letter, especially the vowels. If you are fifty or over, it is probable that you learned to read using some variant of the phonic method.

A wholly different approach, analytical rather than synthetic, originated in Germany and was advocated by Horace Mann and other educators after about 1840. This involved teaching the *visual* recognition of whole words before giving any attention to letter-names or letter-sounds. This so-called sight method was later extended so that whole sentences, representing units of thought, were introduced first, with the pupils only later learning to recognize the constituent words and then, finally, the constituent letters. This method was especially popular during the 1920s and 30s, which period was also characterized by the shift in emphasis from oral reading to silent reading. It was found that ability to read orally did not necessarily mean ability to read silently and that instruction in oral reading was not always adequate if silent reading was the goal. Thus, an almost exclusive emphasis on rapid, comprehensive silent reading was a feature of the years from about 1920 to 1925. More recently, however, the pendulum has swung back again toward phonics, which indeed had never entirely left the curriculum.

All of these different methods of teaching elementary reading were successful for some pupils, unsuccessful for others. In the last two or three decades, it has perhaps been the failures that have attracted the most attention. And here the third historical trend comes into play. It is traditional in America to criticize the schools; for more than a century, parents, self-styled experts, and educators themselves have attacked and indicted the educational system. No aspect of schooling has been more severely criticized than reading instruction. The current books have a long ancestry, and every innovation carries in its train a posse of suspicious and, one feels, unpersuadable observers.

The critics may or may not be right, but in any event the problems have taken on a new urgency as the continuing effort to educate all citizens has entered a new phase, resulting in ever-growing high school and college populations. A young man or woman who cannot read very well is hindered in his pursuit of the American dream, but that remains largely a personal matter if he is not in school. If he remains in school or goes to college, however, it is a matter of concern for his teachers as well, and for his fellow students.

Hence, researchers are very active at the present time, and their work has resulted in numerous new approaches to reading instruction. Among the more important new programs are the so-called eclectic approach, the individualized reading approach, the language-experience approach, the various approaches based on linguistic principles, and others based more or less closely on some kind of programmed instruction. In addition, new mediums such as the Initial Teaching Alphabet (i.t.a.) have been employed, and sometimes these involve new methods as well. Still other devices and programs are the "total immersion method," the "foreign-language-school method," and the method known variously as the "see-say," "look-say," "look-and-say," or "word method." Doubtless experiments are now being undertaken in methods and approaches that differ from all of these. It is perhaps too early to tell whether any of these is the long-sought panacea for all reading ills.

Stages of Learning to Read

One useful finding of recent research is the analysis of stages in learning to read. It is now widely accepted that there are at least four more or less clearly distinguishable stages in the child's progress toward what is called mature reading ability. The first stage is known by the term "reading readiness." This begins, it has been pointed out, at birth, and continues normally until the age of about six or seven.

Reading readiness includes several different kinds of preparation for learning to read. Physical readiness involves good vision and hearing. Intellectual readiness involves a minimum level of visual perception such that the child can take in and remember an entire word and the letters that combine to form it. Language readiness involves the ability to speak clearly and to use several sentences in correct order. Personal readiness involves the ability to work with other children, to sustain attention, to follow directions, and the like.

General reading readiness is assessed by tests and is also estimated by teachers who are often skillful at discerning just when a pupil is ready to learn to read. The important thing to remember is that jumping the gun is usually self-defeating. The child who is not yet ready to read is frustrated if attempts are made to teach him, and he may carry over his dislike for the experience into his later school career and even into adult life. Delaying the beginning of reading instruction beyond the reading readiness stage is not nearly so serious, despite the feelings of parents who may fear that their child is "backward" or is not "keeping up" with his peers.

In the second stage, children learn to read very simple materials. They usually begin, at least in the United States, by learning a few sight words, and typically manage to master perhaps three hundred to four hundred words by the end of the first year. Basic skills are introduced at this time, such as the use of context or meaning clues and the beginning sounds of words. By the end of this period pupils are expected to be reading simple books independently and with enthusiasm.

It is incidentally worth observing that something quite mysterious, almost magical, occurs during this stage. At one moment in the course of his development the child, when faced with a series of symbols on a page, finds them quite meaningless. Not much later—perhaps only two or three weeks later—he has discovered meaning in them; he knows that they say "The cat sat on the hat." How this happens no one really knows, despite the efforts of philosophers and psychologists over two and a half millennia to study the phenomenon. Where does meaning come from? How is it that a French child would find the same meaning in the symbols "*Le chat s'asseyait sur le chapeau*"? Indeed, this discovery of meaning in symbols may be the most astounding intellectual feat that any human being ever performs—and most humans perform it before they are seven years old!

The third stage is characterized by rapid progress in vocabulary building and by increasing skill in "unlocking" the meaning of unfamiliar words through context clues. In addition, children at this stage learn to read for different purposes and in different areas of content, such as science, social studies, language arts, and the like. They learn that reading, besides being something one does at school, is also something one can do on one's own, for fun, to satisfy curiosity, or even to "expand one's horizons."

Finally, the fourth stage is characterized by the refinement and enhancement of the skills previously acquired. Above all, the student begins to be able to assimilate his reading experiences—that is, to carry over concepts from one piece of writing to another, and to compare the views of different writers on the same subject. This, the mature stage of reading, should be reached by young persons in their early teens. Ideally, they should continue to build on it for the rest of their lives.

That they often do not even reach it is apparent to many parents and to most educators. The reasons for the failure are many, ranging all the way from various kinds of deprivations in the home environment—economic, social, and/or intellectual (including parental illiteracy)—to personal problems of all kinds (including total revolt against "the system"). But one cause of the failure is not often noted. The very emphasis on reading readiness and on the methods employed to teach children the rudiments of reading has meant that the other, the higher, levels of reading have tended to be slighted. This is quite understandable, considering the urgency and extent of the problems found on this first level. Nevertheless, effective remedies for the overall reading deficiencies of Americans cannot be found unless efforts are made on *all* levels of reading.

Stages and Levels

We have described four levels of reading, and we have also outlined four stages of learning to read in an elementary fashion. What is the relation between these stages and levels?

It is of paramount importance to recognize that the four stages outlined here are all stages of the first level of reading, as outlined in the previous chapter. They are stages, that is, of elementary reading, which thus can be usefully divided somewhat in the manner of the elementary school curriculum. The first stage of elementary reading—reading readiness—corresponds to pre-school and kindergarten experiences. The second stage—word mastery—corresponds to the first grade experience of the typical child (although many quite normal children are not "typical" in this sense), with the result that the child attains what we can call second-stage reading skills, or first grade ability in reading or first grade literacy. The third stage of elementary reading—vocabulary growth and the utilization of context—is typically (but not universally, even for normal children) acquired at about the end of the fourth grade of elementary school, and results in what is variously called fourth grade, or functional, literacy—the ability, according to one common definition, to read traffic signs or picture captions fairly easily, to fill out the simpler government forms, and the like. The fourth and final stage of elementary reading is attained at about the time the pupil leaves or graduates from elementary school or junior high school. It is sometimes called eighth grade, ninth grade, or tenth grade literacy. The child is a "mature" reader in the sense that he is now capable of reading almost anything, but still in a relatively unsophisticated manner. In the simplest terms, he is mature enough to do high school work.

However, he is not yet a "mature" reader in the sense in which we want to employ the term in this book. He has mastered the first level of reading, that is all; he can read on his own and is prepared to learn more about reading. *But he does not yet know how to read beyond the elementary level.*

We mention all this because it is highly germane to the message of this book. We assume—we must assume—that you, our reader, have attained ninth grade literacy, that you have mastered the elementary level of reading, which means that you have passed successfully through the four stages described. If you think about it, you realize that we could not assume less. No one can learn from a how-to-do-it book until he can read it; and it is particularly true of a book purporting to teach one to read that its readers must be able to read in some sense of the term.

The difference between aided and unaided discovery comes into play here. Typically, the four stages of elementary reading are attained with the help of living teachers. Children differ in their abilities, of course; some need more help than others. But a teacher is usually present to answer questions and smooth over difficulties that arise during the elementary school years. Only when he has mastered all of the four stages of elementary reading is the child prepared to move on to the higher levels of reading. Only then can he read independently and learn on his own. Only then can he begin to become a really good reader.

Higher Levels of Reading and Higher Education

Traditionally, the high schools of America have provided little reading instruction for their students, and the colleges have provided none. That situation has changed in recent years. Two generations ago, when high school enrollments increased greatly within a relatively short period, educators began to realize that it could no longer be assumed that entering students could read effectively. Remedial reading instruction was therefore provided, sometimes for as many as 75% or more students. Within the last decade, the same situation has occurred at the college level. Thus, of approximately 40,000 freshmen entering the City University of New York in the fall of 1971, upwards of half, or more than 20,000 young people, had to be given some kind of remedial training in reading.

That does not mean, however, that *reading instruction beyond the elementary level* is offered in many U.S. colleges to this day. In fact, it is offered in almost none of them. Remedial reading instruction is not instruction in the higher levels of reading. It serves only to bring students up to a level of maturity in reading that they should have attained by the time they graduated from elementary school. To this day, most institutions of higher learning either do not know how to instruct students in reading beyond the elementary level, or lack the facilities and personnel to do so.

We say this despite the fact that a number of four-year and community colleges have recently instituted courses in speed reading, or in "effective" reading, or "competence" in reading. On the whole (though there are exceptions), these courses are remedial. They are designed to overcome various kinds of failures of the lower schools. They are not designed to take the student beyond the first level or to introduce him to the kinds and levels of reading that are the main subject of this book.

This, of course, should not be the case. A good liberal arts high school, if it does nothing else, ought to produce graduates who are competent analytical readers. A good college, if it does nothing else, ought to produce competent syntopical readers. A college degree ought to represent general competence in reading such that a graduate could read any kind of material for general readers and be able to undertake independent research on almost any subject (for that is what syntopical reading, among other things, enables you to do). Often, however, three or four years of graduate study are required before students attain this level of reading ability, and they do not always attain it even then.

One should not have to spend four years in graduate school in order to learn how to read. Four years of graduate school, in addition to twelve years of preparatory education and four years of college—that adds up to twenty full years of schooling. It should not take that long to learn to read. Something is very wrong if it does.

What is wrong can be corrected. Courses could be instituted in many high schools and colleges that are based on the program described in this book. There is nothing arcane or even really new about what we have to propose. It is largely common sense.

Reading and the Democratic Ideal of Education

We do not want to seem to be mere carping critics. We know that the thunder of thousands of freshmen feet upon the stairs makes it hard to hear, no matter how reasonable the message. And as long as a large proportion, even a majority, of these new students cannot read effectively at the elementary level, we are aware that the first task to be faced must be to teach them to read in the lowest, the largest common-denominator, sense of the term.

Nor, for the moment, would we want it any other way. We are on record as holding that unlimited educational opportunity—or, speaking practically, educational opportunity that is limited only by individual desire, ability, and need—is the most valuable service that society can provide for its members. That we do not yet know how to provide that kind of opportunity is no reason to give up the attempt.

But we must also realize—students, teachers, and laymen alike—that even when we have accomplished the task that lies before us, we will not have accomplished the whole task. We must be more than a nation of functional literates. We must become a nation of truly competent readers, recognizing all that the word *competent* implies. Nothing less will satisfy the needs of the world that is coming.

4

The Second Level of Reading: Inspectional Reading

Inspectional reading is a true level of reading. It is quite distinct from the level that precedes it (elementary reading) and from the one that follows it in natural sequence (analytical reading). But, as we noted in Chapter 2, the levels of reading are cumulative. Thus, elementary reading is contained in inspectional reading, as, indeed, inspectional reading is contained in analytical reading, and analytical reading in syntopical reading.

Practically, this means that you cannot read on the inspectional level unless you can read effectively on the elementary level. You must be able to read an author's text more or less steadily, without having to stop to look up the meaning of many words, and without stumbling over the grammar and syntax. You must be able to make sense of a majority of the sentences and paragraphs, although not necessarily the best sense of all of them.

What, then, is involved in inspectional reading? How do you go about doing it?

The first thing to realize is that there are two types of inspectional reading. They are aspects of a single skill, but the beginning reader is well-advised to consider them as two different steps or activities. The experienced reader learns to perform both steps simultaneously, but for the moment we will treat them as if they were quite distinct.

Inspectional Reading I: Systematic Skimming or Pre-reading

Let us return to the basic situation to which we have referred before. There is a book or other reading matter, and here is your mind. What is the first thing that you do?

Let us assume two further elements in the situation, elements that are quite common. First, you do not know whether you want to read the book. You do not know whether it deserves an analytical reading. But you suspect that it does, or at least that it contains both information and insights that would be valuable to you if you could dig them out.

Second, let us assume—and this is very often the case—that you have only a limited time in which to find all this out.

In this case, what you must do is *skim* the book, or, as some prefer to say, pre-read it. Skimming or pre-reading is the first sublevel of inspectional reading. Your main aim is to discover whether the book requires a more careful reading. Secondly, skimming can tell you lots of other things about the book, even if you decide not to read it again with more care.

Giving a book this kind of quick once-over is a threshing process that helps you to separate the chaff from the real kernels of nourishment. You may discover that what you get from skimming is all the book is worth to you for the time being. It may never be worth more. But you will know at least what the author's main contention is, as well as what kind of book he has written, so the time you have spent looking through the book will not have been wasted.

The habit of skimming should not take much time to acquire. Here are some suggestions about how to do it..

1. LOOK AT THE TITLE PAGE AND, IF THE BOOK HAS ONE, AT ITS PREFACE. Read each quickly. Note especially the subtitles or other indications of the scope or aim of the book or of the author's

special angle on his subject. Before completing this step you should have a good idea of the subject, and, if you wish, you may pause for a moment to place the book in the appropriate category in your mind. What pigeonhole that already contains other books does this one belong in?

2. STUDY THE TABLE OF CONTENTS to obtain a general sense of the book's structure; use it as you would a road map before taking a trip. It is astonishing how many people never even glance at a book's table of contents unless they wish to look something up in it. In fact, many authors spend a considerable amount of time in creating the table of contents, and it is sad to think their efforts are often wasted.

It used to be a common practice, especially in expository works, but sometimes even in novels and poems, to write very full tables of contents, with the chapters or parts broken down into many subtitles indicative of the topics covered. Milton, for example, wrote more or less lengthy headings, or "Arguments," as he called them, for each book of *Paradise Lost*. Gibbon published his *Decline and Fall of the Roman Empire* with an extensive analytical table of contents for each chapter. Such summaries are no longer common, although occasionally you do still come across an analytical table of contents. One reason for the decline of the practice may be that people are not so likely to read tables of contents as they once were. Also, publishers have come to feel that a less revealing table of contents is more seductive than a completely frank and open one. Readers, they feel, will be attracted to a book with more or less mysterious chapter titles—they will want to read the book to find out what the chapters are about. Even so, a table of contents can be valuable, and you should read it carefully before going on to the rest of the book.

At this point, you might turn back to the table of contents of this book, if you have not already read it. We tried to make it as full and informative as we could. Examining it should give you a good idea of what we are trying to do.

3. CHECK THE INDEX if the book has one—most expository works do. Make a quick estimate of the range of topics covered and of the kinds of books and authors referred to. When you see terms listed that seem crucial, look up at least some of the passages cited. (We will have much more to say about crucial terms in Part Two. Here you must make your judgment of their importance on the basis of your general sense of the book, as obtained from steps 1 and 2.) The passages you read may contain the crux—the point on which the book hinges— or the new departure which is the key to the author's approach and attitude.

   As in the case of the table of contents, you might at this point check the index of *this* book. You will recognize as crucial some terms that have already been discussed. Can you identify, for example, by the number of references under them, any others that also seem important?

4. If the book is a new one with a dust jacket, READ THE PUBLISH-ER'S BLURB. Some people have the impression that the blurb is never anything but sheer puffery. But this is quite often not true, especially in the case of expository works. The blurbs of many of these books are written by the authors themselves, admittedly with the help of the publisher's public relations department. It is not uncommon for authors to try to summa-rize as accurately as they can the main points in their book. These efforts should not go unnoticed. Of course, if the blurb is nothing but a puff for the book, you will ordinarily be able to discover this at a glance. But that in itself can tell you some-thing about the work. Perhaps the book does not say anything of importance—and that is why the blurb does not say any-thing, either.

   Upon completing these first four steps you may already have enough information about the book to know that you want to read it more carefully, or that you do not want or need to read it at all. In either case, you may put it aside for the moment. If you do not do so, you are now ready to skim the book, properly speaking.

5. From your general and still rather vague knowledge of the book's contents, LOOK NOW AT THE CHAPTERS THAT SEEM TO BE PIVOTAL TO ITS ARGUMENT. If these chapters have summary statements in their opening or closing pages, as they often do, read these statements carefully.

6. Finally, TURN THE PAGES, DIPPING IN HERE AND THERE, READING A PARAGRAPH OR TWO, SOMETIMES SEVERAL PAGES IN SEQUENCE, NEVER MORE THAN THAT. Thumb through the book in this way, always looking for signs of the main contention, listening for the basic pulsebeat of the matter. Above all, do not fail to read the last two or three pages, or, if these are an epilogue, the last few pages of the main part of the book. Few authors are able to resist the temptation to sum up what they think is new and important about their work in these pages. You do not want to miss this, even though, as sometimes happens, the author himself may be wrong in his judgment.

You have now skimmed the book systematically; you have given it the first type of inspectional reading. You should know a good deal about the book at this point, after having spent no more than a few minutes, at most an hour, with it. In particular, you should know whether the book contains matter that you still want to dig out, or whether it deserves no more of your time and attention. You should also be able to place the book even more accurately than before in your mental card catalogue, for further reference if the occasion should ever arise.

Incidentally, this is a very active sort of reading. It is impossible to give any book an inspectional reading without being alert, without having all of one's faculties awake and working. How many times have you daydreamed through several pages of a good book only to wake up to the realization that you have no idea of the ground you have gone over? That cannot happen if you follow the steps outlined here—that is, if you have a system for following a general thread.

Think of yourself as a detective looking for clues to a book's general theme or idea, alert for anything that will make it clearer. Heeding the suggestions we have made will help you sustain this attitude. You will be surprised to find out how much time you will save, pleased to see how much more you will grasp, and relieved to discover how much easier it all can be than you supposed.

Inspectional Reading II: Superficial Reading

The title of this section is intentionally provocative. The word "superficial" ordinarily has a negative connotation. We are quite serious, however, in using the term.

Everyone has had the experience of struggling fruitlessly with a difficult book that was begun with high hopes of enlightenment. It is natural enough to conclude that it was a mistake to try to read it in the first place. But that was not the mistake. Rather it was in expecting too much from the first going over of a difficult book. Approached in the right way, no book intended for the general reader, no matter how difficult, need be a cause for despair.

What is the right approach? The answer lies in an important and helpful rule of reading that is generally overlooked. That rule is simply this: *In tackling a difficult book for the first time, read it through without ever stopping to look up or ponder the things you do not understand right away.*

Pay attention to what you can understand and do not be stopped by what you cannot immediately grasp. Go right on reading past the point where you have difficulties in understanding, and you will soon come to things you do understand. Concentrate on these. Keep on in this way. Read the book through, undeterred and undismayed by the paragraphs, footnotes, comments, and references that escape you. If you let yourself get stalled, if you allow yourself to be tripped up by any one of these stumbling blocks, you are lost. In most cases, you will not be able to puzzle the thing out by sticking to it. You will have a much better chance of understanding it on a second reading, but that requires you to have read the book *through* at least once.

What you understand by reading the book through to the end—even if it is only fifty percent or less—will help you when you make the additional effort later to go back to the places you passed by on your first reading. And even if you never go back, understanding half of a really tough book is much better than not understanding it at all, which will be the case if you allow yourself to be stopped by the first difficult passage you come to.

Most of us were taught to pay attention to the things we did not understand. We were told to go to a dictionary when we met an unfamiliar word. We were told to go to an encyclopedia or some other reference work when we were confronted with allusions or statements we did not comprehend. We were told to consult footnotes, scholarly commentaries, or other secondary sources to get help. But when these things are done *prematurely,* they only impede our reading, instead of helping it.

The tremendous pleasure that can come from reading Shakespeare, for instance, was spoiled for generations of high school students who were forced to go through *Julius Caesar, As You Like It,* or *Hamlet,* scene by scene, looking up all the strange words in a glossary and studying all the scholarly footnotes. As a result, they never really read a Shakespearean play. By the time they reached the end, they had forgotten the beginning and lost sight of the whole. Instead of being forced to take this pedantic approach, they should have been encouraged to read the play at one sitting and discuss what they got out of that first quick reading. Only then would they have been ready to study the play carefully and closely because then they would have understood enough of it to learn more.

The rule applies with equal force to expository works. Here, indeed, the best proof of the soundness of the rule—give a book a first superficial reading—is what happens when you do *not* follow it. Take a basic work in economics, for example, such as Adam Smith's classic *The Wealth of Nations.* (We choose this book as an example because it is more than a textbook or a work for specialists in the field. It is a book for the *general* reader.) If you insist on understanding everything on every page before you go on to the next, you will not get very far. In your effort to master the fine points, you will miss the big points that Smith makes so clearly about the factors of wages, rents, profits, and interest that enter into the cost of things, the role of the market in determining prices, the evils of monopoly, the reasons for free trade. You will miss the forest for the trees. You will not be reading well on *any* level.

On Reading Speeds

We described inspectional reading in Chapter 2 as the art of getting the most out of a book in a limited time. In describing it further in the present chapter, we have in no way changed that definition. The two steps involved in inspectional reading are both taken rapidly. The competent inspectional reader will accomplish them both quickly, no matter how long or difficult the book he is trying to read.

That working definition, however, inevitably raises the question, What about speed reading? What is the relation between the levels of reading and the many speed reading courses, both academic and commercial, that are offered at the present day?

We have already suggested that such courses are basically remedial—that is, that they provide instruction mainly, if not exclusively, in reading on the elementary level. But more needs to be said.

Let it be understood at once that we are wholly in favor of the proposition that most people ought to be *able* to read faster than they do. Too often, there are things we *have* to read that are not really worth spending a lot of time reading; if we cannot read them quickly, it will be a terrible waste of time. It is true enough that many people read some things too slowly, and that they ought to read them faster. But many people also read some things too fast, and they ought to read those things more slowly. A good speed reading course should therefore teach you to read at many different speeds, not just one speed that is faster than anything you can manage now. It should enable you to vary your rate of reading in accordance with the nature and complexity of the material.

Our point is really very simple. Many books are hardly worth even skimming; some should be read quickly; and a few should be read at a rate, usually quite slow, that allows for complete comprehension. It is wasteful to read a book slowly that deserves only a fast reading; speed reading skills can help you solve that problem. But this is only one reading problem. The obstacles that stand in the way of comprehension of a difficult book are not ordinarily, and perhaps never primarily, physiological or psychological. They arise because the reader simply does not know what to do when approaching a difficult—and rewarding—book. He does not know the rules of reading; he does not know how to marshal his intellectual resources for the task. No matter how quickly he reads, he will be no better off if, as is too often true, he does not know what he is looking for and does not know when he has found it.

With regard to rates of reading, then, the ideal is not merely to be able to read faster, but to be able to read at *different speeds*—and to know when the different speeds are appropriate. Inspectional reading is accomplished quickly, but that is not only because you read faster, although in fact you do; it is also because you read less of a book when you give it an inspectional reading, and because you read it in a different way, with different goals in mind. Analytical reading is ordinarily much slower than inspectional reading, but even when you are giving a book an analytical reading, you should not read all of it at the same rate of speed. Every book, no matter how difficult, contains interstitial material that can be and should be read quickly;

and every good book also contains matter that is difficult and should be read very slowly.

Fixations and Regressions

Speed reading courses properly make much of the discovery—we have known it for half a century or more—that most people continue to sub-vocalize for years after they are first taught to read. Films of eye movements, furthermore, show that the eyes of young or un-trained readers "fixate" as many as five or six times in the course of each line that is read. (The eye is blind while it moves; it can only see when it stops.) Thus single words or at the most two-word or three-word phrases are being read at a time, in jumps across the line. Even worse than that, the eyes of incompetent readers regress as often as once every two or three lines—that is, they return to phrases or sentences previously read.

All of these habits are wasteful and obviously cut down reading speed. They are wasteful because the mind, unlike the eye, does not need to "read" only a word or short phrase at a time. The mind, that astounding instrument, can grasp a sentence or even a paragraph at a "glance"—if only the eyes will provide it with the information it needs. Thus the primary task—recognized as such by all speed reading courses—is to correct the fixations and regressions that slow so many readers down. Fortunately, this can be done quite easily. Once it is done, the student can read as fast as his mind will let him, not as slow as his eyes make him.

There are various devices for breaking the eye fixations, some of them complicated and expensive. Usually, however, it is not necessary to employ any device more sophisticated than your own hand, which you can train yourself to follow as it moves more and more quickly across and down the page. You can do this yourself. Place your thumb and first two fingers together. Sweep this "pointer" across a line of type, a little faster than it is comfortable for your eyes to move. Force yourself to keep up with your hand. You will very soon be able to read the words as you follow your hand. Keep practicing this, and keep increasing the speed at which your hand moves, and before you know it you will have doubled or trebled your reading speed.

The Problem of Comprehension

But what exactly have you gained if you increase your reading speed significantly? It is true that you have saved time—but what about comprehension? Has that also increased, or has it suffered in the process?

There is no speed reading course that we know of that does not claim to be able to increase your comprehension along with your reading speed. And on the whole, there is probably some foundation for these claims. The hand (or some other device) used as a timer tends not only to increase your reading rate, but also to improve your concentration on what you are reading. As long as you are following your hand it is harder to fall asleep, to daydream, to let your mind wander. So far, so good. Concentration is another name for what we have called activity in reading. The good reader reads actively, with concentration.

But concentration alone does not really have much of an effect on comprehension, when that is properly understood. Comprehension involves much more than merely being able to answer simple questions of fact about a text. This limited kind of comprehension, in fact, is nothing but the elementary ability to answer the question about a book or other reading material: "What does it say?" The many further questions that, when correctly answered, imply higher levels of comprehension are seldom asked in speed reading courses, and instruction in how to answer them is seldom given.

To make this clearer, let us take an example of something to read. Let us take the Declaration of Independence. You probably have a copy of it available. Take it down and look at it. It occupies less than three pages when printed. How fast should you read it?

The second paragraph of the Declaration ends with the sentence: "To prove this, let facts be submitted to a candid world." The following two pages of "facts," some of which, incidentally, are quite dubious, can be read quickly. It is not necessary to gain more than a general idea of the *kind* of facts that Jefferson is citing, unless, of course, you are a scholar concerned with the historical circumstances in which he wrote. Even the last paragraph, ending with the justly celebrated statement that the signers "mutually pledge to each other our lives, our fortunes, and our sacred honour," can be read quickly. This is a rhetorical flourish, and it deserves what mere rhetoric always deserves. But the first two paragraphs of the Declaration of Independence require more than a first rapid reading.

We doubt that there is anyone who can read those first two paragraphs at a rate much faster than 20 words a minute. Indeed, individual words in the famous second paragraph—words like "inalienable," "rights," "liberty," "happiness," "consent," "just powers"—are worth dwelling over, puzzling about, considering at length. Properly read, for full comprehension, those first two paragraphs of the Declaration might require days, or weeks, or even years.

The problem of speed reading, then, is the problem of comprehension. Practically, this comes down to defining comprehension at levels beyond the elementary. Speed reading courses, for the most part, do not attempt this. It is worth emphasizing, therefore, that it is precisely comprehension in reading that this book seeks to improve. You cannot comprehend a book without reading it analytically; analytical reading, as we have noted, is undertaken primarily for the sake of comprehension (or understanding).

Summary of Inspectional Reading

A few words in summary of this chapter. There is no single right speed at which you should read; the ability to read at various speeds and to know when each speed is appropriate is the ideal. Great speed in reading is a dubious achievement; it is of value only if what you have to read is not really worth reading. A better formula is this: *Every book should be read no more slowly than it deserves, and no more quickly than you can read it with satisfaction and comprehension.* In any event, the speed at which they read, be it fast or slow, is but a fractional part of most people's problem with reading.

Skimming or pre-reading a book is always a good idea; it is necessary when you do not know, as is often the case, whether the book you have in hand is worth reading carefully. You will find that out by skimming it. It is generally desirable to skim even a book that you intend to read carefully, to get some idea of its form and structure.

Finally, do not try to understand every word or page of a difficult book the first time through. This is the most important rule of all; it is the essence of inspectional reading. Do not be afraid to be, or to seem to be, superficial. Race through even the hardest book. You will then be prepared to read it well the second time.

We have now completed our initial discussion of the second level of reading—inspectional reading. We will return to the subject when we come to Part Four, where we will show what an important role inspectional reading plays in syntopical reading, the fourth and highest level of reading.

However, you should keep in mind during our discussion of the third level of reading—analytical reading—which is described in the second part of this book, that inspectional reading serves an important function at that level, too. The two stages of inspectional reading can both be thought of as anticipations of steps that the reader takes when he reads analytically. The first stage of inspectional reading—the stage we have called systematic skimming— serves to prepare the analytical reader to answer the questions that must be asked during the first stage of that level. Systematic skimming, in other words, anticipates the comprehension of a book's structure. And the second stage of inspectional reading—the stage we have called superficial reading—serves the reader when he comes to the second stage of reading at the analytical level. Superficial reading is the first necessary step in the interpretation of a book's contents.

Before going on to explain analytical reading, we want to pause for a moment to consider again the nature of reading as an activity. There are certain actions the active or demanding reader must perform in order to read well. We will discuss them in the next chapter.

5

How to Be a Demanding Reader

The rules for reading yourself to sleep are easier to follow than are the rules for staying awake while reading. Get into bed in a comfortable position, make sure the light is inadequate enough to cause a slight eyestrain, choose a book that is either terribly difficult or terribly boring—in any event, one that you do not really care whether you read or not—and you will be asleep in a few minutes. Those who are experts in relaxing with a book do not have to wait for nightfall. A comfortable chair in the library will do any time.

Unfortunately, the rules for keeping awake do not consist in doing just the opposite. It is *possible* to keep awake while reading in a comfortable chair or even in bed, and people have been known to strain their eyes by reading late in light too dim. What kept the famous candlelight readers awake? One thing certainly—it made a difference to them, a great difference, whether or not they read the book they had in hand.

Whether you manage to keep awake or not depends in large part on your goal in reading. If your aim in reading is to profit from it—to grow somehow in mind or spirit—you have to keep awake. That means reading as actively as possible. It means making an effort—an effort for which you expect to be repaid.

Good books, fiction or nonfiction, deserve such reading. To use a good book as a sedative is conspicuous waste. To fall asleep or, what is the same, to let your mind wander during the hours you planned to devote to reading for profit—that is, primarily for understanding—is clearly to defeat your own ends.

But the sad fact is that many people who can distinguish between profit and pleasure—between understanding, on the one hand, and entertainment or the mere satisfaction of curiosity, on the other hand—nevertheless fail to carry out their reading plans. They fail even if they know which books give which. The reason is that they do not know how to be demanding readers, how to keep their mind on what they are doing by making it do the work without which no profit can be earned.

The Essence of Active Reading: The Four Basic Questions a Reader Asks

We have already discussed active reading extensively in this book. We have said that active reading is better reading, and we have noted that inspectional reading is always active. It is an effortful, not an effortless, undertaking. But we have not yet gone to the heart of the matter by stating the one simple prescription for active reading. It is: *Ask questions while you read—questions that you yourself must try to answer in the course of reading.*

Any questions? No. The art of reading on any level above the elementary consists in the habit of asking the right questions in the right order. There are four main questions you must ask about any book.*

1. WHAT IS THE BOOK ABOUT AS A WHOLE? You must try to discover the leading theme of the book, and how the author develops

---

* These four questions, as stated, together with the discussion of them that follows, apply mainly to expository or nonfiction works. However, the questions, when adapted, apply to fiction and poetry as well. The adaptations required are discussed in Chapters 14 and 15.

this theme in an orderly way by subdividing it into its essential subordinate themes or topics.

2. WHAT IS BEING SAID IN DETAIL, AND HOW? You must try to discover the main ideas, assertions, and arguments that constitute the author's particular message.

3. IS THE BOOK TRUE, IN WHOLE OR PART? You cannot answer this question until you have answered the first two. You have to know what is being said before you can decide whether it is true or not. When you understand a book, however, you are obligated, if you are reading seriously, to make up your own mind. Knowing the author's mind is not enough.

4. WHAT OF IT? If the book has given you information, you must ask about its significance. Why does the author think it is important to know these things? Is it important to you to know them? And if the book has not only informed you, but also enlightened you, it is necessary to seek further enlightenment by asking what else follows, what is further implied or suggested.

We will return to these four questions at length in the rest of this book. Stated another way, they become the basic rules of reading with which Part Two is mainly concerned. They are stated here in question form for a very good reason. Reading a book on any level beyond the elementary is essentially an effort on your part to ask it questions (and to answer them to the best of your ability). That should never be forgotten. And that is why there is all the difference in the world between the demanding and the undemanding reader. The latter asks no questions—and gets no answers.

The four questions stated above summarize the whole obligation of a reader. They apply to anything worth reading—a book or an article or even an advertisement. Inspectional reading tends to provide more accurate answers to the first two questions than to the last two, but it nevertheless helps with those also. An analytical reading of a book has not been accomplished satisfactorily until you have answers to those last questions—until you have some idea of the book's truth, in whole or part, and of its significance, if only in your own scheme of things. The last question—What of it?—is probably the most important one in syntopical reading. Naturally, you will have to answer the first three questions before attempting the final one.

Knowing what the four questions are is not enough. You must remember to ask them as you read. The *habit* of doing that is the mark of a demanding reader. More than that, you must know how to answer them precisely and accurately. The trained ability to do that is the *art* of reading.

People go to sleep over good books not because they are unwilling to make the effort, but because they do not know how to make it. Good books are over your head; they would not be good for you if they were not. And books that are over your head weary you unless you can reach up to them and pull yourself up to their level. It is not the stretching that tires you, but the frustration of stretching unsuccessfully because you lack the skill to stretch effectively. To keep on reading actively, you must have not only the will to do so, but also the skill—the art that enables you to elevate yourself by mastering what at first sight seems to be beyond you.

How to Make a Book Your Own

If you have the habit of asking a book questions as you read, you are a better reader than if you do not. But, as we have indicated, merely asking questions is not enough. You have to try to answer them. And although that could be done, theoretically, in your mind only, it is much easier to do it with a pencil in your hand. The pencil then becomes the sign of your alertness while you read.

It is an old saying that you have to "read between the lines" to get the most out of anything. The rules of reading are a formal way of saying this. But we want to persuade you to "write between the lines," too. Unless you do, you are not likely to do the most efficient kind of reading.

When you buy a book, you establish a property right in it, just as you do in clothes or furniture when you buy and pay for them. But the act of purchase is actually only the prelude to possession in the case of a book. Full ownership of a book only comes when you have made it a part of yourself, and the best way to make yourself a part of it—which comes to the same thing—is by writing in it.

Why is marking a book indispensable to reading it? First, it keeps you awake—not merely conscious, but wide awake. Second, reading, if it is active, is thinking, and thinking tends to express itself in words, spoken or written. The person who says he knows what he thinks but cannot express it usually does not know what he thinks. Third, writing your reactions down helps you to remember the thoughts of the author.

Reading a book should be a conversation between you and the author. Presumably he knows more about the subject than you do; if not, you probably should not be bothering with his book. But understanding is a two-way operation; the learner has to question himself and question the teacher. He even has to be willing to argue with the teacher, once he understands what the teacher is saying. Marking a book is literally an expression of your differences or your agreements with the author. It is the highest respect you can pay him.

There are all kinds of devices for marking a book intelligently and fruitfully. Here are some devices that can be used:

1. UNDERLINING—of major points; of important or forceful statements.

2. VERTICAL LINES AT THE MARGIN—to emphasize a statement already underlined or to point to a passage too long to be underlined.

3. STAR, ASTERISK, OR OTHER DOODAD AT THE MARGIN—to be used sparingly, to emphasize the ten or dozen most important statements or passages in the book. You may want to fold a corner of each page on which you make such marks or place a

slip of paper between the pages. In either case, you will be able to take the book off the shelf at any time and, by opening it to the indicated page, refresh your recollection.

4. NUMBERS IN THE MARGIN—to indicate a sequence of points made by the author in developing an argument.

5. NUMBERS OF OTHER PAGES IN THE MARGIN—to indicate where else in the book the author makes the same points, or points relevant to or in contradiction of those here marked; to tie up the ideas in a book, which, though they may be separated by many pages, belong together. Many readers use the symbol "Cf" to indicate the other page numbers; it means "compare" or "refer to."

6. CIRCLING OF KEY WORDS OR PHRASES—This serves much the same function as underlining.

7. WRITING IN THE MARGIN, OR AT THE TOP OR BOTTOM OF THE PAGE—to record questions (and perhaps answers) which a passage raises in your mind; to reduce a complicated discussion to a simple statement; to record the sequence of major points right through the book. The endpapers at the back of the book can be used to make a personal index of the author's points in the order of their appearance.

To inveterate book-markers, the front endpapers are often the most important. Some people reserve them for a fancy bookplate. But that expresses only their financial ownership of the book. The front endpapers are better reserved for a record of your thinking. After finishing the book and making your personal index on the back endpapers, turn to the front and try to outline the book, not page by page or point by point (you have already done that at the back), but as an integrated structure, with a basic outline and an order of parts. That outline will be the measure of your understanding of the work; unlike a bookplate, it will express your intellectual ownership of the book.

The Three Kinds of Note-making

There are three quite different kinds of notes that you will make in your books as well as about them. Which kind you make depends upon the level at which you are reading.

When you give a book an inspectional reading, you may not have much time to make notes in it; inspectional reading, as we have observed, is always limited as to time. Nevertheless, you are asking important questions about a book when you read it at this level, and it would be desirable, even if it is not always possible, to record your answers when they are fresh in your mind.

The questions answered by inspectional reading are: first, what kind of book is it? second, what is it about as a whole? and third, what is the structural order of the work whereby the author develops his conception or understanding of that general subject matter? You may and probably should make notes concerning your answers to these questions, especially if you know that it may be days or months before you will be able to return to the book to give it an analytical reading. The best place to make such notes is on the contents page, or perhaps on the title page, which are otherwise unused in the scheme we have outlined above.

The point to recognize is that these notes primarily concern the structure of the book, and not its substance—at least not in detail. *We therefore call this kind of note-making structural.*

In the course of an inspectional reading, especially of a long and difficult book, you may attain some insights into the author's ideas about his subject matter. Often, however, you will not; and certainly you should put off making any judgment of the accuracy or truth of the statements until you have read the book more carefully. Then, during an analytical reading, you will need to give answers to questions about the truth and significance of the book. The notes you make at this level of reading are, therefore, not structural but *conceptual*. They concern the author's concepts, and also your own, as they have been deepened or broadened by your reading of the book.

There is an obvious difference between structural and conceptual note-making. What kind of notes do you make when you are giving several books a syntopical reading—when you are reading more than one book on a single subject? Again, such notes will tend to be conceptual; and the notes on a page may refer you not only to other pages in that book, but also to pages in other books.

There is a step beyond even that, however, and a truly expert reader can take it when he is reading several books syntopically. That is to make notes about the *shape of the discussion*—the discussion that is engaged in by all of the authors, even if unbeknownst to them. For reasons that will become clear in Part Four, we prefer to call such notes *dialectical*. Since they are made concerning several books, not just one, they often have to be made on a separate sheet (or sheets) of paper. Here, a structure of concepts is implied—an order of statements and questions about a single subject matter. We will return to this kind of note-making in Chapter 20.

Forming the Habit of Reading

Any art or skill is possessed by those who have formed the habit of operating according to its rules. This is the way the artist or craftsman in any field differs from those who lack his skill.

Now there is no other way of forming a habit of operation than by operating. That is what it means to say one learns to do by doing. The difference between your activity before and after you have formed a habit is a difference in facility and readiness. After practice, you can do the same thing much better than when you started. That is what it means to say practice makes perfect. What you do very imperfectly at first, you gradually come to do with the kind of almost automatic perfection that an instinctive performance has. You do something as if you were born to it, as if the activity were as natural to you as walking or eating. That is what it means to say that habit is second nature.

Knowing the rules of an art is not the same as having the habit.

When we speak of a man as skilled in any way, we do not mean that he knows the rules of making or doing something, but that he possesses the habit of making or doing it. Of course, it is true that knowing the rules, more or less explicitly, is a condition of getting the skill. You cannot follow rules you do not know. Nor can you acquire an artistic habit—any craft or skill—without following rules. The art as something that can be taught consists of rules to be followed in operation. The art as something learned and possessed consists of the habit that results from operating according to the rules.

Incidentally, not everyone understands that being an artist consists in operating according to rules. People point to a highly original painter or sculptor and say, "He isn't following rules. He's doing something entirely original, something that has never been done before, something for which there are no rules." But they fail to see what rules it is that the artist follows. There are no final, unbreakable rules, strictly speaking, for making a painting or sculpture. But there are rules for preparing canvas and mixing paints and applying them, and for molding clay or welding steel. Those rules the painter or sculptor must have followed, or else he could not have made the thing he has made. No matter how original his final production, no matter how little it seems to obey the "rules" of art as they have traditionally been understood, he must be skilled to produce it. And this is the art—the skill or craft—that we are talking about here.

From Many Rules to One Habit

Reading is like skiing. When done well, when done by an expert, both reading and skiing are graceful, harmonious activities. When done by a beginner, both are awkward, frustrating, and slow.

Learning to ski is one of the most humiliating experiences an adult can undergo (that is one reason to start young). After all, an adult has been walking for a long time; he knows where his feet are; he knows how to put one foot in front of the other in order to get somewhere. But as soon as he puts skis on his feet, it is as though he had to learn to walk all over again. He slips and slides, falls down, has trouble getting up, gets his skis crossed, tumbles again, and generally looks—and feels—like a fool.

Even the best instructor seems at first to be no help. The ease with which the instructor performs actions that he says are simple but that the student secretly believes are impossible is almost insulting. How can you remember everything the instructor says you have to remember? Bend your knees. Look down the hill. Keep your weight on the downhill ski. Keep your back straight, but nevertheless lean forward. The admonitions seem endless—how can you think about all that and still ski?

The point about skiing, of course, is that you should not be thinking about the separate acts that, together, make a smooth turn or series of linked turns—instead, you should merely be looking ahead of you down the hill, anticipating bumps and other skiers, enjoying the feel of the cold wind on your cheeks, smiling with pleasure at the fluid grace of your body as you speed down the mountain. In other words, you must learn to forget the separate acts in order to perform all of them, and indeed any of them, well. But in order *to forget them as separate acts, you have to learn them first as separate acts.* Only then can you put them together to become a good skier.

It is the same with reading. Probably you have been reading for a long time, too, and starting to learn all over again can be humiliating. But it is just as true of reading as it is of skiing that you cannot coalesce a lot of different acts into one complex, harmonious performance until you become expert at each of them. You cannot telescope the different parts of the job so that they run into one another and fuse intimately. Each separate act requires your full attention while you are doing it. After you have practiced the parts separately, you can not only do each with greater facility and less attention but can also gradually put them together into a smoothly running whole.

All of this is common knowledge about learning a complex skill. We say it here merely because we want you to realize that learning to read is at least as complex as learning to ski or to typewrite or to play tennis. If you can recall your patience in any other learning experience you have had, you will be more tolerant of instructors who will shortly enumerate a long list of rules for reading.

The person who has had one experience in acquiring a complex skill knows that he need not fear the array of rules that present themselves at the beginning of something new to be learned. He knows that he does not have to worry about how all the separate acts in which he must become separately proficient are going to work together.

The multiplicity of the rules indicates the complexity of the one habit to be formed, not a plurality of distinct habits. The parts coalesce and telescope as each reaches the stage of automatic execution. When all the subordinate acts can be done more or less automatically, you have formed the habit of the whole performance. Then you can think about tackling an expert run you have never skied before, or reading a book that you once thought was too difficult for you. At the beginning, the learner pays attention to himself and his skill in the separate acts. When the acts have lost their separateness in the skill of the whole performance, the learner can at last pay attention to the goal that the technique he has acquired enables him to reach.

We hope we have encouraged you by the things we have said in these pages. It is hard to learn to read well. Not only is reading, especially analytical reading, a very complex activity—much more complex than skiing—it is also much more of a mental activity. The beginning skier must think of physical acts that he can later forget and perform almost automatically. It is relatively easy to think of and be conscious of physical acts. It is much harder to think of mental acts, as the beginning analytical reader must do; in a sense, he is thinking about his own thoughts. Most of us are unaccustomed to doing this. Nevertheless, it can be done, and a person who does it cannot help learning to read much better.

PART 2

The Third Level of Reading:
Analytical Reading

6

Pigeonholing a Book

We said at the beginning of this book that the instruction in reading that it provides applies to anything you have to or want to read. However, in expounding the rules of analytical reading, as we will do in Part Two, we may seem to be ignoring that fact. We will usually, if not always, refer to the reading of whole books. Why is this so?

The answer is simple. Reading a whole book, and especially a long and difficult one, poses the severest problems any reader can face. Reading a short story is almost always easier than reading a novel; reading an article is almost always easier than reading a book on the same subject. If you can read an epic poem or a novel, you can read a lyric or a short story; if you can read an expository book—a history, a philosophical work, a scientific treatise—you can read an article or abstract in the same field.

Hence everything that we will say about reading books applies to reading other materials of the kinds indicated. You are to understand, when we refer to the reading of books, that the rules expounded refer to lesser and more easily understood materials, too. Sometimes the rules do not apply to the latter in quite the same way, or to the extent that they apply to whole books. Nevertheless, it will always be easy for you to adapt them so that they are applicable.

The Importance of Classifying Books

The first rule of analytical reading can be expressed as follows: RULE 1. YOU MUST KNOW WHAT KIND OF BOOK YOU ARE READING, AND YOU SHOULD KNOW THIS AS EARLY IN THE PROCESS AS POSSIBLE, PREFERABLY BEFORE YOU BEGIN TO READ.

You must know, for instance, whether you are reading fiction—a novel, a play, an epic, a lyric—or whether it is an expository work of some sort. Almost every reader knows a work of fiction when he sees it. Or so it seems—and yet this is not always easy. Is *Portnoy's Complaint* a novel or a psychoanalytical study? Is *Naked Lunch* a fiction or a tract against drug abuse, similar to the books that used to recount the horrors of alcohol for the betterment of readers? Is *Gone with the Wind* a romance or a history of the South before and during the Civil War? Do *Main Street* and *The Grapes of Wrath* belong in the category of belles-lettres or are both of them sociological studies, the one concentrating on urban experiences, the other on agrarian life?

All of these, of course, are novels; all of them appeared on the fiction side of the best-seller lists. Yet the questions are not absurd. Just by their titles, it would be hard to tell in the case of *Main Street* and *Middletown* which was fiction and which was social science. There is so much social science in some contemporary novels, and so much fiction in much of sociology, that it is hard to keep them apart. But there is another kind of science, too—physics and chemistry, for instance—in books like *The Andromeda Strain* or the novels of Robert Heinlein or Arthur C. Clarke. And a book like *The Universe and Dr. Einstein,* while clearly not fiction, is almost as "readable" as a novel, and probably more readable than some of the novels of, say, William Faulkner.

An expository book is one that conveys knowledge primarily, "knowledge" being construed broadly. Any book that consists primarily of opinions, theories, hypotheses, or speculations, for which the claim is made more or less explicitly that they are true in some sense, conveys knowledge in this meaning of knowledge and is an expository work. As with fiction, most people know an expository work when they see it. Here, however, the problem is not to distinguish nonfiction from fiction, but to recognize that there are various kinds of expository books. It is not merely a question of knowing which books are primarily instructive, but also which are instructive in a particular way. The kinds of information or enlightenment that a history and a philosophical work afford are not the same. The problems dealt with by a book on physics and one on morals are not the same, nor are the methods the writers employ in solving such different problems.

Thus this first rule of analytical reading, though it is applicable to all books, applies particularly to nonfictional, expository works. How do you go about following the rule, particularly its last clause?

As we have already suggested, you do so by first inspecting the book—giving it an inspectional reading. You read the title, the subtitle, the table of contents, and you at least glance at the preface or introduction by the author and at the index. If the book has a dust jacket, you look at the publisher's blurb. These are the signal flags the author waves to let you know which way the wind is blowing. It is not his fault if you will not stop, look, and listen.

What You Can Learn from the Title of a Book

The numbers of readers who pay no attention to the signals is larger than you might expect. We have had this experience again and again with students. We have asked them what a book was about. We have asked them, in the most general terms, to tell us what sort of book it was. This is a good way, almost an indispensable way, to begin a discussion of a book. Nevertheless, it is often hard to get any kind of answer to the question.

Let us take a couple of examples of the kind of confusion that can occur. In 1859, Darwin published a very famous book. A century later the entire English-speaking world celebrated the publication of the book. It was discussed endlessly, and its influence was assessed by learned and not-so-learned commentators. The book was about the theory of evolution, and the word "species" was in the title. What was the title?

Probably you said *The Origin of Species,* in which case you were correct. But you might not have said that. You might have said that the title was *The Origin of the Species.* Recently, we asked some twenty-five reasonably well-read persons what the title of Darwin's book was and more than half said *The Origin of the Species.* The reason for the mistake is obvious; they supposed, never having read the book, that it had something to do with the development of the human species. In fact, it has little or nothing to do with that subject, which Darwin covered in a later book, *The Descent of Man. The Origin of Species* is about what its title says it is about—namely the proliferation in the natural world of a vast number of species of plants and animals from an originally much smaller number of species, owing mainly to the principle of natural selection. We mention this common error because many think they know the title of the book, although few have actually ever read the title carefully and thought about what it means.

Here is another example. In this case we will not ask you to remember the title, but to think about what it means. Gibbon wrote a famous, and famously long, book about the Roman Empire. He called it *The Decline and Fall of the Roman Empire.* Almost everybody who takes up the book recognizes that title; and most people, even without the book in their hand, know the title. Indeed, the phrase "decline and fall" has become proverbial. Nevertheless, when we asked the same twenty-five well-read people why the first chapter is called "The Extent and Military Force of the Empire in the Age of the Antonines," they had no idea. They did not see that if the book as a whole was titled *Decline and Fall,* then it might be assumed that the narrative would begin with the high point of the Roman Empire, and continue through to the end. Unconsciously, they had translated "decline and fall" into "rise and fall." They were puzzled because there was no discussion of the Roman Republic, which ended a century and a half before the Age of the Antonines. If they had read the title carefully they could have assumed that the Age of the Antonines was the high point of the Empire, even if they had not known it before. Reading the title, in other words, could have given them essential information about the book before they started to read it; but they had failed to do that, as most people fail to do even with an unfamiliar book.

One reason why titles and prefaces are ignored by many readers is that they do not think it important to classify the book they are reading. They do not follow this first rule of analytical reading. If they tried to follow it, they would be grateful to the author for helping them. Obviously, the author thinks it is important for the reader to know the kind of book he is being given. That is why he goes to the trouble of making it plain in the preface, and usually tries to make his title—or at least his subtitle—descriptive. Thus, Einstein and Infeld, in their preface to *The Evolution of Physics,* tell the reader that they expect him to know "that a scientific book, even though popular, must not be read in the same way as a novel." They also construct an analytical table of contents to advise the reader in advance of the details of their treatment. In any event, the chapter headings listed in the front serve the purpose of amplifying the significance of the main title.

The reader who ignores all these things has only himself to blame if he is puzzled by the question, What kind of book is this? He is going to become more perplexed. If he cannot answer that question, and if he never asks it of himself, he is going to be unable to answer a lot of other questions about the book.

Important as reading titles is, it is not enough. The clearest titles in the world, the most explicit front matter, will not help you to classify a book unless you have the broad lines of classification already in your mind.

You will not know the sense in which Euclid's *Elements of Geometry* and William James' *Principles of Psychology* are books of the same sort if you do not know that psychology and geometry are both sciences—and, incidentally, if you do not know that "elements" and "principles" mean much the same thing in these two titles (though not in general), nor will you further be able to distinguish them as different unless you know there are different kinds of science. Similarly, in the case of Aristotle's *Politics* and Adam Smith's *The Wealth of Nations,* you can tell how these books are alike and different only if you know what a practical problem is, and what different kinds of practical problems there are.

Titles sometimes make the grouping of books easy. Anyone would know that Euclid's *Elements,* Descartes' *Geometry,* and Hilbert's *Foundations of Geometry* are three mathematical books, more or less closely related in subject matter. This is not always the case. It might not be so easy to tell from the titles that Augustine's *The City of God,* Hobbes' *Leviathan,* and Rousseau's *Social Contract* are political treatises, although a careful perusal of their chapter headings would reveal the problems that are common to these three books.

Again, however, to group books as being of the same kind is not enough; to follow this first rule of reading you must know *what that kind is.* The title will not tell you, nor all the rest of the front matter, nor even the whole book itself sometimes, unless you have some categories you can apply to classify books intelligently. In other words, this rule has to be made a little more intelligible if you are to follow it intelligently. It can only be made intelligible by drawing distinctions and thus creating categories that make sense and will stand up to the test of time.

We have already discussed a rough classification of books. The main distinction, we said, was between works of fiction, on the one hand, and works conveying knowledge, or expository works, on the other hand. Among expository works, we can further distinguish history from philosophy, and both from science and mathematics.

Now this is all very well as far as it goes. This is a classification scheme with fairly perspicuous categories, and most people could probably place most books in the right category if they thought about it. But not all books in all categories.

The trouble is that as yet we have no principles of classification. We will have more to say about these principles as we proceed in our discussion of the higher levels of reading. For the moment, we want to confine ourselves to one basic distinction, a distinction that applies across the board to all expository works. It is the distinction between theoretical and practical works.

Practical vs. Theoretical Books

Everyone uses the words "theoretical" and "practical," but not everyone knows what they mean, perhaps least of all the hardheaded practical man who distrusts all theorists, especially if they are in the government. For such persons, "theoretical" means visionary or even mystical; "practical" means something that works, something that has an immediate cash return. There is an element of truth in this. The practical has to do with what works in some way, at once or in the long run. The theoretical concerns something to be seen or understood. If we polish the rough truth that is here being grasped, we come to the distinction between knowledge and action as the two ends a writer may have in mind.

But, you may say, in dealing with expository books, are we not dealing with books that convey knowledge? How does action come into it? The answer, of course, is that intelligent action depends on knowledge. Knowledge can be used in many ways, not only for controlling nature and inventing useful machines or instruments but also for directing human conduct and regulating man's operations in various fields of skill. What we have in mind here is exemplified by the distinction between pure and applied science, or, as it is sometimes very inaccurately expressed, between science and technology.

Some books and some teachers are interested only in the knowledge itself that they have to communicate. This does not mean that they deny its utility, or that they insist that knowledge is good *only* for its own sake. They simply limit themselves to one kind of communication or teaching, and leave the other kind to other men. These others have an interest beyond knowledge for its own sake. They are concerned with the problems of human life that knowledge can help to solve. They communicate knowledge, too, but always with a view to and an emphasis upon its application.

To make knowledge practical we must convert it into rules of operation. We must pass from knowing *what is the case* to knowing *what to do about it if we wish to get somewhere.* This can be summarized in the distinction between knowing *that* and knowing *how.* Theoretical books teach you *that* something is the case. Practical books teach you *how* to do something you want to do or think you should do.

This book is practical, not theoretical. Any guidebook is a practical book. Any book that tells you either what you *should* do or *how* to do it is practical. Thus you see that the class of practical books includes all expositions of arts to be learned, all manuals of practice in any field, such as engineering or medicine or cooking, and all treatises that are conveniently classified as moral, such as books on economic, ethical, or political problems. We will later explain why this last group of books, properly called "normative," constitutes a very special category of practical books.

Probably no one would question our calling expositions of arts to be learned and manuals or rule books, practical works. But the "practical" man to whom we have referred might object to the notion that a book on ethics, say, or one on economics, was practical. He might say that such a book was not practical because it was not true or would not work.

In fact, this is irrelevant to the point, although a book about economics that is not true is a bad book. Strictly speaking, any ethical work teaches us how to live our lives, tells us what we should do and not do, and often informs us of the rewards and punishments attached to doing and not doing it. Thus, whether or not we agree with its conclusions, any such work is practical. (Some modern sociological studies merely report the actual behavior of men, without judging it. These are neither ethical nor practical books. They are theoretical works—works of science.)

Similarly with a work on economics. Apart from reportorial, mathematical, or statistical studies of economic behavior, which are theoretical rather than practical, such works usually teach us how to organize our economic life, either as individuals or as societies or states, tell us what we should do and not do, and also inform us of the penalties involved if we do not do what we should. Again, we may disagree, but our disagreement does not make the book unpractical.

Immanuel Kant wrote two famous philosophical works, one called *The Critique of Pure Reason,* the other, *The Critique of Practical Reason.* The first is about what is and how we know it—not how *to* know it, but how we in fact *do* know it—as well as about what can and cannot be known. It is a theoretical book *par excellence. The Critique of Practical Reason* is about how men should conduct themselves and about what constitutes virtuous or right conduct. This book places great emphasis on duty as the basis of all right action, and that emphasis may seem repellent to many modern readers. They may even say it is "impractical" to believe that duty is any longer a useful ethical concept. What they mean, of course, is that Kant is wrong, in their opinion, in his basic approach. But that does not mean that his book is any less a practical work in the sense we are employing here.

Apart from manuals and moral treatises (in the broad sense) one other instance of practical writing should be mentioned. An oration—a political speech or moral exhortation—certainly tries to tell you what you should do or how you should feel about something. Anyone who writes practically about anything not only tries to advise you but also tries to persuade you to follow his advice. Hence there is an element of oratory or exhortation in every moral treatise. It is also present in books that try to teach an art, such as this one. Thus, in addition to trying to teach you to read better, we have tried, and will continue to try, to persuade you to make the effort to do so.

Although every practical book is somewhat oratorical and hortatory, it does not follow that oratory and exhortation are coextensive with the practical. There is a difference between a political harangue and a treatise on politics, between economic propaganda and an analysis of economic problems. The *Communist Manifesto* is a piece of oratory, but Marx's *Capital* is much more than that.

Sometimes you can detect that a book is practical by its title. If the title contains such phrases as "the art of" or "how to," you can spot it at once. If the title names fields that you know are practical, such as ethics or politics, engineering or business, and in many cases economics, law, or medicine, you can classify the book fairly readily.

Titles can tell you even more than that. John Locke wrote two books with similar titles: *An Essay Concerning Human Understanding* and *A Treatise Concerning the Origin, Extent, and End of Civil Government*. Which of these is theoretical, which practical?

From the titles alone we may conclude that the first is theoretical, because any analysis of understanding would be theoretical, and that the second is practical, because problems of government are themselves practical. But one could go beyond that, employing the techniques of inspectional reading that we have described. Locke wrote an introduction to the book on understanding. There he expressed his intention as being to inquire into the "origin, certainty, and extent of human knowledge." The phrasing resembles the title of the book on government, but with one important difference. Locke was concerned with the *certainty* or validity of knowledge in the one case, and with the *end* or purpose of government in the other. Questions about the validity of something are theoretical, whereas to raise questions about the end of anything, the purpose it serves, is practical.

In describing the art of inspectional reading, we noted that you should not ordinarily stop after reading the front matter of a book and perhaps its index. You should read passages in the book that appear to be of a summary nature. You should also read the beginning and end of the book and of its major parts.

This becomes necessary when, as is sometimes the case, it is impossible to classify a book from its title and other front matter. In that case, you have to depend on signs to be found in the main body of the text. By paying attention to the words and keeping the basic categories in mind, you should be able to classify a book without reading very far.

A practical book will soon betray its character by the frequent occurrence of such words as "should" and "ought," "good" and "bad," "ends" and "means." The characteristic statement in a practical book is one that says that something should be done (or made); or that this is the right way of doing (or making) something; or that one thing is better than another as an end to be sought, or a means to be chosen. In contrast, a theoretical book keeps saying "is," not "should" or "ought." It tries to show that something is true, that these are the facts; not that things would be better if they were otherwise, and here is the way to make them better.

Before turning to theoretical books, let us caution you against supposing that the problem is as simple as telling whether you are drinking coffee or milk. We have merely suggested some signs whereby you can begin to make discriminations. The better you understand everything that is involved in the distinction between the theoretical and the practical, the better you will be able to use the signs.

For one thing, you will have to learn to mistrust them. You have to be suspicious in classifying books. We have noted that although economics is primarily and usually a practical matter, there are nevertheless books on economics that are purely theoretical. Similarly, although understanding is primarily and usually a theoretical matter, there are books (most of them are terrible) that purport to teach you "how to think." You will also find authors who do not know the difference between theory and practice, just as there are novelists who do not know the difference between fiction and sociology. You will find books that are partly of one sort and partly of another, such as Spinoza's *Ethics*. It remains, nevertheless, to your advantage as a reader to detect the way an author approaches his problem.

Kinds of Theoretical Books

The traditional subdivision of theoretical books classifies them as history, science, and philosophy. Everybody knows the differences here in a rough way. It is only when you try to refine the obvious, and give the distinctions greater precision, that you get into difficulties. For the moment, let us try to skirt that danger and let rough approximations suffice.

In the case of history, the title usually does the trick. If the word "history" does not appear in the title, the rest of the front matter is likely to inform us that this is a book about something that happened in the past—not necessarily in the far past, of course, because it may have happened only yesterday. The essence of history is narration. History is knowledge of particular events or things that not only existed in the past but also underwent a series of changes in the course of time. The historian narrates these happenings and often colors his narrative with comment on, or insight into, the significance of the events.

History is chronotopic. *Chronos* is the Greek word for time, *topos* the Greek word for place. History always deals with things that existed or events that occurred on a particular date and in a particular place. The word "chronotopic" can remind you of that.

Science is not concerned with the past as such. It treats of matters than can happen at *any* time or place. The scientist seeks laws or generalizations. He wants to find out how things happen for the most part or in every case, not, as the historian does, how some particular things happened at a given time and place in the past.

The title of a scientific work is usually less revealing than the title of a history book. The word "science" sometimes appears, but more often the name of the subject matter appears, such as psychology or geology or physics. Then we must know whether that subject matter belongs to the scientist, as geology clearly does, or to the philosopher, as metaphysics clearly does. The trouble comes with the cases that are not so clear, such as physics and psychology, which have been claimed, at various times, by both scientists and philosophers. There is even trouble with the very words "philosophy" and "science," for they have been variously used. Aristotle called his book on *Physics* a scientific treatise, although according to current usage we should regard it as philosophical; and Newton titled his great work *Mathematical Principles of Natural Philosophy,* though for us it is one of the masterpieces of science.

Philosophy is like science and unlike history in that it seeks general truths rather than an account of particular events, either in the near or distant past. But the philosopher does not ask the same questions as the scientist, nor does he employ the same kind of method to answer them.

Since titles and subject-matter names are not likely to help us determine whether a book is philosophical or scientific, how can we tell? There is one criterion that we think always works, although you may have to read a certain amount of the book before you can apply it. If a theoretical book emphasizes things that lie outside the scope of your normal, routine, daily experience, it is a scientific work. If not, it is philosophical.

The distinction may be surprising. Let us illustrate it. (Remember that it applies only to books that are either science or philosophy, not to books that are neither.) Galileo's *Two New Sciences* requires you to imagine, or to repeat for yourself in a laboratory, certain experiments with inclined planes. Newton's *Opticks* refers to experiences in dark rooms with prisms, mirrors, and specially controlled rays of light. The special experience to which the author refers may not have been obtained by him in a laboratory. The facts that Darwin reported in *The Origin of Species* he observed in the course of many years of work in the field. They are facts that can be and have been rechecked by other observers making a similar effort. But they are not facts that can be checked in terms of the ordinary daily experience of the average man.

In contrast, a philosophical book appeals to no facts or observations that lie outside the experience of the ordinary man. A philosopher refers the reader to his own normal and common experience for the verification or support of anything the writer has to say. Thus, Locke's *Essay Concerning Human Understanding* is a philosophical work in psychology, whereas many of Freud's writings are scientific. Locke makes every point in terms of the experience all of us have of our own mental processes. Freud can make many of his points only by reporting what he observed under the clinical conditions of the psychoanalyst's office.

William James, another great psychologist, took an interesting middle course. He reports many examples of the special experience that only the careful, trained observer can know about, but he also frequently asks the reader to judge whether what is being said is not true from his own experience. Thus James' *Principles of Psychology* is both a scientific and a philosophical work, although it is primarily scientific.

The distinction proposed here is popularly recognized when we say that science is experimental or depends upon elaborate observational researches, whereas philosophy is merely armchair thinking. The contrast should not be invidious. There are certain problems, some of them very important, that can be solved in an armchair by a man who knows how to think about them in the light of common, human experience. There are other problems that no amount of the best armchair thinking can solve. What is needed to solve them is investigation of some sort—experiments in the laboratory or research in the field—extending experience beyond the normal, everyday routine. Special experience is required.

This does not mean that the philosopher is a pure thinker and the scientist merely an observer. Both have to observe and think, but they think about different sorts of observations. And however they may have arrived at the conclusions that they want to prove, they prove them in different ways, the scientist by pointing to the results of his special experiences, the philosopher by pointing to experiences that are common to all.

This difference in method always reveals itself in philosophical and scientific books, and that is how you can tell which sort of book you are reading. If you note the sort of experience that is being referred to as a condition of understanding what is being said, you will know whether the book is scientific or philosophical.

It is important to know this because, apart from the different kinds of experiences that they depend on, scientists and philosophers do not think in exactly the same way. Their styles in arguing are different. You must be able to find the terms and propositions—here we are getting a little ahead of ourselves—that constitute these different sorts of argumentation.

The same is true of history. Historical statements are different from scientific and philosophical ones. A historian argues differently and interprets facts differently. Furthermore, the typical history book is narrative in form. A narrative is a narrative, whether it be fact or fiction. The historian must write poetically, which means he must obey the rules for telling a good story. Whatever other excellences Locke's *Essay on Human Understanding* or Newton's *Principia* may have, neither is a good story.

You may object that we are making too much of the classification of books, at least before one has read them. Is it really all that important?

We may be able to meet the objections by calling your attention to one obvious fact. If you walked into a classroom in which a teacher was lecturing or otherwise instructing students, you could tell very soon whether the class was one in history, science, or philosophy. There would be something in the way the teacher proceeded, the kind of words he used, the type of arguments he employed, the sort of problems he proposed, and the kind of responses he expected from his students, that would give him away as belonging to one department or another. And it would make a difference to you to know this, if you were going to try to listen intelligently to what went on.

In short, the methods of teaching different kinds of subject matter are different. Any teacher knows this. Because of the difference in method and subject matter, the philosopher usually finds it easier to teach students who have not been previously taught by his colleagues, whereas the scientist prefers the student whom his colleagues have already prepared. And so forth and so on.

Now, just as there is a difference in the art of teaching in different fields, so there is a reciprocal difference in the art of being taught. The activity of the student must somehow be responsive to the activity of the instructor. The relation between books and their readers is the same as that between teachers and their students. Hence, as books differ in the kinds of knowledge they have to communicate, they proceed to instruct us differently; and, if we are to follow them, we must learn to read each kind in an appropriate manner.

7

X-raying a Book

Every book has a skeleton hidden between its covers. Your job as an analytical reader is to find it.

A book comes to you with flesh on its bare bones and clothes over its flesh. It is all dressed up. You do not have to undress it or tear the flesh off its limbs to get at the firm structure that underlies the soft surface. But you must read the book with X-ray eyes, for it is an essential part of your apprehension of any book to grasp its structure.

Recognition of the need to see the structure of a book leads to the discovery of the second and third rules for reading any book. We say "any book." These rules apply to poetry as well as to science, and to any kind of expository work. Their application will be different, of course, according to the kind of book they are used on. The unity of a novel is not the same as the unity of a treatise on politics; nor are the parts of the same sort, or ordered in the same way. But every book without exception that is worth reading at all has a unity and an organization of parts. A book that did not would be a mess. It would be relatively unreadable, as bad books actually are.

We will state these two rules as simply as possible. Then we will explain and illustrate them.

The second rule of analytical reading can be expressed as follows: RULE 2. STATE THE UNITY OF THE WHOLE BOOK IN A SINGLE SENTENCE, OR AT MOST A FEW SENTENCES (A SHORT PARAGRAPH).

This means that you must say what the whole book is about as briefly as possible. To say what the whole book is about is not the same as saying what kind of book it is. (That was covered by Rule 1.) The word "about" may be misleading here. In one sense, a book is *about* a certain type of subject matter, which it treats in a certain way. If you know this, you know what *kind* of book it is. But there is another, more colloquial sense of "about." We ask a person what he is about, what he is up to. So we can wonder what an author is up to, what he is trying to do. To find out what a book is about in this sense is to discover its *theme* or main *point*.

A book is a work of art. (Again, we want to warn you against too narrow a conception of "art." We do not mean, or we do not only mean, "fine art" here. A book is the product of someone who has a certain skill in making. He is a maker of books and he has made one here for our benefit.) In proportion as it is good, as a book and as a work of art, it has a more nearly perfect, a more pervasive unity. This is true of music and paintings, of novels and plays; it is no less true of books that convey knowledge.

But it is not enough to acknowledge this fact vaguely. You must apprehend the unity with definiteness. There is only one way to know that you have succeeded. You must be able to tell yourself or anybody else what the unity is, and in a few words. (If it requires too many words, you have not seen the unity but a multiplicity.) Do not be satisfied with "feeling the unity" that you cannot express. The reader who says, "I know what it is, but I just can't say it," probably does not even fool himself.

The third rule can be expressed as follows: RULE 3. SET FORTH THE MAJOR PARTS OF THE BOOK, AND SHOW HOW THESE ARE ORGANIZED INTO A WHOLE, BY BEING ORDERED TO ONE ANOTHER AND TO THE UNITY OF THE WHOLE.

The reason for this rule should be obvious. If a work of art were absolutely simple, it would, of course, have no parts. But that is never the case. None of the sensible, physical things man knows is simple in this absolute way, nor is any human production. They are all complex unities. You have not grasped a complex unity if all you know about it is *how it is one*. You must also know *how it is many*, not a many that consists of a lot of separate things, but an organized many. If the parts were not organically related, the whole that they composed would not be one. Strictly speaking, there would be no whole at all but merely a collection.

There is a difference between a heap of bricks, on the one hand, and the single house they can constitute, on the other. There is a difference between a single house and a collection of houses. A book is like a single house. It is a mansion having many rooms, rooms on different levels, of different sizes and shapes, with different outlooks, with different uses. The rooms are independent, in part. Each has its own structure and interior decoration. But they are not absolutely independent and separate. They are connected by doors and arches, by corridors and stairways, by what architects call a "traffic pattern." Because they are connected, the partial function that each performs contributes its share to the usefulness of the whole house. Otherwise the house would not be livable.

The analogy is almost perfect. A good book, like a good house, is an orderly arrangement of parts. Each major part has a certain amount of independence. As we will see, it may have an interior structure of its own, and it may be decorated in a different way from other parts. But it must also be connected with the other parts—that is, related to them functionally—for otherwise it would not contribute its share to the intelligibility of the whole.

As houses are more or less livable, so books are more or less readable. The most readable book is an architectural achievement on the part of the author. The best books are those that have the most intelligible structure. Though they are usually more complex than poorer books, their greater complexity is also a greater simplicity, because their parts are better organized, more unified.

That is one of the reasons why the best books are also the most readable. Lesser works are really more bothersome to read. Yet to read them well—that is, as well as they can be read—you must try to find some plan in them. They would have been better books if their authors had themselves seen the plan a little more clearly. But if they hang together at all, if they are a complex unity to any degree and not mere collections, there must be a plan and you must find it.

Of Plots and Plans: Stating the Unity of a Book

Let us return now to the second rule, which requires you to state the unity of a book. A few illustrations of the rule in operation may guide you in putting it into practice.

Let us begin with a famous case. You probably read Homer's *Odyssey* in school. If not, you must know the story of Odysseus, or Ulysses, as the Romans call him, the man who took ten years to return from the siege of Troy only to find his faithful wife Penelope herself besieged by suitors. It is an elaborate story as Homer tells it, full of exciting adventures on land and sea, replete with episodes of all sorts and many complications of plot. But it also has a single unity of action, a main thread of plot that ties everything together.

Aristotle, in his *Poetics,* insists that this is the mark of *every* good story, novel, or play. To support his point, he shows how the unity of the *Odyssey* can be summarized in a few sentences.

> A certain man is absent from home for many years; he is jealously watched by Poseidon, and left desolate. Meanwhile his home is in a wretched plight; suitors are wasting his substance and plotting against his son. At length, tempest-tossed, he himself arrives; he makes certain persons acquainted with him; he attacks the suitors with his own hand, and is himself preserved while he destroys them.

"This," says Aristotle, "is the essence of the plot; the rest is episode." After you know the plot in this way, and through it the unity of the whole narrative, you can put the parts into their proper places.

You might find it a good exercise to try this with some novels you have read. Try it on some good ones, such as Fielding's *Tom Jones* or Dostoevsky's *Crime and Punishment* or Joyce's modern *Ulysses*. The plot of *Tom Jones,* for instance, can be reduced to the familiar formula: Boy meets girl, boy loses girl, boy gets girl. That, indeed, is the plot of every romance. To recognize this is to learn what it means to say that there are only a small number of plots in the world. The difference between good and bad stories having the same essential plot lies in what the author does with it, how he dresses up the bare bones.

You do not always have to find out the unity of a book all by yourself. The author often helps you. Sometimes, the title is all you have to read. In the eighteenth century, writers had the habit of composing elaborate titles that told the reader what the whole book was about. Here is a title by Jeremy Collier, an English divine who attacked what he considered to be the obscenity—we would say pornography, perhaps—of Restoration drama much more learnedly than is customary nowadays: *A Short View of the Immorality and Profaneness of the English Stage, together with the Sense of Antiquity upon this Argument.* You can guess from this that Collier recites many flagrant instances of the abuse of morals and that he supports his protest by quoting texts from those ancients who argued, as Plato did, that the stage corrupts youth, or, as the early Church fathers did, that plays are seductions of the flesh and the devil.

Sometimes the author tells you the unity of his plan in his preface. In this respect, expository books differ radically from fiction. A scientific or philosophical writer has no reason to keep you in suspense. In fact, the less suspense he keeps you in, the more likely you are to sustain the effort of reading his work through. Like a newspaper article, an expository book may summarize itself in its first paragraph.

Do not be too proud to accept the author's help if he proffers it, but do not rely too completely on what he says in the preface, either.

The best-laid plans of authors, like those of mice and other men, often go awry. Be guided by the prospectus the author gives you, but always remember that the obligation of finding the unity belongs finally to the reader, as much as the obligation of having one belongs to the writer. You can discharge that obligation honestly only by reading the whole book.

The introductory paragraph of Herodotus' history of the war between the Greeks and the Persians provides an excellent summary of the whole. It runs:

These are the researches of Herodotus of Halicarnassus, which he publishes, in the hope of thereby preserving from decay the remembrance of what men have done, and of preventing the great and wonderful actions of the Greeks and the Barbarians from losing their due meed of glory; and withal to put on record what were their grounds of feud.

That is a good beginning for you as a reader. It tells you succinctly what the whole book is about.

But you had better not stop there. After you have read the nine parts of Herodotus' history through, you will probably find it necessary to elaborate on that statement to do justice to the whole. You might want to mention the Persian kings—Cyrus, Darius, and Xerxes; the Greek heroes of the war—primarily Themistocles; and the major events—the crossing of the Hellespont and the decisive battles, notably Thermopylae and Salamis.

All the rest of the fascinating details, with which Herodotus richly prepares you for his climax, can be left out of your summary of the plot. Note, here, that the unity of a history is a single thread of plot, very much as in fiction. So far as unity is concerned, this rule of reading elicits the same kind of answer in history and in fiction.

A few more illustrations may suffice. Let us take a practical book first. The unity of Aristotle's *Ethics* can be stated thus:

This is an inquiry into the nature of human happiness and an analysis of the conditions under which happiness may be gained or lost, with an indication of what men must do in their conduct and thinking in order to become happy or to avoid unhappiness, the principal emphasis being placed on the cultivation of the virtues, both moral and intellectual, although other goods are also recognized as necessary for happiness, such as wealth, health, friends, and a just society in which to live.

Another practical book is Adam Smith's *The Wealth of Nations*. Here the reader is aided by the author's own statement of "the plan of the work" at the very beginning. But that takes several pages. The unity can be more briefly stated as follows:

This is an inquiry into the source of national wealth in any economy that is built on a division of labor, considering the relation of the wages paid labor, the profits returned to capital, and the rent owed the landowner, as the prime factors in the price of commodities. It discusses the various ways in which capital can be more or less gainfully employed, and relates the origin and use of money to the accumulation and employment of capital. Examining the development of opulence in different nations and under different conditions, it compares the several systems of political economy, and argues for the beneficence of free trade.

If a reader grasped the unity of *The Wealth of Nations* in this way, and did a similar job for Marx's *Das Kapital,* he would be well on the way toward seeing the relation between two of the most influential books of the past two centuries.

Darwin's *The Origin of Species* provides us with a good example of the unity of a theoretical book in science. Here is a statement of it:

This is an account of the variation of living things during the course of countless generations and the way in which this results in new groupings of plants and animals; it treats both of the variability of domesticated animals and of variability under natural conditions, showing how such factors as the struggle for existence and natural selection operate to bring about and sustain such groupings; it argues that species are not fixed and immutable groups, but that they are merely varieties in transition from a less to a more marked and permanent status, supporting this argument by evidences from extinct animals found in the earth's crust, and from comparative embryology and anatomy.

That may seem like a big mouthful, but the book was an even bigger one for a great many readers in the nineteenth century, partly because they did not go to the trouble of finding out what it was really about.

Finally, let us take Locke's *Essay Concerning Human Understanding* as a theoretical book in philosophy. You may recall our observing that Locke himself summarized his work by saying that it was "an inquiry into the origin, certainty and extent of human knowledge, together with the grounds and degrees of belief, opinion and assent." We would not quarrel with so excellent a statement of plan by the author, except to add two subordinate qualifications to do justice to the first and third parts of the essay: it will be shown, we would add, that there are no innate ideas, but that all human knowledge is acquired from experience; and language will be discussed as a medium for the expression of thought, its proper use and most familiar abuses to be indicated.

There are two things we want you to note before we proceed. The first is how frequently you can expect the author, especially a good one, to help you to state the plan of his book. Despite that fact, most readers are at a total loss if you ask them to say briefly what the whole book is about. Partly this is owing to the widespread inability to speak concise English sentences. Partly it is owing to neglect of this rule in reading. But it also indicates that many readers pay as little attention to the author's introductory words as they ordinarily do to his title.

The second point is a word of caution. Do not take the sample summaries we have given you as if they were, in each case, a final and absolute formulation of the book's unity. A unity can be variously stated. There is no one right way to do it. One statement is better than another, of course, in proportion as it is brief, accurate, and comprehensive. But quite different statements may be equally good, or equally bad.

We have here sometimes stated the unity of a book quite differently from the author's expression of it, and without apologies to him. You may differ similarly from us. After all, a book is something different to each reader. It would not be surprising if that difference expressed itself in the way the reader stated its unity. This does not mean, however, that anything goes. Though readers are different, the book is the same, and there can be an objective check upon the accuracy and fidelity of the statements anyone makes about it.

Mastering the Multiplicity: The Art of Outlining a Book

Let us turn now to the other structural rule, the rule that requires us to set forth the major parts of the book in their order and relation. This third rule is closely related to the second. A well-stated unity indicates the major parts that compose the whole; you cannot comprehend a whole without somehow seeing its parts. But it is also true that unless you grasp the organization of its parts, you cannot know the whole comprehensively.

Why, then, make two rules here instead of one? It is primarily a matter of convenience. It is easier to grasp a complex and unified structure in two steps than in one. The second rule directs your attention toward the unity, the third toward the complexity, of a book. There is another reason for the separation. The major parts of a book may be seen at the moment when you grasp its unity. But these parts are themselves usually complex and have an interior structure you must see. Hence the third rule involves more than just an enumeration of the parts. It means outlining them, that is, treating the parts as if they were subordinate wholes, each with a unity and complexity of its own.

A formula can be stated for operating according to this third rule. It will guide you in a general way. According to the second rule, we had to say: The whole book is about so and so and such and such. That done, we might obey the third rule by proceeding as follows: (1) The author accomplished this plan in five major parts, of which the first part is about so and so, the second part is about such and such, the third part is about this, the fourth part about that, and the fifth part about still another thing. (2) The first of these major parts is divided into three sections, of which the first considers X, the second considers Y, and the third considers Z. (3) In the first section of the first part, the author makes four points, of which the first is A, the second B, the third C, and the fourth D. And so on and so forth.

You may object to this much outlining. It would take a lifetime to read a book that way. But of course this is only a formula. The rule looks as if it required an impossible amount of work from you. In fact, the good reader does this sort of thing habitually, and hence easily and naturally. He may not write it all out. He may not even at the time of reading have made it all verbally explicit. But if he were called upon to give an account of the structure of the book, he would do something that approximated the formula we have described.

The word "approximation" should relieve your anxiety. A good rule always describes the ideal performance. But a person can be skilled in an art without being the ideal artist. He can be a good practitioner if he merely approximates the rule. We have stated the rule here for the ideal case. You should be satisfied if you make a very rough approximation to what is required.

Even when you become more skilled, you will not want to read every book with the same degree of effort. You will not find it profitable to expend all your skill on some books. Even the best readers try to make a fairly close approximation to the requirements of this rule for only a relatively few books. For the most part, they are satisfied with a rough notion of the book's structure. The degree of approximation varies with the character of the book and your purpose in reading it. Regardless of this variability, the rule remains the same. You must know how to follow it, whether you follow it closely or only in a rough fashion.

You should understand that the limitations on the degree to which you can approximate the rule are not only ones of time and effort. You are a finite, mortal creature; but a book is also finite and, if not mortal, at least defective in the way all things made by man are. No book deserves a perfect outline because no book is perfect. It goes only so far, and so must you. This rule, after all, does not call for your putting things into the book that the author did not put there. Your outline is of the book itself, not the subject matter that the book is about. Perhaps the outline of a subject matter could be extended indefinitely, but not your outline of the book, which gives the subject matter only more or less definitive treatment. Hence you should not feel that we are urging you merely to be lazy about following this rule. You could not follow it out to the bitter end even if you wanted to.

The forbidding aspect of the formula for setting forth the order and relation of the parts may be somewhat lessened by a few illustrations of the rule in operation. Unfortunately, it is more difficult to illustrate this rule than the other one about stating the unity. A unity, after all, can be stated in a sentence or two, at most a short paragraph. But in the case of a large and complex book, a careful and adequate outline of the parts, and their parts, and *their* parts down to the least structural unit that is comprehensible and worthwhile identifying, would take a great many pages to write out.

Theoretically, the outline could be longer than the original. Some of the great medieval commentaries on the works of Aristotle *are* longer than the works they comment on. They include, of course, more than an outline, for they undertake to interpret the author sentence by sentence. The same is true of certain modern commentaries, such as the great ones on Kant's *Critique of Pure Reason*. And a variorum edition of a Shakespeare play, which includes an exhaustive outline as well as other things, is many times as long—perhaps ten times as long—as the original. You might look into a commentary of this sort if you want to see the rule followed as close to perfection as man can do. Aquinas, for instance, begins each section of his commentary with a beautiful outline of the points that Aristotle has made in a particular part of his work; and he always says explicitly how that part fits the structure of the whole, especially in relation to the parts that come before and after.

Let us take something easier than a treatise of Aristotle. Aristotle is probably the most compact of prose writers; you would expect that an outline of one of his works would be extensive and difficult. Let us also agree that, for the sake of the example, we will not carry the process out to the relative perfection that would be possible if we had a great number of pages available.

The United States Constitution is an interesting, practical document, and a very well-organized piece of writing. If you examine it, you should have no difficulty in finding its major parts. They are pretty clearly indicated, though you have to do some thinking to make the main divisions. Here is a suggested outline of the document:

FIRST: The Preamble, setting forth the purpose(s) of the Constitution;

SECOND: The first Article, dealing with the legislative department of the government;

THIRD: The second Article, dealing with the executive department of the government;

FOURTH: The third Article, dealing with the judicial department of the government;

FIFTH: The fourth Article, dealing with the relationship between the state governments and the federal government;

SIXTH: The fifth, sixth, and seventh Articles, dealing with the amendment of the Constitution, its status as the supreme law of the land, and provisions for its ratifications;

SEVENTH: The first ten amendments, constituting the Bill of Rights;
EIGHTH: The remaining amendments up to the present day.

Those are the major divisions. Now let us outline one of them, the *Second,* comprising the Constitution's first Article. Like most of the other Articles, it is divided into Sections. Here is a suggested outline.

II, 1: Section 1, establishing legislative powers in a Congress of the United States, divided into two bodies, a Senate and a House of Representatives;

II, 2: Sections 2 and 3, respectively describing the composition of the House and Senate and stating the qualifications of members. In addition, it is stated that the House has the sole power of impeachment, while the Senate has the sole power of trying impeachments;

II, 3: Sections 4 and 5, having to do with the election of members of both branches of Congress and with the internal organization and affairs of each;

II, 4: Section 6, stating the perquisites and emoluments of members of both branches, and stating one limitation on civil employment of members;

II, 5: Section 7, defining the relationship between the legislative and executive departments of the government and describing the President's veto power;

II, 6: Section 8, stating the powers of Congress;

II, 7: Section 9, stating some limitations on the powers outlined in Section 8;

II, 8: Section 10, stating limitations on the powers of the states and the extent to which they must give over certain powers to the Congress.

We could then proceed to make a similar outline of all the other major divisions, and, after completing that, return to outline the Sections in turn. Some of these, for example Section 8 in Article I, would require the identification of many different topics and sub-topics.

Of course, this is only one way of doing the job. There are many others. The first three Articles could be grouped together in one major division, for instance; or instead of two divisions with respect to the amendments, more major divisions could be introduced, grouping the amendments according to the problems they dealt with. We suggest that you try your hand at making your own division of the Constitution into its main parts. Go even further than we did, and try to state the parts of the parts as well. You may have read the Constitution many times, but if you have not applied this rule before, you will find that it reveals much in the document that you never saw.

Here is one more example, again very brief. We have already stated the unity of Aristotle's *Ethics*. Now let us attempt a first approximation of its structure. The whole is divided into the following main parts: A first, treating of happiness as the end of life, and discussing it in relation to all other practicable goods; a second, treating of the nature of voluntary action, and its relation to the formation of good and bad habits; a third, discussing the various virtues and vices, both moral and intellectual; a fourth, dealing with moral states that are neither virtuous nor vicious; a fifth, treating of friendship; and a sixth and last, discussing pleasure, and completing the account of human happiness begun in the first.

These divisions obviously do not correspond to the ten books of the *Ethics*. Thus, the first part is accomplished in the first book; the second part runs through Book II and the first half of Book III; the third part extends from the rest of Book III through the end of Book VI; the discussion of pleasure occurs at the end of Book VII and again at the beginning of Book X.

We mention this to show you that you need not follow the apparent structure of a book as indicated by its chapter divisions. That structure may, of course, be better than the outline you develop, but it may also be worse; in any event, the point is to make your own outline. The author made his in order to write a good book. You must make yours in order to read it well. If he were a perfect writer and you a perfect reader, it would follow that the two would be the same. In proportion as either of you falls away from perfection, all sorts of discrepancies will inevitably result.

This does not mean that you should ignore chapter headings and sectional divisions made by the author; we did not ignore them in our analysis of the Constitution, although we did not slavishly follow them, either. They are intended to help you, just as titles and prefaces are. But you must use them as guides for your own activity, and not rely on them passively. There are few authors who execute their plan perfectly, but there is often more plan in a good book than meets the eye at first. The surface can be deceiving. You must look beneath it to discover the real structure.

How important is it to discover that real structure? We think very important. Another way of saying this is to say that Rule 2—the requirement that you state the unity of a book—cannot be effectively followed without obeying Rule 3—the requirement that you state the parts that make up that unity. You might, from a cursory glance at a book, be able to come up with an adequate statement of its unity in two or three sentences. But you would not really know that it was adequate. Someone else, who had read the book better, might know this, and award you high marks for your efforts. But for you, from your point of view, it would have been merely a good guess, a lucky hit. This is why the third rule is absolutely necessary as a complement to the second one.

A very simple example will show what we mean. A two-year-old child, just having begun to talk, might say that "two plus two is four." Objectively, this is a true statement; but we would be wrong to conclude from it that the child knew much mathematics. In fact, the child probably would not know what the statement meant, and so, although the statement by itself was adequate, we would have to say that the child still needed training in the subject. Similarly, you might be right in your guess about a book's main theme or point, but you still need to go through the exercise of showing *how* and *why* you stated it as you did. The requirement that you outline the parts of a book, and show how they exemplify and develop the main theme, is thus supportive of your statement of the book's unity.

The Reciprocal Arts of Reading and Writing

In general, the two rules of reading that we have been discussing look as if they were rules of writing also. Of course they are. Writing and reading are reciprocal, as are teaching and being taught. If authors and teachers did not organize their communications, if they failed to unify them and order their parts, there would be no point in directing readers or listeners to search for the unity and uncover the structure of the whole.

Nevertheless, although the rules are reciprocal, they are not followed in the same way. The reader tries to *uncover* the skeleton that the book conceals. The author starts with the skeleton and tries to *cover it up*. His aim is to conceal the skeleton artistically or, in other words, to put flesh on the bare bones. If he is a good writer, he does not bury a puny skeleton under a mass of fat; on the other hand, neither should the flesh be too thin, so that the bones show through. If the flesh is thick enough, and if flabbiness is avoided, the joints will be detectable and the motion of the parts will reveal the articulation.

Why is this so? Why should not an expository book, one that attempts to present a body of knowledge in an ordered way, be merely an outline of the subject? The reason is not only that most readers cannot read outlines, and that such a book would be repellent to a self-respecting reader who thought that if he could do his job, the author ought to do his. There is more to it than that. The flesh of a book is as much a part of it as the skeleton. This is as true of books as it is of animals and human beings. The flesh—the outline spelled out, "read out," as we sometimes say—adds an essential dimension. It adds life, in the case of the animal. Just so, actually writing the book from an outline, no matter how detailed, gives the work a kind of life that it would not otherwise have had.

We can summarize all of this by recalling the old-fashioned maxim that a piece of writing should have unity, clarity, and coherence. That is, indeed, a basic maxim of good writing. The two rules we have been discussing in this chapter relate to writing that follows that maxim. If the writing has unity, we must find it. If the writing has clarity and coherence, we must appreciate it by finding the distinction and the order of the parts. What is clear is so by the distinctness of its outlines. What is coherent hangs together in an orderly disposition of parts.

These two rules, therefore, can be used to distinguish well made books from badly made ones. If, after you have attained sufficient skill, no amount of effort on your part results in your apprehension of the unity of a book, and if you are also not able to discern its parts and their relation to one another, then very likely the book is a bad one, whatever its reputation. You should not be too quick to make this judgment; perhaps the fault is in you instead of the book. However, neither should you fail *ever* to make it and always assume that the fault is in you. In fact, whatever your own failings as a reader, the fault is usually in the book, for most books—the very great majority—are badly made books in the sense that their authors did not write them according to these rules.

These two rules can also, we might add, be used in reading any substantial part of an expository book, as well as the whole. If the part chosen is itself a relatively independent, complex unity, its unity and complexity must be discerned for it to be well read. Here there is a significant difference between books conveying knowledge and poetical works, plays, and novels. The parts of the former can be much more autonomous than the parts of the latter. The person who says of a novel that he has "read enough to get the idea" does not know what he is talking about. He cannot be correct, for if the novel is any good at all, the idea is in the whole and cannot be found short of reading the whole. But you can get the idea of Aristotle's *Ethics* or

Darwin's *Origin of Species* by reading some parts carefully, although you would not, in that case, be able to observe Rule 3.

Discovering the Author's Intentions

There is one more rule of reading that we want to discuss in this chapter. It can be stated briefly. It needs little explanation and no illustration. It really repeats in another form what you have already done if you have applied the second and third rules. But it is a useful repetition because it throws the whole and its parts into another light.

This fourth rule can be stated thus: RULE 4. FIND OUT WHAT THE AUTHOR'S PROBLEMS WERE. The author of a book starts with a question or a set of questions. The book ostensibly contains the answer or answers.

The writer may or may not tell you what the questions were as well as give you the answers that are the fruits of his work. Whether he does or does not, and especially if he does not, it is your task as a reader to formulate the questions as precisely as you can. You should be able to state the main question that the book tries to answer, and you should be able to state the subordinate questions if the main question is complex and has many parts. You should not only have a fairly adequate grasp of all the questions involved but should also be able to put the questions in an intelligible order. Which are primary and which secondary? Which questions must be answered first, if others are to be answered later?

You can see how this rule duplicates, in a sense, work you have already done in stating the unity and finding its parts. It may, however, actually help you to do that work. In other words, following the fourth rule is a useful procedure in conjunction with obeying the other two.

And since the rule is a little more unfamiliar than the other two, it may be even more helpful to you in tackling a difficult book. We want to emphasize, however, that we do not mean for you to fall into what is called by critics the intentional fallacy. That is the fallacy of thinking you can discover what was in an author's mind from the book he has written. This applies particularly to literary works; it is a grave error, for example, to try to psychoanalyze Shakespeare from the evidence of *Hamlet*. Nevertheless, even with a poetical work, it is often extremely helpful to try to say what the author was trying to do. In the case of expository works, the rule has obvious merit. And yet most readers, no matter how skilled in other respects, very often fail to observe it. As a result, their conception of a book's main point or theme may be extremely deficient, and of course their outline of its structure will be chaotic. They will fail to see the unity of a book because they do not see *why it has the unity it has;* and their apprehension of the book's skeletal structure will lack comprehension of *the end that it serves.*

If you know the kinds of questions anyone can ask about anything, you will become adept in detecting an author's problems. They can be formulated briefly: Does something exist? What kind of thing is it? What caused it to exist, or under what conditions can it exist, or why does it exist? What purpose does it serve? What are the consequences of its existence? What are its characteristic properties, its typical traits? What are its relations to other things of a similar sort, or of a different sort? How does it behave? *These are all theoretical questions.* What ends should be sought? What means should be chosen to a given end? What things must one do to gain a certain objective, and in what order? Under these conditions, what is the right thing to do, or the better rather than the worse? Under what conditions would it be better to do this rather than that? *These are all practical questions.*

This list of questions is far from being exhaustive, but it does represent the types of most frequently asked questions in the pursuit of theoretical or practical knowledge. It may help you discover the problems a book has tried to solve. The questions have to be adapted when applied to works of imaginative literature, and there too they will be useful.

The First Stage of Analytical Reading

We have now stated and explained the first four rules of reading. They are rules of analytical reading, although if you inspect a book well before reading it, that will help you to apply them.

It is important at this point to recognize that these first four rules are connected and form a group of rules having a single aim. Together, they provide the reader who applies them with a knowledge of a book's structure. When you have applied them to a book, or indeed to anything fairly lengthy and difficult that you may be reading, you will have accomplished the first stage of reading it analytically.

You should not take the term "stage" in a chronological sense, unless perhaps at the very beginning of your exercise as an analytical reader. That is, it is not necessary to read a book through in order to apply the first four rules, then to read it again and again in order to apply the other rules. The practiced reader accomplishes all of these stages at once. Nevertheless, you must realize that knowing a book's structure does constitute a stage toward reading it analytically.

Another way to say this is that applying these first four rules helps you to answer the first basic question about a book. You will recall that that first question is: *What is the book about as a whole?* You will also recall that we said that this means discovering the leading theme of the book, and how the author develops this theme in an orderly way by subdividing it into its essential subordinate themes or topics. Clearly, applying the first four rules of reading will provide most of what you need to know in order to answer this question— although it should be pointed out that your answer will improve in accuracy as you proceed to apply the other rules and to answer the other questions.

Since we have now described the first stage of analytical reading, let us pause a moment to write out the first four rules in order, under the appropriate heading, for review.

THE FIRST STAGE OF ANALYTICAL READING, OR RULES FOR FINDING WHAT A BOOK IS ABOUT

1. Classify the book according to kind and subject matter.

2. State what the whole book is about with the utmost brevity.

3. Enumerate its major parts in their order and relation, and outline these parts as you have outlined the whole.

4. Define the problem or problems the author is trying to solve.

8

Coming to Terms with an Author

The first stage of analytical reading has been accomplished when you have applied the four rules listed at the end of the last chapter, which together allow you to tell what a book is about and to outline its structure. You are now ready to go on to the next stage, which also comprises four rules of reading. The first of these we call, for short, coming to terms.

Coming to terms is usually the last step in any successful business negotiation. All that remains is to sign on the dotted line. But in the analytical reading of a book, coming to terms is the first step beyond the outline. Unless the reader comes to terms with the author, the communication of knowledge from one to the other does not take place. For *a term is the basic element of communicable knowledge.*

Words vs. Terms

A *term* is not a *word*—at least, not just a word without further qualifications. If a term and a word were exactly the same, you would only have to find the important words in a book in order to come to terms with it. But a word can have many meanings, especially an important word. If the author uses a word in one meaning, and the reader reads it in another, words have passed between them, but they have not come to terms. Where there is unresolved ambiguity in communication, there is no communication, or at best communication must be incomplete.

Just look at the word "communication" for a moment. Its root is related to the word "common." We speak of a community as a group of people who have something in common. Communication is an effort on the part of one person to share something with another person (or with an animal or a machine): his knowledge, his decisions, his sentiments. It succeeds only when it results in a common something, such as an item of information or knowledge that two parties share.

When there is ambiguity in the communication of knowledge, all that is in common are the words that one person speaks or writes and another hears or reads. So long as ambiguity persists, there is no meaning in common between writer and reader. For the communication to be successfully completed, therefore, it is necessary for the two parties to use the same words *with the same meanings*—in short, to come to terms. When that happens, communication happens, the miracle of two minds with but a single thought.

A term can be defined as an unambiguous word. That is not quite accurate, for strictly there are no unambiguous words. What we should have said is that a term is a word *used unambiguously*. The dictionary is full of words. They are almost all ambiguous in the sense that they have many meanings. But a word that has several meanings can be used in one sense at a time. When writer and reader somehow manage for a time to use a given word with one and only one meaning, then, during that time of unambiguous usage, they have come to terms.

You cannot find terms in dictionaries, though the materials for making them are there. Terms occur only in the process of communication. They occur when a writer tries to avoid ambiguity and a reader helps him by trying to follow his use of words. There are, of course, many degrees of success in this. Coming to terms is the ideal toward which writer and reader should strive. Since this is one of the primary achievements of the art of writing and reading, we can think of terms as *a skilled use of words for the sake of communicating knowledge.*

At this point it is probably clear that we are speaking exclusively of expository writers and expository books. Poetry and fiction are not nearly so concerned with the unambiguous use of words as expository works—works that convey knowledge in the broad sense of the word that we have been employing. It can even be argued that the best poetry is that which is the most richly ambiguous, and it has been said with justice that any good poet is sometimes intentionally ambiguous in his writing. This is an important insight about poetry to which we will return later. It is obviously one of the primary differences between the poetical and the expository or scientific realms of literary art.

We are now ready to state the fifth rule of reading (an expository work). Stated roughly, it is this: You must spot the important words in a book and figure out how the author is using them. But we can make that a little more precise and elegant: RULE 5. FIND THE IMPORTANT WORDS AND THROUGH THEM COME TO TERMS WITH THE AUTHOR. Note that the rule has two parts. The first part is to locate the important words, the words that make a difference. The second part is to determine the meaning of these words, as used, with precision.

This is the first rule for the second stage of analytical reading, the aim of which is not the outlining of a book's structure but the interpretation of its contents or message. The other rules for this stage, to be discussed in the next chapter, are like this one in an important respect. They also require you to take two steps: a step dealing with the language as such, and a step beyond the language to the thought that lies behind it.

If language were a pure and perfect medium for thought, these steps would not be separate. If every word had only one meaning, if words could not be used ambiguously, if, in short, each word was an ideal term, language would be a diaphanous medium. The reader would see straight through the writer's words to the content of his mind. If that were the case, there would be no need at all for this second stage of analytical reading. Interpretation would be unnecessary.

But of course that is far from the case. There is no use crying about it, no use making up impossible schemes for an ideal language, as the philosopher Leibniz and some of his followers have tried to do. Indeed, if they succeeded, there would be no more poetry. The only thing to do, therefore, in expository works, is to make the best of language as it is, and the only way to do that is to use language as skillfully as possible when you want to convey, or to receive, knowledge.

Because language is imperfect as a medium for conveying knowledge, it also functions as an obstacle to communication. The rules of interpretive reading are directed to overcoming that obstacle. We can expect a good writer to do his best to reach us through the barrier language inevitably sets up, but we cannot expect him to do the job all by himself. We must meet him halfway. We, as readers, must try to tunnel through from our side of the barrier. The likelihood of a meeting of minds *through* language depends on the willingness of both reader and writer to work together. Just as teaching will not avail unless there is *a reciprocal activity of being taught,* so no author, regardless of his skill in writing, can achieve communication without *a reciprocal skill on the part of readers.* If that were not so, the diverse skills of writing and reading would not bring minds together, however much effort was expended, any more than the men who tunnel through from opposite sides of a mountain would ever meet unless they made their calculations according to the same principles of engineering.

As we have pointed out, each of the rules of interpretive reading involves two steps. To get technical for a moment, we may say that these rules have a grammatical and a logical aspect. The grammatical aspect is the one that deals with words. The logical step deals with their meanings or, more precisely, with terms. So far as communication is concerned, both steps are indispensable. If language is used without thought, nothing is being communicated. And thought or knowledge cannot be communicated without language. As arts, grammar and logic are concerned with language in relation to thought and thought in relation to language. That is why skill in both reading and writing is gained through these arts.

This business of language and thought—especially the distinction between words and terms—is so important that we are going to risk being repetitious to be sure the main point is understood. The main point is that *one* word can be the vehicle for *many* terms, and *one* term can be expressed by *many* words. Let us illustrate this schematically in the following manner. The word "reading" has been used in many senses in the course of our discussion. Let us take three of these senses: By the word "reading" we may mean (1) reading to be entertained, (2) reading to get information, and (3) reading to achieve understanding.

Now let us symbolize the word "reading" by the letter X, and the three meanings by the letters a, b, and c. What is symbolized in this scheme by Xa, Xb, and Xc, are not three words, for X remains the same throughout. But they are three terms, on the condition, of course, that you, as reader, and we, as writers know when X is being used in one sense and not another. If we write Xa in a given place, and you read Xb, we are writing and you are reading the same word, but not in the same way. The ambiguity prevents or at least impedes communication. Only when you think the word as we think it, do we have one thought between us. Our minds cannot meet in X, but only in Xa or Xb or Xc. Thus we come to terms.

Finding the Key Words

We are now prepared to put flesh on the rule that requires the reader to come to terms. How does he go about doing it? How does he find the important or key words in a book?

You can be sure of one thing. Not all the words an author uses are important. Better than that, you can be sure that most of his words are not. Only those words that he uses in a special way are important for him, and for us as readers. This is not an absolute matter, of course, but one of degree. Words may be more or less important. Our only concern is with the fact that some words in a book are more important than others. At one extreme are the words that the author uses as the proverbial man in the street does. Since the author is using these words as everyone does in ordinary discourse, the reader should have no trouble with them. He is familiar with their ambiguity and he has grown accustomed to the variation in their meanings as they occur in this context or that.

For example, the word "reading" occurs in A. S. Eddington's book, *The Nature of the Physical World*. He speaks of "pointer-readings," the readings of dials and gauges on scientific instruments. He is using the word "reading" in one of its ordinary senses. It is not for him a technical word. He can rely on ordinary usage to convey what he means to the reader. Even if he used the word "reading" in a different sense somewhere else in the book—in a phrase, let us say, such as "reading nature"—he could be confident that the reader would note the shift to another of the word's ordinary meanings. The reader who could not do this could not talk to his friends or carry on his daily business.

But Eddington is not able to use the word "cause" so lightheartedly. That may be a word of common speech, but he is using it in a definitely special sense when he discusses the theory of causation. How that word is to be understood makes a difference that both he and the reader must bother about. For the same reason, the word "reading" is important in this book. We cannot get along with merely using it in an ordinary way.

An author uses most words as men ordinarily do in conversation, with a range of meanings, and trusting to the context to indicate the shifts. Knowing this fact is some help in detecting the more important words. We must not forget, however, that at different times and places the same words are not equally familiar items in daily usage. Contemporary writers will employ most words as they are ordinarily used *today,* and you will know which words these are because you are alive today. But in reading books written in the past, it may be more difficult to detect the words the author is using as most people did at the time and place he was writing. The fact that some authors intentionally employ archaic words, or archaic senses of words, complicates the matter further, as does the translation of books from foreign languages.

Nevertheless, it remains true that most of the words in any book can be read just as one would use them in talking to one's friends. Take any page of this book and count the words we are using in that way: all the prepositions, conjunctions, and articles, and almost all of the verbs, nouns, adverbs, and adjectives. In this chapter so far, there have been only a few important words: "word," "term," "ambiguity," "communication," and perhaps one or two more. Of these, "term" is clearly the most important; all the others are important in relation to it.

You cannot locate the key words without making an effort to understand the passage in which they occur. This situation is somewhat paradoxical. If you do understand the passage, you will, of course, know which words in it are the most important. If you do not fully understand the passage, it is probably because you do not know the way the author is using certain words. If you mark the words that trouble you, you may hit the very ones the author is using specially. That this is likely to be so follows from the fact that you should have no trouble with the words the author uses in an ordinary way.

From your point of view as a reader, therefore, the most important words are *those that give you trouble.* It is likely that these words are important for the author as well. However, they may not be.

It is also possible that words that are important for the author do not bother you, and precisely because you understand them. In that case, you have already come to terms with the author. Only where you fail to come to terms have you work still to do.

Technical Words and Special Vocabularies

So far we have been proceeding negatively by eliminating the ordinary words. You discover some of the important words by the fact that they are *not ordinary for you.* That is why they bother you. But is there any other way of spotting the important words? Are there any positive signs that point to them?

There are several. The first and most obvious sign is the explicit stress an author places upon certain words and not others. He may do this in many ways. He may use such typographical devices as quotation marks or italics to mark the word for you. He may call your attention to the word by explicitly discussing its various senses and indicating the way he is going to use it here and there. Or he may emphasize the word by defining the thing that the word is used to name.

No one can read Euclid without knowing that such words as "point," "line," "plane," "angle," "parallel," and so forth are of the first importance. These are the words that name geometrical entities defined by Euclid. There are other important words, such as "equals," "whole," and "part," but these do not name anything that is defined. You know they are important from the fact that they occur in the axioms. Euclid helps you here by making his primary propositions explicit at the very beginning. You can guess that the terms composing such propositions are basic, and that underlines for you the words that express these terms. You may have no difficulty with these words, because they are words of common speech, and Euclid appears to be using them that way.

If all authors wrote as Euclid did, you may say, this business of reading would be much easier. But that of course is not possible, although there have in fact been men who thought that any subject matter could be expounded in the geometrical manner. The procedure—the method of exposition and proof—that works in mathematics is not applicable in every field of knowledge. In any event, for our purposes it is sufficient to note what is common to every sort of exposition. *Every field of knowledge has its own technical vocabulary.* Euclid makes his plain right at the beginning. The same is true of any writer, such as Galileo or Newton, who writes in the geometrical manner. In books differently written or in other fields, the technical vocabulary must be discovered by the reader.

If the author has not pointed out the words himself, the reader may locate them through having some prior knowledge of the subject matter. If he knows something about biology or economics before he begins to read Darwin or Adam Smith, he certainly has some leads toward discerning the technical words. The rules of analyzing a book's structure may help here. If you know what kind of book it is, what it is about as a whole, and what its major parts are, you are greatly aided in separating the technical vocabulary from the ordinary words. The author's title, chapter headings, and preface may be useful in this connection.

From this you know, for example, that "wealth" is a technical word for Adam Smith, and "species" for Darwin. Since one technical word leads to another, you cannot help but discover other technical words in a similar fashion. You can soon make a list of the important words used by Adam Smith: labor, capital, land, wages, profits, rent, commodity, price, exchange, productive, unproductive, money, and so forth. And here are some you cannot miss in Darwin: variety, genus, selection, survival, adaptation, hybrid, fittest, creation.

Where a field of knowledge has a well-established technical vocabulary, the task of locating the important words in a book treating that subject matter is relatively easy. You can spot them *positively* through having some acquaintance with the field, or *negatively* by knowing what words must be technical, because they are not ordinary. Unfortunately, there are many fields in which a technical vocabulary is not well established.

Philosophers are notorious for having private vocabularies. There are some words, of course, that have a traditional standing in philosophy. Though they may not be used by all writers in the same sense, they are nevertheless technical words in the discussion of certain problems. But philosophers often find it necessary to coin new words, or to take some word from common speech and *make it a technical word.* This last procedure is likely to be most misleading to the reader who supposes that he knows what the word means, and therefore treats it as an ordinary word. Most good authors, however, anticipating just this confusion, give very explicit warning whenever they adopt the procedure.

In this connection, one clue to an important word is that the author quarrels with other writers about it. When you find an author telling you how a particular word has been used by others, and why he chooses to use it otherwise, you can be sure that word makes a great difference to him.

We have here emphasized the notion of technical vocabulary, but you must not take this too narrowly. The relatively small set of words that express an author's main ideas, his leading concepts, constitutes his special vocabulary. They are the words that carry his analysis, his argument. If he is making an original communication, some of these words are likely to be used by him in a very special way, although he may use others in a fashion that has become traditional in the field. In either case, these are the words that are most important *for him.* They should be important *for you* as a reader also, but in addition any other word whose meaning is not clear is important for you.

The trouble with most readers is that they simply do not pay enough attention to words to locate their difficulties. They fail to distinguish the words that they do not understand sufficiently from those they do. All the things we have suggested to help you find the important words in a book will be of no avail unless you make a deliberate effort to note the words you must work on to find the terms they convey. The reader who fails to ponder, or at least to mark, the words he does not understand is headed for disaster.

If you are reading a book that can increase your understanding, it stands to reason that not all of its words will be completely intelligible to you. If you proceed as if they were all ordinary words, all on the same level of general intelligibility as the words of a newspaper article, you will make no headway toward interpretation of the book. You might just as well be reading a newspaper, for the book cannot enlighten you if you do not try to understand it.

Most of us are addicted to non-active reading. The outstanding fault of the non-active or undemanding reader is his inattention to words, and his consequent failure to come to terms with the author.

Finding the Meanings

Spotting the important words is only the beginning of the task. It merely locates the places in the text where you have to go to work. There is another part of this fifth rule of reading. Let us turn to that now. Let us suppose you have marked the words that trouble you. What next?

There are two main possibilities. Either the author is using these words in a single sense throughout or he is using them in two or more senses, shifting his meaning from place to place. In the first alternative, the word stands for a single term. A good example of the use of important words so that they are restricted to a single meaning is found in Euclid. In the second alternative, the word stands for several terms.

In the light of these alternatives, your procedure should be as follows. First, try to determine whether the word has one or many meanings. If it has many, try to see how they are related. Finally, note the places where the word is used in one sense or another, and see if the context gives you any clue to the reason for the shift in meaning. This last will enable you to follow the word in its change of meanings with the same flexibility that characterizes the author's usage.

But, you may complain, everything is clear except the main thing. How does one find out what the meanings are? The answer, though simple, may appear unsatisfactory. But patience and practice will show you otherwise. The answer is that *you have to discover the meaning of a word you do not understand by using the meanings of all the other words in the context that you do understand.* This must be the way, no matter how merry-go-roundish it may seem at first.

The easiest way to illustrate this is to consider a definition. A definition is stated in words. If you do not understand any of the words used in the definition, you obviously cannot understand the meaning of the word that names the thing defined. The word "point" is a basic word in geometry. You may think you know what it means (in geometry), but Euclid wants to be sure you use it in only one way. He tells you what he means by first defining the thing he is later going to use the word to name. He says: "A point is that which has no part."

How does that help to bring you to terms with him? You know, he assumes, what every other word in the sentence means with sufficient precision. You know that whatever has parts is a complex whole. You know that the opposite of complex is simple. To be simple is the same as to lack parts. You know that the use of the words "is" and "that which" means that the thing referred to must be an entity of some sort. Incidentally, it follows from all this that, if there are no physical things without parts, a point, as Euclid speaks of it, cannot be physical.

This illustration is typical of the process by which you acquire meanings. You operate with meanings you already possess. If every word that was used in a definition had itself to be defined, nothing could ever be defined. If every word in a book you were reading was entirely strange to you, as in the case of a book in a totally foreign language, you could make no progress at all.

That is what people mean when they say of a book that it is all Greek to them. They simply have not tried to understand it, which would be justifiable if it were really in Greek. But most of the words in any English book are familiar words. These words surround the strange words, the technical words, the words that may cause the reader some trouble. The surrounding words are the *context* for the words to be interpreted. The reader has all the materials he needs to do the job.

We are not pretending the job is an easy one. We are only insisting that it is not an impossible one. If it were, no one could read a book to gain in understanding. The fact that a book can give you new insights or enlighten you indicates that it probably contains words you may not readily understand. If you could not come to understand those words by your own efforts, then the kind of reading we are talking about would be impossible. It would be impossible to pass from understanding less to understanding more by your own operations on a book.

There is no rule of thumb for doing this. The process is something like the trial-and-error method of putting a jigsaw puzzle together. The more parts you put together, the easier it is to find places for the remaining parts, if only because there are fewer of them. A book comes to you with a large number of words already in place. *A word in place is a term.* It is definitely located by the meaning that you and the author share in using it. The remaining words must be put in place. You do this by trying to make them fit this way or that. The better you understand the picture that the words so far in place already partially reveal, the easier it is to complete the picture by making terms of the remaining words. Each word put into place makes the next adjustment easier.

You will make errors, of course, in the process. You will think you have managed to find where a word belongs and how it fits, only to discover later that the placement of another word requires you to make a whole series of readjustments. The errors will get corrected because, so long as they are not found out, the picture cannot be completed. Once you have had any experience at all in this work of coming to terms, you will soon be able to check yourself. You will know whether you have succeeded or not. You will not blithely think you understand when you do not.

In comparing a book to a jigsaw puzzle, we have made one assumption that is not true. A good puzzle is, of course, one all of whose parts fit. The picture can be perfectly completed. The same is true of the ideally good book, but there is no such book. In proportion as books are good, their terms will be so well made and put together by the author that the reader can do the work of interpretation fruitfully. Here, as in the case of every other rule of reading, bad books are less readable than good ones. The rules do not work on them, except to show you how bad they are. If the author uses words ambiguously you cannot find out what he is trying to say. You can only find out that he has not been precise.

But, you may ask, does not an author who uses a word in more than a single sense use it ambiguously? And is it not the usual practice for authors to use words in several senses, especially their most important words?

The answer to the first question is No; to the second, Yes. To use a word ambiguously is to use it in several senses without distinguishing or relating their meanings. (For example, we have probably used the word "important" ambiguously in this chapter, for we were not always clear as to whether we meant important for the author or important for you.) The author who does that has not made terms that the reader can come to. But the author who distinguishes the several senses in which he is using a critical word and enables the reader to make a responsive discrimination is offering terms.

You should not forget that one word can represent several terms. One way to remember this is to distinguish between the author's *vocabulary* and his *terminology*. If you make a list in one column of the important words, and in another of their important meanings, you will see the relation between the vocabulary and the terminology.

There are several further complications. In the first place, a word that has several distinct meanings can be used either in a single sense or in a combination of senses. Let us take the word "reading" again as an example. In some places, we have used it to stand for reading any kind of book. In others, we have used it to stand for reading books that instruct rather than entertain. In still others, we have used it to stand for reading that enlightens rather than informs.

Now if we symbolize here, as we did before, these three distinct meanings of "reading" by $Xa, Xb,$ and $Xc,$ then the first usage just mentioned is *Xabc,* the second is *Xbc,* and the third *Xc.* In other words, if several meanings are related, one can use a word to stand for all of them, for some of them, or for only one of them at a time. So long as each usage is definite, the word so used is a term.

In the second place, there is the problem of synonyms. The repetition of a single word over and over is awkward and boring, except in mathematical writing, and so good authors often substitute different words having the same or very similar meanings for important words in their text. This is just the opposite of the situation where one word can stand for several terms; here, one and the same term is represented by two or more words used synonymously.

We can express this symbolically as follows. Let X and Y be two different words, such as "enlightenment" and "insight." Let the letter a stand for the same meaning that each can express, namely, a gain in understanding. Then Xa and Ya represent the same term, though they are distinct as words. When we speak of reading "for insight" and reading "for enlightenment," we are referring to the same kind of reading, because the two phrases are being used with the same meaning. The words are different, but there is only one term for you as a reader to grasp.

This is important, of course. If you supposed that every time an author changed his words, he was shifting his terms, you would make as great an error as to suppose that every time he used the same words, the terms remained the same. Keep this in mind when you list the author's vocabulary and terminology in separate columns. You will find two relationships. On the one hand, a single word may be related to several terms. On the other hand, a single term may be related to several words.

In the third place, and finally, there is the matter of phrases. If a phrase is a unit, that is, if it is a whole that can be the subject or predicate of a sentence; it is like a single word. Like a single word, it can refer to something being talked about in some way.

It follows, therefore, that a term can be expressed by a phrase as well as by a word. And all the relations that exist between words and terms hold also between terms and phrases. Two phrases may express the same term, and one phrase may express several terms, according to the way its constituent words are used.

In general, a phrase is less likely to be ambiguous than a word. Because it is a group of words, each of which is in the context of the others, the single words are more likely to have restricted meanings. That is why a writer is likely to substitute a fairly elaborate phrase for a single word if he wants to be sure that you get his meaning.

One illustration should suffice. To be sure that you come to terms with us about reading, we substitute phrases like "reading for enlightenment" for the single word "reading." To make doubly sure, we may substitute a more elaborate phrase, such as "the process of passing from understanding less to understanding more by the operation of your mind upon a book." There is only one term here, a term referring to the kind of reading that this book is mostly about. But that one term has been expressed by a single word, a short phrase, and a longer one.

This has been a hard chapter to write, and probably a hard one to read. The reason is clear. The rule of reading we have been discussing cannot be made fully intelligible without going into all sorts of grammatical and logical explanations about words and terms.

In fact, we have actually done very little explaining. To give an adequate account of these matters would take many chapters. We have merely touched upon the most essential points. We hope we have said enough to make the rule a useful guide in practice. The more you put it into practice, the more you will appreciate the intricacies of the problem. You will want to know something about the literal and metaphorical use of words. You will want to know about the distinction between abstract and concrete words, and between proper and common names. You will become interested in the whole business of definition: the difference between defining words and defining things; why some words are indefinable, and yet have definite meanings, and so forth. You will seek light on what is called "the emotive use of words," that is, the use of words to arouse emotions, to move men to action or change their minds, as distinct from the communication of knowledge. And you may even become interested in the relation between ordinary "rational" speech and "bizarre" or "crazy" talk—the speech of the mentally disturbed, where almost every word carries weird and unexpected but nevertheless identifiable connotations.

If the practice of analytical reading elicits these further interests, you will be in a position to satisfy them by reading books on these special subjects. And you will profit more from reading such books, because you will go to them with questions born of your own experience in reading. The study of grammar and logic, the sciences that underlie these rules, is practical only to the extent you can relate it to practice.

You may never wish to go further. But even if you do not, you will find that your comprehension of any book will be enormously increased if you only go to the trouble of finding its important words, identifying their shifting meanings, and coming to terms. Seldom does such a small change in a habit have such a large effect.

9

Determining an Author's Message

Not only coming to terms but also making propositions occurs among traders as well as in the world of books. What a buyer or seller means by a proposition is some sort of proposal, some sort of offer or acceptance. In honest dealings, the person who makes a proposition in this sense is declaring his intention to act in a certain way. More than honesty is required for successful negotiations. The proposition should be clear and, of course, attractive. Then the traders can come to terms.

A proposition in a book is also a declaration. It is an expression of the author's judgment about something. He affirms something he thinks to be true, or denies something he judges to be false. He asserts this or that to be a fact. A proposition of this sort is a declaration of knowledge, not intentions. The author may tell us his intentions at the beginning in a preface. In an expository book, he usually promises to instruct us about something. To find out whether he keeps those promises, we must look for his propositions.

Generally, the order of reading reverses the order of business. Businessmen usually come to terms after they find out what the proposition is. But the reader must usually come to terms with an author first, before he can find out what the author is proposing, what judgment he is declaring. That is why the fifth rule of analytical reading concerns words and terms, and the sixth, which we are about to discuss, concerns sentences and propositions.

There is a seventh rule that is closely related to the sixth. The author may be honest in declaring himself on matters of fact or knowledge. We usually proceed in that trust. But unless we are exclusively interested in the author's personality, we should not be satisfied with knowing what his opinions are. *His propositions are nothing but expressions of personal opinion unless they are supported by reasons.* If it is the book and the subject with which it deals that we are interested in, and not just the author, we want to know not merely what his propositions are, but *also why he thinks we should be persuaded to accept them.*

The seventh rule, therefore, deals with arguments of all sorts. There are many kinds of reasoning, many ways of supporting what one says. Sometimes it is possible to argue that something is true; sometimes no more than a probability can be defended. But every sort of argument consists of a number of statements related in a certain way. *This* is said *because* of *that.* The word "because" here signifies a reason being given.

The presence of arguments is indicated by other words that relate statements, such as: *if* this is so, *then* that; or, *since* this, *therefore* that; or, it *follows* from this, that that is the case. In the course of earlier chapters in this book, such sequences occurred. For those of us who are no longer in school, we observed, it is necessary, if we want to go on learning and discovering, to know how to make books teach us well. In that situation, *if* we want to go on learning, *then* we must know how to learn from books, which are absent teachers.

An argument is always a set or series of statements of which some provide the grounds or reasons for what is to be concluded. A paragraph, therefore, or at least a collection of sentences, is required to express an argument. The premises or principles of an argument may not always be stated first, but they are the *source* of the conclusion, nevertheless. If the argument is valid, the conclusion follows from the premises. That does not necessarily mean that the conclusion is true, since one or all of the premises that support it may be false.

There is a grammatical as well as a logical aspect to the order of these rules of interpretation. We go from terms to propositions to arguments, by going from words (and phrases) to sentences to collections of sentences (or paragraphs). We are building up from simpler to more complex units. The smallest significant element in a book is, of course, a single word. It would be true but not adequate to say that a book consists of words. It also consists of groups of words, taken as units, and similarly of groups of sentences, taken as units. The active reader is attentive not only to the words but also to the sentences and paragraphs. There is no other way of discovering the author's terms, propositions, and arguments.

The movement at this stage of analytical reading—*when interpretation is our goal*—seems to be in the opposite direction from the movement in the first stage—*when the goal was a structural outline.* There we went from the book as a whole to its major parts, and then to their subordinate divisions. As you might suspect, the two movements meet somewhere. The major parts of a book and their principal divisions contain many propositions and usually several arguments. But if you keep on dividing the book into its parts, at last you have to say: "In this part, the following points are made." Now each of these points is likely to be a proposition, and some of them taken together probably form an argument.

Thus, the two processes, outlining and interpretation, meet at the level of propositions and arguments. You work down to propositions and arguments by dividing the book into its parts. You work up to arguments by seeing how they are composed of propositions and ultimately of terms. When you have completed the two processes, you can really say that you know the contents of a book.

Sentences vs. Propositions

We have already noticed another thing about the rules we are going to discuss in this chapter. As in the case of the rule about words and terms, we are here also dealing with the relation of language and thought. Sentences and paragraphs are grammatical units. They are units of language. Propositions and arguments are logical units, or units of thought and knowledge.

We have to face here a problem similar to the one we faced in the last chapter. Because language is not a perfect medium for the expression of thought, because one word can have many meanings and two or more words can have the same meaning, we saw how complicated was the relation between an author's *vocabulary* and his *terminology*. One word may represent several terms, and one term may be represented by several words.

Mathematicians describe the relation between the buttons and the buttonholes on a well-made coat as a one-to-one relationship. There is a button for every buttonhole, and a hole for every button. Well, the point is that words and terms do *not* stand in a one-to-one relation. The greatest error you can make in applying these rules is to suppose that a one-to-one relationship exists between the elements of language and those of thought or knowledge.

As a matter of fact, it would be wise not to make too easy assumptions even about buttons and buttonholes. The sleeves of most men's suit jackets bear buttons that have no corresponding buttonholes. And if you have worn the coat for a while, it may have a hole with no corresponding button.

Let us illustrate this in the case of sentences and propositions. Not every sentence in a book expresses a proposition. For one thing, some sentences express questions. They state problems rather than answers. *Propositions are the answers to questions.* They are declarations of knowledge or opinion. That is why we call sentences that express them declarative, and distinguish sentences that ask questions as interrogative. Other sentences express wishes or intentions. They may give us some knowledge of the author's purpose, but they do not convey the knowledge he is trying to expound.

Moreover, not all the declarative sentences can be read as if each expressed one proposition. There are at least two reasons for this. The first is the fact that words are ambiguous and can be used in various sentences. Thus, it is possible for the same sentence to express different propositions if there is a shift in the terms the words express. "Reading is learning" is a simple sentence; but if at one place we mean by "learning" the acquisition of information, and at another we mean the development of understanding, the proposition is not the same, because the terms are different. Yet the sentence is the same.

The second reason is that all sentences are not as simple as "Reading is learning." When its words are used unambiguously, a simple sentence *usually* expresses a single proposition. But even when its words are used unambiguously, a compound sentence expresses two or more propositions. A compound sentence is really a collection of sentences, connected by such words as "and," or "if . . . then," or "not only . . . but also." You may rightly conclude that the line between a long compound sentence and a short paragraph may be difficult to draw. A compound sentence can express a number of propositions related in the form of an argument.

Such sentences can be very difficult to interpret. Let us take an interesting sentence from Machiavelli's *The Prince* to show what we mean:

> A prince ought to inspire fear in such a way that, if he does not win love, he avoids hatred; because he can endure very well being feared whilst he is not hated, which will always be as long as he abstains from the property of his citizens and from their women.

This is grammatically a *single* sentence, though it is extremely complex. The semicolon and the "because" indicate the major break in it. The first proposition is that a prince ought to inspire fear in a certain way.

Beginning with the word "because," we have what is in effect another sentence. (It could be made independent by saying: "The reason for this is that he can endure," and so forth.) And this sentence expresses two propositions at least: (1) the reason why the prince ought to inspire fear in a certain way is that he can endure being feared so long as he is not hated; (2) he can avoid being hated only by keeping his hands off the property of his citizens and their women.

It is important to distinguish the various propositions that a long, complex sentence contains. In order to agree or disagree with Machiavelli, you must first understand what he is saying. But he is saying three things in this one sentence. You may disagree with one of them and agree with the others. You may think Machiavelli is wrong in recommending terrorism to a prince on any grounds; but you may acknowledge his shrewdness in saying that the prince had better not arouse hatred along with fear, and you may also agree that keeping his hands off his subjects' property and women is an in-dispensable condition of not being hated. Unless you recognize the distinct propositions in a complicated sentence, you cannot make a discriminating judgment on what the writer is saying.

Lawyers know this fact very well. They have to examine sen-tences carefully to see what is being alleged by the plaintiff or denied by the defendant. The single sentence, "John Doe signed the lease on March 24," looks simple enough, but still it says several things, some of which may be true and the others false. John Doe may have signed the lease, but not on March 24, and that fact may be important. In short, even a grammatically simple sentence sometimes expresses two or more propositions.

We have said enough to indicate what we mean by the differ-ence between sentences and propositions. They are not related as one to one. Not only can a single sentence express several propo-sitions, either through ambiguity or complexity, but one and the same proposition can also be expressed by two or more different sentences. If you grasp our terms through the words and phrases we use synonymously, you will know that we are saying the same thing when we say, "Teaching and being taught are correlative functions," and "Initiating and receiving communication are re-lated processes."

We are going to stop explaining the grammatical and logical points involved and turn to the rules. The difficulty in this chapter, as in the last, is to stop explaining. Instead, we will assume that you know some grammar. We do not necessarily mean that you must understand everything about syntax, but you should be concerned about the ordering of words in sentences and their relation to one another. Some knowledge of grammar is indispensable to a reader. You cannot begin to deal with terms, propositions, and arguments—the elements of thought—until you can penetrate beneath the surface of language. So long as words, sentences, and paragraphs are opaque and unanalyzed, they are a barrier to, rather than a medium of, communication. You will read words but not receive knowledge.

Here are the rules. The fifth rule of reading, as you will recall from the last chapter, was: RULE 5. FIND THE IMPORTANT WORDS AND COME TO TERMS. The sixth rule can be expressed thus: RULE 6. MARK THE MOST IMPORTANT SENTENCES IN A BOOK AND DISCOVER THE PROPOSITIONS THEY CONTAIN. The seventh rule is this: RULE 7. LOCATE OR CONSTRUCT THE BASIC ARGUMENTS IN THE BOOK BY FINDING THEM IN THE CONNECTION OF SENTENCES. You will see later why we did not say "paragraphs" in the formulation of this rule.

Incidentally, it is just as true of these new rules as it was of the rule about coming to terms that they apply primarily to expository works. The rules about propositions and arguments are quite different when you are reading a poetical work—a novel, play, or poem. We will discuss the changes that are required in applying them to such works later.

Finding the Key Sentences

How does one locate the most important sentences in a book? How, then, does one interpret these sentences to discover the one or more propositions they contain?

Again, we are placing emphasis on what is important. To say that there is only a relatively small number of key sentences in a book does not mean that you need pay no attention to all the rest. Obviously, you have to understand every sentence. But most of the sentences, like most of the words, will cause you no difficulty. As we pointed out in our discussion of reading speeds, you will read them relatively quickly. From your point of view as a reader, the sentences important *for you* are those that require an effort of interpretation because, at first sight, they are not perfectly intelligible. You understand them just well enough to know there is more to understand. They are the sentences that you read much more slowly and carefully than the rest. These may not be the sentences that are most important *for the author,* but they are likely to be, because you are likely to have the greatest difficulty with the most important things the author has to say. And it hardly needs remarking that those are the things you should read most carefully.

From the author's point of view, the important sentences are the ones that express the judgments on which his whole argument rests. A book usually contains much more than the bare statement of an argument, or a series of arguments. The author may explain how he came to the point of view he now holds, or why he thinks his position has serious consequences. He may discuss the words he has to use. He may comment on the work of others. He may indulge in all sorts of supporting and surrounding discussion. But *the heart of his communication lies in the major affirmations and denials he is making, and the reasons he gives for so doing.* To come to grips, therefore, you have to see the main sentences as if they were raised from the page in high relief.

Some authors help you do this. They underline the sentences for you. They either tell you that this is an important point when they make it, or they use one or another typographical device to make their leading sentences stand out. Of course, nothing helps those who will not keep awake while reading. We have met many readers and students who paid no attention even to such clear signs. They preferred to read on rather than stop and examine the important sentences carefully.

There are a few books in which the leading propositions are set forth in sentences that occupy a special place in the order and style of the exposition. Euclid, again, gives us the most obvious example of this. He not only states his definitions, his postulates, and his axioms—his principal propositions—at the beginning, but he also labels every proposition to be proved. You may not understand all of his statements. You may not follow all of his arguments. But you cannot miss the important sentences or the grouping of sentences for the statement of the proofs.

The *Summa Theologica* of St. Thomas Aquinas is another book whose style of exposition puts the leading sentences into high relief. It proceeds by raising questions. Each section is headed by a question. There are many indications of the answer that Aquinas is trying to defend. A whole series of objections opposing the answer is stated. The place where Aquinas begins to argue his own point is marked by the words, "I answer that." There is no excuse for not being able to locate the important sentences in such a book—those expressing the reasons as well as the conclusions—yet even here it remains all a blur for those readers who treat everything they read as equally important—and read it all at the same speed, either fast or slow. That usually means that everything is equally unimportant.

Apart from books whose style or format calls attention to what most needs interpretation by the reader, the spotting of the important sentences is a job the reader must perform for himself. There are several things he can do. We have already mentioned one. If he is sensitive to the difference between passages he can understand readily and those he cannot, he will probably be able to locate the sentences that carry the main burden of meaning. Perhaps you are beginning to see how essential a part of reading it is to *be perplexed and know it.* Wonder is the beginning of wisdom in learning from books as well as from nature. If you never ask yourself any questions about the meaning of a passage, you cannot expect the book to give you any insight you do not already possess.

Another clue to the important sentences is found in the words that compose them. If you have already marked the important words, they should lead you to the sentences that deserve further attention. Thus the first step in interpretive reading prepares for the second. But the reverse may also be the case. It may be that you will mark certain words only after you have become puzzled by the meaning of a sentence. The fact that we have stated these rules in a fixed order does not mean that you have to follow them in that order. Terms constitute propositions. Propositions contain terms. If you know the terms the words express, you have caught the proposition in the sentence. If you understand the proposition conveyed by a sentence, you have arrived at the terms also.

This suggests one further clue to the location of the principal propositions. They must belong to the main argument of the book. They must be either premises or conclusions. Hence, if you can detect those sentences that seem to form a sequence, a sequence in which there is a beginning and an end, you probably have put your finger on the sentences that are important.

We said a sequence in which there is a beginning and an end. Every argument that men can express in words takes time to state. You may speak a sentence in one breath, but there are pauses in an argument. You have to say one thing first, then another, and then another. An argument begins somewhere, goes somewhere, gets somewhere. It is a movement of thought. It may begin with what is really the conclusion and then proceed to give the reasons for it. Or it may start with the evidence and the reasons and bring you to the conclusion that follows therefrom.

Of course, here as elsewhere, the clue will not work unless you know how to use it. You have to recognize an argument when you see one. Despite some disappointing experiences, however, we persist in our opinion that the human mind is as naturally sensitive to arguments as the eye is to colors. (There may be some people who are argument-blind!) But the eye will not see if it is not kept open, and the mind will not follow an argument if it is not awake.

Many persons believe that they know how to read because they read at different speeds. But they pause and go slow *over the wrong sentences*. They pause over the sentences that *interest* them rather than the ones that *puzzle* them. Indeed, this is one of the greatest obstacles to reading a book that is not completely contemporary. Any old book contains facts that are somewhat surprising because they are different from what we know. But when you are reading for understanding it is not that kind of novelty that you are seeking. Your interest in the author himself, or in his language, or in the world in which he wrote, is one thing; your concern to understand his ideas is quite another. It is this concern that the rules we are discussing here can help you to satisfy, not your curiosity about other matters.

Finding the Propositions

Let us suppose that you have located the leading sentences. Another step is required by Rule 6. You must discover the proposition or propositions that each of these sentences contains. This is just another way of saying that you must know what the sentence means. You discover terms by discovering what a word means in a given usage. You discover propositions similarly by interpreting all the words that make up the sentence, and especially its principal words.

Once more, you cannot do this very well unless you know a little grammar. You must know the role that adjectives and adverbs play, how verbs function in relation to nouns, how modifying words and clauses restrict or amplify the meaning of the words they modify, and so forth. Ideally, you should be able to dissect a sentence according to the rules of syntax, although you do not necessarily have to do it in a formal way. Despite the current de-emphasis on teaching grammar in school, we have to assume that you know this much of it. We cannot believe you do not, though you may have grown a little rusty from lack of practice in the rudiments of the art of reading.

There are only two differences between finding the terms that words express and the propositions that sentences express. One is that you employ a larger context in the latter case. You bring all the surrounding sentences to bear on the sentence in question, just as you used the surrounding words to interpret a particular word. In both cases, you proceed from what you do understand to the gradual elucidation of what is at first relatively unintelligible.

The other difference lies in the fact that complicated sentences usually express more than one proposition. You have not completed your interpretation of an important sentence until you have separated out of it all the different, though perhaps related, propositions. Skill in doing this comes with practice. Take some of the complicated sentences in this book and try to state in your own words each of the things that is being asserted. Number them and relate them.

"State in your own words!" That suggests the best test we know for telling whether you have understood the proposition or propositions in the sentence. If, when you are asked to explain what the author means by a particular sentence, all you can do is repeat his very words, with some minor alterations in their order, you had better suspect that you do not know what he means. Ideally, you should be able to say the same thing in totally different words. The idea can, of course, be approximated in varying degrees. But if you cannot get away at all from the author's words, it shows that *only words* have passed from him to you, *not thought or knowledge.* You know his words, not his mind. He was trying to communicate knowledge, and all you received was words.

The process of translation from a foreign language to English is relevant to the test we have suggested. If you cannot state in an English sentence what a French sentence says, you know you do not understand the meaning of the French. But even if you can, your translation may remain only on the verbal level; for even when you have formed a faithful English replica, you still may not know what the writer of the French sentence was trying to convey.

The translation of one English sentence into another, however, is not merely verbal. The new sentence you have formed is not a verbal replica of the original. If accurate, *it is faithful to the thought alone.* That is why making such translations is the best test you can apply to yourself, if you want to be sure you have digested the proposition, not merely swallowed the words. If you fail the test, you have uncovered a failure of understanding. If you say that you know what the author means, but can only repeat the author's sentence to show that you do, then you would not be able to recognize the author's proposition if it were presented to you in other words.

The author may himself express the same proposition in different words in the course of his writing. The reader who has not seen through the words to the proposition they convey is likely to treat the equivalent sentences as if they were statements of different propositions. Imagine a person who did not know that "$2 + 2 = 4$" and "$4 - 2 = 2$" were different notations for the same arithmetic relationship—the relationship of four as the double of two, or two as the half of four.

You would have to conclude that that person simply did not understand the equation. The same conclusion is forced on you concerning yourself or anybody else who cannot tell when equivalent statements of the same proposition are being made, or who cannot himself offer an equivalent statement when he claims to understand the proposition a sentence contains.

These remarks have a bearing on syntopical reading—the reading of several books about the same subject matter. Different authors frequently say the same thing in different words, or different things using almost the same words. The reader who cannot see through the language to the terms and propositions will never be able to compare such related works. Because of their verbal differences, he is likely to misread the authors as disagreeing, or to ignore their real differences because of verbal resemblances in their statements.

There is one other test of whether you understand the proposition in a sentence you have read. Can you point to some experience you have had that the proposition describes or to which the proposition is in any way relevant? Can you exemplify the general truth that has been enunciated by referring to a particular instance of it? To imagine a possible case is often as good as citing an actual one. If you cannot do anything at all to exemplify or illustrate the proposition, either imaginatively or by reference to actual experiences, you should suspect that you do not know what is being said.

Not all propositions are equally susceptible to this test. It may be necessary to have the special experience that only a laboratory can afford to be sure you have grasped certain scientific propositions. But the main point is clear. Propositions do not exist in a vacuum. They refer to the world in which we live. Unless you can show some acquaintance with actual or possible facts to which the proposition refers or is relevant somehow, you are *playing with words,* not dealing with thought and knowledge.

Let us consider one example of this. A basic proposition in metaphysics is expressed by the following words: "Nothing acts except what is actual." We have heard many students repeat those words to us with an air of satisfied wisdom. They have thought they were discharging their duty to us and to the author by so perfect a verbal repetition. But the sham was obvious as soon as we asked them to state the proposition in other words. Seldom could they say, for instance, that if something does not exist, it cannot do anything. Yet this is an immediately apparent translation—apparent, at least, to anyone who understood the proposition in the original sense.

Failing to get a translation, we would then ask for an exemplification of the proposition. If any one of them told us that grass is not made to grow by merely *possible* showers—that one's bank account does not increase on account of a merely *possible* raise—we would know that the proposition had been grasped.

The vice of "verbalism" can be defined as the bad habit of using words without regard for the thoughts they should convey and without awareness of the experiences to which they should refer. It is playing with words. As the two tests we have suggested indicate, "verbalism" is the besetting sin of those who fail to read analytically. Such readers never get beyond the words. They possess what they read as a verbal memory that they can recite emptily. One of the charges made by certain modern educators against the liberal arts is that they tend to verbalism, but just the opposite seems to be the case. The failure in reading—the omnipresent verbalism—of those who have not been trained in the arts of grammar and logic shows how lack of such discipline results in slavery to words rather than mastery of them.

Finding the Arguments

We have spent enough time on propositions. Let us now turn to the seventh rule of analytical reading, which requires the reader to deal with collections of sentences. We said before that there was a reason for not formulating this rule of interpretation by saying that the reader should find the most important paragraphs. The reason is that there are no settled conventions among writers about how to construct paragraphs. Some great writers, such as Montaigne, Locke, or Proust, write extremely long paragraphs; others, such as Machiavelli, Hobbes, or Tolstoy, write relatively short ones. In recent times, under the influence of newspaper and magazine style, most writers tend to cut their paragraphs to fit quick and easy reading. This paragraph, for instance, is probably too long. If we had wanted to coddle our readers, we should have started a new one with the words, "Some great writers."

It is not merely a matter of length. The point that is troublesome here has to do with the relation between language and thought. The logical unit to which the seventh rule directs our reading is the argument—a sequence of propositions, some of which give reasons for another. This logical unit is not uniquely related to any recognizable unit of writing, as terms are related to words and phrases, and propositions to sentences. An argument may be expressed in a single complicated sentence. Or it may be expressed in a number of sentences that are only part of one paragraph. Sometimes an argument may coincide with a paragraph, but it may also happen that an argument runs through several or many paragraphs.

There is one further difficulty. *There are many paragraphs in any book that do not express an argument at all*—perhaps not even part of one. They may consist of collections of sentences that detail evidence or report how the evidence has been gathered. As there are sentences that are of secondary importance, because they are merely digressions or side remarks, so also can there be paragraphs of this sort. It hardly needs to be said that they should be read rather quickly.

Because of all this, we suggest another formulation of RULE 7, as follows: FIND IF YOU CAN THE PARAGRAPHS IN A BOOK THAT STATE ITS IMPORTANT ARGUMENTS; BUT IF THE ARGUMENTS ARE NOT THUS EXPRESSED, YOUR TASK IS TO CONSTRUCT THEM, BY TAKING A SENTENCE FROM THIS PARAGRAPH, AND ONE FROM THAT, UNTIL YOU HAVE GATHERED TOGETHER THE SEQUENCE OF SENTENCES THAT STATE THE PROPOSITIONS THAT COMPOSE THE ARGUMENT.

After you have discovered the leading sentences, the construction of paragraphs should be relatively easy. There are various ways of doing this. You can do it by actually writing out on a piece of paper the propositions that together form an argument. But usually a better way, as we have already suggested, is to put numbers in the margin, together with other marks, to indicate the places where the sentences occur that should be tied together in a sequence.

Authors are more or less helpful to their readers in this matter of making the arguments plain. Good expository authors try to reveal, not conceal, their thought. Yet not even all good authors do this in the same way. Some, such as Euclid, Galileo, Newton (authors who write in a geometrical or mathematical style), come close to the ideal of making a single paragraph an argumentative unit. The style of most writing in non-mathematical fields tends to present two or more arguments in a single paragraph or to have an argument run through several.

In proportion as a book is more loosely constructed, the paragraphs tend to become more diffuse. You often have to search through all the paragraphs of a chapter to find the sentences you can construct into a statement of a single argument. Some books make you search in vain, and some do not even encourage the search.

A good book usually summarizes itself as its arguments develop. If the author summarizes his arguments for you at the end of a chapter, or at the end of an elaborate section, you should be able to look back over the preceding pages and find the materials he has brought together in the summary. In *The Origin of Species,* Darwin summarizes his whole argument for the reader in a last chapter, entitled "Recapitulation and Conclusion." The reader who has worked through the book deserves that help. The one who has not cannot use it.

Incidentally, if you have inspected the book well before beginning to read it analytically, you will know whether the summary passages exist and if they do, where they are. You can then make the best possible use of them when interpreting the book.

Another sign of a bad or loosely constructed book is the omission of steps in an argument. Sometimes they can be omitted without damage or inconvenience, because the propositions left out can be generally supplied from the common knowledge of readers. But sometimes their omission is misleading, and may even be intended to mislead. One of the most familiar tricks of the orator or propagandist is to leave certain things unsaid, things that are highly relevant to the argument, but that might be challenged if they were made explicit. While we do not expect such devices in an honest author whose aim is to instruct us, it is nevertheless a sound maxim of careful reading to make every step in an argument explicit.

Whatever kind of book it is, your obligation as a reader remains the same. If the book contains arguments, you must know what they are, and be able to put them into a nutshell. Any good argument can be put into a nutshell. There are, of course, arguments built upon arguments. In the course of an elaborate analysis, one thing may be proved in order to prove another, and this may be used in turn to make a still further point. The units of reasoning, however, are single arguments. If you can find these in any book you are reading, you are not likely to miss the larger sequences.

This is all very well to say, you may object, but unless one knows the structure of arguments as a logician does, how can one be expected to find them in a book, or worse, to construct them when the author does not state them compactly in a single paragraph?

The answer is that it must be obvious that you do not have to know about arguments "as a logician does." There are relatively few logicians in the world, for better or for worse. Most of the books that convey knowledge and can instruct us contain arguments. They are intended for the general reader, not for specialists in logic.

No great logical competence is needed to read these books. To repeat what we said before, the nature of the human mind is such that if it works at all during the process of reading, if it comes to terms with the author and reaches his propositions, it will see his arguments as well.

There are, however, a few things we can say that may be helpful to you in carrying out this rule of reading. *In the first place,* remember that every argument must involve a number of statements. Of these, some give the reasons why you should accept a conclusion the author is proposing. If you find the conclusion first, then look for the reasons. If you find the reasons first, see where they lead.

In the second place, discriminate between the kind of argument that points to one or more particular facts as evidence for some generalization and the kind that offers a series of general statements to prove some further generalizations. The former kind of reasoning is usually referred to as inductive, the latter as deductive; but the names are not what is important. What is important is the ability to discriminate between the two.

In the literature of science, this distinction is observed whenever the difference is emphasized between the proof of a proposition by reasoning and its establishment by experiment. Galileo, in his *Two*

New Sciences, speaks of illustrating by experiment conclusions that have already been reached by mathematical demonstration. And in a concluding chapter of his book *On the Motion of the Heart,* the great physiologist William Harvey writes: "It has been shown by reason and experiment that blood by the beat of the ventricles flows through the lungs and heart and is pumped to the whole body." Sometimes it is possible to support a proposition both by reasoning from other general truths and by offering experimental evidence. Sometimes only one method of argument is available.

In the third place, observe what things the author says he must *assume,* what he says can be *proved* or otherwise evidenced, and what need not be proved because it is *self-evident.* He may honestly try to tell you what all his assumptions are, or he may just as honestly leave you to find them out for yourself. Obviously, not everything can be proved, just as not everything can be defined. If every proposition had to be proved, there would be no beginning to any proof. Such things as axioms and assumptions or postulates are needed for the proof of other propositions. If these other propositions are proved, they can, of course, be used as premises in further proofs.

Every line of argument, in other words, must start somewhere. Basically, there are two ways or places in which it can start: with *assumptions* agreed on between writer and reader, or with what are called *self-evident propositions,* which neither the writer nor reader can deny. In the first case, the assumptions can be anything, so long as agreement exists. The second case requires some further comment here.

In recent times, it has become commonplace to refer to self-evident propositions as "tautologies"; the feeling behind the term is sometimes one of contempt for the trivial, or a suspicion of legerdemain. Rabbits are being pulled out of a hat. You put the truth in by defining your words, and then pull it out as if you were surprised to find it there. That, however, is not always the case.

For example, there is a considerable difference between a proposition such as "a father of a father is a grandfather," and a proposition such as "the whole is greater than its parts." The former statement *is* a tautology; the proposition is contained in the definition of the words; it only thinly conceals the verbal stipulation, "Let us call the parent of a parent a 'grandparent.'" But that is far from being the case with the second proposition. Let us try to see why.

The statement, "The whole is greater than its parts," expresses our understanding of things as they are and of their relationships, which would be the same no matter what words we used or how we set up our linguistic conventions. Finite quantitative wholes exist and they have definite finite parts; for example, this page can be cut in half or in quarters. Now, as we understand a finite whole (that is, any finite whole) and as we understand a definite part of a finite whole, we understand the whole to be greater than the part, or the part to be less than the whole. So far is this from being a mere verbal matter that we cannot define the meaning of the words "whole" and "part"; these words express primitive or indefinable notions. As we are unable to define them *separately,* all we can do is express our understanding of whole and part by a statement of how wholes and parts are *related*.

The statement is axiomatic or self-evident in the sense that its opposite is immediately seen to be false. We can use the word "part" for this page, and the word "whole" for a half of this page after cutting it in two, but we cannot think that the page before it is cut is less than the half of it that we have in our hand after we have cut it. However we use language, our understanding of finite wholes and their definite parts is such that we are compelled to say that we know that the whole is greater than the part, and what we know is the relation between existent wholes and their parts, not something about the use of words or their meanings.

Such self-evident propositions, then, have the status of indemonstrable but also undeniable truths. They are based on common experience alone and are part of common-sense knowledge, for they belong to no organized body of knowledge; they do not belong to philosophy or mathematics any more than they belong to science or history. That is why, incidentally, Euclid called them "common notions." They are also instructive, despite the fact that Locke, for example, did not think they were. He could see no difference between a proposition that really does not instruct, such as the one about the grandparent, and one that does—one that teaches us something we would not otherwise know—such as the one about parts and wholes. And those moderns who refer to all such propositions as tautologies make the same mistake. They do not see that some of the propositions they call "tautologies" really add to our knowledge, while others, of course, do not.

Finding the Solutions

These three rules of analytical reading—about terms, propositions, and arguments—can be brought to a head in an eighth rule, which governs the last step in the interpretation of a book's content. More than that, it ties together the first stage of analytical reading (outlining the structure) and the second stage (interpreting the contents).

The last step in your attempt to discover what a book is about was the discovery of the major problems that the author tried to solve in the course of his book. (As you will recall, this was covered by Rule 4.) Now, after you have come to terms with him and grasped his propositions and arguments, you should check what you have found by addressing yourself to some further questions. Which of the problems that the author tried to solve did he succeed in solving? In the course of solving these, did he raise any new ones? Of the problems that he failed to solve, old or new, which did the author himself know he had failed on? A good writer, like a good reader, should know whether a problem has been solved or not, although of course it is likely to cost the reader less pain to acknowledge the situation.

This final step in interpretive reading is covered by RULE 8. FIND

OUT WHAT THE AUTHOR'S SOLUTIONS ARE. When you have applied this rule, and the three that precede it in interpretive reading, you can feel reasonably sure that you have managed to understand the book. If you started with a book that was over your head—one, therefore, that was able to teach you something—you have come a long way. More than that, you are now able to complete your analytical reading of the book. The third and last stage of the job will be relatively easy. You have been keeping your eyes and your mind open and your mouth shut. Up to this point, you have been following the author. From this point on, you are going to have a chance to argue with the author and express yourself.

The Second Stage of Analytical Reading

We have now described the second stage of analytical reading. Another way to say this is that we have now set forth the materials for answering the second basic question that you must ask about a book, or indeed anything that you read. You will recall that that second question is *What is being said in detail, and how?* Applying Rules 5 through 8 clearly helps you to answer this question. When you have come to terms with the author, found his key propositions and arguments, and identified his solutions of the problems that he faced, you will know what he is saying in his book, and you are thus prepared to go on to ask the final two basic questions about it.

Since we have now completed another stage in the analytical reading process, let us, as before, pause a moment to write out the rules of this stage for review.

THE SECOND STAGE OF ANALYTICAL READING, OR RULES FOR FINDING WHAT A BOOK SAYS (INTERPRETING ITS CONTENTS)

5. Come to terms with the author by interpreting his key words.

6. Grasp the author's leading propositions by dealing with his most important sentences.

7. Know the author's arguments, by finding them in, or constructing them out of, sequences of sentences.

8. Determine which of his problems the author has solved, and which he has not; and as to the latter, decide which the author knew he had failed to solve.

10

Criticizing a Book Fairly

We said at the end of the last chapter that we had come a long way. We have learned how to outline a book. We have learned the four rules for interpreting a book's contents. We are now ready for the last stage of analytical reading. Here you will reap the reward of all your previous efforts.

Reading a book is a kind of conversation. You may think it is not conversation at all, because the author does all the talking and you have nothing to say. If you think that, you do not realize your full obligation as a reader—and you are not grasping your opportunities.

As a matter of fact, the reader is the one who has the last word. The author has had his say, and then it is the reader's turn. The conversation between a book and its reader would appear to be an orderly one, each party talking in turn, no interruptions, and so forth. If, however, the reader is undisciplined and impolite, it may be anything but orderly. The poor author cannot defend himself. He cannot say, "Here, wait till I've finished, before you start disagreeing." He cannot protest that the reader has misunderstood him, has missed his point.

Ordinary conversations between persons who confront each other are good only when they are carried on civilly. We are not thinking merely of the civilities according to conventions of social politeness. Such conventions are not really important. What is important is that there is an *intellectual* etiquette to be observed. Without it, conversation is bickering rather than profitable communication. We are assuming here, of course, that the conversation is about a serious matter on which men can agree or disagree. Then it becomes important that they conduct themselves well. Otherwise, there is no profit in the enterprise. The profit in good conversation is something learned.

What is true of ordinary conversation is even more true of the rather special situation in which a book has talked to a reader and the reader talks back. That the author is well disciplined, we will take for granted temporarily. That he has conducted his part of the conversation well can be assumed in the case of good books. What *can* the reader do to reciprocate? What *must* he do to hold up his end well?

The reader has an obligation as well as an opportunity to talk back. The opportunity is clear. Nothing can stop a reader from pronouncing judgment. The roots of the obligation, however, lie a little deeper in the nature of the relation between books and readers.

If the book is of the sort that conveys knowledge, the author's aim was to instruct. He has tried to teach. He has tried to convince or persuade his reader about something. His effort is crowned with success only if the reader finally says, "I am taught. You have convinced me that such and such is true, or persuaded me that it is probable." But even if the reader is not convinced or persuaded, the author's intention and effort should be respected. The reader owes him a considered judgment. If he cannot say, "I agree," he should at least have grounds for disagreeing or even for suspending judgment on the question.

We are really saying no more than what we have already said many times. A good book deserves an active reading. The activity of reading does not stop with the work of understanding what a book says. *It must be completed by the work of criticism, the work of judging.* The undemanding reader fails to satisfy this requirement, probably even more than he fails to analyze and interpret. He not only makes no effort to understand; he also dismisses a book simply by putting it aside and forgetting it. Worse than faintly praising it, he damns it by giving it no critical consideration whatever.

Teachability as a Virtue

What we mean by talking back is not something apart from reading. It is the third stage in the analytical reading of a book; and there are rules here as in the case of the first two stages. Some of these rules are general maxims of intellectual etiquette. We will deal with them in this chapter. Others are more specific criteria for defining points of criticism. They will be discussed in the next chapter.

There is a tendency to think that a good book is above the criticism of the average reader. The reader and the author are not peers. The author, according to this view, should be subjected to a trial only by a jury of his peers. Remember Bacon's recommendation to the reader: "Read not to contradict and confute; nor to believe and take for granted; nor to find talk and discourse; but to weigh and consider." Sir Walter Scott casts even more dire aspersions on those "who read to doubt or read to scorn."

There is a certain truth here, of course, but there is also a good deal of nonsense about the aura of impeccability with which books are thus surrounded, and the false piety it produces. Readers may be like children, in the sense that great authors can teach them, but that does not mean they must not be heard from. Cervantes may or not have been right in saying, "There is no book so bad but something good may be found in it." It is more certain that there is no book so good that no fault can be found with it.

It is true that a book that can enlighten its readers, and is in this sense superior to them, should not be criticized by them until they understand it. When they do, they have elevated themselves almost to equality with the author. Now they are fit to exercise the rights and privileges of their new position. Unless they exercise their critical faculties now, they are doing the author an injustice. He has done what he could to make them his equal. He deserves that they act like his peers, that they engage in conversation with him, that they talk back.

We are discussing here the virtue of teachability—a virtue that is almost always misunderstood. Teachability is often confused with subservience. A person is wrongly thought to be teachable if he is passive and pliable. On the contrary, teachability is an extremely active virtue. No one is really teachable who does not freely exercise his power of independent judgment. He can be trained, perhaps, but not taught. *The most teachable reader is, therefore, the most critical.* He is the reader who finally responds to a book by the greatest effort to make up his own mind on the matters the author has discussed.

We say "finally" because teachability requires that a teacher be fully heard and, more than that, understood before he is judged. We should add also that sheer amount of effort is not an adequate criterion of teachability. The reader must know *how* to judge a book, just as he must know how to arrive at an understanding of its contents. This third group of rules for reading, then, is a guide to the last stage in the disciplined exercise of teachability.

The Role of Rhetoric

We have everywhere found a certain reciprocity between the art of teaching and the art of being taught, between the skill of the author that makes him a considerate writer and the skill of the reader that makes him handle a book with consideration. We have seen how the same principles of grammar and logic underlie rules of good writing as well as rules of good reading. The rules we have so far discussed concern the achievement of intelligibility on the part of the writer and the achievement of understanding on the part of the reader. This last set of rules goes beyond understanding to critical judgment. Here is where rhetoric comes in.

There are, of course, many uses of rhetoric. We usually think of it in connection with the orator or the propagandist. But in its most general significance, rhetoric is involved in every situation in which communication takes place among human beings. If we are the talk-ers, we wish not only to be understood but also to be agreed with in some sense. If our purpose in trying to communicate is serious, we wish to convince or persuade—more precisely, to convince about theoretical matters and to persuade about matters that ultimately af-fect action or feeling.

To be equally serious in receiving such communication, one must be not only a *responsive* but also a *responsible* listener. You are responsive to the extent that you follow what has been said and note the intention that prompts it. But you also have the responsibility of taking a position. When you take it, it is yours, not the author's. To regard anyone except yourself as responsible for your judgment is to be a slave, not a free man. It is from this fact that the liberal arts acquire their name.

On the part of the speaker or writer, rhetorical skill is knowing how to convince or persuade. Since this is the ultimate end in view, all the other aspects of communication must serve it. Grammatical and logical skill in writing clearly and intelligibly has merit in itself, but it is also a means to an end. Reciprocally, on the part of the reader or listener, rhetorical skill is knowing how to react to anyone who tries to convince or persuade us. Here, too, grammatical and logical skill, which enables us to understand what is being said, prepares the way for a critical reaction.

The Importance of Suspending Judgment

Thus you see how the three arts of grammar, logic, and rhetoric cooperate in regulating the elaborate processes of writing and read-ing. Skill in the first two stages of analytical reading comes from a mastery of grammar and logic. Skill in the third stage depends on the remaining art. The rules of this stage of reading rest on the principles of rhetoric, conceived in the broadest sense. We will con-sider them as a code of etiquette to make the reader not only polite, but also effective, in talking back. (Although it is not generally recognized, etiquette always serves these two purposes, not just the former.)

You probably also see what the ninth rule of reading is going to be. It has been intimated several times already. Do not begin to talk back until you have listened carefully and are sure you understand. Not until you are honestly satisfied that you have accomplished the first two stages of reading should you feel free to express yourself. When you have, you not only have earned the right to turn critic, you also have the duty to do so.

This means, in effect, that the third stage of analytical reading must always follow the other two in time. The first two stages interpenetrate each other. Even the beginning reader can combine them somewhat, and the expert combines them almost completely. He can discover the contents of a book by breaking down the whole into its parts and at the same time constructing the whole out of its elements of thought and knowledge, its terms, propositions, and arguments. Furthermore, even for the beginner, a certain amount of the work required at those two stages can be performed during a good inspectional reading. But the expert no less than the beginner must wait until he understands before he starts to criticize.

Let us restate this ninth rule of reading in the following form: RULE 9. YOU MUST BE ABLE TO SAY, WITH REASONABLE CERTAINTY, "I UNDERSTAND," BEFORE YOU CAN SAY ANY ONE OF THE FOLLOWING THINGS: "I AGREE," OR "I DISAGREE," OR "I SUSPEND JUDGMENT." These three remarks exhaust all the critical positions you can take. We hope you have not made the error of supposing that to criticize is always to disagree. That is a popular misconception. To agree is just as much an exercise of critical judgment on your part as to disagree. You can be just as wrong in agreeing as in disagreeing. To agree without understanding is inane. To disagree without understanding is impudent.

Though it may not be so obvious at first, suspending judgment is also an act of criticism. It is taking the position that something has not been shown. You are saying that you are not convinced or persuaded one way or the other.

The rule seems to be such obvious common sense that you may wonder why we have bothered to state it so explicitly. There are two reasons. In the first place, many people make the error already mentioned of identifying criticism with disagreement. (Even "constructive" criticism is disagreement.) In the second place, though this rule seems obviously sound, our experience has been that few people observe it in practice. Like the golden rule, it elicits more lip service than intelligent obedience.

Every author has had the experience of suffering book reviews by critics who did not feel obliged to do the work of the first two stages first. The critic too often thinks he does not have to be a reader as well as a judge. Every lecturer has also had the experience of having critical questions asked that were not based on any understanding of what he had said. You yourself may remember an occasion where someone said to a speaker, in one breath or at most two, "I don't know what you mean, but I think you're wrong."

There is actually no point in answering critics of this sort. The only polite thing to do is to ask them to state your position for you, the position they claim to be challenging. If they cannot do it satisfactorily, if they cannot repeat what you have said *in their own words,* you know that they do not understand, and you are entirely justified in ignoring their criticisms. They are irrelevant, as all criticism must be that is not based on understanding. When you find the rare person who shows that he understands what you are saying as well as you do, then you can delight in his agreement or be seriously disturbed by his dissent.

In years of reading books with students of one kind and another, we have found this rule more honored in the breach than in the observance. Students who plainly do not know what the author is saying seem to have no hesitation in setting themselves up as his judges. They not only disagree with something they do not understand but, what is equally bad, they also often agree to a position they cannot express intelligibly in their own words. Their discussion, like their reading, is all words. Where understanding is not present, affirmations and denials are equally meaningless and unintelligible. Nor is a position of doubt or detachment any more intelligent in a reader who does not know what he is suspending judgment about.

There are several further points to note concerning the observance of this rule. If you are reading a good book, you ought to hesitate before you say, "I understand." The presumption certainly is that you have a lot of work to do before you can make that declaration honestly and with assurance. You must, of course, be a judge of yourself in this matter, and that makes the responsibility even more severe.

To say "I don't understand" is, of course, also a critical judgment, but *only after you have tried your hardest does it reflect on the book rather than yourself.* If you have done everything that can be expected of you and still do not understand, it may be because the book is unintelligible. The presumption, however, is in favor of the book, especially if it is a good one. In reading good books, failure to understand is usually the reader's fault. Hence he is obligated to stay with the task imposed by the first two stages of analytical reading a long time before entering on the third. When you say "I don't understand," watch your tone of voice. Be sure it concedes the possibility that it may not be the author's fault.

There are two other conditions under which the rule requires special care. If you are reading only part of a book, it is more difficult to be sure that you understand, and hence you should be more hesitant to criticize. And sometimes a book is related to other books by the same author, and depends upon them for its full significance. In this situation, also, you should be more circumspect about saying "I understand," and slower to raise your critical lance.

A good example of brashness in this last respect is furnished by literary critics who have agreed or disagreed with Aristotle's *Poetics* without realizing that the main principles in Aristotle's analysis of poetry depend in part on points made in other of his works, his treatises on psychology and logic and metaphysics. They have agreed or disagreed without understanding what it is all about.

The same is true of other writers, such as Plato and Kant, Adam Smith and Karl Marx, who have not been able to say everything they knew or thought in a single work. Those who judge Kant's *Critique of Pure Reason* without reading his *Critique of Practical Reason,* or Adam Smith's *Wealth of Nations* without reading his *Theory of the Moral Sentiments,* or *The Communist Manifesto* without Marx's *Capital,* are more likely than not to be agreeing or disagreeing with something they do not fully understand.

The Importance of Avoiding Contentiousness

The second general maxim of critical reading is as obvious as the first, but it needs explicit statement, nevertheless, and for the same reason. It is RULE 10, and it can be expressed thus: WHEN YOU DISAGREE, DO SO REASONABLY, AND NOT DISPUTATIOUSLY OR CONTENTIOUSLY. There is no point in winning an argument if you know or suspect you are wrong. Practically, of course, it may get you ahead in the world for a short time. But honesty is the better policy in the slightly longer run.

We learned this maxim first from Plato and Aristotle. In a passage in the *Symposium,* this interchange occurs:

> I cannot refute you, Socrates, said Agathon: Let us assume that what you say is true.
>
> Say rather, Agathon, that you cannot refute the truth; for Socrates is easily refuted.

The passage is echoed in a remark of Aristotle's in the *Ethics.* "It would be thought to be better," he says,

> indeed to be our duty, for the sake of maintaining the truth even to destroy what touches us closely, especially as we are philosophers or lovers of wisdom; for, while both are dear, piety requires us to honor truth above our friends.

Plato and Aristotle here give us advice that most people ignore. Most people think that winning the argument is what matters, not learning the truth.

He who regards conversation as a battle can win only by being an antagonist, only by disagreeing successfully, whether he is right or wrong. The reader who approaches a book in this spirit reads it only to find something he can disagree with. For the disputatious and the contentious, a bone can always be found to pick a quarrel over. It makes no difference whether the bone is really a chip on your own shoulder.

In a conversation that a reader has with a book in the privacy of his own study, there is nothing to prevent the reader from seeming to win the argument. He can dominate the situation. The author is not there to defend himself. If all he wants is the empty satisfaction of seeming to show the author up, the reader can get it readily. He scarcely has to read the book through to get it. Glancing at the first few pages will suffice.

But if he realizes that the only profit in conversation, with living or dead teachers, is what one can learn from them, if he realizes that you win only by gaining knowledge, not by knocking the other fellow down, he may see the futility of mere contentiousness. We are not saying that a reader should not ultimately disagree and try to show where the author is wrong. We are saying only that *he should be as prepared to agree as to disagree*. Whichever he does should be motivated by one consideration alone—the facts, the truth about the case.

More than honesty is required here. It goes without saying that a reader should admit a point when he sees it. But he also should not feel *whipped* by having to agree with an author, instead of dissenting. If he feels that way, he is inveterately disputatious. In the light of this second maxim, his problem is seen to be emotional rather than intellectual.

On the Resolution of Disagreements

The third maxim is closely related to the second. It states another condition prior to the undertaking of criticism. It recommends that you regard disagreements as capable of being resolved. Where the second maxim urged you not to disagree *disputatiously,* this one warns you against disagreeing *hopelessly.* One is hopeless about the fruitfulness of discussion if he does not recognize that all rational men can agree. Note that we said "can agree." We did not say all rational men *do* agree. Even when they do not agree, they can. The point we are trying to make is that disagreement is futile agitation unless it is undertaken with the hope that it may lead to the resolution of an issue.

These two facts, that people do disagree and can agree, arise from the complexity of human nature. Men are rational animals. Their rationality is the source of their power to agree. Their animality, and the imperfections of their reason that it entails, is the cause of most of the disagreements that occur. Men are creatures of passion and prejudice. The language they must use to communicate is an imperfect medium, clouded by emotion and colored by interest, as well as inadequately transparent for thought. Yet to the extent that men are rational, these obstacles to their understanding can be overcome. The sort of disagreement that is only apparent, the sort that results from misunderstanding, is certainly curable.

There is, of course, another sort of disagreement, which is owing merely to inequalities of knowledge. The relatively ignorant often wrongly disagree with the relatively learned about matters exceeding their knowledge. The more learned, however, have a right to be critical of errors made by those who lack relevant knowledge. Disagreement of this sort can also be corrected. Inequality of knowledge is always curable by instruction.

There may still be other disagreements that are more deeply buried, and that may subsist in the body of reason itself. It is hard to be sure about these, and almost impossible for reason to describe them. In any event, what we have just said applies to the great majority of disagreements. They can be resolved by the removal of misunderstanding or of ignorance. Both cures are usually possible, though often difficult. Hence the person who, at any stage of a conversation, disagrees, should at least hope to reach agreement in the end. He should be as much prepared to have his own mind changed as seek to change the mind of another. He should always keep before him the possibility that he misunderstands or that he is ignorant on some point. No one who looks upon disagreement as an occasion for teaching another should forget that it is also an occasion for being taught.

The trouble is that many people regard disagreement as unrelated to either teaching or being taught. They think that everything is just a matter of opinion. I have mine, and you have yours; and our right to our opinions is as inviolable as our right to private property. On such a view, communication cannot be profitable if the profit to be gained is an increase in knowledge. Conversation is hardly better than a ping-pong game of opposed opinions, a game in which no one keeps score, no one wins, and everyone is satisfied because he does not lose—that is, he ends up holding the same opinions he started with.

We would not—and could not—write this book if we held this view. Instead, we hold that knowledge can be communicated and that discussion can result in learning. If genuine knowledge, not mere personal opinion, is at stake, then, for the most part, either disagreements are apparent only—to be removed by coming to terms and a meeting of minds; or they are real, and the genuine issues can be resolved—in the long run, of course—by appeals to fact and reason. The maxim of rationality concerning disagreements is to be patient for the long run. We are saying, in short, that disagreements are arguable matters. And argument is empty unless it is undertaken on the supposition that there is attainable an understanding that, when attained by reason in the light of all the relevant evidence, resolves the original issues.

How does this third maxim apply to the conversation between reader and writer? How can it be stated as a rule of reading? It deals with the situation in which the reader finds himself disagreeing with something in the book. It requires him first to be sure that the disagreement is not owing to misunderstanding. Suppose that the reader has been careful to observe the rule that he must not render a critical judgment until he understands, and is therefore satisfied that there is no misunderstanding here. What then?

This maxim then requires him to distinguish between genuine knowledge and mere opinion, and to regard an issue where knowledge is concerned as one that can be resolved. If he pursues the matter further, he may be instructed by the author on points that will change his mind. If that does not happen, he may be justified in his criticism, and, metaphorically at least, be able to instruct the author. He can at least hope that were the author alive and present, his mind could be changed.

You may remember something that was said on this subject in the last chapter. If an author does not give reasons for his propositions, they can be treated only as expressions of personal opinions on his part. The reader who does not distinguish between the reasoned statement of knowledge and the flat expression of opinion is not reading to learn. He is at most interested in the author's personality and is using the book as a case history. Such a reader will, of course, neither agree nor disagree. He does not judge the book but the man.

If, however, the reader is primarily interested in the book and not the man, he should take his critical obligations seriously. These involve applying the distinction between real knowledge and mere opinion to himself as well as to the author. Thus the reader must do more than make judgments of agreement or disagreement. He must give reasons for them. In the former case, of course, it suffices if he actively shares the author's reasons for the point on which they agree. But when he disagrees, he must give his own grounds for doing so. Otherwise, he is treating a matter of knowledge as if it were opinion.

RULE 11, therefore, can be stated as follows: RESPECT THE DIFFERENCE BETWEEN KNOWLEDGE AND MERE PERSONAL OPINION BY GIVING REASONS FOR ANY CRITICAL JUDGMENT YOU MAKE.

Incidentally, we would not want to be understood as claiming that there is a great deal of "absolute" knowledge available to men. Self-evident propositions, in the sense in which we defined them in the previous chapter, seem to us to be both indemonstrable and undeniable truths. Most knowledge, however, lacks that degree of absoluteness. What we know, we know subject to correction; we know it because all, or at least the weight, of the evidence supports it, but we are not and cannot be certain that new evidence will not sometime invalidate what we now believe is true.

This, however, does not remove the important distinction between knowledge and opinion that we have been stressing. Knowledge, if you please, consists in those *opinions that can be defended,* opinions for which there is evidence of one kind or another. If we really know something, in this sense, we must believe that we can convince others of what we know. Opinion, in the sense in which we have been employing the word, is unsupported judgment. That is why we have employed the modifiers "mere" or "personal" in conjunction with it. We can do no more than opine that something is true when we have no evidence or reason for the statement other than our personal feeling or prejudice. We can say that it is true and that we know it when we have objective evidence that other reasonable men are likely to accept.

Let us now summarize the three general maxims we have discussed in this chapter. The three together state the conditions of a critical reading and the manner in which the reader should proceed to "talk back" to the author.

The first requires the reader to complete the task of understanding before rushing in. The second adjures him not to be disputatious or contentious. The third asks him to view disagreement about matters of knowledge as being generally remediable. This rule goes further: It also commands him to give reasons for his disagreements so that issues are not merely stated but also defined. In that lies all hope for resolution.

11

Agreeing or Disagreeing with an Author

The first thing a reader can say is that he understands or that he does not. In fact, he must say he understands, in order to say more. If he does not understand, he should keep his peace and go back to work on the book.

There is one exception to the harshness of the second alternative. "I don't understand" may itself be a critical remark. To make it so, the reader must be able to support it. If the fault is with the book rather than himself, the reader must locate the sources of trouble. He should be able to show that the structure of the book is disorderly, that its parts do not hang together, that some of it lacks relevance, or, perhaps, that the author equivocates in the use of important words, with a whole train of consequent confusions. To the extent that a reader can support his charge that the book is unintelligible, he has no further critical obligations.

Let us suppose, however, that you are reading a good book. That means it is a relatively intelligible one. And let us suppose that you are finally able to say "I understand." If, in addition to understanding the book, you agree thoroughly with what the author says, the work is over. The analytical reading is completely done. You have been enlightened, and convinced or persuaded. It is clear that we have additional steps to consider only in the case of disagreement or suspended judgment. The former is the more usual case.

To the extent that authors argue with their readers—and expect their readers to argue back—the good reader must be acquainted with the principles of argument. He must be able to carry on civil, as well as intelligent, controversy. That is why there is need for a chapter of this sort in a book on reading. *Not simply by following an author's arguments, but only by meeting them as well, can the reader ultimately reach significant agreement or disagreement with his author.*

The meaning of agreement and disagreement deserves a moment's further consideration. The reader who comes to terms with an author and grasps his propositions and reasoning shares the author's mind. In fact, the whole process of interpretation is directed toward a meeting of minds through the medium of language. Understanding a book can be described as a kind of agreement between writer and reader. They agree about the use of language to express ideas. Because of that agreement, the reader is able to see through the author's language to the ideas he is trying to express.

If the reader understands a book, how can he disagree with it? Critical reading demands that he make up his own mind. But his mind and the author's have become as one through his success in understanding the book. What mind has he left to make up independently?

There are some people who make the error that causes this apparent difficulty: they fail to distinguish between two senses of "agreement." In consequence, they wrongly suppose that where there is understanding between men, disagreement is impossible. They say that all disagreement is simply owing to misunderstanding.

The error in this becomes obvious as soon as we remember that the author is making judgments about the world in which we live. He claims to be giving us theoretical knowledge about the way things exist and behave, or practical knowledge about what should be done. Obviously, he can be either right or wrong. His claim is justified only to the extent that he speaks truly, to the extent that he says what is probable in the light of evidence. Otherwise, his claim is unfounded.

If you say, for instance, that "all men are equal," we may take you to mean that all men are equally endowed at birth with intelligence, strength, and other abilities. In the light of the facts as we know them, we disagree with you. We think you are wrong. But suppose we have misunderstood you. Suppose you meant by these words that *all men should have equal political rights.* Because we misapprehended your meaning, our disagreement was irrelevant. Now suppose the mistake corrected. Two alternatives still remain. We can agree or disagree, *but now if we disagree, there is a real issue between us.* We understand your political position, but hold a contrary one.

Issues about matters of fact or policy—issues about the way things are or should be—are real in this sense only when they are based on a common understanding of what is being said. Agreement about the use of words is the indispensable condition for genuine agreement or disagreement about the facts being discussed. It is because of, not in spite of, your meeting the author's mind through a sound interpretation of his book that you are able to make up your own mind as concurring in or dissenting from the position he has taken.

Prejudice and Judgment

Now let us consider the situation in which, having said you understand, you proceed to disagree. If you have tried to abide by the maxims stated in the previous chapter, you disagree because you think the author can be shown to be wrong on some point. You are not simply voicing your prejudice or expressing your emotions. Because this is true, then, from an ideal point of view, there are three conditions that must be satisfied if controversy is to be well conducted.

The first is this. Since men are animals as well as rational, it is necessary to acknowledge the emotions you bring to a dispute, or those that arise in the course of it. Otherwise you are likely to be giving vent to feelings, not stating reasons. You may even think you have reasons, when all you have are strong feelings.

Second, you must make your own assumptions explicit. You must know what your prejudices—that is, your prejudgments—are. Otherwise you are not likely to admit that your opponent may be equally entitled to different assumptions. *Good controversy should not be a quarrel about assumptions.* If an author, for example, explicitly asks you to take something for granted, the fact that the opposite can also be taken for granted should not prevent you from honoring his request. If your prejudices lie on the opposite side, and if you do not acknowledge them to be prejudices, you cannot give the author's case a fair hearing.

Third and finally, an attempt at impartiality is a good antidote for the blindness that is almost inevitable in partisanship. Controversy without partisanship is, of course, impossible. But to be sure that there is more light in it, and less heat, each of the disputants should at least try to take the other fellow's point of view. If you have not been able to read a book *sympathetically,* your disagreement with it is probably more contentious than civil.

These three conditions are, ideally, the *sine qua non* of intelligent and profitable conversation. They are obviously applicable to reading, insofar as that is a kind of conversation between reader and author. Each of them contains sound advice for readers who are willing to respect the civilities of disagreement.

But the ideal here, as elsewhere, can only be approximated. The ideal should never be expected from human beings. We ourselves, we hasten to admit, are sufficiently conscious of our own defects. We have violated our own rules about good intellectual manners in controversy. We have caught ourselves attacking a book rather than criticizing it, knocking straw men over, denouncing where we could not support denials, proclaiming our prejudices as if ours were any better than the author's.

We continue to believe, however, that conversation and critical reading *can* be well disciplined. We are therefore going to substitute for those three ideal conditions, a set of prescriptions that may be easier to follow. They indicate the four ways in which a book can be adversely criticized. Our hope is that if a reader confines himself to making these points, he will be less likely to indulge in expressions of emotion or prejudice.

The four points can be briefly summarized by conceiving the reader as conversing with the author, as talking back. After he has said, "I understand but I disagree," he can make the following remarks to the author: (1) *"You are uninformed"*; (2) *"You are misinformed"*; (3) *"You are illogical—your reasoning is not cogent"*; (4) *"Your analysis is incomplete."*

These may not be exhaustive, though we think they are. In any event, they are certainly the principal points a reader who disagrees can make. They are somewhat independent. Making one of these remarks does not prevent you from making another. Each and all can be made, because the defects they refer to are not mutually exclusive.

But, we should add, the reader cannot make any of these remarks without being definite and precise about the respect in which the author is uninformed or misinformed or illogical. A book cannot be uninformed or misinformed about everything. It cannot be totally illogical. Furthermore, the reader who makes any of these remarks must not only make it definitely, by specifying the respect, but he must also support his point. He must give reasons for saying what he does.

Judging the Author's Soundness

The first three remarks are somewhat different from the fourth, as we will presently see. Let us consider each of them briefly, and then turn to the fourth.

1. To say that an author is *uninformed* is to say that he lacks some piece of knowledge that is relevant to the problem he is trying to solve. Notice here that unless the knowledge, if possessed by the author, would have been relevant, there is

no point in making this remark. To support the remark, you must be able yourself to state the knowledge that the author lacks and show how it is relevant, how it makes a difference to his conclusions.

A few illustrations here must suffice. Darwin lacked the knowledge of genetics that the work of Mendel and later experimentalists now provides. His ignorance of the mechanism of inheritance is one of the major defects in *The Origin of Species.* Gibbon lacked certain facts that later historical research has shown to have a bearing on the fall of Rome. Usually, in science and history, the lack of information is discovered by later researches. Improved techniques of observation and prolonged investigation make this the way things happen for the most part. But in philosophy, it may happen otherwise. There is just as likely to be loss as gain with the passage of time. The ancients, for example, clearly distinguished between what men can sense and imagine and what they can understand. Yet, in the eighteenth century, David Hume revealed his ignorance of this distinction between im ages and ideas, even though it had been so well established by the work of earlier philosophers.

2. To say that an author is *misinformed* is to say that he asserts what is not the case. His error here may be owing to lack of knowledge, but the error is more than that. Whatever its cause, it consists in making assertions contrary to fact. The author is proposing as true or more probable what is in fact false or less probable. He is claiming to have knowledge he does not possess. This kind of defect should be pointed out, of course, only if it is relevant to the author's conclusions. And to support the remark you must be able to argue the truth or greater probability of a position contrary to the author's.

For example, in one of his political treatises, Spinoza appears to say that democracy is a more primitive type of government than monarchy. This is contrary to well-ascertained facts of political history. Spinoza's error in this respect has a bearing on his argument. Aristotle was misinformed about the role that the female factor plays in animal reproduction, and consequently came to unsupportable conclusions about the processes of procreation. Aquinas erroneously supposed that the matter of the heavenly bodies is essentially different from that of terrestrial bodies, because he supposed that the former change only in position, and are otherwise unalterable. Modern astrophysics corrects this error and thereby improves on ancient and medieval astronomy. But here is an error that has limited relevance. Making it does not affect Aquinas' metaphysical account of the nature of all sensible things as composed of matter and form.

These first two points of criticism may be related. Lack of information, as we have seen, may be the cause of erroneous assertions. Further, whenever a man is *misinformed* in a certain respect, he is also *uninformed* in the same respect. But it makes a difference whether the defect is simply negative or positive as well. Lack of relevant knowledge makes it impossible to solve certain problems or support certain conclusions. Erroneous suppositions, however, lead to wrong conclusions and untenable solutions. Taken together, these two points charge an author with defects in his premises. He needs more knowledge than he possesses. His evidences and reasons are not good enough in quantity or quality.

3. To say that an author is *illogical* is to say that he has committed a fallacy in reasoning. In general, fallacies are of two sorts. There is the *non sequitur,* which means that what is drawn as a conclusion simply does not follow from the reasons offered. And there is the occurrence of inconsistency, which means that two things the author has tried to say are incompatible. To make either of these criticisms, the reader must be able

to show the precise respect in which the author's argument lacks cogency. One is concerned with this defect only to the extent that the major conclusions are affected by it. A book may safely lack cogency in irrelevant respects.

It is more difficult to illustrate this third point, because few really good books make obvious slips in reasoning. When they do occur, they are usually elaborately concealed, and it requires a very penetrating reader to discover them. But we can show you a patent fallacy in Machiavelli's *The Prince.* Machiavelli writes:

The chief foundations of all states, new as well as old, are good laws. As there cannot be good laws where the state is not well armed, it follows that where they are well armed they have good laws.

Now it simply does not follow from the fact that good laws depend on an adequate police force, that where the police force is adequate, the laws will necessarily be good. We are ignoring the highly questionable character of the first contention. We are only interested in the *non sequitur* here. It is truer to say that happiness depends on health than that good laws depend on an effective police force, but it does not follow that all who are healthy are happy.

In his *Elements of Law,* Hobbes argues in one place that all bodies are nothing but quantities of matter in motion. The world of bodies, he says, has no qualities whatsoever. Then, in another place, he argues that man is himself nothing but a body, or a collection of atomic bodies in motion. Yet, admitting the existence of sensory qualities—colors, odors, tastes, and so forth—he concludes that they are nothing but the motions of atoms in the brain. The conclusion is inconsistent with the position first taken, namely, that the world of bodies in motion is without qualities. What is said of all bodies in motion must apply to any particular group of them, including the atoms of the brain.

This third point of criticism is related to the other two. An author may, of course, fail to draw the conclusions that his evidences or principles imply. Thus his reasoning is incomplete. But we are here concerned primarily with the case in which *he reasons poorly from good grounds.* It is interesting, but less important, to discover lack of cogency in reasoning from premises that are themselves untrue, or from evidences that are inadequate.

A person who from sound premises reaches a conclusion invalidly is, in a sense, misinformed. But it is worthwhile to distinguish the kind of erroneous statement that is owing to bad reasoning from the kind previously discussed, which is owing to other defects, especially insufficient knowledge of relevant details.

Judging the Author's Completeness

The first three points of criticism, which we have just considered, deal with the soundness of the author's statements and reasoning. Let us turn now to the fourth adverse remark a reader can make. It deals with the completeness of the author's execution of his plan— the adequacy with which he discharges the task he has chosen.

Before we proceed to this fourth remark, one thing should be observed. Since you have said you understand, your failure to support any of these first three remarks obligates you to agree with the author as far as he has gone. You have no freedom of will about this. It is not your sacred privilege to decide whether you are going to agree or disagree.

If you have not been able to show that the author is uninformed, misinformed, or illogical on relevant matters, you simply cannot disagree. You must agree. You cannot say, as so many students and others do, "I find nothing wrong with your premises, and no errors in reasoning, but I don't agree with your conclusions." All you can possibly mean by saying something like that is that you do not *like* the conclusions. You are not disagreeing. You are expressing your emotions or prejudices. If you have been convinced, you should admit it.

(If, despite your failure to support one or more of these three critical points, you still honestly feel unconvinced, perhaps you should not have said you understood in the first place.)

The first three remarks are related to the author's terms, propositions, and arguments. These are the elements he used to solve the problems that initiated his efforts. The fourth remark—that the book is incomplete—bears on the structure of the whole.

4. To say that an author's *analysis is incomplete* is to say that he has not solved all the problems he started with, or that he has not made as good a use of his materials as possible, that he did not see all their implications and ramifications, or that he has failed to make distinctions that are relevant to his undertaking. It is not enough to say that a book is incomplete. Anyone can say that of any book. Men are finite, and so are their works, every last one. There is no point in making this remark, therefore, unless the reader can define the inadequacy precisely, either by his own efforts as a knower or through the help of other books.

   Let us illustrate this point briefly. The analysis of types of government in Aristotle's *Politics* is incomplete. Because of the limitations of his time and his erroneous acceptance of slavery, Aristotle fails to consider, or for that matter even to conceive, the truly democratic constitution that is based on universal suffrage; nor can he imagine either representative government or the modern kind of federated state. His analysis would have to be extended to apply to these political realities. Euclid's *Elements of Geometry* is an incomplete account because Euclid failed to consider other postulates about the relation of parallel lines. Modern geometrical works, making these other assumptions, supply the deficiencies. Dewey's *How We Think* is an incomplete analysis of thinking because it fails to treat the sort of thinking that occurs in reading or learning by instruction in addition to the sort that occurs in investigation and discovery. To a Christian who believes in personal immortality, the writings of Epictetus or Marcus Aurelius are an incomplete account of human happiness.

This fourth point is strictly not a basis for disagreement. It is critically adverse only to the extent that it marks the limitations of the author's achievement. A reader who agrees with a book in part—because he finds no reason to make any of the other points of adverse criticism—may, nevertheless, suspend judgment on the whole, in the light of this fourth point about the book's incompleteness. Suspended judgment on the reader's part responds to an author's failure to solve his problems perfectly.

Related books in the same field can be critically compared by reference to these four criteria. One is better than another in proportion as it speaks more truth and makes fewer errors. If we are reading for knowledge, that book is best, obviously, which most adequately treats a given subject matter. One author may lack information that another possesses; one may make erroneous suppositions from which another is free; one may be less cogent than another in reasoning from similar grounds. But the profoundest comparison is made with respect to the completeness of the analysis that each presents. The measure of such completeness is to be found in the number of valid and significant distinctions that the accounts being compared contain. You may see now how useful it is to have a grasp of the author's terms. The number of distinct terms is correlative with the number of distinctions.

You may also see how the fourth critical remark ties together the three stages of analytical reading of any book. The last step of structural outlining is to know the problems that the author is trying to solve. The last step of interpretation is to know which of these problems the author solved and which he did not. The final step of criticism is the point about completeness. It touches structural outlining insofar as it considers how adequately the author has stated his problems, and interpretation insofar as it measures how satisfactorily he has solved them.

The Third Stage of Analytical Reading

We have now completed, in a general way, the enumeration and discussion of the rules of analytical reading. We can now set forth all the rules in their proper order and under appropriate headings.

I. THE FIRST STAGE OF ANALYTICAL READING: RULES FOR FINDING WHAT A BOOK IS ABOUT

1. Classify the book according to kind and subject matter.

2. State what the whole book is about with the utmost brevity.

3. Enumerate its major parts in their order and relation, and outline these parts as you have outlined the whole.

4. Define the problem or problems the author has tried to solve.

II. THE SECOND STAGE OF ANALYTICAL READING: RULES FOR INTERPRETING A BOOK'S CONTENTS

5. Come to terms with the author by interpreting his key words.

6. Grasp the author's leading propositions by dealing with his most important sentences.

7. Know the author's arguments, by finding them in, or constructing them out of, sequences of sentences.

8. Determine which of his problems the author has solved, and which he has not; and of the latter, decide which the author knew he had failed to solve.

III. THE THIRD STAGE OF ANALYTICAL READING: RULES FOR CRITICIZING A BOOK AS A COMMUNICATION OF KNOWLEDGE

A. *General Maxims of Intellectual Etiquette*

9. Do not begin criticism until you have completed your outline and your interpretation of the book. (Do not say you agree, disagree, or suspend judgment, until you can say "I understand.")

10. Do not disagree disputatiously or contentiously.

11. Demonstrate that you recognize the difference between knowledge and mere personal opinion by presenting good reasons for any critical judgment you make.

B. *Special Criteria for Points of Criticism*

12. Show wherein the author is uninformed.

13. Show wherein the author is misinformed.

14. Show wherein the author is illogical.

15. Show wherein the author's analysis or account is incomplete.

Note: Of these last four, the first three are criteria for disagreement. Failing in all of these, you must agree, at least in part, although you may suspend judgment on the whole, in the light of the last point.

We observed at the end of Chapter 7 that applying the first four rules of analytical reading helps you to answer the first basic question you must ask about a book, namely, *What is the book about as a whole?* Similarly, at the end of Chapter 9, we pointed out that applying the four rules for interpretation helps you to answer the second question you must ask, namely, *What is being said in detail, and how?* It is probably clear that the last seven rules of reading—the maxims of intellectual etiquette and the criteria for points of criticism—help you to answer the third and fourth basic questions you must ask. You will recall that those questions are: *Is it true?* and *What of it?*

The question, Is it true? can be asked of anything we read. It is applicable to every kind of writing, in one or another sense of "truth"— mathematical, scientific, philosophical, historical, and poetical. No higher commendation can be given any work of the human mind than to praise it for the measure of truth it has achieved; by the same token, to criticize it adversely for its failure in this respect is to treat it with the seriousness that a serious work deserves. Yet, strangely enough, in recent years, for the first time in Western history, there is a dwindling concern with this criterion of excellence. Books win the plaudits of the critics and gain widespread popular attention almost to the extent that they flout the truth—the more outrageously they do so, the better. Many readers, and most particularly those who review current publications, employ other standards for judging, and praising or condemning, the books they read—their novelty, their sensationalism, their seductiveness, their force, and even their power to bemuse or befuddle the mind, but not their truth, their clarity, or their power to enlighten. They have, perhaps, been brought to this pass by the fact that so much of current writing outside the sphere of the exact sciences manifests so little concern with truth. One might hazard the guess that if saying something that is true, in any sense of that term, were ever again to become the primary concern it should be, fewer books would be written, published, and read.

Unless what you have read is true in some sense, you need go no further. But if it is, you must face the last question. You cannot read for information intelligently without determining what significance is, or should be, attached to the facts presented. Facts seldom come to us without some interpretation, explicit or implied. This is especially true if you are reading digests of information that necessarily select the facts according to some evaluation of their significance, some principle of interpretation. And if you are reading for enlightenment, there is really no end to the inquiry that, at every stage of learning, is renewed by the question, What of it?

These four questions, as we have already pointed out, summarize all the obligations of a reader. The first three, moreover, correspond to something in the very nature of human discourse. If communications were not complex, structural outlining would be unnecessary. If language were a perfect medium instead of a relatively opaque one, there would be no need for interpretation. If error and ignorance did not circumscribe truth and knowledge, we should not have to be critical. The fourth question turns on the distinction between information and understanding. When the material you have read is itself primarily informational, you are challenged to go further and seek enlightenment. Even when you have been somewhat enlightened by what you have read, you are called upon to continue the search for significance.

Before proceeding to Part Three, perhaps we should stress, once again, that these rules of analytical reading describe an ideal performance. Few people have ever read any book in this ideal manner, and those who have, probably read very few books this way. The ideal remains, however, the measure of achievement. You are a good reader to the degree in which you approximate it.

When we speak of someone as "well-read," we should have this ideal in mind. Too often, we use that phrase to mean the quantity rather than the quality of reading. A person who has read widely but not well deserves to be pitied rather than praised. As Thomas Hobbes said, "If I read as many books as most men do, I would be as dull-witted as they are."

The great writers have always been great readers, but that does not mean that they read all the books that, in their day, were listed as the indispensable ones. In many cases, they read fewer books than are now required in most of our colleges, but what they did read, they read well. Because they had mastered these books, they became peers with their authors. They were entitled to become authorities in their own right. In the natural course of events, a good student frequently becomes a teacher, and so, too, a good reader becomes an author.

Our intention here is not to lead you from reading to writing. It is rather to remind you that one approaches the ideal of good reading by applying the rules we have described in the reading of a single book, and not by trying to become superficially acquainted with a larger number. There are, of course, many books worth reading well. There is a much larger number that should be only inspected. To become well-read, in every sense of the word, one must know how to use whatever skill one possesses with discrimination—by reading every book according to its merits.

12

Aids to Reading

Any aid to reading that lies outside the book being read we may speak of as extrinsic. By "intrinsic reading" we mean reading a book in itself, quite apart from all other books. By "extrinsic reading" we mean reading a book in the light of other books. So far we have intentionally avoided mentioning any extrinsic aids to reading. The rules of reading we have set forth are rules of intrinsic reading—they do not include going outside the book to discover what it means. There are good reasons for our having insisted up to now on your primary task as a reader—taking the book into your study and working on it by yourself, with the power of your own mind, and with no other aids. But it would be wrong to continue insisting on this. Extrinsic aids can help. And sometimes they are necessary for full understanding.

One reason why we have said nothing about extrinsic reading up to now is that intrinsic and extrinsic reading tend to fuse in the actual process of understanding and criticizing a book. We really cannot help bringing our experience to bear on the tasks of interpretation and criticism and even outlining. We must have read other books before this one; no one starts his reading career by reading analytically. We may not bring to bear our experience both of other books and of life as systematically as we should, but we nevertheless measure the statements and conclusions of a writer against other things that we know, from many different sources. Thus it is common sense to say that no book should be, because no book can be, read entirely and completely in isolation.

But the main reason for avoiding extrinsic aids up to this point is that many readers depend on them too slavishly, and we wanted you to realize that this is unnecessary. Reading a book with a dictionary in the other hand is a bad idea, although this does not mean you should never go to a dictionary for the meanings of words that are strange to you. And seeking the meaning of a book that puzzles you in a commentary is often ill-advised. On the whole, it is best to do all that you can by yourself before seeking outside help; for if you act consistently on this principle, you will find that you need less and less outside help.

The extrinsic aids to reading fall into four categories. In the order in which we will discuss them in this chapter, they are: first, relevant experiences; second, other books; third, commentaries and abstracts; fourth, reference books.

How and when to use any of these types of extrinsic aids cannot be stated for every particular case. Some general suggestions can be made, however. It is a common-sense maxim of reading that outside help should be sought whenever a book remains unintelligible to you, either in whole or part, *after you have done your best to read it according to the rules of intrinsic reading.*

The Role of Relevant Experience

There are two types of relevant experience that may be referred to for help in understanding difficult books. We have already mentioned the distinction involved, when we spoke in Chapter 6 of the difference between common experience and special experience. Common experience is available to all men and women just because they are alive. Special experience must be actively sought and is available only to those who go to the trouble of acquiring it. The best example of special experience is an experiment in a laboratory, but a laboratory is not always required. An anthropologist may acquire special experience by traveling to the Amazon basin, for example, to study the aboriginal inhabitants of a region that has not yet been explored. He thereby gains experience that is not ordinarily available to others, and that will never be available to many; for if large numbers of scientists invade the region, it will cease to be unique. Similarly, the experience of the astronauts on the moon is highly special, although the moon is not a laboratory in the ordinary sense of the term. Most men do not have the opportunity of knowing what it is like to live on an airless planet, and it will be centuries before this becomes a common experience, if it ever does. Jupiter, too, with its enormously greater gravity, will remain a "laboratory" in this sense for a long time to come, and may always be such.

Common experience does not have to be shared by everyone in order to be common. *Common* is not the same as *universal*. The experience of being a child of parents, for example, is not shared by every human being, for some are orphans from birth. However, family life is nevertheless common experience, because most men and women, in the ordinary course of their lives, share it. Nor is sexual love a universal experience, although it is common, in the sense we are giving the word *common*. Some men and women never experience it, but the experience is shared by such a high proportion of humans that it cannot be called special. (This does not mean that sexual activity cannot be studied in the laboratory, as in fact it has been.) The experience of being taught is not universal, either, for some men and women never go to school. But it, too, is common.

The two kinds of experience are mainly relevant to different kinds of books. Common experience is most relevant to the reading of fiction, on the one hand, and to the reading of philosophy, on the other. Judgments concerning the verisimilitude of a novel are almost wholly based on common experience; the book, we say, is either true or not true to our experience of life as it is led by most people, ourselves included. The philosopher, like the poet, appeals to the common experience of mankind. He does no work in laboratories or research in the field. Hence to understand and test a philosopher's leading principles you do not need the extrinsic aid of special experience. He refers you to your own common sense and your daily observation of the world in which you live.

Special experience is mainly relevant to the reading of scientific works. To understand and judge the inductive arguments in a scientific book, you must be able to follow the evidence that the scientist reports as their basis. Sometimes the scientist's description of an experiment is so vivid and clear that you have no trouble. Sometimes illustrations and diagrams help to acquaint you with the phenomena described.

Both common and special experience are relevant to the reading of history books. This is because history partakes both of the fictional and the scientific. On the one hand, a narrative history is a story, having a plot and characters, episodes, complications of action, a climax, an aftermath. The common experience that is relevant to reading novels and plays is relevant here, too. But history is also like science, in the sense that at least some of the experience on which the historian bases his work is quite special. He may have read a document or many documents that the reader could not manage to see without great trouble. He may have done extensive research, either into the remains of past civilizations or in the form of interviews with living persons in faraway places.

How do you know whether you are making proper use of your experience to help you understand a book? The surest test is one we have already recommended as a test of understanding: ask yourself whether you can give a concrete example of a point that you feel you understand. We have many times asked students to do this, only to find that they could not. The students appeared to have understood the point, but they were completely at a loss when called upon to supply an example. Obviously, they had not really understood the book. Test yourself in this way when you are not quite sure whether you have grasped a book. Take Aristotle's discussion of virtue in the *Ethics,* for example. He says over and over that virtue is a mean between the extremes of defect and excess. He gives some concrete examples; can you supply others? If so, you have understood his general point. If not, you should go back and read his discussion again.

Other Books as Extrinsic Aids to Reading

We will have more to say later about syntopical reading, where more than one book is read on a single subject. For the moment, we want to say a few things about the desirability of reading other books as extrinsic aids to the reading of a particular work.

Our advice applies particularly to the reading of so-called great books. The enthusiasm with which people embark on a course of reading great books often gives way, fairly soon, to a feeling of hopeless inadequacy. One reason, of course, is that many readers do not know how to read a single book very well. But that is not all. There is another reason: namely, that they think they should be able to understand the first book they pick up, without having read the others to which it is closely related. They may try to read *The Federalist Papers* without having first read the Articles of Confederation and the Constitution. Or they may try all these without having read Montesquieu's *The Spirit of Laws,* Rousseau's *The Social Contract,* and Locke's second treatise *Of Civil Government.*

Not only are many of the great books related, but also they were written in a certain order that should not be ignored. A later writer has been influenced by an earlier one. If you read the earlier writer first, he may help you to understand the later one. Reading related books in relation to one another and in an order that renders the later ones more intelligible is a basic common-sense maxim of extrinsic reading.

The utility of this kind of extrinsic reading is simply an extension of the value of context in reading a book by itself. We have seen how the context must be used to interpret words and sentences to find terms and propositions. Just as the whole book is the context for any of its parts, so related books provide an even larger context that helps you interpret the book you are reading.

It has often been observed that the great books are involved in a prolonged conversation. The great authors were great readers, and one way to understand them is to read the books they read. As readers, they carried on a conversation with other authors, just as each of us carries on a conversation with the books we read, though we may not write other books.

To join this conversation, we must read the great books in relation to one another, and in an order that somehow respects chronology. The conversation of the books takes place in time. Time is of the essence here and should not be disregarded. The books can be read from the present into the past or from the past into the present. Though the order from past to present has certain advantages through being more natural, the fact of chronology can be observed in either way.

It should be noted, incidentally, that the need to read books in relation to one another applies more to history and philosophy than to science and fiction. It is most important in the case of philosophy, because philosophers are great readers of each other. It is probably least important in the case of novels or plays, which, if they are really good, can be read in isolation, although of course the literary critic will not want to confine himself to doing so.

How to Use Commentaries and Abstracts

A third category of extrinsic aids to reading includes commentaries and abstracts. The thing to emphasize here is that such works should be used wisely, which is to say sparingly. There are two reasons for this.

The first is that commentators are not always right in their comments on a book. Sometimes, of course, their works are enormously useful, but this is true less often than one could wish. The handbooks and manuals that are widely available in college bookstores and in stores frequented by high school students are often particularly misleading. These works purport to tell the student everything he has to know about a book that has been assigned by one of his teachers, but they are sometimes woefully wrong in their interpretations, and besides, as a practical matter, they irritate some teachers and professors.

In defense of handbooks, it must be conceded that they are often invaluable for passing examinations. Furthermore, to balance the fact that some teachers are irritated by the errors of handbooks, other teachers use them themselves in their teaching.

The second reason for using commentaries sparingly is that, even if they are right, they may not be exhaustive. That is, you may be able to discover important meanings in a book that the author of a commentary about it has not discovered. Reading a commentary, particularly one that seems very self-assured, thus tends to limit your understanding of a book, even if your understanding, as far as it goes, is correct.

Hence, there is one piece of advice that we want to give you about using commentaries. Indeed, this comes close to being a basic maxim of extrinsic reading. Whereas it is one of the rules of intrinsic reading that you should read an author's preface and introduction *before* reading his book, the rule in the case of extrinsic reading is that you should not read a commentary by someone else until *after* you have read the book. This applies particularly to scholarly and critical introductions. They are properly used only if you do your best to read the book first, and then and only then apply to them for answers to questions that still puzzle you. If you read them first they are likely to distort your reading of the book. You will tend to see only the points made by the scholar or critic, and fail to see other points that may be just as important.

There is considerable pleasure associated with the reading of such introductions when it is done in this way. You have read the book and understood it. The writer of the introduction has also read it, perhaps many times, and has his own understanding of it. You approach him, therefore, on essentially equal terms. If you read his introduction before reading the book, however, you are at his mercy.

Heeding this rule, that commentaries should be read after you have read the book that they expound and not before, applies also to handbooks. Such works cannot hurt you if you have already read the book and know where the handbook is wrong, if it is. But if you depend wholly on the handbook, and never read the original book, you may be in bad trouble.

And there is this further point. If you get into the habit of depending on commentaries and handbooks, you will be totally lost if you cannot find one. You may be able to understand a particular book with the help of a commentary, but in general you will be a worse reader.

The rule of extrinsic reading given here applies also to abstracts and plot digests. They are useful in two connections, but in those two only. First, they can help to jog your memory of a book's contents, if you have already read it. Ideally, you made such an abstract yourself, in reading the book analytically, but if you have not done so, an abstract or digest can be an important aid. Second, abstracts are useful when you are engaged in syntopical reading, and wish to know whether a certain work is likely to be germane to your project. An abstract can never replace the reading of a book, but it can sometimes tell you whether you want or need to read the book or not.

How to Use Reference Books

There are many kinds of reference books. In the following section we will confine ourselves mainly to the two most used kinds, dictionaries and encyclopedias. However, many of the things we will have to say apply to other kinds of reference books as well.

It is not always realized, yet it is nevertheless true, that a good deal of knowledge is required before you can use a reference book well. Specifically, four kinds of knowledge are required. Thus a reference book is an antidote to ignorance in only a limited way. It cannot cure total ignorance. It cannot do your thinking for you.

To use a reference book well, you must, *first,* have some idea, however vague it may be, of what you want to know. Your ignorance must be like a circle of darkness surrounded by light. You want to bring light to the dark circle. You cannot do that unless light surrounds the darkness. Another way to say this is that you must be able to ask a reference book an intelligible question. It will be no help to you if you are wandering, lost, in a fog of ignorance.

Second, you must know where to find out what you want to know. You must know what kind of question you are asking, and which kinds of reference books answer that kind of question. There is no reference book that answers all questions; all such works are specialists, as it were. Practically, this comes down to the fact that you must have a fair overall knowledge of *all* of the major types of reference books before you can use *any one* type effectively.

There is a *third,* and correlative, kind of knowledge that is required before a reference book can be useful to you. You must know how the particular work is organized. It will do you no good to know what you want to know, and to know the kind of reference book to use, if you do not know how to use the particular work. Thus there is an art of reading reference books, just as there is an art to reading anything else. There is a correlative art to making reference books, by the way. The author or compiler should know what kind of information readers will seek, and arrange his book to fit their needs. He may not always be able to anticipate these, however, which is why the rule that you should read the introduction and preface to a book before reading the book itself applies particularly here. Do not try to use a reference book before getting the editor's advice on *how* to use it.

Of course, not all kinds of questions can be answered by reference books. You will not find in any reference book the answers to the three questions that God asks the angel in Tolstoy's story, *What Men Live By*—namely, "What dwells in man?" "What is not given to man?" and "What do men live by?" Nor will you find the answers to another question that is also used as the title of a Tolstoy story: "How much land does a man need?" And there are many such questions. Reference books are only useful when you know which kinds of questions can be answered by them, and which cannot. This comes down to knowing the sorts of things that men generally agree on. Only those things about which men generally and conventionally agree are to be found in reference books. Unsupported opinions have no business there, though they sometimes creep in.

We agree that it is possible to know when a man was born, when he died, and facts about similar matters. We agree that it is possible to define words and things, and that it is possible to sketch the history of almost anything. We do not agree on moral questions or on questions about the future, and so these sorts of things are not to be found in reference books. We assume in our time that the physical world is orderable, and thus almost everything about it is to be found in reference books. This was not always so; as a result, the history of reference books is interesting in itself, for it can tell us much about changes in men's opinions as to what is knowable.

As you can see, we have just been suggesting that there is a *fourth* requirement for the intelligent use of reference books. You must know *what* you want to know; you must know *in what reference work* to find it; you must know *how* to find it in the reference work; and you must know that it is *considered knowable* by the authors or compilers of the book. All this indicates that you must know a good deal before you can use a work of reference. Reference books are useless to people who know nothing. They are not guides to the perplexed.

How to Use a Dictionary

As a reference book, the dictionary is subject to all the considerations outlined above. But the dictionary also invites a playful reading. It challenges anyone to sit down with it in an idle moment. There are worse ways to kill time.

Dictionaries are full of arcane knowledge and witty oddments. Over and above that, of course, they have their more sober employments. To make the most of these, one has to know how to read the special kind of book a dictionary is.

Santayana's remark about the Greeks—that they were the only uneducated people in European history—has a double significance. The masses were, of course, uneducated, but even the learned few—

the leisure class—were not educated in the sense that they had to sit at the feet of foreign masters. Education, in that sense, begins with the Romans, who went to school to Greek pedagogues, and became cultivated through contact with the Greek culture they had conquered.

It is not surprising, therefore, that the first dictionaries were glossaries of Homeric words, intended to help Romans read the *Iliad* and *Odyssey* as well as other Greek literature employing the "archaic" Homeric vocabulary. In the same way, many of us today need a glossary to read Shakespeare, or if not Shakespeare, Chaucer.

There were dictionaries in the Middle Ages, but they were usually encyclopedias of worldly knowledge comprised of discussions of the most important technical terms employed in learned discourse. There were foreign-language dictionaries in the Renaissance (both Greek and Latin), made necessary by the fact that the works that dominated the education of the period were in the ancient languages. Even when the so-called vulgar tongues—Italian, French, English—gradually replaced Latin as the language of learning, the pursuit of learning was still the privilege of the few. Under such circumstances, dictionaries were intended for a limited audience, mainly as an aid to reading and writing worthy literature.

Thus we see that from the beginning the educational motive dominated the making of dictionaries, although there was also an interest in preserving the purity and order of the language. As contrasted with the latter purpose, the *Oxford English Dictionary* (known familiarly as the OED), begun in 1857, was a new departure, in that it did not try to dictate usage but instead to present an accurate historical record of every type of usage—the worst as well as the best, taken from popular as well as elegant writing. But this conflict between the lexicographer as self-appointed arbiter and the lexicographer as historian can be regarded as a side-issue, for the dictionary, however constructed, is primarily an educational instrument.

This fact is relevant to the rules for using a dictionary well, as an extrinsic aid to reading. The first rule of reading any book is to know what kind of book it is. That means knowing what the author's intention was and what sort of thing you can expect to find in his work. If you look upon a dictionary merely as a spelling book or guide to pronunciation, you will use it accordingly, which is to say not well. If you realize that it contains a wealth of historical information, crystallized in the growth and development of language, you will pay attention, not merely to the variety of meanings listed under each word, but also to their order and relation.

Above all, if you are interested in advancing your own education, you will use a dictionary according to its primary intention—as a help in reading books that might otherwise be too difficult because their vocabulary includes technical words, archaic words, literary allusions, or even familiar words used in obsolete senses.

Of course, there are many problems to be solved in reading a book well other than those arising from an author's vocabulary. And we have warned against—particularly on the first reading of a difficult book—sitting with the book in one hand and the dictionary in the other. If you have to look up too many words at the beginning, you will certainly lose track of the book's unity and order. The dictionary's primary service is on those occasions when you are confronted with a technical word or with a word that is wholly new to you. Even then, we would not recommend looking up even these during your first reading of a good book unless they seem to be important to the author's general meaning.

This suggests several other negative injunctions. There is no more irritating fellow than the one who tries to settle an argument about communism, or justice, or freedom, by quoting from the dictionary. Lexicographers may be respected as authorities on word usage, but they are not the ultimate founts of wisdom. Another negative rule is: Don't swallow the dictionary. Don't try to get word-rich quick by memorizing a fancy list of words whose meanings are unconnected with any actual experience. In short, do not forget that the dictionary is a book about words, not about things.

If we remember this, we can derive from that fact all the rules for using a dictionary intelligently. Words can be looked at in four ways.

1. WORDS ARE PHYSICAL THINGS—writable words and speakable sounds. There must, therefore, be uniform ways of spelling and pronouncing them, though the uniformity is often spoiled by variations, and in any event is not as eternally important as some of your teachers may have indicated.
2. WORDS ARE PARTS OF SPEECH. Each single word plays a grammatical role in the more complicated structure of a phrase or sentence. The same word can vary in different usages, shifting from one part of speech to another, especially in a non-inflected language like English.
3. WORDS ARE SIGNS. They have meanings, not one but many. These meanings are related in various ways. Sometimes they shade from one into another; sometimes a word will have two or more sets of totally unrelated meanings. Through their meanings, different words are related to one another—as synonyms sharing in the same meaning even though they differ in shading; or as antonyms through opposition or contrast of meanings. Furthermore, it is in their capacity as signs that we distinguish words as proper or common names (according as they name just one thing or many that are alike in some respect); and as concrete or abstract names (according as they point to something we can sense, or refer to some aspect of things that we can understand by thought but not observe through our senses).

Finally, 4. WORDS ARE CONVENTIONAL. They are man-made signs. That is why every word has a history, a cultural career in the course of which it goes through certain transformations. The history of words is given by their etymological derivation from original word-roots, prefixes, and suffixes; it includes the account of their physical changes, both in spelling and pronunciation; it tells of the shifting meanings, and which among them are archaic and obsolete, which are current and regular, which are idiomatic, colloquial, or slang.

A good dictionary will answer all of these four different kinds of questions about words. The art of using a dictionary consists in knowing what questions to ask about words and how to find the answers. We have suggested the questions. The dictionary itself tells you how to find the answers.

As such, it is a perfect self-help book, because it tells you what to pay attention to and how to interpret the various abbreviations and symbols it uses in giving you the four varieties of information about words. Anyone who fails to consult the explanatory notes and the list of abbreviations at the beginning of a dictionary has only himself to blame if he is not able to use it well.

How to Use an Encyclopedia

Many of the things we have said about dictionaries apply to encyclopedias also. Like the dictionary, the encyclopedia invites a playful reading. It too is diverting, entertaining, and, for some people, soothing. But it is just as vain to try to read an encyclopedia through as a dictionary. The man who knew an encyclopedia by heart would be in grave danger of incurring the title *idiot savant*—"learned fool."

Many people use a dictionary to find out how to spell and pronounce words. The analogous employment of an encyclopedia is to use it only to look up dates and places and other such simple facts. But this is to under-use, or misuse, an encyclopedia. Like dictionaries, such works are educational as well as informational tools. A glance at their history will confirm this.

Though the word "encyclopedia" is Greek, the Greeks had no encyclopedia, and for the same reason that they had no dictionary. The word meant to them not a book about knowledge, a book in which knowledge reposed, but knowledge itself—all the knowledge that an educated man should have. It was again the Romans who first found encyclopedias necessary; the oldest extant example is that of Pliny.

Interestingly enough, the first alphabetically-arranged encyclopedia did not appear until about 1700. Most of the great encyclopedias since then have been alphabetical. It is the easiest of all arrangements, and it made possible great strides in encyclopedia-making.

Encyclopedias present a different problem from word-books. An alphabetical arrangement is natural for a dictionary. But is the world, which is the subject matter of an encyclopedia, arranged alphabetically? Obviously not. Well then, how is the world arranged and ordered? This comes down to asking how knowledge is ordered.

The ordering of knowledge has changed with the centuries. All knowledge was once ordered in relation to the seven liberal arts—grammar, rhetoric, and logic, the trivium; arithmetic, geometry, astronomy, and music, the quadrivium. Medieval encyclopedias reflected this arrangement. Since the universities were arranged according to the same system, and students studied according to it also, the arrangement was useful in education.

The modern university is very different from the medieval one, and the change is reflected in modern encyclopedias. The knowledge that they report is divided up in fiefs, or specialties, that are roughly equivalent to the various departments of the university. But this arrangement, although it forms the backbone structure of an encyclopedia, is masked by the alphabetical arrangement of the material.

It is this infra-structure—to take a term from the sociologists—that the good reader and user of an encyclopedia will seek to discover. It is true that it is primarily factual information that he wants from his set. But he should not be content with facts in isolation. The encyclopedia presents him with an arrangement of facts—facts in relation to other facts. The understanding, as contrasted with the mere information, that an encyclopedia can provide depends on the recognition of such relations.

In an alphabetically-arranged encyclopedia, these relations are to a large extent obscured. In a topically-arranged encyclopedia, they are, of course, highlighted. But topical encyclopedias have many disadvantages, among them the fact that most readers are not accustomed to using them. Ideally, the best encyclopedia would be one that had both a topical and an alphabetical arrangement. Its presentation of material in the form of separate articles would be alphabetical, but it would also contain some kind of topical key or outline—essentially, a table of contents. (A table of contents is a topical arrangement of a book, as opposed to an index, which is an alphabetical arrangement.) As far as we know, there is no such encyclopedia on the market today, but it would be worth the effort to try to make one.

In default of the ideal, the reader must fall back on the help and advice provided him by an encyclopedia's editors. Any good encyclopedia includes directions about how to use it effectively, and these should be read and followed. Often, these directions require that the user go first to the set's index, before turning to one of the alphabetically-arranged volumes. Here, the index is serving the function of a table of contents, though not very well; for it gathers together, under one heading, references to discussions in the encyclopedia that may be widely separated in space but that are nevertheless about the same general subject. This reflects the fact that although an index is of course alphabetically arranged, its so-called analyticals—that is, the breakdowns under a main entry—are topically arranged. But the topics themselves must be in alphabetical order, which is not necessarily the best arrangement. Thus the index of a really good encyclopedia such as Britannica goes part of the way toward revealing the arrangement of knowledge that the work reflects. For this reason, any reader who fails to use the index has only himself to blame if the work does not serve his needs.

There are negative injunctions associated with the use of encyclopedias, just as there are for dictionaries. Encyclopedias, like dictionaries, are valuable adjuncts to the reading of good books—bad books do not ordinarily require their presence; but, as before, it is wise not to enslave yourself to an encyclopedia. Again, as with dictionaries, encyclopedias are not to be used for the settling of arguments where these are based on differences of opinion. Nevertheless, they *should* be used to end disputes about matters of fact as quickly and permanently as possible. Facts should never be argued about in the first place. An encyclopedia makes this vain effort unnecessary, because encyclopedias are full of facts. Ideally, they are filled with nothing else. Finally, although dictionaries usually agree in their accounts of words, encyclopedias often do not agree in their accounts of facts. Hence, if you are really interested in a subject and are depending on encyclopedic treatments of it, do not restrict yourself to just one encyclopedia. Read more than one, and preferably ones written at different times.

We noted several points about words that the user should keep in mind when he consults a dictionary. In the case of encyclopedias, the analogous points are about facts, for an encyclopedia is about facts as a dictionary is about words.

1. FACTS ARE PROPOSITIONS. Statements of fact employ words in combination, such as "Abraham Lincoln was born on February 12, 1809," or "the atomic number of gold is 79." Facts are not physical things, as words are, but they do require to be explained. For thorough knowledge, for understanding, you must also know what the significance of a fact is—how it affects the truth you are seeking. You do not know much if all you know is what the fact is.

2. FACTS ARE "TRUE" PROPOSITIONS. Facts are not opinions. When someone says "it is a fact that," he means that it is generally agreed that such is the case. He never means, or never should mean, that he alone, or he together with a minority of observers, believes such and such to be the case. It is this characteristic of facts that gives the encyclopedia its tone and style. An encyclopedia that contains the unsupported opinions of its editors is dishonest; and although an encyclopedia may report opinions (for example, in a phrase like "it is held by some that this is the case, by others that that is the case"), it must clearly label them. The requirement that an encyclopedia report the facts of the case and not opinions about it (except as noted

above) also limits the work's coverage. It cannot properly deal with matters about which there is no consensus—with moral questions, for example. If it does deal with such questions, it can only properly report the disagreements among men about them.

3. FACTS ARE REFLECTIONS OF REALITY. Facts may be either (a) informational singulars or (b) relatively unquestioned generalizations, but in either case they are held to represent the way things really are. (The birth date of Lincoln is an informational singular; the atomic number of gold implies a relatively unquestioned generalization about matter.) Thus facts are not ideas or concepts, nor are they theories in the sense of being mere speculations about reality. Similarly, an explanation of reality (or of part of it) is not a fact until and unless there is general agreement that it is correct.

There is one exception to the last statement. An encyclopedia can properly describe a theory that is no longer held to be correct, in whole or in part, or one that has not yet been fully validated, when it is associated with a topic, person or school that is the subject of an article. Thus, for example, Aristotle's views on the nature of celestial matter could be expounded in an article on Aristoteleanism even though we no longer believe them to be true.

Finally, 4. FACTS ARE TO SOME EXTENT CONVENTIONAL. Facts change, we say. We mean that some propositions that are considered to be facts in one epoch are no longer considered to be facts in another. Insofar as facts are "true" and represent reality, they cannot change, of course, because truth, strictly speaking, does not change, nor does reality. But not all propositions that we take to be true are really true; and we must concede that almost any given proposition that we take to be true can be falsified by more patient or more accurate observation and investigation. This applies particularly to the facts of science.

Facts are also—again to some extent—culturally determined. An atomic scientist, for example, maintains a complicated, hypothetical structure of reality in his mind that determines—for him—certain facts that are different from the facts that are determined for and accepted by a primitive. This does not mean that the scientist and the primitive cannot agree on any facts; they must agree, for instance, that two plus two is four, or that a physical whole is greater than any of its parts. But the primitive may not agree with the scientist's facts about nuclear particles, just as the scientist may not agree with the primitive's facts about ritual magic. (That was a hard sentence to write, because, being culturally determined ourselves, we tend to agree with the scientist rather than the primitive and were thus tempted to put the second "fact" in quotation marks. But that is precisely the point.)

A good encyclopedia will answer your questions about facts if you remember the points about facts that we have outlined above. The art of using an encyclopedia as an aid to reading is the art of asking the proper questions about facts. As with the dictionary, we have merely suggested the questions; the encyclopedia will supply the answers.

You should also remember that an encyclopedia is not the best place to pursue understanding. Insights may be gained from it about the order and arrangement of knowledge; but that, although an important subject, is nonetheless a limited one. There are many matters required for understanding that you will not find in an encyclopedia.

There are two particularly striking omissions. An encyclopedia, properly speaking, contains no arguments, except insofar as it reports the course of arguments that are now widely accepted as correct or at least as of historical interest. Thus a major element in expository writing is lacking. An encyclopedia also contains no poetry or imaginative literature, although it may contain facts about poetry and poets. Since both the imagination and the reason are required for understanding, this means that the encyclopedia must be a relatively unsatisfying tool in the pursuit of it.

PART 3

*Approaches to Different Kinds
of Reading Matter*

13

How to Read Practical Books

In any art or field of practice, rules have a disappointing way of being too general. The more general, of course, the fewer, and that is an advantage. The more general, too, the more intelligible—it is easier to understand the rules in and by themselves. But it is also true that the more general the rules, the more remote they are from the intricacies of the actual situation in which you try to follow them.

We have stated the rules of analytical reading generally so that they apply to any expository book—any book that conveys knowledge, in the sense in which we have been using that term. But you cannot read a book in general. You read this book or that, and every particular book is of a particular sort. It may be a history or a book in mathematics, a political tract or a work in natural science, or a philosophical or theological treatise. Hence, you must have some flexibility and adaptability in following the rules. Fortunately, you will gradually get the feeling of how they work on different kinds of books as you apply them.

It is important to note here that the fifteen rules of reading, in the form in which they were presented toward the end of Chapter 11, do not apply to the reading of fiction and poetry. The outlining of the structure of an imaginative work is a different matter from the outlining of an expository book. Novels and plays and poems do not proceed by terms, propositions, and arguments—their fundamental content, in other words, is not logical, and the criticism of such works is based on different premises. Nevertheless, it would be a mistake to think that no rules at all apply to reading imaginative literature. In fact, there is a parallel set of rules for reading such books that we will describe in the next chapter. These are useful in themselves; but the examination of them and their differences from the rules for reading expository works also throws light on the latter rules.

You need not fear that you will have to learn a whole new set of fifteen or more rules for reading fiction and poetry. The connection between the two kinds of rules is easy to see and state. It consists in the underlying fact, which we have emphasized over and over, that you must ask questions when you read, and specifically that you must ask four particular questions of whatever you are reading. These four questions are relevant to any book, whether fiction or nonfiction, whether poetry or history or science or philosophy. We have seen how the rules of reading expository works connect with and are developed from these four questions. Similarly, the rules of reading imaginative literature are also developed from them, although the difference in the nature of the materials read causes some dissimilarities in the development.

That being the case, in this part of the book we will have more to say about these questions than about the rules for reading. We will occasionally refer to a new rule, or to a revision or adaptation of an old one. But most of the time, as we proceed to suggest approaches to the reading of different kinds of books and other materials, we will emphasize the different questions that must be primarily asked, and the different kinds of answers that can be expected.

In the expository realm, we have noted that the basic division is into the practical and the theoretical—books that are concerned with the problems of action, and books that are concerned only with something to be known. The theoretical is further divisible, as we have noted, into history, science (and mathematics), and philosophy. The practical division cuts across all boundaries, and we therefore propose to examine the nature of such books a little further, and to suggest some guidelines and precautions when you read them.

The Two Kinds of Practical Books

The most important thing to remember about any practical book is that *it can never solve the practical problems with which it is concerned.* A theoretical book can solve its own problems. But a practical problem can only be solved by action itself. When your practical problem is how to earn a living, a book on how to make friends and influence people cannot solve it, though it may suggest things to do. Nothing short of the doing solves the problem. It is solved only by earning a living.

Take this book, for example. It is a practical book. If your interest in it is practical (it might, of course, be only theoretical), you want to solve the problem of learning to read. You would not regard that problem as solved and done away with until you did learn. This book cannot solve the problem for you. It can only help. You must actually go through the activity of reading, not only this book but many others. That is what it means to say that nothing but action solves practical problems, and action occurs only in the world, not in books.

Every action takes place in a particular situation, always in the here and now and under a particular set of circumstances. You cannot act in general. The kind of practical judgment that immediately precedes action must be highly particular. It can be expressed in words, but it seldom is. It is almost never found in books, because the author of a practical book cannot envisage the concrete practical situations in which his readers may have to act. Try as he will to be helpful, he cannot give them concrete practical advice. Only another person in exactly the same situation could do that.

Practical books can, however, state more or less general rules that apply to a lot of particular situations of the same sort. Whoever tries to use such books must apply the rules to particular cases and, therefore, must exercise practical judgment in doing so. In other words, the reader himself must add something to the book to make it applicable in practice. He must add his knowledge of the particular situation and his judgment of how the rule applies to the case.

Any book that contains rules—prescriptions, maxims, or any sort of general directions—you will readily recognize as a practical book. But a practical book may contain more than rules. It may try to state the principles that underlie the rules and make them intelligible. For example, in this practical book about reading, we have tried here and there to explain the rules by brief expositions of grammatical, rhetorical, and logical principles. The principles that underlie rules are usually in themselves scientific, that is, they are items of theoretical knowledge. Taken together, they are the theory of the thing. Thus, we talk about the theory of bridge building or the theory of contract bridge. We mean *the theoretical principles that make the rules of good procedure what they are.*

Practical books thus fall into two main groups. Some, like this one, or a cookbook, or a driver's manual, are primarily presentations of rules. Whatever other discussion they contain is for the sake of the rules. There are few great books of this sort. The other kind of practical book is primarily concerned with the principles that generate rules. Most of the great books in economics, politics, and morals are of this sort.

This distinction is not sharp and absolute. Both principles and rules may be found in the same book. The point is one of relative emphasis. You will have no difficulty in sorting books into these two piles. The book of rules in any field will always be immediately recognizable as practical. The book of practical principles may look at first like a theoretical book. In a sense it is, as we have seen. It deals with the theory of a particular kind of practice. You can always tell it is practical, however. The nature of its problems gives it away. It is always about a field of human behavior in which men can do better or worse.

In reading a book that is primarily a rule-book, the major propositions to look for, of course, are the rules. A rule is most directly expressed by an imperative rather than a declarative sentence. It is a command. It says: "Save nine stitches by taking a stitch in time." That rule can also be expressed declaratively, as when we say, "A stitch in time saves nine." Both forms of statement suggest—the imperative a little more emphatically, but not necessarily more memorably—that it is worth while to be prompt.

Whether it is stated declaratively or in the form of a command, you can always recognize a rule because it recommends something as worth doing to gain a certain end. Thus, the rule of reading that commands you to come to terms can also be stated as a recommendation: good reading involves coming to terms. The word "good" is the giveaway. That such reading is worth doing is implied.

The arguments in a practical book of this sort will be attempts to show you that the rules are sound. The writer may have to appeal to principles to persuade you that they are, or he may simply illustrate their soundness by showing you how they work in concrete cases. Look for both sorts of arguments. The appeal to principles is usually less persuasive, but it has one advantage. It can explain the reason for the rules better than examples of their use.

In the other kind of practical books, the kind dealing mainly with the principles underlying rules, the major propositions and arguments will, of course, look exactly like those in a purely theoretical book. The propositions will say that something is the case, and the arguments will try to show that it is so.

But there is an important difference between reading such a book and reading a purely theoretical one. Since the ultimate problems to be solved are practical—problems of action, in fields where men can do better or worse—an intelligent reader of such books about "practical principles" always reads between the lines or in the margins. He tries to see the rules that may not be expressed but that can, nevertheless, be derived from the principles. He goes further. He tries to figure out how the rules should be applied in practice.

Unless it is so read, a practical book is not read *as practical*. To fail to read a practical book *as practical* is to read it poorly. You really do not understand it, and you certainly cannot criticize it properly in any other way. If the intelligibility of rules is to be found in principles, it is no less true that the significance of practical principles is to be found in the rules they lead to, the actions they recommend.

This indicates what you must do to understand either sort of practical book. It also indicates the ultimate criteria for critical judgment. In the case of purely theoretical books, the criteria for agreement or disagreement relate to the truth of what is being said. But practical truth is different from theoretical truth. A rule of conduct is practically true on two conditions: one is that it works; the other is that its working leads you to the right end, an end you rightly desire.

Suppose that the end an author thinks you should seek does not seem like the right one to you. Even though his recommendations may be practically sound, in the sense of getting you to that end, you will not agree with him ultimately. And your judgment of his book as practically true or practically false will be made accordingly. If you do not think careful and intelligent reading is worth doing, this book has little practical truth for you, however sound its rules may be.

Notice what this means. In judging a theoretical book, the reader must observe the identity of, or the discrepancy between, his own basic principles or assumptions and those of the author. *In judging a practical book, everything turns on the ends or goals.* If you do not share Karl Marx's fervor about economic justice, his economic doctrine and the reforms it suggests are likely to seem to you practically false or irrelevant. You may think, as Edmund Burke did, for example, that preserving the *status quo* is the most desirable objective; everything considered, you believe that to be more important than removing the inequities of capitalism. In that case, you are likely to think that a book like *The Communist Manifesto* is preposterously false. Your main judgment will always be in terms of the ends, not the means. We have no practical interest in even the soundest means to reach ends we disapprove of or do not care about.

The Role of Persuasion

This brief discussion gives you a clue to the two major questions you must ask yourself in reading any sort of practical book. The first is: What are the author's objectives? The second is: What means for achieving them is he proposing? It may be more difficult to answer these questions in the case of a book about principles than in the case of one about rules. The ends and means are likely to be less obvious. Yet answering them in either case is necessary for the understanding and criticism of a practical book.

It also reminds you of one aspect of practical writing that we noted earlier. There is an admixture of oratory or propaganda in every practical book. We have never read a book of political philosophy—however theoretical it may have appeared, however "abstract" the principles with which it dealt—that did not try to persuade the reader about "the best form of government." Similarly, moral treatises try to persuade the reader about "the good life" as well as recommend ways of leading it. And we have tried continuously to persuade you to read books in a certain way, for the sake of the understanding that you may attain.

You can see why the practical author must always be something of an orator or propagandist. Since your ultimate judgment of his work is going to turn on *your acceptance of the goal for which he is proposing means,* it is up to him to win you to his ends. To do this, he has to argue in a way that appeals to your heart as well as your mind. He may have to play on your emotions and gain direction of your will.

There is nothing wrong or vicious about this. It is of the very nature of practical affairs that men have to be persuaded to think and act in a certain way. Neither practical thinking nor action is an affair of the mind alone. The emotions cannot be left out. No one makes serious practical judgments or engages in action without being moved somehow from below the neck. The world might be a better place if we did, but it would certainly be a different world. The writer of practical books who does not realize this will be ineffective.

The reader of them who does not is likely to be sold a bill of goods without his knowing it.

The best protection against propaganda of any sort is the recognition of it for what it is. Only hidden and undetected oratory is really insidious. What reaches the heart without going through the mind is likely to bounce back and put the mind out of business. Propaganda taken in that way is like a drug you do not know you are swallowing. The effect is mysterious; you do not know afterwards why you feel or think the way you do.

The person who reads a practical book intelligently, who knows its basic terms, propositions, and arguments, will always be able to detect its oratory. He will spot the passages that make an "emotive use of words." Aware that he must be subject to persuasion, he can do something about weighing the appeals. He has sales resistance; but this need not be one hundred percent. Sales resistance is good when it prevents you from buying hastily and thoughtlessly. But the reader who supposes he should be totally deaf to all appeals might just as well not read practical books.

There is a further point here. Because of the nature of practical problems and because of the admixture of oratory in all practical writing, the "personality" of the author is more important in the case of practical books than theoretical. You need know nothing whatever about the author of a mathematical treatise; his reasoning is either good or not, and it makes no difference what kind of man he is. But in order to understand and judge a moral treatise, a political tract, or an economic discussion, you should know something about the character of the writer, something about his life and times. In reading Aristotle's *Politics,* for example, it is highly relevant to know that Greek society was based on slavery. Similarly, much light is thrown on *The Prince* by knowing the Italian political situation at the time of Machiavelli, and his relation to the Medicis; or, in the case of Hobbes' *Leviathan,* that Hobbes lived during the English civil wars and was almost pathologically distressed by social violence and disorder.

What Does Agreement Entail in the Case of a Practical Book?

We are sure that you can see that the four questions you must ask about any book are somewhat changed in the case of reading a practical book. Let us try to spell out these changes.

The first question, What is the book about?, does not change very much. Since a practical book is an expository one, it is still necessary, in the course of answering this first question, to make an outline of the book's structure.

However, although you must always try to find out (Rule 4 covers this) what an author's problems were, here, in the case of practical books, this requirement becomes the dominant one. We have said that you must try to discern the author's objectives. That is another way of saying you must know what problems he was trying to solve. You must know what he wanted to do—because, in the case of a practical work, knowing what *he* wants to do comes down to knowing what he wants *you* to do. And that is obviously of considerable importance.

The second question does not change very much, either. You must still, in order to answer the question about the book's meaning or contents, discover the author's terms, propositions, and arguments. But here again it is the last aspect of that task (covered by Rule 8) that now looms most important. Rule 8, you will recall, required you to say which of the author's problems he solved and which he did not. The adaptation of this rule that applies in the case of practical books has already been stated. You must discover and understand the means the author recommends for achieving what he is proposing. In other words, if Rule 4 as adapted for practical books is FIND OUT WHAT THE AUTHOR WANTS YOU TO DO, then Rule 8, as similarly adapted, is FIND OUT HOW HE PROPOSES THAT YOU DO THIS.

The third question, Is it true?, is changed somewhat more than the first two. In the case of a theoretical book, the question is answered when you have compared the author's description and explanation of what is or happens in the world with your own knowledge thereof. If the book accords generally with your own experience of the way things are, then you must concede its truthfulness, at least in part. In the case of a practical book, although there is some such comparison of the book and reality, the main consideration is whether the author's objectives—that is, the ends that he seeks, together with the means he proposes to reach them—accord with your conception of what it is right to seek, and of what is the best way of seeking it.

The fourth question, What of it?, is changed most of all. If, after reading a theoretical book, your view of its subject matter is altered more or less, then you are required to make some adjustments in your general view of things. (If no adjustments are called for, then you cannot have learned much, if anything, from the book.) But these adjustments need not be earth-shaking, and above all they do not necessarily imply action on your part.

Agreement with a practical book, however, *does* imply action on your part. If you are convinced or persuaded by the author that the ends he proposes are worthy, and if you are further convinced or persuaded that the means he recommends are likely to achieve those ends, then it is hard to see how you can refuse to act in the way the author wishes you to.

We recognize, of course, that this does not always happen. But we want you to realize what it means when it does not. It means that despite his apparent agreement with the author's ends and acceptance of his means, the reader really does not agree or accept. If he did both, he could not reasonably fail to act.

Let us give an example of what we mean. If, after completing Part Two of this book, you (1) agreed that reading analytically is worthwhile, and (2) accepted the rules of reading as essentially supportive of that aim, then you must have begun to try to read in the manner we have described. If you did not, it is not just because you were lazy or tired. It is because you did not really mean either (1) or (2).

There is one apparent exception to this contention. Suppose, for example, that you read an article about how to make a chocolate mousse. You like chocolate mousse, and so you agree with the author of the article that the end in view is good. You also accept the author's proposed means for attaining the end—his recipe. But you are a male reader who never goes into the kitchen, and so you do not make a mousse. Does this invalidate our point?

It does not, although it does indicate an important distinction between types of practical books that should be mentioned. With regard to the ends proposed by the authors of such works, these are sometimes general or universal—applicable to all human beings—and sometimes applicable only to a certain portion of human beings. If the end is universal—as it is, for example, with this book, which maintains that *all* persons should read better, not just some—then the implication discussed in this section applies to every reader. If the end is selective, applying only to a certain class of human beings, then the reader must decide whether or not he belongs to that class. If he does, then the implication applies to him, and he is more or less obligated to act in the ways specified by the author. If he does not, then he may not be so obligated.

We say "may not be so obligated" because there is a strong possibility that the reader may be fooling himself, or misunderstanding his own motives, in deciding that he does not belong to the class to which the end is relevant. In the case of the reader of the article about chocolate mousse, he is probably, by his inaction, expressing his view that, although mousse is admittedly delicious, someone else—perhaps his wife—should be the one to make it. And in many cases, we concede the desirability of an end and the feasibility of the means, but in one way or another express our reluctance to perform the action ourselves. Let someone else do it, we say, more or less explicitly.

This, of course, is not primarily a reading problem but rather a psychological one. Nevertheless, the psychological fact has bearing on how effectively we read a practical book, and so we have discussed the matter here.

14

How to Read Imaginative Literature

So far, this book has been concerned with only half the reading that most people do. Even that is too liberal an estimate. Probably the greater part of anybody's reading time is spent on newspapers and magazines, and on things that have to be read in connection with one's job. And so far as books are concerned, most of us read more fiction than nonfiction. Furthermore, of the nonfiction books, the most popular are those that, like newspapers and magazines, deal journalistically with matters of contemporary interest.

We have not deceived you about the rules set forth in the preceding chapters. Before undertaking to discuss them in detail, we explained that we would have to limit ourselves to the business of reading serious nonfiction books. To have expounded the rules for reading imaginative and expository literature *at the same time* would have been confusing. But now we cannot ignore the other types of reading any longer.

Before embarking on the task, we want to emphasize one rather strange paradox. The problem of knowing how to read imaginative literature is inherently much more difficult than the problem of knowing how to read expository books. Nevertheless, it seems to be a fact that such skill is more widely possessed than the art of reading science and philosophy, politics, economics, and history. How can this be true?

It may be, of course, that people deceive themselves about their ability to read novels intelligently. From our teaching experience, we know how tongue-tied people become when asked to say what they liked about a novel. That they enjoyed it is perfectly clear to them, but they cannot give much of an account of their enjoyment or tell what the book contained that caused them pleasure. This might indicate that people can be good readers of fiction without being good critics. We suspect this is, at best, a half-truth. A critical reading of anything depends upon the fullness of one's apprehension. Those who cannot say what they like about a novel probably have not read it below its most obvious surfaces. However, there is more to the paradox than that. Imaginative literature primarily *pleases* rather than teaches. It is much easier to be pleased than taught, but much harder to know *why* one is pleased. Beauty is harder to analyze than truth.

To make this point clear would require an extensive analysis of aesthetic appreciation. We cannot undertake that here. We can, however, give you some advice about how to read imaginative literature. We will proceed, first, by the *way of negation,* stating the obvious "don'ts" instead of the constructive rules. Next, we will proceed by the *way of analogy,* briefly translating the rules for reading nonfiction into their equivalents for reading fiction. Finally, in the next chapter, we will proceed to examine the problems of reading specific types of imaginative literature, namely, novels, plays, and lyric poems.

How Not to Read Imaginative Literature

In order to proceed by the way of negation, it is first of all necessary to grasp the basic differences between expository and imaginative literature. These differences will explain why we cannot read a novel as if it were a philosophical argument, or a lyric as if it were a mathematical demonstration.

The most obvious difference, already mentioned, relates to the purposes of the two kinds of writing. Expository books *try to convey knowledge*—knowledge about experiences that the reader has had or could have. Imaginative ones *try to communicate an experience it-self*—one that the reader can have or share *only* by reading—and if they succeed, they give the reader something to be enjoyed. Because of their diverse intentions, the two sorts of work appeal differently to the intellect and the imagination.

We *experience* things through the exercise of our senses and imagination. To *know* anything we must use our powers of judgment and reasoning, which are intellectual. This does not mean that we can think without using our imagination, or that sense experience is ever wholly divorced from rational insight or reflection. The matter is only one of emphasis. Fiction appeals primarily to the imagination. That is one reason for calling it imaginative literature, in contrast to science and philosophy which are intellectual.

This fact about imaginative literature leads to what is probably the most important of the negative injunctions we want to suggest. *Don't try to resist the effect that a work of imaginative literature has on you.*

We have discussed at length the importance of reading actively. This is true of all books, but it is true in quite different ways of expository works and of poetry. The reader of the former should be like a bird of prey, constantly alert, always ready to pounce. The kind of activity that is appropriate in reading poetry and fiction is not the same. It is a sort of passive action, if we may be allowed the expression, or, better, active passion. We must act in such a way, when reading a story, that we let it act on us. We must allow it to move us, we must let it do whatever work it wants to do on us. We must somehow make ourselves open to it.

We owe much to the expository literature—the philosophy, science, mathematics—that has shaped the real world in which we live. But we could not live in this world if we were not able, from time to time, to get away from it. We do not mean that imaginative literature is always, or essentially, escapist. In the ordinary sense of that term, the idea is contemptible. If we must escape from reality, it should be to a deeper, or greater, reality. This is the reality of our inner life, of our own unique vision of the world. To discover this reality makes us happy; the experience is deeply *satisfying* to some part of ourselves we do not ordinarily touch. In any event, the rules of reading a great work of literary art should have as an end or goal just such a profound experience. The rules should clear away all that stops us from feeling as deeply as we possibly can.

The basic difference between expository and imaginative literature leads to another difference. Because of their radically diverse aims, these two kinds of writing necessarily use language differently. The imaginative writer tries to maximize the latent ambiguities of words, in order thereby to gain all the richness and force that is inherent in their multiple meanings. He uses metaphors as the units of his construction just as the logical writer uses words sharpened to a single meaning. What Dante said of *The Divine Comedy,* that it must be read as having several distinct though related meanings, generally applies to poetry and fiction. The logic of expository writing aims at an ideal of unambiguous explicitness. Nothing should be left between the lines. Everything that is relevant and statable should be said as explicitly and clearly as possible. In contrast, imaginative writing relies as much upon what is implied as upon what is said. The multiplication of metaphors puts almost more content between the lines than in the words that compose them. The whole poem or story says something that none of its words say or can say.

From this fact we obtain another negative injunction. *Don't look for terms, propositions, and arguments in imaginative literature.* Such things are logical, not poetic, devices. "In poetry and in drama," the poet Mark Van Doren once observed, "statement is one of the obscurer mediums." What a lyric poem "states," for instance, cannot be found in any of its sentences. And the whole, comprising all its words in their relations to and reactions upon each other, says something that can never be confined within the straitjacket of propositions. (However, imaginative literature contains elements that are *analogous* to terms, propositions, and arguments, and we will discuss them in a moment.)

Of course, we can learn from imaginative literature, from poems and stories and especially, perhaps, plays—but not in the same way as we are taught by scientific and philosophical books. We learn from experience—the experience that we have in the course of our daily lives. So, too, we can learn from the vicarious, or artistically created, experiences that fiction produces in our imagination. In this sense, poems and stories teach as well as please. But the sense in which science and philosophy teach us is different. Expository works do not provide us with novel experiences. They comment on such experiences as we already have or can get. That is why it seems right to say that expository books teach primarily, while imaginative books teach only derivatively, by creating experiences from which we can learn. In order to learn from such books, we have to do our own thinking about experience; in order to learn from scientists and philosophers, we must first try to understand the thinking they have done.

Finally, one last negative rule. *Don't criticize fiction by the standards of truth and consistency that properly apply to communication of knowledge.* The "truth" of a good story is its verisimilitude, its intrinsic probability or plausibility. It must be a likely story, but it need not describe the facts of life or society in a manner that is verifiable by experiment or research. Centuries ago, Aristotle remarked that "the standard of correctness is not the same in poetry as in politics," or in physics or psychology for that matter. Technical inaccuracies about anatomy or errors in geography or history should be criticized when the book in which they occur offers itself as a treatise on those subjects. But misstatements of fact do not mar a story if its teller succeeds in surrounding them with plausibility. When we read history, we want the truth in some sense, and we have a right to complain if we do not get it. When we read a novel we want a story that must be true only in the sense that it *could have happened* in the world of characters and events that the novelist has created, and re-created in us.

What do we do with a philosophical book, once we have read it and understood it? We test it—against the common experience that was its original inspiration, and that is its only excuse for being. We say, is this true? Have we felt this? Have we always thought this without realizing it? Is this obvious now, though it was not previously? Complicated as the author's theory or explanation may be, is it actually simpler than the chaotic ideas and opinions we had about this subject before?

If we can answer most of these questions in the affirmative, then we are bound by the community of understanding that is between ourselves and the author. When we understand and do not disagree, we must say, "This is our common sense of the matter. We have tested your theory and found it correct."

Not so with poetry. We cannot test *Othello*, say, against our own experience, unless we too are Moors and wedded to Venetian ladies whom we suspect of treachery. But even if this were so, Othello is not every Moor, and Desdemona is not every Venetian lady; and most such couples would have the good fortune not to know an Iago. In fact, all but one would be so fortunate; Othello, the character as well as the play, is unique.

General Rules for Reading Imaginative Literature

To make the "don'ts" discussed in the last section more helpful, they must be supplemented by constructive suggestions. These suggestions can be developed by analogy from the rules of reading expository works.

There are, as we have seen, three groups of such rules. The first group consists of rules for discovering the unity and part-whole structure; the second consists of rules for identifying and interpreting the book's component terms, propositions, and arguments; the third consists of rules for criticizing the author's doctrine so that we can reach intelligent agreement or disagreement with him. We called these three groups of rules structural, interpretive, and critical. By analogy, we can find similar sets of rules to guide us in reading poems, novels, and plays.

First, we can translate the structural rules—the rules of outlining—into their fictional analogues as follows.

(1) You must classify a work of imaginative literature according to its kind. A lyric tells its story primarily in terms of a single emotional experience, whereas novels and plays have much more complicated plots, involving many characters, their actions and their reactions upon one another, as well as the emotions they suffer in the process. Everyone knows, furthermore, that a play differs from a novel by reason of the fact that it narrates entirely by means of actions and speeches. (There are some interesting exceptions to this, which we will mention later.) The playwright can never speak in his own person, as the novelist can, and frequently does, in the course of a novel. All of these differences in manner of writing call for differences in the reader's receptivity. Therefore, you should recognize at once the kind of fiction you are reading.

(2) You must grasp the unity of the whole work. Whether you have done this or not can be tested by whether you are able to express that unity in a sentence or two. The unity of an expository work resides ultimately in the main problem that it tries to solve. Hence its unity can be stated by the formulation of this question, or by the propositions that answer it. The unity of fiction is also connected with the problem the author has faced, but we have seen that that problem is the attempt to convey a concrete experience, and so *the unity of a story is always in its plot.* You have not grasped the whole story until you can summarize its plot in a brief narration—*not* a proposition or an argument. Therein lies its unity.

Note that there is no real contradiction here between what we have just said about the unity of plot and what we said about the uniqueness of the language of a fictional work. Even a lyric has a "plot" in the sense in which we are using the term here. But the plot is not the concrete experience that is re-created in the reader by the work, be it lyric, play, or novel; it is only the framework of it, or perhaps the occasion of it. It stands for the unity of the work, which is properly in the experience itself, just as the logical summation of the meaning of an expository work stands for the argument of the whole.

(3) You must not only reduce the whole to its simplest unity, but you must also discover how that whole is constructed out of all its parts. The parts of an expository book are concerned with parts of the whole problem, the partial solutions contributing to the solution of the whole. The parts of fiction are the various steps that the author takes to develop his plot—the details of characterization and incident. The way in which the parts are arranged differs in the two cases. In science and philosophy, they must be ordered logically. In a story, the parts must somehow fit into a temporal scheme, a progress from a beginning through the middle to its end. To know the structure of a narrative, you must know where it begins—which is not necessarily on the first page, of course—what it goes through, and where it comes out at. You must know the various crises that lead up to the climax, where and how the climax occurs, and what happens in the aftermath. (By "aftermath" we do not mean what happens after the story is over. Nobody can know that. We mean only what happens, within the narrative, after the climax has occurred.)

An important consequence follows from the points we have just made. The parts or sub-wholes of an expository book are more likely to be independently readable than the parts of fiction. Euclid published his *Elements* in thirteen parts, or books, as he called them, and the first of them can be read by itself. That is more or less the case with every well-organized expository book. Its sections or chapters, taken separately or in subgroups, make sense. But the chapters of a novel, the acts of a play, or the verses of a lyric often become relatively meaningless when wrenched from the whole.

Second, what are the interpretive rules for reading fiction? Our prior consideration of the difference between a poetic and a logical use of language prepares us to make a translation of the rules that direct us to find the terms, the propositions, and the arguments. We know we should not do that, but we must do something analogous to it.

(1) The elements of fiction are its episodes and incidents, its characters, and their thoughts, speeches, feelings, and actions. Each of these is an element in the world the author creates. By manipulating these elements, the author tells his story. They are like the terms in logical discourse. Just as you must come to terms with an expository writer, so here you must become acquainted with the details of incident and characterization. You have not grasped a story until you are familiar with its characters, until you have lived through its events.

(2) Terms are connected in propositions. The elements of fiction are connected by the total scene or background against which they stand out in relief. The imaginative writer, we have seen, creates a world in which his characters "live, move, and have their being." The fictional analogue of the rule that directs you to find the author's propositions can, therefore, be stated as follows: become at home in this imaginary world; know it as if you were an observer on the scene; become a member of its population, willing to befriend its characters, and able to participate in its happenings by sympathetic insight, as you would do in the actions and sufferings of a friend. If you can do this, the elements of fiction will cease to be so many isolated pawns moved about mechanically on a chessboard. You will have found the connections that vitalize them into members of a living society.

(3) If there is any motion in an expository book, it is the movement of the argument, a logical transition from evidences and reasons to the conclusions they support. In the reading of such books, it is necessary to follow the argument. Hence, after you have discovered its terms and propositions, you are called upon to analyze its reasoning. There is an analogous last step in the interpretive reading of fiction. You have become acquainted with the characters. You have joined them in the imaginary world wherein they dwell, consented to the laws of their society, breathed its air, tasted its food, traveled its highways. Now you must follow them through their adventures. The scene or background, the social setting, is (like the proposition) a kind of *static* connection of the elements of fiction. The unraveling

of the plot (like the arguments or reasoning) is the dynamic connection. Aristotle said that plot is the soul of a story. It is its life. To read a story well you must have your finger on the pulse of the narrative, be sensitive to its very beat.

Before leaving these fictional equivalents for the interpretive rules of reading, we must caution you not to examine the analogy too closely. An analogy of this sort is like a metaphor that will disintegrate if you press it too hard. The three steps we have suggested outline the way in which one becomes progressively aware of the artistic achievement of an imaginative writer. Far from spoiling your enjoyment of a novel or play, they should enable you to enrich your pleasure by knowing intimately the sources of your delight. You will not only know *what* you like but also *why* you like it.

One other caution: the foregoing rules apply mainly to novels and plays. To the extent that lyric poems have some narrative line, they apply to lyrics also. But the rules do not cease to apply to non-narrative lyrics, although the connection is much less close. A lyric is the representation of a concrete experience, just like a long story, and it attempts to re-create that experience in the reader. There is a beginning, middle, and end of even the shortest lyric, just as there is a temporal sequence in any experience, no matter how brief and fleeting. And though the cast of characters may be very small in a short lyric, there is always at least one character—namely, the speaker of the poem.

Third, and last, what are the critical rules for reading fiction? You may remember that we distinguished, in the case of expository works, between the general maxims governing criticism and a number of particular points—specific critical remarks. With respect to the general maxims, the analogy can be sufficiently drawn by one translation. Where, in the case of expository works, the advice was not to criticize a book—not to say you agree or disagree—until you can first say you understand, so here the maxim is: *don't criticize imaginative writing until you fully appreciate what the author has tried to make you experience.*

There is an important corollary to this. The good reader of a story does not question the world that the author creates—the world that is re-created in himself. "We must grant the artist his subject, his idea, his *donné,*" said Henry James in *The Art of Fiction;* "our criticism is applied only to what he makes of it." That is, we must merely appreciate the fact that a writer sets his story in, say, Paris, and not object that it would have been better to set it in Minneapolis; but we have a right to criticize what he does with his Parisians and with the city itself.

In other words, we must remember the obvious fact that we do not agree or disagree with fiction. We either like it or we do not. Our critical judgment in the case of expository books concerns their *truth,* whereas in criticizing belles-lettres, as the word itself suggests, we consider chiefly their *beauty.* The beauty of any work of art is related to the pleasure it gives us when we know it well.

Let us restate the maxims, then, in the following manner. Before you express your likes and dislikes, you must first be sure that you have made an honest effort to appreciate the work. By appreciation, we mean having the experience that the author tried to produce for you by working on your emotions and imagination. Thus, you cannot *appreciate* a novel by reading it passively (indeed, as we have remarked, you must read it passionately) any more than you can *understand* a philosophical book that way. To achieve appreciation, as to achieve understanding, you must read actively, and that means performing all the acts of analytical reading that we have briefly outlined.

After you have completed such a reading, you are competent to judge. Your first judgment will naturally be one of taste. You will say not only *that* you like or dislike the book, but also *why.* The reasons you give will, of course, have some critical relevance to the book itself, but in their first expression they are more likely to be about you— your preferences and prejudices—than about the book. Hence, to complete the task of criticism, you must objectify your reactions by pointing to those things in the book that caused them. You must pass from saying what *you* like or dislike and why, to saying what is good or bad about the *book* and why.

The better you can reflectively discern the causes of your pleasure in reading fiction or poetry, the nearer you will come to knowing the artistic virtues in the literary work itself. You will thus gradually develop a standard of criticism. And you will probably find a large company of men and women of similar taste to share your critical judgments. You may even discover, what we think is true, that good taste in literature is acquired by anyone who learns to read.

15

Suggestions for Reading Stories, Plays, and Poems

The parallel rules for reading imaginative literature that were discussed in the last chapter were general ones, applying across the board to all kinds of imaginative literature—novels and stories, whether in prose or verse (including epics); plays, whether tragedies or comedies or something in between; and lyric poems, of whatever length or complexity.

These rules, being general, must be adapted somewhat when they are applied to the different kinds of imaginative literature. In this chapter we want to suggest the adaptations that are required. We will have something particular to say about the reading of stories, plays, and lyric poems, and we will also include notes on the special problems presented by the reading of epic poems and the great Greek tragedies.

Before proceeding to those matters, however, it is desirable to make some remarks about the last of the four questions that the active and demanding reader must ask of any book, when that question is asked of a work of imaginative literature.

You will recall that the first three questions are: first, What is the book about as a whole?; second, What is being said in detail, and how?; and third, Is the book true, in whole or part? The application of these three questions to imaginative literature was covered in the last chapter. The first question is answered when you are able to describe the unity of the plot of a story, play, or poem—"plot" being construed broadly to include the action or movement of a lyric poem as well as of a story. The second question is answered when you are able to discern the role that the various characters play, and recount, in your own words, the key incidents and events in which they are involved. And the third question is answered when you are able to give a reasoned judgment about the poetical truth of the work. Is it a likely story? Does the work satisfy your heart and your mind? Do you appreciate the beauty of the work? In each case, can you say why?

The fourth question is, What of it? In the case of expository books, an answer to this question implies some kind of action on your part. "Action," here, does not always mean going out and doing something. We have suggested that that kind of action is an obligation for the reader when he agrees with a practical work—that is, agrees with the ends proposed—and accepts as appropriate the means by which the author says they can be attained. Action in this sense is not obligatory when the expository work is theoretical. There, mental action alone is required. But if you are convinced that such a book is true, in whole or part, then you must agree with its conclusions, and if they imply some adjustment of your views of the subject, then you are more or less required to make those adjustments.

Now it is important to recognize that, in the case of a work of imaginative literature, this fourth and final question must be interpreted quite differently. In a sense, the question is irrelevant to the reading of stories and poems. Strictly speaking, no action whatever is called for on your part when you have read a novel, play, or poem well—that is, analytically. You have discharged all of your responsibilities as a reader when you have applied the parallel rules of analytical reading to such works, and answered the first three questions.

We say "strictly speaking," because it is obvious that imaginative works have often led readers to act in various ways. Sometimes a story is a better way of getting a point across—be it a political, economic, or moral point—than an expository work making the same point. George Orwell's *Animal Farm* and his *1984* are both powerful attacks on totalitarianism. Aldous Huxley's *Brave New World* is an eloquent diatribe against the tyranny of technological progress. Alexander Solzhenitsyn's *The First Circle* tells us more about the petty cruelty and inhumanity of the Soviet bureaucracy than a hundred factual studies and reports. Such works have been banned and censored many times in the history of mankind, and the reason for that is clear. As E. B. White once remarked, "A despot doesn't fear eloquent writers preaching freedom—he fears a drunken poet who may crack a joke that will take hold."

Nevertheless, such practical consequences of the reading of stories and poems are not of the essence of the matter. Imaginative writings *can* lead to action, but they do not *have to*. They belong in the realm of fine art.

A work of fine art is "fine" not because it is "refined" or "finished," but because it is an end (*finis,* Latin, means end) in itself. It does not move toward some result beyond itself. It is, as Emerson said of beauty, its own excuse for being.

Therefore, when it comes to applying this last question to works of imaginative literature, you should do so with caution. If you feel impelled because of a book you have read to go out and do something, ask yourself whether the work contains some implied statement that has produced this feeling. Poetry, properly speaking, is not the realm of statement, although many stories and poems have statements in them, more or less deeply buried. And it is quite right to take heed of them, and to react to them. But you should remember that you are then taking heed of and reacting to something other than the story or poem itself. That subsists in its own right. To read it well, all you have to do is experience it.

How to Read Stories

The first piece of advice we would like to give you for reading a story is this: Read it quickly and with total immersion. Ideally, a story should be read at one sitting, although this is rarely possible for busy people with long novels. Nevertheless, the ideal should be approximated by compressing the reading of a good story into as short a time as feasible. Otherwise you will forget what happened, the unity of the plot will escape you, and you will be lost.

Some readers, when they really like a novel, want to savor it, to pause over it, to draw out the reading of it for as long as they can. But in this case they are probably not so much reading the book as satisfying their more or less unconscious feelings about the events and the characters. We will return to that in a moment.

Read quickly, we suggest, and with total immersion. We have indicated the importance of letting an imaginative book work on you. That is what we mean by the latter phrase. Let the characters into your mind and heart; suspend your disbelief, if such it is, about the events. Do not disapprove of something a character does before you understand why he does it—if then. Try as hard as you can to live in his world, not in yours; there, the things he does may be quite understandable. And do not judge the world as a whole until you are sure that you have "lived" in it to the extent of your ability.

Following this rule will allow you to answer the first question you should ask about any book—What is it about, as a whole? Unless you read it quickly you will fail to see the unity of the story. Unless you read intensely you will fail to see the details.

The terms of a story, as we have observed, are its characters and incidents. You must become acquainted with them, and be able to sort them out. But here a word of warning. To take *War and Peace* as an example, many readers start this great novel and are overwhelmed by the vast number of characters to whom they are introduced, especially since they all have strange-sounding names. They soon give up on the book in the belief that they will never be able to sort out all the complicated relationships, to know who is who. This is true of any big novel—and if a novel is really good, we want it to be as big as possible.

It does not always occur to such fainthearted readers that exactly the same thing happens to them when they move to a new town or part of a town, when they go to a new school or job, or even when they arrive at a party. They do not give up in those circumstances; they know that after a short while individuals will begin to be visible in the mass, friends will emerge from the faceless crowd of fellow-workers, fellow-students, or fellow-guests. We may not remember the names of everyone we met at a party, but we will recall the name of the man we talked to for an hour, or the girl with whom we made a date for the next evening, or the mother whose child goes to the same school as ours. The same thing happens in a novel. We should not expect to remember every character; many of them are merely background persons, who are there only to set off the actions of the main characters. However, by the time we have finished *War and Peace* or any big novel, we know who is important, and we do not forget. Pierre, Andrew, Natasha, Princess Mary, Nicholas—the names are likely to come immediately to memory, although it may have been years since we read Tolstoy's book.

We also, despite the plethora of incidents, soon learn *what* is important. Authors generally give a good deal of help in this respect; they do not want the reader to miss what is essential to the unfolding of the plot, so they flag it in various ways. But our point is that you should not be anxious if all is not clear from the beginning. Actually, it should *not* be clear then. A story is like life itself; in life, we do not expect to understand events as they occur, at least with total clarity, but looking back on them, we do understand. So the reader of a story, looking back on it after he has finished it, understands the relation of events and the order of actions.

All of this comes down to the same point: you must finish a story in order to be able to say that you have read it well. Paradoxically, however, a story ceases to be like life on its last page. Life goes on, but the story does not. Its characters have no vitality outside the book, and your imagination of what happens to them before the first page and after the last is only as good as the next reader's. Actually, all such speculations are meaningless. Preludes to *Hamlet* have been written, but they are ridiculous. We should not ask what happens to Pierre and Natasha after *War and Peace* ends. We are satisfied with Shakespeare's and Tolstoy's creations partly because they are limited in time. We need no more.

The great majority of books that are read are stories of one kind or another. People who cannot read listen to stories. We even make them up for ourselves. Fiction seems to be a necessity for human beings. Why is this?

One reason why fiction is a human necessity is that it satisfies many unconscious as well as conscious needs. It would be important if it only touched the conscious mind, as expository writing does. But fiction is important, too, because it also touches the unconscious.

On the simplest level—and a discussion of this subject could be very complex—we like or dislike certain kinds of people more than others, without always being sure why. If, in a novel, such people are rewarded or punished, we may have stronger feelings, either pro or con, about the book than it merits artistically.

For example, we are often pleased when a character in a novel inherits money, or otherwise comes into good fortune. However, this tends to be true only if the character is "sympathetic"—meaning that we can identify with him or her. We do not admit to ourselves that we would like to inherit the money, we merely say that we like the book.

Perhaps we would all like to love more richly than we do. Many novels are about love—most are, perhaps—and it gives us pleasure to identify with the loving characters. They are free, and we are not. But we may not want to admit this; for to do so might make us feel, consciously, that our own loves are inadequate.

Again, almost everyone has some unconscious sadism and masochism in his makeup. These are often satisfied in novels, where we can identify with either the conqueror or victim, or even with both. In each case, we are prone to say simply that we like "that kind of book"—without specifying or really knowing why.

Finally, we suspect that life as we know it is unjust. Why do good people suffer, and bad ones prosper? We do not know, we cannot know, but the fact causes great anxiety in everyone. In stories, this chaotic and unpleasant situation is adjusted, and that is extremely satisfying to us.

In stories—in novels and narrative poems and plays—justice usually does exist. People get what they deserve; the author, who is like a god to his characters, sees to it that they are rewarded or punished according to their true merit. In a good story, in a satisfying one, this is usually so, at least. One of the most irritating things about a bad story is that the people in it seem to be punished or rewarded with no rhyme or reason. The great storyteller makes no mistakes. He is able to convince us that justice—poetic justice, we call it—has been done.

This is true even of high tragedy. There, terrible things happen to good men, but we see that the hero, even if he does not wholly deserve his fate, at least comes to understand it. And we have a profound desire to share his understanding. If we only *knew*—then we could withstand whatever the world has in store for us. "I Want to Know Why" is the title of a story by Sherwood Anderson. It could be the title of many stories. The tragic hero does learn why, though often, of course, only after the ruin of his life. We can share his insight without sharing his suffering.

Thus, in criticizing fiction we must be careful to distinguish those books that satisfy our own particular unconscious needs—the ones that make us say, "I like this book, although I don't really know why"—from those that satisfy the deep unconscious needs of almost everybody. The latter are undoubtedly the great stories, the ones that live on and on for generations and centuries. As long as man is man, they will go on satisfying him, giving him something that he needs to have—a belief in justice and understanding and the allaying of anxiety. We do not know, we cannot be sure, that the real world is good. But the world of a great story *is* somehow good. We want to live there as often and as long as we can.

A Note About Epics

Perhaps the most honored but probably the least read books in the great tradition of the Western World are the major epic poems, particularly the *Iliad* and *Odyssey* of Homer, Virgil's *Aeneid,* Dante's *Divine Comedy,* and Milton's *Paradise Lost.* This paradox requires some comment.

Judging by the very small number that have been completed successfully in the past 2,500 years, a long epic poem is apparently the most difficult thing a man can write. This is not for want of trying; hundreds of epics have been begun, and some—for example, Wordsworth's *Prelude* and Byron's *Don Juan*—have grown to extensive proportions without ever really being finished. So honor is due the poet who sticks to the task and completes it. Greater honor is due him if he produces a work that has the qualities of the five just mentioned. But they are certainly not easy to read.

This is not only because they are written in verse—for in every case except that of *Paradise Lost,* prose translations are available to us. The difficulty seems rather to lie in their elevation, in their approach to their subject matter. Any of these major epics exerts enormous demands on the reader—demands of attention, of involvement, and of imagination. The effort required to read them is very great indeed.

Most of us are not aware of the loss we suffer by not making that effort. For the rewards to be gained from a good reading—an analytical reading, as we should say—of these epics are at least as great as those to be gained from the reading of any other books, certainly any other works of fiction. Unfortunately, however, these rewards are not gained by readers who do less than a good job on these books.

We hope that you will take a stab at reading these five great epic poems, and that you will manage to get through all of them. We are certain you will not be disappointed if you do. And you will be able to enjoy a further satisfaction. Homer, Virgil, Dante, and Milton—they are the authors that every good poet, to say nothing of other writers, has read. Along with the Bible, they constitute the backbone of any serious reading program.

How to Read Plays

A play is fiction, a story, and insofar as that is true, it should be read like a story. Perhaps the reader has to be more active in creating the background, the world in which the characters live and move, for there is no description in plays such as abounds in novels. But the problems are essentially similar.

However, there is one important difference. When you read a play, you are not reading a *complete* work. The complete play (the work that the author intended you to apprehend) is only apprehended when it is acted on a stage. Like music, which must be heard, a play lacks a physical dimension when we read it in a book. The reader must supply that dimension.

The only way to do that is to make a pretense of seeing it acted. Therefore, once you have discovered what the play is about, as a whole and in detail, and once you have answered the other questions you must ask about any story, then try *directing* the play. Imagine that you have half a dozen good actors before you, awaiting your commands. Tell them how to say this line, how to play that scene. Explain the importance of these few words, and how that action is the climax of the work. You will have a lot of fun, and you will learn a lot about the play.

An example will show what we mean. In *Hamlet,* Act II, Scene ii, Polonius announces to the king and queen that Hamlet is insane because of his love for Ophelia, who has spurned the prince's advances. The king and queen are doubtful, whereupon Polonius proposes that the king and he hide behind an arras, in order to overhear a conversation between Hamlet and Ophelia. This proposal occurs in Act II, Scene ii, at lines 160–170; immediately thereafter Hamlet enters, reading. His speeches to Polonius are enigmatic; as Polonius says, "though this be madness, yet there is method in't!" Later on, early in Act III, Hamlet enters and delivers the famous soliloquy, beginning "To be or not to be," and then is interrupted by catching sight of Ophelia. He speaks to her quite reasonably for a time, but suddenly he cries: "Ha, ha! are you honest?" (III, i, line 103). Now the question is, has Hamlet overheard Polonius say earlier that he and the king planned to spy on him? And did he perhaps also hear Polonius say that he would "loose my daughter to him"? If so Hamlet's conversations with both Polonius and Ophelia would mean one thing; if he did not overhear the plotting, they would mean another. Shakespeare left no stage directions; the reader (or director) must decide for himself. Your own decision will be central to your understanding of the play.

Many of Shakespeare's plays require this kind of activity on the part of the reader. Our point is that it is always desirable, no matter how explicit the playwright was in telling us exactly what we should expect to see. (We cannot question what we are to hear, since the play's words are before us.) Probably you have not read a play really well until you have pretended to put it on the stage in this way. At best, you have given it only a partial reading.

Earlier, we suggested that there were interesting exceptions to the rule that the playwright cannot speak directly to the reader as the author of a novel can and often does. (Fielding, in *Tom Jones,* is an example of this direct addressing of the reader in one great novel.) Two of these exceptions are separated by nearly twenty-five centuries of time. Aristophanes, the ancient Greek comic playwright, wrote the only examples of what is called Old Comedy that survive. From time to time in an Aristophanic play, and always at least once, the leading actor would step out of character, perhaps move forward toward the audience, and deliver a political speech that had nothing whatever to do with the action of the drama. It is felt that these speeches were expressions of the author's personal feelings. This is occasionally done nowadays—no useful artistic device is ever really lost—but perhaps not as effectively as Aristophanes did it.

The other example is that of Shaw, who not only expected his plays to be acted but also hoped that they would be read. He published them all, at least one (*Heartbreak House*) before it was ever acted, and accompanied the publication with long prefaces in which he explained the meaning of the plays and told his readers how to understand them. (He also included very extensive stage directions in the published versions.) To read a Shavian play without reading the preface Shaw wrote for it is to turn one's back intentionally on an important aid to understanding. Again, other modern playwrights have imitated Shaw in this device, but never as effectively as he did.

One other bit of advice may be helpful, particularly in reading Shakespeare. We have already suggested the importance of reading the plays through, as nearly as possible at one sitting, in order to get a feel for the whole. But, since the plays are mostly in verse, and since the verse is more or less opaque in places because of changes in the language that have occurred since 1600, it is often desirable to read a puzzling passage out loud. Read slowly, as if an audience were listening, and with "expression"—that is, try to make the words meaningful to you as you read them. This simple device will clear up many difficulties. Only after it has failed should you turn to the glossary or notes.

A Note About Tragedy

Most plays are not worth reading. This, we think, is because they *are* incomplete. They were not meant to be read—they were meant to be acted. There are many great expository works, and many great novels, stories, and lyric poems, but there are only a few great plays. However, those few—the tragedies of Aeschylus, Sophocles, and Euripides, the plays of Shakespeare, Molière's comedies, the works of a very few moderns—are very great indeed, for they contain within them some of the deepest and richest insights men have ever expressed in words.

Among these, Greek tragedy is probably the toughest nut to crack for beginning readers. For one thing, in the ancient world three tragedies were presented at one time, the three often dealing with a common theme, but except in one case (the *Oresteia* of Aeschylus) only single plays (or acts) survive. For another, it is almost impossible to stage the plays mentally, since we know almost nothing about how the Greek directors did it. For still another, the plays often are based on stories that were well known to their audiences but are known to us only through the plays. It is one thing to know the story of Oedipus, for example, as well as we know the story of George Washington and the Cherry Tree, and thus to view Sophocles' masterpiece as a commentary on a familiar tale; and it is quite another to see *Oedipus Rex* as the primary story and try to imagine the familiar tale that provided the background.

Nevertheless, the plays are so powerful that they triumph over even these obstacles, as well as others. It is important to read them well, for they not only can tell us much about life as we still live it, but they also form a kind of literary framework for many other plays written much later—for example, Racine's and O'Neill's. We have two bits of advice that may help.

The first is to remember that the essence of tragedy is time, or rather the lack of it. There is no problem in any Greek tragedy that could not have been solved if there had been enough time, but there is never enough. Decisions, choices have to be made in a moment, there is no time to think and weigh the consequences; and, since even tragic heroes are fallible—especially fallible, perhaps—the decisions are wrong. It is easy for us to see what should have been done, but would we have been able to see in time? That is the question that you should always ask in reading any Greek tragedy.

The second bit of advice is this. One thing we do know about the staging of Greek plays is that the tragic actors wore buskins on their feet that elevated them several inches above the ground. (They also wore masks.) But the members of the chorus did not wear buskins, though they sometimes wore masks. The comparison between the size of the tragic protagonists, on the one hand, and the members of the chorus, on the other hand, was thus highly significant. Therefore you should always imagine, when you read the words of the chorus, that the words are spoken by persons of your own stature; while the words spoken by the protagonists proceed from the mouths of giants, from personages who did not only seem, but actually were, larger than life.

How to Read Lyric Poetry

The simplest definition of poetry (in the somewhat limited sense implied by the title of this section) is that it is what poets write. That seems obvious enough, and yet there are those who would dispute the definition. Poetry, they hold, is a kind of spontaneous overflowing of the personality, which may be expressed in written words but may also take the form of physical action, or more or less musical sound, or even just feeling. There is something to this, of course, and poets have always recognized it. It is a very old notion that the poet reaches down deep into himself to produce his poems, that their place of origin is a mysterious "well of creation" within the mind or soul. In this sense of the term, poetry can be made by anyone at any time, in a kind of solitary sensitivity session. But although we admit that there is a kernel of truth in this definition, the meaning of the term that we will be employing in what follows is much narrower. Whatever may be the origin of the poetic impulse, poetry, for us, consists of words, and what is more, of words that are arranged in a more or less orderly and disciplined way.

Other definitions of the term that similarly contain a kernel of truth are that poetry (again, primarily lyric poetry) is not truly poetry unless it praises, or unless it rouses to action (usually revolutionary), or unless it is written in rhyme, or unless it employs a specialized language that is called "poetic diction." In that sentence we have intentionally mixed together some very modern and some very antiquated notions. Our point is that all of these definitions, and a dozen more that we might mention, are too narrow, just as the definition discussed in the last paragraph was too broad (for us).

Between such very broad and such very narrow definitions lies a central core that most people, if they were feeling reasonable about the matter, would admit was poetry. If we tried to state precisely what the central core consisted in, we would probably get into trouble, and so we will not try. Nevertheless, we are certain that you know what we mean. We are certain that nine times out of ten, or perhaps even ninety-nine times out of a hundred, you would agree with us that X was a poem and Y was not. And that is fully sufficient for our purposes in the following pages.

Many people believe that they cannot read lyric poetry—especially modern poetry. They think that it is often difficult, obscure, complex, and that it demands so much attention, so much work on their part, that it is not worthwhile. We would say two things. First, lyric poetry, even modern poetry, does not always demand as much work as you may think if you go about reading it in the right way. Second, it is often worth whatever effort you are willing to spend.

We do not mean that you should not work on a poem. A good poem can be worked at, re-read, and thought about over and over for the rest of your life. You will never stop finding new things in it, new pleasures and delights, and also new ideas about yourself and the world. We mean that the initial task of bringing a poem close enough to you to work on it is not as hard as you may have believed.

The first rule to follow in reading a lyric is to read it through without stopping, whether you think you understand it or not. This is the same rule that we have suggested for many different kinds of books, but it is more important for a poem than it is for a philosophical or scientific treatise, and even for a novel or play.

In fact, the trouble so many people seem to have in reading poems, especially the difficult modern ones, stems from their unawareness of this first rule of reading them. When faced by a poem of T. S. Eliot or Dylan Thomas or some other "obscure" modern, they plunge in with a will, but are brought up short by the first line or stanza. They do not understand it immediately and in its entirety, and they think they should. They puzzle over the words, try to unwind the complicated skein of the syntax, and soon give up, concluding that, as they suspected, modern poetry is just too difficult for them.

It is not only modern lyrics that are difficult. Many of the best poems in the language are complicated and involved in their language and thought. Besides, many apparently simple poems have immense complexity under the surface.

But any good lyric poem has a unity. Unless we read all of it, and all at once, we cannot comprehend its unity. We cannot discover, except possibly by accident, the basic feeling or experience that underlies it. In particular, the essence of a poem is almost never to be found in its first line, or even in its first stanza. It is to be found only in the whole, and not conclusively in any part.

The second rule for reading lyrics is this: Read the poem through again—but read it *out loud*. We have suggested this before, in the case of poetic dramas like Shakespeare's. There it was helpful; here it is essential. You will find, as you read the poem out loud, that the very act of speaking the words forces you to understand them better. You cannot glide over a misunderstood phrase or line quite so easily if you are speaking it. Your ear is offended by a misplaced emphasis that your eyes might miss. And the rhythm of the poem, and its rhymes, if it has them, will help you to understand by making you place the emphasis where it belongs. Finally, you will be able to open yourself to the poem, and let it work on you, as it should.

In the reading of lyrics, these first two suggestions are more important than anything else. We think that if readers who believe they cannot read poems would obey these rules first, they would have little difficulty afterwards. For once you have apprehended a poem in its unity, even if this apprehension is vague, you can begin to ask it questions. And as with expository works, that is the secret of understanding.

The questions you ask of an expository work are grammatical

and logical. The questions you ask of a lyric are usually rhetorical, though they may also be syntactical. You do not come to terms with a poem; but you must discover the key words. You discover them not primarily by an act of grammatical discernment, however, but by an act of rhetorical discernment. Why do certain words pop out of the poem and stare you in the face? Is it because the rhythm marks them? Or the rhyme? Or are the words repeated? Do several stanzas seem to be about the same ideas; if so, do these ideas form any kind of sequence? Anything of this sort that you can discover will help your understanding.

In most good lyrics there is some kind of conflict. Sometimes two antagonists—either individual people, or images, or ideas—are named, and then the conflict between them is described. If so, this is easy to discover. But often the conflict is only implied and not stated. For example, a large number of great lyric poems—perhaps even the majority of them—are about the conflict between love and time, between life and death, between the beauty of transient things and the triumph of eternity. But these words may not be mentioned in the poem itself.

It has been said that almost all of Shakespeare's sonnets are about the ravages of what he calls "Devouring time." It is clear that some of them are, for he explicitly says so again and again.

> *When I have seen by Time's fell hand defaced*
> *The rich-proud cost of outworn buried age*

he writes in the 64th sonnet and lists other victories that time gains over all that man wishes were proof against it. Then he says:

> *Ruin hath taught me thus to ruminate,*
> *That Time will come and take my love away.*

There is no question what that sonnet is about. Similarly with the famous 116th sonnet, which contains these lines:

> *Love's not Time's fool, though rosy lips and cheeks*
> *Within his bending sickle's compass come;*
> *Love alters not with his brief hours and weeks,*
> *But bears it out even to the edge of doom.*

But the almost equally famous 138th sonnet, which begins with the lines:

> *When my love swears that she is made of truth*
> *I do believe her, though I know she lies,*

is also about the conflict between love and time, although the word "time" appears nowhere in the poem.

That you will see without much difficulty. Nor is there any difficulty in seeing that Marvell's celebrated lyric "To His Coy Mistress" is about the same subject, for he makes this clear right at the beginning:

> *Had we but world enough, and time,*
> *This coyness, lady, were no crime.*

We do not have all the time in the world, Marvell says—for

> *. . . at my back I always hear*
> *Time's wingèd chariot hurrying near;*
> *And yonder all before us lie*
> *Deserts of vast eternity.*

Therefore, he adjures his mistress,

> *Let us roll all our strength and all*
> *Our sweetness up into one ball,*
> *And tear our pleasures with rough strife*
> *Thorough the iron gates of life.*

> *Thus, though we cannot make our sun*
> *Stand still, yet we will make him run.*

It is perhaps a bit harder to see that the subject of "You, Andrew Marvell," by Archibald MacLeish, is exactly the same. The poem begins:

> *And here face down beneath the sun*
> *And here upon earth's noonward height*
> *To feel the always coming on*
> *The always rising of the night*

Thus MacLeish asks us to imagine someone (the poet? the speaker? the reader?) as lying in the noonday sun—but all the same, in the midst of that brightness and warmth, aware of "the earthly chill of dusk." He imagines the line of the shadow of the setting sun—of all the cumulative successive setting suns of history—moving across the world, across Persia, and Baghdad . . . he feels "Lebanon fade out and Crete," "And Spain go under and the shore / Of Africa the gilded sand," and . . . "now the long light on the sea" vanishes, too. And he concludes:

> *And here face downward in the sun*
> *To feel how swift, how secretly,*
> *The shadow of the night comes on. . . .*

The word "time" is not used in the poem, nor is there any mention of a lover. Nevertheless, the title reminds us of Marvell's lyric with its theme of "Had we but world enough and time," and thus the combination of the poem itself and its title invokes the same conflict, between love (or life) and time, that was the subject of the other poems we have considered here.

One final piece of advice about reading lyric poems. In general, readers of such works feel that they must know more about the authors and their times than they really have to. We put much faith in commentaries, criticism, biographies—but this may be only because we doubt our own ability to read. Almost everyone can read any poem, if he will go to work on it. Anything you discover about an author's life or times is valid and may be helpful. But a vast knowledge of the context of a poem is no guarantee that the poem itself will be understood. To be understood it must be read—over and over. Reading any great lyric poem is a lifetime job—not, of course, in the sense that it should go on and on throughout a lifetime, but rather that as a great poem, it deserves many return visits. And during vacations from a given poem, we may learn more about it than we realize.

16

How to Read History

"History," like "poetry," is a word of many meanings. In order for this chapter to be useful to you, we must come to terms with you about the word—that is, explain how we will be using it.

First of all, there is the difference between history as fact and history as a written record of the facts. We are obviously, here, employing the term in the latter sense, since in our sense of "read" you cannot read facts. But there are many kinds of written record that are called historical. A collection of documents pertaining to a certain event or period could be called a history of it. A transcription of an oral interview with a participant, or a collection of such transcriptions, could similarly be called a history of the event in which he or they participated. A work having quite a different intention, such as a personal diary or collection of letters, could be construed as being a history of the time. The word could be applied, and indeed has been applied, to almost every kind of writing that originated in a time period, or in the context of an event, in which the reader was interested.

The sense in which we use the word "history" in what follows is both narrower and broader than any of those. It is narrower because we want to restrict ourselves to essentially narrative accounts, presented in a more or less formal manner, of a period or event or series of events in the past. This is a traditional use of the term, and we do not apologize for it. Again, as with our definition of lyric poetry, we think you will agree with us that this is the ordinary meaning of the term, and we want to stick to the ordinary here.

But our meaning is also broader than many of the definitions of the term that are current today. We think, although not all historians agree with us, that the essence of history is narration, that the last five letters of the word—"story"—help us to understand the basic meaning. Even a collection of documents, *as a collection,* tells a story. That story may not be explicit—that is, the historian may try not to arrange the documents in any "meaningful" order. But it is implicit in them, whether they are ordered or not. Otherwise, we think, the collection would not be called a history of its time.

It is not important, however, whether all historians agree with us in our notion of what history is. There is a great deal of history of the kind we are discussing, and you will want to or have to read at least some of it. We will try to aid you in that task.

The Elusiveness of Historical Facts

Probably you have been a member of a jury, listening to the testimony about a simple matter of fact, such as an automobile accident. Or you may have been on a blue ribbon jury, and have had to decide whether one person killed another or not. If you have done either, you know how difficult it is to reconstruct the past, even a single event in the past, from the memories of persons who actually saw it happen.

A court concerns itself with events that have happened fairly recently and in the presence of living witnesses. In addition, there are stringent rules of evidence. A witness cannot *suppose* anything, he cannot guess or hypothecate or estimate (except under very carefully controlled conditions). And of course he is not supposed to lie.

With all the careful rules of evidence, and cross-examination besides, have you ever been absolutely sure, as a member of a jury, that you really knew what *happened*?

The law assumes that you will not be absolutely sure. It assumes that there will always be some doubt in a juror's mind. As a matter of practice, in order that trials may be decided one way or the other, it says that the doubt must be "reasonable" if it is to be allowed to affect your judgment. The doubt must be, in other words, sufficient to trouble your conscience.

A historian is concerned with events that occurred, most of them, a long time ago. All the witnesses to the events are usually dead. What evidence they give is not given in a courtroom—that is, it is not governed by stringent and careful rules. Such witnesses as there are often guess, hypothecate, estimate, assume, and suppose. We cannot see their faces in order to judge whether they are lying (if we ever really can know that about anybody). They are not cross-examined. And there is no guarantee whatever that they know what they are talking about.

If, then, it is difficult to be sure that one knows about the truth of a relatively simple matter, such as is decided by a jury in a court of law, how much more difficult it is to know what really happened in history. A historical *fact,* though we may have a feeling of trust and solidity about the word, is one of the most elusive things in the world.

Of course, about some kinds of historical fact we can be pretty certain. America was involved in a Civil War that began with the firing on Fort Sumter, on April 12, 1861, and ended with the surrender of General Lee to General Grant at Appomattox Court House, on April 9, 1865. Everyone agrees about those dates. It is not likely (though it is not totally impossible) that every American calendar was incorrect at that time.

But how much have we learned if we know exactly when the Civil War started and when it ended? Indeed, those dates have been disputed—not on the grounds that the calendars were wrong, but that the war really started with the election of Lincoln in the fall of 1860 and ended with his assassination five days after Lee's surrender. Others have claimed that the war started even earlier—as much as five or ten or twenty years before 1861—and we know that it was still actually being fought in outlying parts of the United States, to which word had not yet come of the Northern triumph, as late as May, June, and July, 1865. And there are those, too, who feel that the Civil War is not over yet, that it will never be over until black Americans are completely free and equal, or until the South manages to secede from the Union, or until the right of the federal government to control all the states is finally established and accepted by every American everywhere.

At least we do know, one might say, that whether or not the firing on Fort Sumter started the Civil War, it did occur on April 12, 1861. That is true—within the limits of possibility we referred to before. But why was Sumter fired on? That is an obvious next question. And could war still have been avoided after the attack? If it had been, would we care that such and such an assault occurred on such and such a spring day more than a century ago? If we did not care—and we do not care about many attacks on forts that have doubtless occurred, but about which we know nothing whatever—would the firing on Sumter still be a significant historical fact?

Theories of History

We class history, the *story* of the past, more often under fiction than under science—if it must be affiliated with one or the other. If not, if history, that is, is allowed to rest somewhere in between the two main divisions of the kinds of books, then it is usually admitted that history is *closer* to fiction than to science.

This does not mean that a historian *makes up* his facts, like a poet or story teller. However, we might get into trouble if we insisted too strongly that a writer of fiction makes up *his* facts. He creates a world, as we have said. But this new world is not totally different from our own—indeed, it had better not be—and a poet is an ordinary man, with ordinary senses by and through which he has learned. He does not see things that we cannot see (he may see better or in a slightly different way). His characters use words that we use (otherwise we could not believe in them). It is only in dreams that human beings create really strange new worlds—yet even in the most fantastic dream the events and creatures of the imagination are made up out of elements of everyday experience. They are merely put together in strange new ways.

A good historian does not, of course, make up the past. He considers himself responsibly bound by some concept or criterion of accuracy or facts. Nevertheless, it is important to remember that the historian must always make up something. He must either find a general pattern in, or impose one on, events; or he must suppose that he knows why the persons in his story did the things they did. He may have a general theory or philosophy, such as that Providence rules human affairs, and make his history fit that. Or he may abjure any such pattern, imposed as it were from the outside or above, and instead insist that he is merely reporting the real events that have occurred. But in that case he is likely to be forced to assign causes for events and motivations for actions. It is essential to recognize which way the historian you are reading is operating.

The only way to avoid taking either one or the other position is to assume that men do not do things for a purpose, or that the purpose, if it exists, is undiscoverable—in other words, that there is no pattern to history at all.

Tolstoy had such a theory about history. He was not a historian, of course; he was a novelist. But many historians have held the same view, particularly in modern times. The causes of every human action, Tolstoy thought, were so manifold, so complex, and so deeply hidden in unconscious motivations that it is impossible to know why anything ever happened.

Because theories of history differ, and because a historian's theory affects his account of events, it is necessary to read more than one account of the history of an event or period if we want to understand it. Indeed, this is the first rule of reading history. And it is all the more important if the event in which we are interested has practical significance for us. It is probably of practical significance to all Americans that they know something about the history of the Civil War. We still live in the backwash of that great and sorry conflict; we live in a world it helped to make. But we cannot hope to understand it if we look at it through the eyes of only one man, or one side, or one faction of modern academic historians. The other day we opened a new Civil War history and noted that its author offered it as "an impartial, objective history of the Civil War from the point of view of the South." The author appeared to be serious. Maybe he was; maybe such a thing is possible. At any rate, we would admit that every narrative history has to be written from *some* point of view. But to get at the truth, we ought to look at it from more than one viewpoint.

The Universal in History

We are not always able to read more than one history of an event. When we are not, we must admit that we do not have much chance of learning the truth of the matter in question—of learning *what really happened*. However, that is not the only reason to read history. It might be claimed that only the professional historian, the man who is writing a history himself, is required to cross-examine his sources by exhaustively checking one against the other. He must leave no stone unturned if he is to know what he ought to know about his subject. We, as lay readers of history, stand somewhere between the professional historian, on the one hand, and the irresponsible amateur, on the other hand, who reads history only for amusement.

Let us take the example of Thucydides. You may be aware that he wrote the only major contemporary history of the Peloponnesian War at the end of the fifth century B.C. In a sense, there is nothing to check his work against. What, then, can we expect to learn from it?

Greece is now a tiny country; a war that occurred there twenty-five centuries ago can have little real effect on our life today. Everyone who fought in it is long dead, and the specific things for which they fought are long dead, too. The victories are now meaningless, and the defeats without pain. The cities that were taken and lost have crumbled into dust. Indeed, if we stop to think of it, almost all that remains of the Peloponnesian War is Thucydides' account of it.

Yet that account is still important. For Thucydides' story—we might as well use that word—has had an influence on the subsequent history of man. Leaders in later eras read Thucydides. When they found themselves in situations that even faintly approximated that of the tragically divided Greek city-states, they compared their own position to that of Athens or Sparta. They used Thucydides as an excuse and a justification, and even as a pattern of conduct. The result was that by ever so little, perhaps, but perceptibly, the history of the world was changed by the view held of a small portion of it by Thucydides in the fifth century B.C. Thus we read Thucydides not because he described perfectly what happened before he wrote his book, but because he to a certain extent determined what happened after. And we read him, strange as this may seem, to know what is happening now.

"Poetry is more philosophical than history," wrote Aristotle. By this he meant that poetry is more general, more universal. A good poem is true not only in its own time and place, but in all times and places. It has meaning and force for all men. History is not quite so universal as that. It is tied to events in a way that poetry is not. But any good history is also universal.

Thucydides himself said that he was writing his history so that men of the future would not have to repeat the mistakes he had seen made and from which he had suffered personally and through the agony of his country. He described the kinds of human mistakes that would have meaning to men other than himself, to men other than Greeks. Yet some of the very same errors that the Athenians and the Spartans made 2,500 years ago, or at least very similar ones, are being made now, as they have been made over and over again since Thucydides' time.

If your view of history is limited, if you go to it to discover only what really happened, you will not learn the main thing that Thucydides, or indeed any good historian, has to teach. If you read Thucydides well, you may even decide to give up trying to discover what really happened in the past.

History is the story of what led up to now. It is the present that interests us—that and the future. The future will be partly determined by the present. Thus, you can learn something about the future, too, from a historian, even from one who like Thucydides lived more than two thousand years ago.

Let us sum up these two suggestions for reading history. The first is: if you can, read more than one history of an event or period that interests you. The second is: read a history not only to learn what really happened at a particular time and place in the past, but also to learn the way men act in all times and places, especially now.

Questions to Ask of a Historical Book

Despite the fact that most histories are closer to fiction than to science, they can be read as expository works, and therefore they should be. Hence, we must ask the same questions of a historical book that we ask of any expository book. Because of the special nature of history, we must ask those questions a little differently and must expect to receive slightly different kinds of answers.

As far as the first question is concerned, every history has a particular and limited subject. It is surprising, then, how often readers do not trouble to find out what this is. In particular, they do not always note carefully what limitations the author sets for himself. A history of the Civil War is not a history of the world in the nineteenth century. It probably will not be a history of the American West in the 1860s. It could, though perhaps it should not, ignore the state of American education in that decade, or the movement of the American frontier, or the progress of American freedom. Hence, if we are to read a history well, it is necessary to know precisely what it is about and what it is not about. Certainly, if we are to criticize it, we must know the latter. An author cannot be blamed for not doing what he did not try to do.

With regard to the second question, the historian tells a story, and that story, of course, occurred in time. Its general outlines are thus determined, and we do not have to search for them. But there is more than one way to tell a story, and we must know how the historian has chosen to tell his. Does he divide his work into chapters that correspond to years or decades or generations? Or does he divide it according to other rubrics of his own choosing? Does he discuss, in one chapter, the economic history of his period, and cover its wars and religious movements and literary productions in others? Which of these is most important to him? If we discover that, if we can say which aspect of the story he is telling seems to him most fundamental, we can understand him better. We may not agree with his judgment about what is basic, but we can still learn from him.

Criticism of history takes two forms. We can judge—but only, as always, after we understand what is being said—that a historian's work lacks verisimilitude. People just do not act that way, we may feel. Even if the historian documents his statements by giving us access to his sources, and even if to our knowledge they are relevant, we can still feel that he has misunderstood them, that he has judged them in the wrong way, perhaps through some deficiency in his grasp of human nature or human affairs. We tend to feel this, for example, about many older historians who do not include much discussion of economic matters in their work. People, we may be inclined to think now, act out of self-interest; too much nobility ascribed to the "hero" of a history may make us suspicious.

On the other hand, we may think, especially if we have some special knowledge of the subject, that the historian has misused his sources. We may be indignant to discover that he has not read a certain book that we have read. And he may be misinformed about the facts of the matter. In that case, he cannot have written a good history of it. We expect a historian to be informed.

The first criticism is, however, more important. A good historian must combine the talents of the storyteller and the scientist. He must know what is *likely* to have happened as well as what some witnesses or writers said actually *did* happen.

With regard to the last question, What of it?, it is possible that no kind of literature has a greater effect on the actions of men than history. Satires and pictures of philosophical utopias have little effect; we would all like the world to be better, but we are seldom inspired by the recommendations of authors who do no more than describe, often bitterly, the difference between the real and the ideal. History, which tells us of the actions of men of the past, often does lead us to make changes, to try to better our lot. In general, statesmen have been more learned in history than in other disciplines. History suggests the possible, for it describes things that have already been done. If they have been done, perhaps they can be done again—or perhaps they can be avoided.

The main answer to the question, What of it?, therefore, lies in the direction of practical, political action. For this reason it is of great importance that history be read well. Unfortunately, leaders have often acted with some knowledge of history but not enough. With the world as small and dangerous as it has become, it would be a good idea for all of us to start reading history better.

How to Read Biography and Autobiography

A biography is a story about a real person. This mixed patrimony causes it to have a mixed character.

Some biographers would object to this description. But ordinarily, at least, a biography is a narrative account of the life, the history, of a man or woman or of a group of people; thus, a biography poses many of the same problems as a history. The reader must ask the same sort of questions—what is the author's purpose? What are his criteria of truth?—as well, of course, as asking the questions we must ask of any book.

There are several kinds of biographies. The *definitive* biography is intended to be the final, exhaustive, scholarly work on the life of someone important enough to deserve a definitive biography. Definitive biographies cannot be written about living persons. They are seldom written until several non-definitive biographies have first appeared, all of them often somewhat inadequate. All sources are gone through, all letters read, and a great deal of contemporary history examined by the author. Since the ability to gather the materials is somewhat different from the talent for shaping them into a good book, definitive biographies are not always easy reading. This is too bad. A scholarly book does not have to be dull. One of the greatest of all biographies is Boswell's *Life of Johnson,* and it is continuously fascinating. It is certainly definitive (though other biographies of Dr. Johnson have since appeared), but it is also uniquely interesting.

A definitive biography is a slice of history—the history of a man and of his times, as seen through his eyes. It should be read as history. An *authorized* biography is not the same thing at all. Such works are usually commissioned by the heirs or friends of some important person, and they are carefully written so that the errors the person made and the triumphs he achieved are seen in the best light possible. They can sometimes be very good indeed, because the author has the advantage—not as a rule accorded to other writers—of being allowed access to all pertinent material by those who control it. But, of course, an authorized biography cannot be trusted in the same way that a definitive biography can be. Instead of reading it simply as history, the reader should understand that it may be biased—that this is the way the reader is expected to think of the book's subject; this is the way his friends and associates want him to be known to the world.

The authorized biography is a kind of history, but it is history with a difference. We may be curious to know what interested persons want the public to know about someone's private life, but we should not expect to know what the private life really was. The reading of an authorized biography will thus often tell us much about the time in which it was written, about its customs and manners, about those actions and attitudes that were acceptable—and, by implication and with a little extrapolation, about those that were not. But we should not hope to discover the real life of a human being any more than we would hope to know the real story of a war if we read the communiqués of only one side. To get at the truth we must read all the communiqués, ask people who were there, and use our own minds to make sense out of the muddle. A definitive biography has already done this work; in the case of an authorized biography (and most biographies of living persons are of this sort), there is still much to do.

There remain those biographies that are neither definitive nor authorized. Perhaps we may call them ordinary biographies. In such works, we expect the author to be accurate, to know his facts. We want above all to be given the feeling that we are viewing the life of a real person in another time and place. Human beings are curious, and especially curious about other human beings.

Such books, although not trustworthy in the way definitive biographies are, are often very good reading. The world would be the poorer without Izaak Walton's *Lives* of his friends, the poets John Donne and George Herbert, for example (Walton is of course better known for his *The Compleat Angler*); or John Tyndall's account of his friend Michael Faraday in *Faraday the Discoverer*.

Some biographies are didactic. They have a moral purpose. Not many of this sort are written any more, but they used to be common. (They are still written for children, of course.) Plutarch's *Lives of the Noble Grecians and Romans* is such a work. Plutarch told the stories of great men of the Greek and Roman past in order to help his contemporaries to be great also, and to help them avoid the errors into which the great so often fall—or so he felt. The *Lives* is a marvelous book; but, although many of the accounts are the only ones we have of their subjects, we do not read it so much for its biographical information as for its view of life in general. Its subjects are interesting people, good and bad, but never indifferent. Plutarch realized this himself. His original intention in writing had been to instruct others, he said, but in the course of the work he discovered that more and more it was he himself who was deriving profit and stimulation from "lodging these men one after the other in his house."

Incidentally, Plutarch's is another historical work that has exercised a profound influence on subsequent history. For example, just as Plutarch shows Alexander the Great modeling his own life on that of Achilles (whose life he learned about from Homer), so many later conquerors have tried to model their lives on that of Plutarch's Alexander.

Autobiographies present some different and interesting problems. First of all, it is questionable whether anyone has ever written a true autobiography. If it is difficult to know the life of anyone else, it is even more difficult to know one's own. And, of course, all autobiographies have to be written about lives that are not yet complete.

The temptation to tell either less or more than the truth (the latter may be more common), when there is no one to contradict you, is almost irresistible. Everybody has some secrets he cannot bear to divulge; everybody also has some illusions about himself, which it is almost impossible for him to regard as illusions. However, although it is not possible to write a wholly true autobiography, neither is it possible to write one that contains no truth at all. Just as no man can be a perfect liar, so every autobiography tells us something about its author, if only that there are things that he wants to conceal.

It is customary to say that the *Confessions* of Rousseau, or some other book written about the same time (about the middle of the eighteenth century), is the first real autobiography. This is to overlook Augustine's *Confessions,* for example, and Montaigne's *Essays;* but the error is more serious than that. In fact, much of what anyone writes on any subject is autobiographical. There is a great deal of Plato in the *Republic,* of Milton in *Paradise Lost,* of Goethe in *Faust*—though we may not be able to put our finger on it exactly. If we are interested in humanity, we will tend, within reasonable limits, to read any book partly with an eye to discovering the character of its author.

This should never be the primary consideration, and it leads, when it is overdone, to the so-called pathetic fallacy. But we should remember that words do not write themselves—the ones we read have been found and written down by a living man. Plato and Aristotle said some similar, and some dissimilar, things; but even if they had agreed completely, they could not have written the same books, for they were different men. We may even discover something of St. Thomas Aquinas in such an apparently unrevealing work as the *Summa Theologica*.

Thus it matters very little that *formal* autobiography is a relatively new literary genre. No one has ever been able to keep himself entirely out of his book. "I have no more made my book," said Montaigne, "than my book has made me; a book co-substantial with its author, concerned with my own self, an integral part of my life." And he added, "Everyone recognizes me in my book, and my book in me." This is true, and not only of Montaigne. "This is no book," says Whitman of his *Leaves of Grass*. "Who touches this touches a man."

Are there any additional hints for reading biographies and autobiographies? Here is one that is important. Despite the fact that such books, and especially the autobiographies, reveal much about their authors, we should not spend so much time trying to discover a writer's secrets that we do not find out what he says plainly. Apart from this, given the fact that such books are often more poetical than discursive or philosophical, and that they are special kinds of history, there is perhaps little more to add. You should remember, of course, that if you wish to know the truth about a person's life, you should read as many biographies of him as you can find, including his own account of his life, if he wrote one. Read biography as history and as the cause of history; take all autobiographies with a grain of salt; and never forget that you must not argue with a book until you fully understand what it is saying. As to the question, What of it?, we would only say this: biography, like history, can be a cause of practical, moral action. A biography can be inspiring. It is the story of a life, usually a more or less successful one—and we too have lives to lead.

How to Read About Current Events

We have said that our exposition of the art of analytical reading applies to everything you have to read, not just to books. Now we want to qualify that statement a little. Analytical reading is not always necessary. There are many things that we read that do not require the kind of effort and skill that is called for at this third level of reading ability. Nevertheless, although the rules of reading do not all always have to be applied, the four questions must always be asked of anything you read. That means, of course, that they must be asked when you are faced with the kind of things to which most of us devote much of our reading time: newspapers, magazines, books about current events, and the like.

After all, history did not stop a thousand years ago, or a hundred. The world goes on, and men and women continue to write about what is happening and how things are changing. Perhaps no modern history is as great as Thucydides' work; posterity will have to be the judge of that. But we do have an obligation, as human beings and as citizens, to try to understand the world around us.

The problem comes down to knowing what is actually happening now. We have chosen the word "actually" in the last sentence intentionally. The French word for newsreel is *actualités;* the whole concept of current events literature is somehow the same as that of the "news." How do we get the news, and how do we know that what we get is true?

You can see at once that we are faced with the same problem that is posed by history itself. We cannot be sure that we are getting at the facts—we cannot be sure that we know what is happening now any more than we can be sure about what happened in the past. And yet we must try to know, so far as that is possible.

If we could be everywhere at once, overhear all conversations on earth, look into the heart of every living person, we might be able to make a stab at the truth of current events. Being human and hence limited, we must fall back on the services of reporters. Reporters are persons who are supposed to know what is happening in a small area. They report it in newspaper stories, in magazines, or in books. What we can know depends on them.

Ideally, a reporter, of whatever kind, is a clear glass in which reality is reflected—or through which it shines. But the human mind is not a clear glass. It is not a good reflector, and when reality shines through it, the mind is not a very good filter. It separates out what it considers to be unreality, untruth. That is proper, of course; a reporter should not report what he thinks is false. But he may be mistaken.

Thus the most important thing to know, when reading any report of current happenings, is *who is writing the report*. What is involved here is not so much an acquaintance with the reporter himself as with the *kind* of mind he has. The various sorts of filter-reporters fall into groups. To understand what kind of filter our reporter's mind is, we must ask a series of questions about it. This amounts to asking a series of questions about any material dealing with current events. The questions are these:

1. What does the author want to prove?
2. Whom does he want to convince?
3. What special knowledge does he assume?
4. What special language does he use?
5. Does he really know what he is talking about?

For the most part it is safe to assume that all current events books want to prove something. Often it is easy enough to discover what this is. The blurb often states the main contention or thesis of such books. If it does not appear there, it may be stated by the author in a preface.

Having asked what the book is trying to prove, you should next ask whom the author is trying to convince. Is the book intended for those "in the know"—and are you in that category? Is it for that small group of persons who can do something, and quickly, about the situation the author describes? Or is it for everyone? If you do not belong to the audience for which the book is intended, you may not want to read it.

You must next discover what special knowledge the author assumes that you have. The word "knowledge" is intended here to cover a lot of ground. "Opinion" or "prejudice" might have been a better choice. Many authors write only for readers who agree with them. If you disagree sharply with a reporter's assumptions, you may only be irritated if you try to read his book.

The assumptions that an author makes, and that he assumes you share, are sometimes very difficult to discover. In *The Seventeenth Century Background*, Basil Willey has this to say:

> . . . it is almost insuperably difficult to become critically conscious
> of one's own habitual assumptions; "doctrines felt as facts" can only
> be seen to be doctrines, and not facts, after great efforts of thought,
> and usually only with the aid of a first-rate metaphysician.

He goes on to suggest that it is easier to discover the "doctrines felt as facts" of an age different from our own, and that is what he attempts to do in his book. In reading books about our own time, however, we do not have the advantage of distance. Thus we must try to see through the filter not only of the author-reporter's mind, but also of our own.

Next, you must ask if there is a special language that the author uses. This is particularly important in reading magazines and newspapers, but it also applies to all books about current history. Certain words provoke special responses from us, responses that they might not provoke from other readers a century hence. An example of such a word is "Communism" or "Communist." We should try to control these responses, or at least know when they occur.

Finally, you must consider the last of the five questions, which is probably the hardest to answer. Does the reporter whose work you are reading himself know the facts? Is he privy to the perhaps secret thoughts and decisions of the persons about whom he is writing? Does he know all that he should know in order to give a fair and balanced account of the situation?

What we are suggesting, in other words, is that the possible bias of the author-reporter is not the only thing that has to be considered. We have heard a good deal lately about the "management of the news"; it is important to realize that this applies not only to us, as members of the public, but also to reporters who are supposed to be "in the know." They may not be. With the best good will in the world, with every intention of providing us with the truth of the matter, a reporter may still be "uninformed" with regard to secret actions, treaties, and so forth. He himself may be aware of this, or he may not. In the latter case, of course, the situation is especially perilous for his reader.

You will note that these five questions are really only variations on the questions we have said you must ask of any expository book. Knowing an author's special language, for example, is nothing more than coming to terms with him. But because current books and other material about the contemporary world pose special problems for us as readers, we have stated the questions in a different way.

Perhaps it is most useful to sum up the difference in a warning rather than a set of rules for reading books of this kind. The warning is this: *Caveat lector*—"Let the reader beware." Readers do not have to be wary when reading Aristotle, or Dante, or Shakespeare. But the author of any contemporary book may have—though he does not necessarily have—an interest in your understanding it in a certain way. Or if he does not, the sources of his information may have such an interest. You should know that interest, and take it into account in whatever you read.

A Note on Digests

There is another consequence of our basic distinction—the distinction between reading for information and reading for understanding—

that underlies everything we have said about reading. And this is that sometimes we have to read for information about understanding— to find out how others have interpreted the facts. Let us try to explain what this means.

For the most part, we read newspapers and magazines, and even advertising matter, for the information they contain. The amount of such material is vast, so vast that no one today has time to read more than a small fraction of it. Necessity has been the mother of a number of good inventions in the field of such reading. The news magazines, for instance, such as *Time* and *Newsweek,* perform an invaluable function for most of us by *reading* the news and reducing it to its essential elements of information. The men who write these magazines are primarily readers. They have developed the art of reading for information to a point far beyond the average reader's competence.

The same is true of a publication like *Reader's Digest,* which professes to bring us in condensed form much that is worth our attention in current general magazines to the compact scope of a single, small volume. Of course, the very best articles, like the best books, cannot be condensed without loss. If the essays of Montaigne, for example, were appearing in a current periodical, we would scarcely be satisfied to read a digest of them. A summary, in this case, would function well only if it impelled us to read the original. For the average article, however, a condensation is usually adequate, and often even better than the original, because the average article is mainly informational. The skill that produces *Reader's Digest* and the scores of similar periodicals is, first of all, a skill in reading, and only then one of writing simply and clearly. It does for us what few of us have the technique—even if we had the time—to do for ourselves. It cuts the core of solid information out of pages and pages of less substantial stuff.

But, after all, we still have to read the periodicals that accomplish these digests of current news and information. If we wish to be informed, we cannot avoid the task of reading, no matter how good the digests are. And the task of reading them is, in the last analysis, the same task as that which is performed by the editors of these magazines on the original material that they make available in more compact form. They have saved us labor, so far as the extent of our reading is concerned, but they have not saved us and cannot entirely save us the trouble of reading. In a sense, the function they perform profits us only if we can read their digests of information as well as they have done the prior reading in order to give us the digests.

And that involves reading for understanding as well as information. Obviously, the more condensed a digest is, the more selection has occurred. We may not have to worry about this very much if 1,000 pages are cut down to 900, say; but if 1,000 pages are cut to ten, or even one, then the question of what has been left out becomes critical. Hence the greater the condensation, the more important it is that we know something of the character of the condenser; the same *caveat* we mentioned before applies here with even greater force. Ultimately, perhaps, this comes down to reading between the lines of an expert condensation. You cannot refer to the original to find out what was left out; you must somehow infer this from the condensation itself. Reading digests, therefore, is sometimes the most demanding and difficult reading that you can do.

17

How to Read Science and Mathematics

The title of this chapter may be misleading. We do not propose to give you advice about how to read every kind of science and mathematics. We will confine ourselves to discussing only two kinds: the great scientific and mathematical classics of our tradition, on the one hand, and modern scientific popularizations, on the other hand. What we say will often be applicable to the reading of specialized monographs on abstruse and limited subjects, but we cannot help you to read those. There are two reasons for this. One is, simply, that we are not qualified to do it.

The other is this. Until approximately the end of the nineteenth century, the major scientific books were written for a lay audience. Their authors—men like Galileo, and Newton, and Darwin—were not averse to being read by specialists in their fields; indeed, they wanted to reach such readers. But there was as yet no institutionalized specialization in those days, days which Albert Einstein called "the happy childhood of science." Intelligent and well-read persons were expected to read scientific books as well as history and philosophy; there were no hard and fast distinctions, no boundaries that could not be crossed. There was also none of the disregard for the general or lay reader that is manifest in contemporary scientific writing. Most modern scientists do not care what lay readers think, and so they do not even try to reach them.

Today, science tends to be written by experts for experts. A serious communication on a scientific subject assumes so much specialized knowledge on the part of the reader that it usually cannot be read at all by anyone not learned in the field. There are obvious advantages to this approach, not least that it serves to advance science more quickly. Experts talking to each other about their expertise can arrive very quickly at the frontiers of it—they can see the problems at once and begin to try to solve them. But the cost is equally obvious. You—the ordinary intelligent reader whom we are addressing in this book—are left quite out of the picture.

In fact, this situation, although it is more extreme in science than elsewhere, obtains in many other fields as well. Nowadays, philosophers seldom write for anyone except other philosophers; economists write for economists; and even historians are beginning to find that the kind of shorthand, monographic communication to other experts that has long been dominant in science is a more convenient way of getting ideas across than the more traditional narrative work written for everyone.

What does the general reader do in these circumstances? He cannot become expert in all fields. He must fall back, therefore, on scientific popularizations. Some of these are good, and some are bad. But it is not only important to know the difference; it is also important to be able to read the good ones with understanding.

Understanding the Scientific Enterprise

One of the fastest growing academic disciplines is the history of science. We have seen marked changes in this area within the past few years. It was not so long ago that "serious" scientists looked down upon historians of science. The latter were thought of as men who studied the history of a subject because they were not capable of expanding its frontiers. The attitude of scientists to historians of science could be summed up in that famous remark of George Bernard Shaw's: "Those who can, do; those who can't, teach."

Expressions of this attitude are seldom heard nowadays. Departments of the history of science have become respectable, and excellent scientists study and write about the history of their subject. An example is what has been called the "Newton industry." At the present time, intensive and extensive research is being undertaken in many countries on the work and strange personality of Sir Isaac Newton. Half a dozen books have been recently published or announced. The reason is that scientists are more concerned than ever before about the nature of the scientific enterprise itself.

Thus we have no hesitation in recommending that you try to read at least some of the great scientific classics of our tradition. In fact, there is really no excuse for not *trying* to read them. None of them is impossibly difficult, not even a book like Newton's *Mathematical Principles of Natural Philosophy,* if you are willing to make the effort.

The most helpful advice we can give you is this. You are required by one of the rules for reading expository works to state, as clearly as you can, the problem that the author has tried to solve. This rule of analytical reading is relevant to all expository works, but *it is particularly relevant to works in the fields of science and mathematics.*

There is another way of saying this. As a layman, you do not read the classical scientific books to become knowledgeable in their subject matters in a contemporary sense. Instead, you read them to understand the history and philosophy of science. That, indeed, is the layman's responsibility with regard to science. The major way in which you can discharge it is to become aware of the problems that the great scientists were trying to solve—aware of the problems, and aware, also, of the background of the problems.

To follow the strands of scientific development, to trace the ways in which facts, assumptions, principles, and proofs are interrelated, is to engage in the activity of the human reason where it has probably operated with the most success. That is enough by itself, perhaps, to justify the historical study of science. In addition, such study will serve to dispel, in some measure, the apparent unintelligibility of science. Most important of all, it is an activity of the mind that is essential to education, the central aim of which has always been recognized, from Socrates' day down to our own, as the freeing of the mind through the discipline of wonder.

Suggestions for Reading Classical Scientific Books

By a scientific book, we mean the report of findings or conclusions in some field of research, whether carried on experimentally in a laboratory or by observations of nature in the raw. The scientific problem is always to describe the phenomena as accurately as possible, and to trace the interconnections between different kinds of phenomena.

In the great works of science, there is no oratory or propaganda, though there may be bias in the sense of initial presuppositions. You detect this, and take account of it, by distinguishing what the author *assumes* from what he *establishes* through argument. The more "objective" a scientific author is, the more he will explicitly ask you to take this or that for granted. Scientific objectivity is not the *absence of initial bias*. It is attained by *frank confession of it*.

The leading terms in a scientific work are usually expressed by uncommon or technical words. They are relatively easy to spot, and through them you can readily grasp the propositions. The main propositions are always general ones. Science thus is not chronotopic. Just the opposite; a scientist, unlike a historian, tries to get away from locality in time and place. He tries to say how things are generally, how things generally behave.

There are likely to be two main difficulties in reading a scientific book. One is with respect to the arguments. Science is primarily inductive; that is, its primary arguments are those that establish a general proposition by reference to observable evidence—a single case created by an experiment, or a vast array of cases collected by patient investigation. There are other arguments, of the sort that are called deductive. These are arguments in which a proposition is proved by other propositions already somehow established. So far as proof is concerned, science does not differ much from philosophy. But the inductive argument is characteristic of science.

This first difficulty arises because, in order to understand the inductive arguments in a scientific book, you must be able to follow the evidence that the scientist reports as their basis. Unfortunately, this is not always possible with nothing but the book in hand. If the book itself fails to enlighten him, the reader has only one recourse, which is to get the necessary special experience for himself at first hand. He may have to witness a laboratory demonstration. He may have to look at and handle pieces of apparatus similar to those referred to in the book. He may have to go to a museum and observe specimens or models.

Anyone who desires to acquire an understanding of the history of science must not only read the classical texts, but must also become acquainted, through direct experience, with the crucial experiments in that history. There are classical experiments as well as classical books. The scientific classics become more intelligible to those who have seen with their own eyes and done with their own hands what a great scientist describes as the procedure by which he reached his insights.

This does not mean that you cannot make a start without going through all the steps described. Take a book like Lavoisier's *Elements of Chemistry*, for instance. Published in 1789, the work is no longer considered to be useful as a textbook in chemistry, and indeed a student would be unwise to study it for the purpose of passing even a high school examination in the subject. Nevertheless, its method was revolutionary at the time, and its conception of a chemical element is still, on the whole, the one that we have in modern times. Now the point is that you do not have to read the book through, and in detail, to receive these impressions of it. The Preface, for example, with its emphasis on the importance of method in science, is enlightening. "Every branch of physical science," wrote Lavoisier,

> must consist of three things: the series of facts which are the objects
> of the science, the ideas which represent these facts, and the words

by which these facts are expressed. . . . And, as ideas are preserved and communicated by means of words, it necessarily follows that we cannot improve the language of any science without at the same time improving the science itself; neither can we, on the other hand, improve a science without improving the language or nomenclature which belongs to it.

This was exactly what Lavoisier did. He improved chemistry by improving its language, just as Newton, a century before, had improved physics by systematizing and ordering *its* language—in the process, as you may recall, developing the differential and integral calculus.

Mention of the calculus leads us to consider the second main difficulty in reading scientific books. And that is the problem of mathematics.

Facing the Problem of Mathematics

Many people are frightened of mathematics and think they cannot read it at all. No one is quite sure why this is so. Some psychologists think there is such a thing as "symbol blindness"—the inability to set aside one's dependence on the concrete and to follow the controlled shifting of symbols. There may be something to this, except, of course, that words shift, too, and their shifts, being more or less uncontrolled, are perhaps even more difficult to follow. Others believe that the trouble lies in the teaching of mathematics. If so, we can be gratified that much recent research has been devoted to the question of how to teach it better.

The problem is partly this. We are not told, or not told early enough so that it sinks in, that mathematics is a language, and that we can learn it like any other, including our own. We have to learn our own language twice, first when we learn to speak it, second when we learn to read it. Fortunately, mathematics has to be learned only once, since it is almost wholly a written language.

As we have already observed, learning a new written language always involves us in problems of elementary reading. When we underwent our initial reading instruction in elementary school, our problem was to learn to recognize certain arbitrary symbols when they appeared on a page, and to memorize certain relations among these symbols. Even the best readers continue to read, at least occasionally, at the elementary level: for example, whenever we come upon a word that we do not know and have to look up in the dictionary. If we are puzzled by the syntax of a sentence, we are also working at the elementary level. Only when we have solved these problems can we go on to read at higher levels.

Since mathematics is a language, it has its own vocabulary, grammar, and syntax, and these have to be learned by the beginning reader. Certain symbols and relationships between symbols have to be memorized. The problem is different, because the language is different, but it is no more difficult, *theoretically,* than learning to read English or French or German. At the elementary level, in fact, it may even be easier.

Any language is a medium of communication among men on subjects that the communicants can mutually comprehend. The subjects of ordinary discourse are mainly emotional facts and relations. Such subjects are not *entirely* comprehensible by any two different persons. But two different persons *can* comprehend a third thing that is outside of and emotionally separated from both of them, such as an electrical circuit, an isosceles triangle, or a syllogism. It is mainly when we invest these things with emotional connotations that we have trouble understanding them. Mathematics allows us to avoid this. There are no emotional connotations of mathematical terms, propositions, and equations when these are properly used.

We are also not told, at least not early enough, how beautiful and how intellectually satisfying mathematics can be. It is probably not too late for anyone to see this if he will go to a little trouble. You might start with Euclid, whose *Elements of Geometry* is one of the most lucid and beautiful works of any kind that has ever been written.

Let us consider, for example, the first five propositions in Book

I of the *Elements*. (If a copy of the book is available, you should look at it.) Propositions in elementary geometry are of two kinds: (1) the statement of problems in the construction of figures, and (2) theorems about the relations between figures or their parts. Construction problems require that something be done, theorems require that something be proved. At the end of a Euclidean construction problem, you will find the letters Q.E.F., which stand for *Quod erat faciendum,* "(Being) what it was required to do." At the end of a Euclidean theorem, you will find the letters Q.E.D., which stand for *Quod erat demonstrandum,* "(Being) what it was required to prove."

The first three propositions in Book I of the *Elements* are all problems of construction. Why is this? One answer is that the constructions are needed in the proofs of the theorems. This is not apparent in the first four propositions, but we can see it in the fifth proposition, which is a theorem. It states that in an isosceles triangle (a triangle with two equal sides) the base angles are equal. This involves the use of Proposition 3, for a shorter line is cut off from a longer line. Since Proposition 3, in turn, depends on the use of the construction in Proposition 2, while Proposition 2 involves Proposition 1, we see that these three constructions are needed for the sake of Proposition 5.

Constructions can also be interpreted as serving another purpose. They bear an obvious similarity to postulates; both constructions and postulates assert that geometrical operations can be performed. In the case of the postulates, the possibility is *assumed;* in the case of the propositions, it is *proved.* The proof, of course, involves the use of the postulates. Thus, we might wonder, for example, whether there is really any such thing as an equilateral triangle, which is defined in Definition 20. Without troubling ourselves here about the thorny question of the existence of mathematical objects, we can at least see that Proposition 1 shows that, from the *assumption* that there are such things as straight lines and circles, it *follows* that there are such things as equilateral triangles.

Let us return to Proposition 5, the theorem about the equality of the base angles of an isosceles triangle. When the conclusion has been reached, in a series of steps involving reference to previous propositions and to the postulates, the proposition has been proved. It has then been shown that *if something is true* (namely, the hypothesis that we have an isosceles triangle), and if some additional things are valid (the definitions, postulates, and prior propositions), *then something else is also true,* namely, the conclusion. The proposition asserts this *if-then* relationship. It does not assert the truth of the hypothesis, nor does it assert the truth of the conclusion, except when the hypothesis is true. Nor is this connection between hypothesis and conclusion seen to be true until the proposition is proved. It is precisely the truth of this connection that is proved, and nothing else.

Is it an exaggeration to say that this is beautiful? We do not think so. What we have here is a *really logical exposition* of a *really limited problem.* There is something very attractive about both the clarity of the exposition and the limited nature of the problem. Ordinary discourse, even very good philosophical discourse, finds it difficult to limit its problems in this way. And the use of logic in the case of philosophical problems is hardly ever as clear as this.

Consider the difference between the argument of Proposition 5, as outlined here, and even the simplest of syllogisms, such as the following:

> All animals are mortal;
> All men are animals;
> Therefore, all men are mortal.

There is something satisfying about that, too. We can treat it as though it were a piece of mathematical reasoning. Assuming that there are such things as animals and men, and that animals are mortal, then the conclusion follows with the same certainty as the one about the angles of the triangle. But the trouble is that there really are animals and men; we are assuming something about real things, something that may or may not be true. We have to examine our assumptions in a way that we do not have to do in mathematics. Euclid's proposition does not suffer from this. It does not really matter to him whether there are such things as isosceles triangles. *If* there are, he is saying, and *if* they are defined in such and such a way, *then* it follows absolutely that their base angles are equal. There can be no doubt about this whatever—now and forever.

Handling the Mathematics in Scientific Books

This digression on Euclid has led us a little out of our way. We were observing that the presence of mathematics in scientific books is one of the main obstacles to reading them. There are a couple of things to say about that.

First, you can probably read at least elementary mathematics better than you think. We have already suggested that you should begin with Euclid, and we are confident that if you spent several evenings with the *Elements* you would overcome much of your fear of the subject. Having done some work on Euclid, you might proceed to glance at the works of other classical Greek mathematicians—Archimedes, Apollonius, Nicomachus. They are not really very difficult, and besides, you can skip.

That leads to the second point we want to make. If your intention is to read *a mathematical book in and for itself,* you must read it, of course, from beginning to end—and with a pencil in your hand, for writing in the margins and even on a scratch pad is more necessary here than in the case of any other kinds of books. But your intention may not be that, but instead to read *a scientific work that has mathematics in it.* In this case, skipping is often the better part of valor.

Take Newton's *Principia* for an example. The book contains many propositions, both construction problems and theorems, but it is not necessary to read all of them in detail, especially the first time through. Read the statement of the proposition, and glance down the proof to get an idea of how it is done; read the statements of the so-called lemmas and corollaries; and read the so-called scholiums, which are essentially discussions of the relations between propositions and of their relations to the work as a whole. You will begin to see that whole if you do this, and so to discover how the system that Newton is constructing is built—what comes first and what second, and how the parts fit together. Go through the whole work in this way, avoiding the diagrams if they trouble you (as they do many readers), merely glancing at much of the interstitial matter, but being sure to find and read the passages where Newton is making his main points. One of these comes at the very end of the work, at the close of Book III, which is titled "The System of the World." This *General Scholium,* as Newton called it, not only sums up what has gone before but also states the great problem of almost all subsequent physics.

Newton's *Optics* is another scientific classic that you might want to try to read. There is actually very little mathematics in it, although at first glance that does not appear to be so because the pages are sprinkled with diagrams. But these diagrams are merely illustrations describing Newton's experiments with holes for the sun to shine through into a dark room, with prisms to intercept the sunbeam, and with pieces of white paper placed so that the various colors of the beam can shine on them. You can quite easily repeat some of these experiments yourself, and this is fun to do, for the colors are beautiful, and the descriptions are eminently clear. You will want to read, in addition to the descriptions of the experiments, the statements of the various theorems or propositions, and the discussions that occur at the end of each of the three Books, where Newton sums up his discoveries and suggests their consequences. The end of Book III is famous, for it contains some statements by Newton about the scientific enterprise itself that are well worth reading.

Mathematics is very often employed by scientific writers, mainly because it has the qualities of preciseness, clarity, and limitedness that we have described. Usually you can understand something of the matter without going very deeply into the mathematics, as in the case of Newton. Oddly enough, however, even if mathematics is absolutely terrifying to you, its absence from certain works may cause you even more trouble. A case in point is Galileo's *Two New Sciences,* his famous treatise on the strength of materials and on motion. This work is particularly difficult for modern readers because it is *not* primarily mathematical; instead, it is presented in the form of a dialogue. The dialogue form, though appropriate to the stage and useful in philosophy when employed by such a master as Plato, is not really appropriate to science. It is therefore hard to discover what Galileo is saying, although when you do you will discover that he is stating some revolutionary things.

Not all of the scientific classics, of course, employ mathematics or even need to employ it. The works of Hippocrates, the founder of Greek medicine, are not mathematical. You might well read them to discover Hippocrates' view of medicine—namely, that it is the art of keeping people well, rather than that of curing them when they are sick. That is unfortunately an uncommon idea nowadays. Nor is William Harvey's discourse on the circulation of the blood mathematical, or William Gilbert's book on magnets. They can be read without too much difficulty if you always keep in mind that your primary obligation is *not to become competent in the subject matter but instead to understand the problem.*

A Note on Popular Science

In a sense, there is little more to say about reading scientific popularizations. By definition, these are works—either books or articles—written for a wide audience, not just for specialists. Thus, if you have managed to read some of the classics of the scientific tradition, you should not have much trouble with them. This is because, although they are about science, they generally skirt or avoid the two main problems that confront the reader of an original contribution in science. First, *they contain relatively few descriptions of experiments* (instead, they merely report the results of experiments). Second, *they contain relatively little mathematics* (unless they are popular books about mathematics itself)

Popular scientific articles are usually easier to read than popular scientific books, although not always. Sometimes such articles are very good—for example, articles found in *Scientific American,* a monthly magazine, or *Science,* a somewhat more technical weekly publication. Of course, these publications, no matter how good they are or how carefully and responsibly edited, pose the problem that was discussed at the end of the last chapter. In reading them, we are at the mercy of reporters who filter the information for us. If they are good reporters, we are fortunate. If they are not, we have almost no recourse.

Scientific popularizations are never easy reading in the sense that a story is or seems to be. Even a three-page article on DNA containing no reports of experiments and no diagrams or mathematical formulas demands considerable effort on the part of the reader. You cannot read it for understanding without keeping your mind awake. Thus, the requirement that you read actively is more important here than almost anywhere else. Identify the subject matter. Discover the relation between the whole and its parts. Come to terms and plot the propositions and arguments. Work at achieving understanding before you begin to criticize or to assess significance. These rules, by now, are all familiar. But they apply here with particular force.

Short articles are usually primarily informational, and as such they require less active thinking on your part. You must make an effort to understand, to follow the account provided by the author, but you often do not have to go beyond that. In the case of such excellent popular books as Whitehead's *Introduction to Mathematics,* Lincoln Barnett's *The Universe and Dr. Einstein,* and Barry Commoner's *The Closing Circle,* something more is required. This is particularly true of a book like Commoner's, on a subject—the environmental crisis—of special interest and importance to all of us today. The writing is compact and requires constant attention. But the book as a whole has implications that the careful reader will not miss. Although it is not a practical work, in the sense described above in Chapter 13, its theoretical conclusions have important consequences. The mere mention of the book's subject matter—the environmental crisis—suggests this. The environment in question is our own; if it is undergoing a crisis of some sort, then it inevitably follows, even if the author had not said so—though in fact he has—that we are also involved in the crisis. The thing to do in a crisis is (usually) to act in a certain way, or to stop acting in a certain way. Thus Commoner's book, though essentially theoretical, has a significance that goes beyond the theoretical and into the realm of the practical.

This is not to suggest that Commoner's work is important and the books by Whitehead and Barnett unimportant. When *The Universe and Dr. Einstein* was written, as a theoretical account (written for a popular audience) of the history of researches into the atom, people were widely aware of the perils inherent in atomic physics, as represented mainly but not exclusively by the recently discovered atomic bomb. Thus that theoretical book also had practical consequences. But even if people are today not so worried about the imminence of an atomic or nuclear war, there is still what may be called a practical necessity to read this theoretical book, or one like it. The reason is that atomic and nuclear physics is one of the great achievements of our age. It promises great things for man, at the same time that it poses great perils. An informed and concerned reader should know everything he can about the subject.

A slightly different urgency is exerted by Whitehead's *Introduction to Mathematics*. Mathematics is one of the major modern mysteries. Perhaps it is the leading one, occupying a place in our society similar to the religious mysteries of another age. If we want to know something about what our age is all about, we should have some understanding of what mathematics is, and of how the mathematician operates and thinks. Whitehead's book, although it does not go very deeply into the more abstruse branches of the subject, is remarkably eloquent about the principles of mathematical reasoning. If it does nothing else, it shows the attentive reader that the mathematician is an ordinary man, not a magician. And that discovery, too, is important for any reader who desires to expand his horizons beyond the immediate here and now of thought and experience.

18

How to Read Philosophy

Children ask magnificent questions. "Why are people?" "What makes the cat tick?" "What's the world's first name?" "Did God have a reason for creating the earth?" Out of the mouths of babes comes, if not wisdom, at least the search for it. Philosophy, according to Aristotle, begins in wonder. It certainly begins in childhood, even if for most of us it stops there, too.

The child is a natural questioner. It is not the number of questions he asks but their character that distinguishes him from the adult. Adults do not lose the curiosity that seems to be a native human trait, but their curiosity deteriorates in quality. They want to know whether something is so, not why. But children's questions are not limited to the sort that can be answered by an encyclopedia.

What happens between the nursery and college to turn the flow of questions off, or, rather, to turn it into the duller channels of adult curiosity about matters of fact? A mind not agitated by good questions cannot appreciate the significance of even the best answers. It is easy enough to learn the answers. But to develop actively inquisitive minds, alive with real questions, profound questions—that is another story.

Why should we have to try to develop such minds, when children are born with them? Somewhere along the line, adults must fail somehow to sustain the infant's curiosity at its original depth.

School itself, perhaps, dulls the mind—by the dead weight of rote learning, much of which may be necessary. The failure is probably even more the parents' fault. We so often tell a child there is no answer, even when one is available, or demand that he ask no more questions. We thinly conceal our irritation when baffled by the apparently unanswerable query. All this discourages the child. He may get the impression that it is impolite to be too inquisitive. Human inquisitiveness is never killed; but it is soon debased to the sort of questions asked by most college students, who, like the adults they are soon to become, ask only for information.

We have no solution for this problem; we are certainly not so brash as to think we can tell you how to answer the profound and wondrous questions that children put. But we do want you to recognize that one of the most remarkable things about the great philosophical books is that they ask the same sort of profound questions that children ask. The ability to retain the child's view of the world, with at the same time a mature understanding of what it means to retain it, is extremely rare—and a person who has these qualities is likely to be able to contribute something really important to our thinking.

We are not required to think as children in order to understand existence. Children certainly do not, and cannot, understand it—if, indeed, anyone can. But we must be able to see as children see, to wonder as they wonder, to ask as they ask. The complexities of adult life get in the way of the truth. The great philosophers have always been able to clear away the complexities and see simple distinctions—simple once they are stated, vastly difficult before. If we are to follow them we too must be childishly simple in our questions—and maturely wise in our replies.

The Questions Philosophers Ask

What are these "childishly simple" questions that philosophers ask? When we write them down, they do not seem simple, because to answer them is so difficult. Nevertheless, they are initially simple in the sense of being basic or fundamental.

Take the following questions about *being or existence,* for example: What is the difference between existing and not existing? What is common to all the things that do exist, and what are the properties of everything that does exist? Are there different ways in which things can exist—different modes of being or existence? Do some things exist only in the mind or for the mind, whereas others exist outside the mind, and whether or not they are known to us, or even knowable by us? Does everything that exists exist physically, or are there some things that exist apart from material embodiment? Do all things change, or is there anything that is immutable? Does anything exist necessarily, or must we say that everything that does exist might not have existed? Is the realm of possible existence larger than the realm of what actually does exist?

These are typically the kind of questions that a philosopher asks when he is concerned to explore the nature of being itself and the realms of being. As questions, they are not difficult to state or understand, but they are enormously difficult to answer—so difficult, in fact, that there are philosophers, especially in recent times, who have held that they cannot be answered in any satisfactory manner.

Another set of philosophical questions concerns *change or becoming* rather than being. Of the things in our experience to which we would unhesitatingly attribute existence, we would also say that all of them are subject to change. They come into being and pass away; while in being, most of them move from one place to another; and many of them change in quantity or in quality: they become larger or smaller, heavier or lighter; or, like the ripening apple and the aging beefsteak, they change in color.

What is involved in any change? In every process of change, is there something that endures unchanged as well as some respect or aspect of that enduring thing which undergoes change? When you learn something that you did not know before, you have certainly changed with respect to the knowledge you have acquired, but you are also the same individual that you were before; if that were not the case, *you* could not be said to have changed through learning. Is this true of all change? For example, is it true of such remarkable changes as birth and death—of coming to be and passing away—or only of less fundamental changes, such as local motion, growth, or alteration in quality? How many different kinds of change are there? Do the same fundamental elements or conditions enter into all processes of change, and are the same causes operative in all? What do we mean by a cause of change? Are there different types of causes responsible for change? Are the causes of change—of becoming—the same as the causes of being, or existence?

Such questions are asked by the philosopher who turns his attention from being to becoming and also tries to relate becoming to being. Once again, they are not difficult questions to state or understand, though they are extremely difficult to answer clearly and well. In any case, you can see how they begin with a childishly simple attitude toward the world and our experience of it.

Unfortunately, we do not have space to go into the whole range of questions more deeply. We can only list some other questions that philosophers ask and try to answer. There are questions not only about being and becoming, but also about necessity and contingency; about the material and the immaterial; about the physical and the non-physical; about freedom and indeterminacy; about the powers of the human mind; about the nature and extent of human knowledge; about the freedom of the will.

All these questions are speculative or theoretical in the sense of those terms that we have employed in distinguishing between the theoretical and practical realms. But philosophy, as you know, is not restricted to theoretical questions only.

Take *good and evil,* for instance. Children are much concerned with the difference between good and bad; their behinds are likely to suffer if they make mistakes about it. But we do not stop wondering about the difference when we grow up. Is there a universally valid distinction between good and evil? Are there certain things that are always good, others that are always bad, whatever the circumstances? Or was Hamlet right when, echoing Montaigne, he said: "There is nothing either good or bad but thinking makes it so."

Good and evil, of course, are not the same as right and wrong; the two pairs of terms seem to refer to different classes of things. In particular, even if we feel that whatever is right is good, we probably do not feel that whatever is wrong is evil. But how do we make this distinction precise?

"Good" is an important philosophical word, but it is an important word in our everyday vocabulary, too. Trying to say what it means is a heady exercise; it will involve you very deeply in philosophy before you know it. There are many things that are good, or, as we would prefer to say, there are many goods. Is it possible to order the goods? Are some more important than others? Do some depend on others? Are there circumstances in which goods conflict, so that you have to choose one good at the expense of forgoing another?

Again, we do not have space to go more extensively into these questions. We can only list some other questions in the practical realm. There are questions not only about good and evil, right and wrong, and the order of goods, but also about duties and obligations; about virtues and vices; about happiness, life's purpose or goal; about justice and rights in the sphere of human relations and social interaction; about the state and its relation to the individual; about the good society, the just polity, and the just economy; about war and peace.

The two groups of questions that we have discussed determine or identify two main divisions of philosophy. The questions in the first group, the questions about being and becoming, have to do with what *is* or *happens* in the world. Such questions belong to the division of philosophy that is called theoretical or speculative. The questions in the second group, the questions concerning good and evil, or right and wrong, have to do with what *ought* to be done or sought, and they belong to the division of philosophy that is sometimes called practical, and is more accurately called normative. Books that tell you how to make something, such as a cookbook, or how to do something, such as a driver's manual, need not try to argue that you ought to become a good cook, or learn to drive a car well; they can assume that you want to make or do something and merely tell you how to succeed in your efforts. In contrast, books of normative philosophy concern themselves primarily with the goals all men *ought* to seek—goals such as leading a good life or instituting a good society—and, unlike cookbooks and driving manuals, they go no further than prescribing in the most universal terms the means that *ought* to be employed in order to achieve these goals.

The questions that philosophers ask also serve to distinguish subordinate branches of the two main divisions of philosophy. A work of speculative or theoretical philosophy is metaphysical if it is mainly concerned with questions about being or existence. It is a work in the philosophy of nature if it is concerned with becoming—with the nature and kinds of changes, their conditions and causes. If its primary concern is with knowledge—with questions about what is involved in our knowing anything, with the causes, extent, and limits of human knowledge, and with its certainties and uncertainties—then it is a work in epistemology, which is just another name for theory of knowledge. Turning from theoretical to normative philosophy, the main distinction is between questions about the good life and what is right or wrong in the conduct of the individual, all of which fall within the sphere of ethics, and questions about the good society and the conduct of the individual in relation to the community—the sphere of politics or political philosophy.

Modern Philosophy and the Great Tradition

For the sake of brevity in what follows, let us call questions about what is and happens in the world, or about what men ought to do or seek, "first-order questions." We should recognize, then, that there are also "second-order questions" that can be asked: questions about our first-order knowledge, questions about the content of our thinking when we try to answer first-order questions, questions about the ways in which we express such thoughts in language.

This distinction between first-order and second-order questions is useful, because it helps to explain what has happened to philosophy in recent years. The majority of professional philosophers at the present day no longer believe that first-order questions can be answered by philosophers. Most professional philosophers today devote their attention exclusively to second-order questions, very often to questions having to do with the language in which thought is expressed.

That is all to the good, for it is never harmful to be critical. The trouble is the wholesale giving up of first-order philosophical questions, which are the ones that are most likely to interest lay readers. In fact, philosophy today, like contemporary science or mathematics, is no longer being written for lay readers. Second-order questions are, almost by definition, ones of narrow appeal; and professional philosophers, like scientists, are not interested in the views of anyone but other experts.

This makes modern philosophy very hard to read for non-philosophers—as difficult, indeed, as science for non-scientists. We cannot in this book give you any advice about how to read modern philosophy as long as it is concerned exclusively with second-order questions. However, there are philosophical books that you can read, and that we believe you should read. These books ask the kinds of questions that we have called first-order ones. It is not accidental that they were also written primarily for a lay audience rather than exclusively for other philosophers.

Up to about 1930, or perhaps even a little later, philosophical books were written for the general reader. Philosophers hoped to be read by their peers, but they also wanted to be read by ordinary, intelligent men and women. Since the questions that they asked and tried to answer were of concern to everyone, they thought that everyone should know what they thought.

All of the great classical works in philosophy, from Plato onward, were written from this point of view. These books are accessible to the lay reader; you can succeed in reading them if you wish to. Everything that we have to say in this chapter is intended to help you do that.

On Philosophical Method

It is important to understand what philosophical method consists in—at least insofar as philosophy is conceived as asking and trying to answer *first-order questions.* Suppose that you are a philosopher who is troubled by one of the childishly simple questions we have mentioned—the question, for instance, about the properties of everything that exists, or the question about the nature and causes of change. How do you proceed?

If your question were scientific, you would know that to answer it you would have to perform some kind of special research, either by way of developing an experiment to test your answer, or by way of observing a wide range of phenomena. If your question were historical, you would know that you would also have to perform research, although of a different kind. But there is no experiment that will tell you what all existing things have in common, precisely in respect to having existence. There are no special kinds of phenomena that you can observe, no documents that you can seek out and read, in order to find out what change is or why things change. All you can do is reflect upon the question. There is, in short, nothing to do but think.

You are not thinking in a total vacuum, of course. Philosophy, when it is good, is not "pure" speculation—thinking divorced from experience. Ideas cannot be put together just any way. There are stringent tests of the validity of answers to philosophical questions. But such tests are based on common experience alone—on the experience that you already have because you are a human being, not a philosopher. You are as well acquainted through common experience with the phenomena of change as anybody else; everything in the world about you manifests mutability. As far as the mere experience of change goes, you are in as good a position to think about its nature and causes as the greatest philosophers. What distinguishes them is that they thought about it extremely well: they formulated the most penetrating questions that could be asked about it, and they undertook to develop carefully and clearly worked-out answers. By what means? Not by investigation. Not by having or trying to get more experience than the rest of us have. Rather, by thinking more profoundly about the experience than the rest of us have.

Understanding this is not enough. We must also realize that not all of the questions that philosophers have asked and tried to answer are truly philosophical. They themselves were not always aware of this, and their ignorance or mistake in this crucial respect can cause unperceptive readers considerable difficulty. To avoid such difficulties, it is necessary to be able to distinguish the truly philosophical questions from the other questions that a philosopher may deal with, but that he should have waived and left for later scientific investigation to answer. The philosopher was misled by failing to see that such questions can be answered by scientific investigation, though he probably could not have known this at the time of his writing.

An example of this is the question that ancient philosophers asked about the difference between the matter of terrestrial and celestial bodies. To their observation, unaided by telescopes, it appeared to be the case that the heavenly bodies changed only in place; they did not appear to come into being or to pass away, like plants and animals; nor did they appear to change in size or quality. Because celestial bodies were subject to one kind of change only—local motion—whereas all terrestrial bodies change in other respects as well, the ancients concluded that they had to be composed of a different kind of matter. They did not surmise, nor could they probably have surmised, that with the invention of the telescope, the heavenly bodies would give us knowledge of their mutability beyond anything we can know through common experience. Hence they took as a question that they thought it proper for philosophers to answer one that should have been reserved for later scientific investigation. Such investigation began with Galileo's use of the telescope and his discovery of the moons of Jupiter; this led to the revolutionary assertion by Kepler that the matter of the heavenly bodies is exactly the same as the matter of bodies on earth; and this in turn laid the groundwork for Newton's formulation of a celestial mechanics in which the same laws of motion apply without qualification to all bodies wherever they are in the physical universe.

On the whole, apart from the confusions that may result, the misinformation or lack of information about scientific matters that mars the work of the classical philosophers is irrelevant. The reason is that it is philosophical questions, not scientific or historical ones, that we are interested in when we read a philosophical work. And, at the risk of repeating ourselves, we must emphasize that there is no other way than thinking to answer such questions. If we could build a telescope or microscope to examine the properties of existence, we should do so, of course. But no such instruments are possible.

We do not want to give the impression that it is only philosophers who make mistakes of the sort we are discussing here. Suppose a scientist becomes troubled by the question about the kind of life a man ought to lead. This is a question in normative philosophy, and the only way to answer it is by thinking about it. But the scientist may not realize that, and instead suppose that some kind of experiment or research will give him an answer. He may decide to ask 1,000 persons what kind of life they would like to lead, and base his answer to the question on their answers. But it should be obvious that his answer, in that case, would be as irrelevant as Aristotle's speculations about the matter of the celestial bodies.

On Philosophical Styles

Although there is only one philosophical method, there are at least five styles of exposition that have been employed by the great philosophers of the Western tradition. The student or reader of philosophy should be able to distinguish between them and know the advantages and disadvantages of each.

1. THE PHILOSOPHICAL DIALOGUE: The first philosophical style of exposition, first in time if not in effectiveness, is the one adopted by Plato in his *Dialogues.* The style is conversational, even colloquial; a number of men discuss a subject with Socrates (or, in the later dialogues, with a speaker known as The Athenian Stranger); often, after a certain amount of fumbling, Socrates embarks on a series of questions and comments that help to elucidate the subject. In the hands of a master like Plato, this style is heuristic, that is, it allows the reader, indeed leads him, to discover things for himself. When the style is enriched by the high drama—some would say the high comedy—of the story of Socrates, it becomes enormously powerful.

"A master like Plato," we said—but there is no one "like" Plato. Other philosophers have attempted dialogues—for example, Cicero and Berkeley—but with little success. Their dialogues are flat, dull, almost unreadable. It is a measure of the greatness of Plato that he was able to write philosophical dialogues that, for wit, charm, and profundity are the equal of any books ever produced by anyone, on any subject. Yet it may be a sign of the inappropriateness of this style of philosophizing that no one except Plato has ever been able to handle it effectively.

That Plato did so, goes without saying. All Western philosophy, Whitehead once remarked, is but "a footnote to Plato"; and the later Greeks themselves had a saying: "Everywhere I go in my head, I meet Plato coming back." Those statements, however, should not be misunderstood. Plato himself had apparently no philosophical system, no doctrine—unless it was that there is no doctrine, that we should simply keep talking. And asking questions. For Plato, and Socrates before him, did indeed manage to raise most of the important questions that subsequent philosophers have felt it necessary to deal with.

? THE PHILOSOPHICAL TREATISE OR ESSAY: Aristotle was Plato's best pupil; he studied under him for twenty years. He is said to have also written dialogues, but none of these survives entirely. What does survive are curiously difficult essays or treatises on a number of different subjects. Aristotle was obviously a clear thinker, but the difficulty of the surviving works has led scholars to suggest that they were originally notes for lectures or books—either Aristotle's own notes, or notes taken down by a student who heard the master speak. We may never know the truth of the matter, but in any event the Aristotelean treatise was a new style in philosophy.

The subjects covered by Aristotle in his treatises, and the various styles adopted by him in presenting his findings, also helped to establish the branches and approaches of philosophy in the succeeding centuries. There are, first of all, the so-called popular works—mostly dialogues, of which only fragments have come down to us. Then there are the documentary collections. The major one that we know about was a collection of 158 separate constitutions of Greek states. Only one of these survives, the constitution of Athens, which was recovered from a papyrus in 1890. Finally, there are the major treatises, some of which, like the *Physics* and *Metaphysics,* or the *Ethics, Politics,* and *Poetics,* are purely philosophical works, theoretical or normative; some of which, like the book *On the Soul,* are mixtures of philosophical theory and early scientific investigation; and some of which, like the biological treatises, are mainly scientific works in the field of natural history.

Immanuel Kant, although he was probably more influenced by Plato in a philosophical sense, adopted Aristotle's style of exposition. His treatises are finished works of art, unlike Aristotle's in this respect. They state the main problem first, go through the subject matter in a thorough and business-like way, and treat special problems by the way or at the last. The clarity of both Kant and Aristotle may be said to consist in the order that they impose on a subject. We see a philosophical beginning, middle, and end. We also, particularly in the case of Aristotle, are provided with accounts of the views and objections of others, both philosophers and ordinary men. Thus, in one sense the style of the treatise is similar to the style of the dialogue. But the element of drama is missing from the Kantian or Aristotelean treatise; a philosophical view is developed through straightforward exposition rather than through the conflict of positions and opinions, as in Plato.

3. THE MEETING OF OBJECTIONS: The philosophical style developed in the Middle Ages and perfected by St. Thomas Aquinas in his *Summa Theologica* has likenesses to both of those already discussed. Plato, we have pointed out, raises most of the persistent philosophical problems; and Socrates, as we might have observed, asks in the course of the dialogues the kind of simple but profound questions that children ask. And Aristotle, as we have also pointed out, recognizes the objections of other philosophers and replies to them.

Aquinas' style is a combination of question-raising and objection-meeting. The *Summa* is divided into parts, treatises, questions, and articles. The form of all the articles is the same. A question is posed; the opposite (wrong) answer to it is given; arguments are educed in support of that wrong answer; these are countered first by an authoritative text (often a quotation from Scripture); and finally, Aquinas introduces his own answer or solution with the words "I answer that." Having given his own view of the matter, he then replies to each of the arguments for the wrong answer.

The neatness and order of this style are appealing to men with orderly minds, but that is not the most important feature of the Thomistic way of philosophizing. Rather, it is Aquinas' explicit recognition of conflicts, his reporting of different views, and his attempt to meet all possible objections to his own solutions. The idea that the truth somehow evolves out of opposition and conflict was a common medieval one. Philosophers in Aquinas' time accepted as a matter of course that they should be prepared to defend their views in open, public disputes, which were often attended by crowds of students and other interested persons. The civilization of the Middle Ages was essentially oral, partly because books were few and hard to come by. A proposition was not accepted as true unless it could meet the test of open discussion; the philosopher was not a solitary thinker, but instead faced his opponents in the intellectual market place (as Socrates might have said). Thus, the *Summa Theologica* is imbued with the spirit of debate and discussion.

4. THE SYSTEMIZATION OF PHILOSOPHY: In the seventeenth century, a fourth style of philosophical exposition was developed by two notable philosophers, Descartes and Spinoza. Fascinated by the promised success of mathematics in organizing man's knowledge of nature, they attempted to organize philosophy itself in a way akin to the organization of mathematics.

Descartes was a great mathematician and, although perhaps wrong on some points, a redoubtable philosopher. What he tried to do, essentially, was to clothe philosophy in mathematical dress—to give it the certainty and formal structure that Euclid, two thousand years before, had given geometry. Descartes was not wholly unsuccessful in this, and his demand for clarity and distinctness in thinking was to some extent justified in the chaotic intellectual climate of his time. He also wrote philosophical treatises in a more or less traditional form, including a set of replies to objections to his views.

Spinoza carried the conception even farther. His *Ethics* is written in strict mathematical form, with propositions, proofs, corollaries, lemmas, scholiums, and the like. However, the subject matter of metaphysics and of morals is not very satisfactorily handled in this manner, which is more appropriate for geometry and other mathematical subjects than for philosophical ones. A sign of this is that when reading Spinoza you can skip a great deal, in exactly the same way that you can skip in Newton. You cannot skip anything in Kant or Aristotle, because the line of reasoning is continuous; and you cannot skip anything in Plato, any more than you would skip a part of a play or poem.

Probably there are no absolute rules of rhetoric. Nevertheless, it is questionable whether it is possible to write a satisfactory philosophical work in mathematical form, as Spinoza tried to do, or a satisfactory scientific work in dialogue form, as Galileo tried to do. The fact is that both of these men failed to some extent to communicate what they wished to communicate, and it seems likely that the form they chose was a major reason for the failure.

5. THE APHORISTIC STYLE: There is one other style of philosophical exposition that deserves mention, although it is probably not as important as the other four. This is the aphoristic style adopted by Nietzsche in such works as *Thus Spake Zarathustra* and by certain modern French philosophers. The popularity of this style during the past century is perhaps owing to the great interest, among Western readers, in the wisdom books of the East, which are written in an aphoristic style. This style may also owe something to the example of Pascal's *Pensées*. But of course Pascal did not intend to leave his great work in the form of short, enigmatic statements; he died before he could finish writing out the book in essay form.

The great advantage of the aphoristic form in philosophy is that it is heuristic; the reader has the impression that more is being said than is actually said, for he does much of the work of thinking—of making connections between statements and of constructing arguments for positions—himself. At the same time, however, this is the great disadvantage of the style, which is really not expositional at all. The author is like a hit-and-run driver; he touches on a subject, he suggests a truth or insight about it, and then runs off to another subject without properly defending what he has said. Thus, although the aphoristic style is enjoyable for those who are poetically inclined, it is irritating for serious philosophers who would rather try to follow and criticize an author's line of thought.

As far as we know, there is no other important style of philosophical exposition that has been employed in our Western tradition. (A work like Lucretius' *On the Nature of Things* is not an exception. It was originally in verse; but as far as its style goes, it is no different from other philosophical essays; and in any event we ordinarily read it nowadays in prose translations.) This means that all of the great philosophers have employed one or the other of these five styles; sometimes, of course, a philosopher tries more than one. The treatise or essay is probably the most common form, both in the past and in the present. It can range all the way from highly formal and difficult works like those of Kant, to popular philosophical essays or letters. Dialogues are notoriously hard to write, and the geometrical style is enormously difficult both to write and to read. The aphoristic style is highly unsatisfactory from a philosophical point of view. The Thomistic style has not been used very much in recent times. Perhaps it would not be acceptable to modern readers, but that seems a shame, considering all its advantages.

Hints for Reading Philosophy

It is perhaps clear from the discussion so far that the most important thing to discover in reading any philosophical work is the question or questions it tries to answer. The questions may be stated explicitly, or they may be implicit to a certain extent. In either case, you must try to find out what they are.

How the author answers these questions will be deeply affected by his controlling principles. These may be stated, too, but that is not always the case. We have already quoted Basil Willey on the difficulty—and the importance—of discovering the hidden and unstated assumptions of an author, to say nothing of our own. This goes for any book. It applies to works in philosophy with particular force.

The great philosophers cannot be charged with having tried to hide their assumptions dishonestly, or with having been unclear in their definitions and postulations. It is precisely the mark of a great philosopher that he makes these things clearer than other writers can. Nevertheless, every great philosopher has certain controlling principles that underlie his work. These are easy enough to see if he states them in the book you are reading. But he may not have done so, reserving their treatment for another book. Or he may never treat them explicitly, but instead allow them to pervade every one of his works.

It is difficult to give examples of such controlling principles. Any that we might proffer would probably be disputed by philosophers, and we do not here have space to defend our choices. Nevertheless, we could mention the controlling idea of Plato that conversation about philosophical subjects is perhaps the most important of all human activities. Now this idea is seldom explicitly stated in the dialogues, although Socrates may be saying it when, in the *Apology,* he asserts that the unexamined life is not worth living, and Plato mentions it in the *Seventh Letter.* The point is that Plato expresses this view in a number of other places, though not in so many words—for example, in the *Protagoras,* where the audience is shown as disapproving of

Protagoras' unwillingness to continue talking to Socrates. Another example is that of Cephalus, in Book I of the *Republic,* who happens to have other business to attend to and so departs. Plato seems to be saying here, though not explicitly, that it is a betrayal of man's deepest nature to refuse to join, for whatever reason, in the search for truth. But, as we have noted, this is not ordinarily cited as one of Plato's "ideas," because it is seldom explicitly discussed in his works.

We can find other examples in Aristotle. In the first place, it is always important to recognize, in reading any Aristotelean work, that things said in other works are relevant to the discussion. Thus the basic principles of logic, expounded in the *Organon,* are assumed in the *Physics.* In the second place, owing partly to the fact that the treatises are not finished works of art, their controlling principles are not always stated with satisfactory clarity. The *Ethics* is about many things: happiness, habit, virtue, pleasure, and so forth—the list could be very long. But the controlling insight is discovered only by the very careful reader. This is the insight that happiness is the *whole* of the good, not the *highest* good, for in that case it would be only one good among others. Recognizing this, we see that happiness does not consist in self-perfection, or the goods of self-improvement, even though these constitute the highest among partial goods. Happiness, as Aristotle says, is the quality of a *whole* life, and he means "whole" not only in a temporal sense but also in terms of all the aspects from which a life can be viewed. The happy man is one, as we might say nowadays, who puts it all together—and keeps it there throughout his life. This insight is controlling in the sense that it affects almost all of the other ideas and insights in the *Ethics,* but it is not stated nearly as explicitly as it might be.

One more example. Kant's mature thought is often known as critical philosophy. He himself contrasted "criticism" to "dogmatism," which he imputed to many previous philosophers. By "dogmatism" he meant the presumption that the human intellect can arrive at the most important truths by pure thinking, without being aware of its own limitations. What is first required, according to

Kant, is a critical survey and assessment of the mind's resources and powers. Thus, the limitation of the mind is a controlling principle in Kant in a way that it is not in any philosopher who precedes him in time. But while this is perfectly clear because explicitly stated in the *Critique of Pure Reason,* it is not stated, because it is assumed, in the *Critique of Judgment,* Kant's major work in aesthetics. Nevertheless, it is controlling there as well.

This is all we can say about finding the controlling principles in a philosophical book, because we are not sure that we can tell you how to discover them. Sometimes it takes years to do this, and many readings and rereadings. Nevertheless, it is the ideal goal of a good and thorough reading, and you should keep in mind that it is ultimately what you must try to do if you are to understand your author. Despite the difficulty of discovering these controlling principles, however, we do not recommend that you take the shortcut of reading books about the philosophers, their lives and opinions. The discovery you come to on your own will be much more valuable than someone else's ideas.

Once you have found an author's controlling principles, you will want to decide whether he adheres to them throughout his work. Unfortunately, philosophers, even the best of them, often do not do so. Consistency, Emerson said, "is the hobgoblin of little minds." That is a very carefree statement, but although it is probably wise to remember it, there is no doubt, either, that inconsistency in a philosopher is a serious problem. If a philosopher is inconsistent, you have to decide which of two sets of propositions he really means—the first principles, as he states them; or the conclusions, which do not in fact follow from the principles as stated. Or you may decide that neither is valid.

The reading of philosophical works has special aspects that relate to the difference between philosophy and science. We are here considering only theoretical works in philosophy, such as metaphysical treatises or books about the philosophy of nature.

The philosophical problem is to explain, not to describe, as science does, the nature of things. Philosophy asks about more than the connections of phenomena. It seeks to penetrate to the ultimate causes and conditions that underlie them. Such problems are satisfactorily explored only when the answers to them are supported by clear arguments and analysis.

The major effort of the reader, therefore, must be with respect to the terms and the initial propositions. Although the philosopher, like the scientist, has a technical terminology, the words that express his terms are usually taken from common speech, but used in a very special sense. This demands special care from the reader. If he does not overcome the tendency to use familiar words in a familiar way, he will probably make gibberish and nonsense of the book.

The basic terms of philosophical discussions are, of course, abstract. But so are those of science. No general knowledge is expressible except in abstract terms. There is nothing particularly difficult about abstractions. We use them every day of our lives and in every sort of conversation. However, the words "abstract" and "concrete" seem to trouble many persons.

Whenever you talk generally about anything, you are using abstractions. What you perceive through your senses is always concrete and particular. What you think with your mind is always abstract and general. To understand an "abstract word" is to have the idea it expresses. "Having an idea" is just another way of saying that you understand some general aspect of the things you experience concretely. You cannot see or touch or even imagine the general aspect thus referred to. If you could, there would be no difference between the senses and the mind. People who try to imagine what ideas refer to befuddle themselves, and end up with a hopeless feeling about all abstractions.

Just as inductive arguments should be the reader's main focus in the case of scientific books, so here, in the case of philosophy, you must pay closest attention to the philosopher's principles. They may be either things he asks you to assume with him, or matters that he calls self-evident. There is no trouble about assumptions. Make them to see what follows, even if you yourself have contrary presuppositions. It is a good mental exercise to pretend that you believe something you really do not believe. And the clearer you are about your own prejudgments, the more likely you will be not to misjudge those made by others.

It is the other sort of principles that may cause trouble. Few philosophical books fail to state some propositions that the author regards as self-evident. Such propositions are drawn directly from experience rather than proved by other propositions.

The thing to remember is that the experience from which they are drawn, as we have noted more than once, is, unlike the scientist's special experience, the common experience of mankind. The philosopher does no work in laboratories, no research in the field. Hence to understand and test a philosopher's leading principles you do not need the extrinsic aid of special experience, obtained by methodical investigation. He refers you to your own common sense and daily observation of the world in which you live.

In other words, the method according to which you should read a philosophical book is very similar to the method according to which it is written. A philosopher, faced with a problem, can do nothing but think about it. A reader, faced with a philosophical book, can do nothing but read it—which means, as we know, thinking about it. There are no other aids except the mind itself.

But this essential loneliness of reader and book is precisely the situation that we imagined at the beginning of our long discussion of the rules of analytical reading. Thus you can see why we say that the rules of reading, as we have stated and explained them, apply more directly to the reading of philosophical books than to the reading of any other kind.

On Making Up Your Own Mind

A good theoretical work in philosophy is as free from oratory and propaganda as a good scientific treatise. You do not have to be concerned about the "personality" of the author, or investigate his social and economic background. There is utility, however, in reading the works of other great philosophers who have dealt with the same problems as your author. The philosophers have carried on a long conversation with each other in the history of thought. You had better listen in on it before you make up your mind about what any of them says.

The fact that philosophers disagree should not trouble you, for two reasons. First, the fact of disagreement, if it is persistent, may point to a great unsolved and, perhaps, insoluble problem. It is good to know where the true mysteries are. Second, the disagreements of others are relatively unimportant. Your responsibility is only to make up your own mind. In the presence of the long conversation that the philosophers have carried on through their books, you must judge what is true and what is false. When you have read a philosophical book well—and that means reading other philosophers on the same subject, too—you are in a position to judge.

It is, indeed, the most distinctive mark of philosophical questions that everyone must answer them for himself. Taking the opinions of others is not solving them, but evading them. And your answers must be solidly grounded, with arguments to back them up. This means, above all, that you cannot depend on the testimony of experts, as you may have to do in the case of science.

The reason is that the questions philosophers ask are simply more important than the questions asked by anyone else. Except children.

A Note on Theology

There are two kinds of theology, natural theology and dogmatic theology. Natural theology is a branch of philosophy; it is the last chapter, as it were, in metaphysics. If you ask, for example, whether causation is an endless process, whether everything is caused, you may find yourself, if you answer in the affirmative, involved in an infinite regress. Therefore you may have to posit some originating cause that is not itself caused. Aristotle called this uncaused cause an unmoved mover. You could give it other names—you could even say that it was merely another name for God—but the point is that you would have arrived at the conception by the unaided effort—the natural working—of your mind.

Dogmatic theology differs from philosophy in that its first principles are articles of faith adhered to by the communicants of some religion. A work of dogmatic theology always depends upon dogmas and the authority of a church that proclaims them.

If you are not of the faith, if you do not belong to the church, you can nevertheless read such a theological book *well* by treating its dogmas with the same respect you treat the assumptions of a mathematician. But you must always keep in mind that an article of faith is not something that the faithful *assume*. Faith, for those who have it, is the most certain form of knowledge, not a tentative opinion.

Understanding this seems to be difficult for many readers today. Typically, they make either or both of two mistakes in dealing with dogmatic theology. The first mistake is to refuse to accept, even temporarily, the articles of faith that are the first principles of the author. As a result, the reader continues to struggle with these first principles, never really paying attention to the book itself. The second mistake is to assume that, because the first principles are dogmatic, the arguments based on them, the reasoning that they support, and the conclusions to which they lead are all dogmatic in the same way. It is true enough, of course, if certain principles are accepted, and the reasoning that is based on them is cogent, that the conclusions must then be accepted too—at least to the extent that the principles are. But if the reasoning is defective, the most acceptable first principles will lead to invalid conclusions.

We are speaking here, as you can see, of the difficulties that face a non-believing reader of a theological work. His task is to accept the first principles as true while he is reading the book, and then to read it with all the care that any good expository work deserves. The

faithful reader of a work that is essential to his faith has other difficulties to face. However, these problems are not confined to reading
theology.

How to Read "Canonical" Books

There is one very interesting kind of book, one kind of reading, that
has not yet been discussed. We use the term "canonical" to refer to
such books; in an older tradition we might have called them "sacred"
or "holy," but those words no longer apply to all such works, though
they still apply to some of them.

A prime example is the Holy Bible, when it is read not as literature but instead as the revealed Word of God. For orthodox Marxists,
however, the works of Marx must be read in much the same way as
the Bible must be read by orthodox Jews or Christians. And Mao
Tse-tung's Little Red Book has an equally canonical character for a
"faithful" Chinese Communist.

The notion of a canonical book can be extended beyond these
obvious examples. Consider any institution—a church, a political
party, a society—that among other things (1) is a teaching institution, (2) has a body of doctrine to teach, and (3) has a faithful and
obedient membership. The members of any such organization read
reverentially. They do not—even cannot—question the authorized
or right reading of the books that to them are canonical. The faithful
are debarred by their faith from finding error in the "sacred" text, to
say nothing of finding nonsense there.

Orthodox Jews read the Old Testament in this way; Christians,
the New Testament; Muslims, the Koran; orthodox Marxists, the
works of Marx and Lenin and, depending on the political climate,
those of Stalin; orthodox Freudian psychoanalysts, the works of
Freud; U.S. Army officers, the infantry manual. And you can think
of many more examples by yourself.

In fact, almost all of us, even if we have not quite reached it,
have approached the situation in which we must read canonically.

A fledgling lawyer, intent on passing the bar exams, must read certain texts in a certain way in order to attain a perfect score. So with doctors and other professionals; and indeed so with all of us when, as students, we were required at the peril of "failure" to read a text according to our professor's interpretation of it. (Of course, not all professors fail their students for disagreeing with them!)

The characteristics of this kind of reading are perhaps summed up in the word "orthodox," which is almost always applicable. The word comes from two Greek roots, meaning "right opinion." These are books for which there is *one and only one right reading;* any other reading or interpretation is fraught with peril, from the loss of an "A" to the damnation of one's soul. This characteristic carries with it an obligation. The faithful reader of a canonical book *is obliged to make sense out of it* and to find it true in one or another sense of "true." If he cannot do this by himself, *he is obliged to go to someone who can.* This may be a priest or a rabbi, or it may be his superior in the party hierarchy, or it may be his professor. In any case, he is obliged to accept the resolution of his problem that is offered him. He reads essentially without freedom; but in return for this he gains a kind of satisfaction that is possibly never obtained when reading other books.

Here, in fact, we must stop. The problem of reading the Holy Book—if you have faith that it is the Word of God—is the most difficult problem in the whole field of reading. There have been more books written about how to read Scripture than about all other aspects of the art of reading together. The Word of God is obviously the most difficult writing men can read; but it is also, if you believe it *is* the Word of God, the most important to read. The effort of the faithful has been duly proportionate to the difficulty of the task. It would be true to say that, in the European tradition at least, the Bible is *the* book in more senses than one. It has been not only the most widely read, but also the most carefully read, book of all.

19

How to Read Social Science

The concepts and terminology of the social sciences pervade almost everything we read today.

Modern journalism, for example, does not limit itself to reporting facts, except in the kind of shorthand, "who-what-why-when-where" news story that one finds on the front page of a newspaper. Journalists, much more commonly, enmesh the facts in interpretation, commentary, analysis of the news. These interpretations and comments draw on the concepts and terminology of the social sciences.

These concepts and this terminology are also reflected in the vast number of current books and articles that may be grouped together under the heading of social criticism. We are confronted with a continuous flow of literature on such subjects as race problems, crime, law enforcement, poverty, education, welfare, war and peace, good and bad government. Much of this literature borrows its ideology and language from the social sciences.

The literature of social science is not confined to nonfiction. There is also a large and important category of contemporary writing that might be termed social-science fiction. Here the aim is to create artificial models of society that allow us, for example, to explore the social consequences of technological innovation. The organization of social power, the kinds of property and ownership, and the distribution of wealth are variously described, deplored, or lauded in novels, plays, stories, moving pictures, television shows. Insofar as they do this they may be said to have social significance or to contain "relevant messages." At the same time they draw on and disseminate elements of the social sciences.

Furthermore, there is hardly any social, economic, or political problem that has not been tackled by specialists in these fields, either on their own or by invitation from officials who are actively coping with these problems. Specialists in the social sciences help to formulate the problems and are called upon to help in dealing with them.

Far from the least important factor in the growing pervasiveness of the social sciences is their introduction at the high school level and in the junior and community colleges. In fact, student enrollments in social science courses are running far ahead of enrollments in the more traditional literature and language courses. And enrollments in social science courses greatly exceed those in courses dealing with the "pure" sciences.

What Is Social Science?

We have been talking of social science as if it were a single entity. That is hardly the case.

Which, in fact, are the social sciences? One way to answer the question is to see what departments and disciplines universities group under this name. Social science divisions usually include departments of anthropology, economics, politics, and sociology. Why do they not ordinarily include as well schools of law, education, business, social service, and public administration, all of which draw on the concepts and methods of the social sciences for their development? The reason commonly given for the separation of these schools from the social science divisions is that the main purpose of such schools is to train for professional work outside of the university, while the previously mentioned departments are more exclusively dedicated to the pursuit of systematic knowledge of human society, an activity that usually goes on within the university.

There is presently a trend in universities toward the establishment of centers and institutes for interdisciplinary studies. These centers cut across the conventional social science departments and professional schools, and include studies in the theories and methods of statistics, demography, psephology (the science of elections and polling), policy- and decision-making, recruitment and treatment of personnel, public administration, human ecology, and many more. Such centers are producing studies and reports that incorporate findings of a dozen or more of these specialties. Considerable sophistication is required even to discern the various strands of these efforts, let alone judge the validity of the findings and conclusions.

What about psychology? Those social scientists who interpret their field strictly tend to exclude psychology on the grounds that it concerns itself with individual and personal characteristics, while the social sciences proper focus on cultural, institutional, and environmental factors. Those who are less strict, while conceding that physiological psychology should be subsumed under the biological sciences, hold that psychology, both normal and abnormal, should be regarded as a social science on the grounds of the inseparability of the individual from his social environment.

Psychology, incidentally, is a prime example of a social science area that is currently enjoying great popularity among students. It is possible that enrollments in psychology across the country are larger than in any other subject. And the literature of psychology, at every level from the most technical to the most popular, is enormous.

What of the behavioral sciences? Where do they fit into the social science picture? As originally used, the term behavioral science included sociology and anthropology and the behavioral aspects of biology, economics, geography, law, psychology and psychiatry, and political science. The accent on behavior served to emphasize observable, measurable behavior capable of being systematically investigated and of producing verifiable findings. Recently, the term behavioral sciences has come to be used almost as a synonym of the term social sciences, but many purists object to this usage.

Finally, what about history? It is acknowledged that the social sciences draw on the study of history for data and for exemplifications of their generalizations. However, although history, viewed as accounts of particular events and persons, may be scientific in the minimal sense of constituting systematic knowledge, it is not a science in the sense that of itself it yields systematic knowledge of patterns or laws of behavior and development.

Is it possible, then, to define what we mean by social science? We think so, at least for the purposes of this chapter. Such fields as anthropology, economics, politics, and sociology constitute a kind of central core of social science, which almost all social scientists would include in any definition. In addition, we think it would be conceded by most social scientists that much, though not all, of the literature of such fields as law, education, and public administration, and some of the literature of such fields as business and social service, together with a considerable portion of psychological literature, falls within the confines of a reasonable definition. We will assume that such a definition, although admittedly imprecise, is clear to you in what follows.

The Apparent Ease of Reading Social Science

A great deal of social science writing seems like the easiest possible material to read. The data are often drawn from experiences familiar to the reader—in this respect, social science is like poetry or philosophy—and the style of exposition is usually narrative, already familiar to the reader through his reading of fiction and history.

In addition, we have all become familiar with the jargon of social science and use it often. Such terms as culture (cross, counter, and sub), in-group, alienation, status, input/output, infra-structure, ethnic, behavioral, consensus, and scores like them, tend to appear in almost every conversation and in almost everything we read.

Consider the word "society" itself. What a chameleon-like word it is, what a host of adjectives can be placed in front of it, while throughout it continues to convey the broad notion of people living together rather than in isolation. We hear of the aberrant society, the abortive society, the acquiescent society, the acquisitive society, the affluent society, and we can continue on through the alphabet until we arrive at the zymotic society, which is one that is in a continuous state of ferment, not unlike our own.

"Social," as an adjective, is also a word of many and familiar meanings. There is social power, social pressure, and social promise—and then, of course, there are the ubiquitous social problems. The last phrase, indeed, is a fine example of the specious ease that is involved in both the reading and the writing of social science literature. We would be willing to wager that in the last few months, if not the last few weeks, you have read and even possibly written the phrase "political, economic, and social problems." When you read or wrote it, you were probably clear as to what was meant by political and economic problems. But what did you, or the author, mean by social problems?

The jargon and metaphors of much social science writing, together with the deep feeling that often imbues it, make for deceptively easy reading. The references are to matters that are readily familiar to the reader; indeed, he reads or hears about them almost daily. Furthermore, his attitudes and feelings regarding them are usually firmly developed. Philosophy, too, deals with the world as we commonly know it, but we are not ordinarily "committed" on philosophical questions. But on matters with which social science deals, we are likely to have strong opinions.

Difficulties of Reading Social Science

Paradoxically, the very factors we have discussed, the factors which make social science seem easy to read, also make it difficult to read. Consider the last factor mentioned, for instance—the commitment that you as a reader are likely to have to some view of the matter your author is considering. Many readers fear that it would be disloyal to their commitment to stand apart and impersonally question what they are reading. Yet this is necessary whenever you read analytically. Such a stance is implied by the rules of reading, at least by the rules of structural outlining and interpretation. If you are going to answer the first two questions that should be asked of anything you read, you must, as it were, check your opinions at the door. You cannot understand a book if you refuse to hear what it is saying.

The very familiarity of the terms and propositions in social science writing is also an obstacle to understanding. Many social scientists recognize this themselves. They object vigorously to the use of more or less technical terms and concepts in popular journalism and other writings. An example of such a concept is that of the Gross National Product (GNP). In serious economic writing, the concept is employed in a relatively limited sense. But many reporters and columnists, some social scientists say, make the concept do too much work. They use it too widely, without really understanding what it means. Obviously, if the writer of something you are reading is confused about his use of a key term, you, as reader, must be so, too.

Let us try to make this point clear by drawing a distinction between the social sciences, on the one hand, and the so-called hard sciences—physics, chemistry, and the like—on the other hand. We have observed that the author of a scientific book (taking "scientific" in the latter sense) makes clear what he assumes and what he desires to prove, and also makes sure that his terms and propositions are easy to spot. Since coming to terms and finding the propositions is a main part of reading any expository work, this means that much of the work is done for you in the case of such books. You may still have difficulty with the mathematical form of presentation; and if you do not have a firm grasp of the arguments and of the experimental or observational basis of the conclusions, you will find it hard to criticize the book—that is, to answer the questions, Is it true? and What of it? Nevertheless, there is an important sense in which the reading of this kind of scientific books is easier than the reading of most other kinds of expository works.

Another way to say what it is that the hard scientist does is to say that he "stipulates his usage"—that is, he informs you what terms are essential to his argument and how he is going to use them. Such stipulations usually occur at the beginning of the book, in the form of definitions, postulates, axioms, and so forth. Since stipulation of usage is characteristic of these fields, it has been said that they are like games or have a "game structure." Stipulation of usage is like establishing the rules of a game. If you want to play poker, you do not dispute the rule that three of a kind is a better hand than two pairs; if you want to play bridge, you do not argue with the convention that a queen takes a jack (in the same suit), or that the highest trump takes any other card (in a suit contract). Similarly, you do not dispute a hard scientist's stipulations in reading his book. You accept them, and go on from there.

Until quite recently, at least, stipulation of usage was not as common in the social sciences as it is in the hard sciences. One reason for this is that the social sciences were typically not mathematicized. Another is that stipulation of usage in the social or behavioral sciences is *harder to do*. It is one thing to define a circle or an isosceles triangle; it is quite another to define an economic depression or mental health. Even if a social scientist attempts to define such terms, his readers are inclined to question his usage. As a result, the social scientist must continue to struggle with his own terms throughout his work—and his struggle creates problems for his reader.

The most important source of difficulty in reading social science derives from the fact that this field of literature is a mixed, rather than a pure, kind of expository writing. We have seen how history is a mixture of fiction and science, and how we must read it with that in mind. We are familiar with this kind of mixture; we have had a great deal of experience with it. The situation in social science is quite different. Much social science is a mixture of science, philosophy, and history, often with some fiction thrown in for good measure.

If social science were always the same kind of mixture, we could become familiar with it as we have with history. But this is far from the case. The mixture itself shifts from book to book, and the reader is confronted with the task of identifying the various strands that go to make up what he is reading. These strands may change in the course of a single book as well as in different books. It is no easy job to separate them out.

You will recall that the first step the analytical reader has to take is to answer the question, What kind of book is this? In the case of fiction, that question is relatively easy to answer. In the case of science and philosophy, it is also relatively easy; and even if history is a mixed form, at least the reader ordinarily knows that he is reading history. But the various strands that go to make up social science— sometimes interwoven in this pattern, sometimes in that, sometimes in still another—make the question very hard to answer when we are reading a work in any of the fields involved. The problem, in fact, *is precisely as difficult as the problem of defining social science.*

Nevertheless, the analytical reader must somehow manage to answer the question. It is not only his first task, but also his most important. If he is able to say what strands go to make up the book he is reading, he will have moved a good way toward understanding it.

Outlining a work in social science poses no special problems, but coming to terms with the author, as we have already suggested, may be extremely difficult, owing to the relative inability of the author to stipulate his usage. Nevertheless, some common understanding of the key terms is usually possible. From terms we move to propositions and arguments, and here again there is no special problem if the book is a good one. But the last question, What of it?, requires considerable restraint on the part of the reader. It is here that the situation we described earlier may occur—namely, the situation in which the reader says, "I cannot fault the author's conclusions, but I nevertheless disagree with them." This comes about, of course, because of the prejudgments that the reader is likely to have concerning the author's approach and his conclusions.

Reading Social Science Literature

More than once in the course of this chapter we have employed the phrase "social science literature" instead of "social science book." The reason is that it is customary in social science to read several books about a subject rather than one book for its own sake. This is not only because social science is a relatively new field with as yet but few classic texts. It is also because when reading social science, we often have our eye primarily on *a particular matter or problem,* rather than on *a particular author or book.* We are interested in law enforcement, for example, and we read half a dozen works on the subject. Or our interest may concern race relations, or education, or taxation, or the problems of local government. Typically, there is no single, authoritative work on any of these subjects, and we must therefore read several. One sign of this is that social science authors themselves, in order to keep up with the times, must constantly bring out new, revised editions of their works; and new works supersede older ones and rapidly render them obsolete.

To some extent, a similar situation obtains in philosophy, as we have already observed. Fully to understand a philosopher, you should make some attempt to read the philosophers your author himself has read, the philosophers who have influenced him. To some extent it is also true in history, where we suggested that, if you want to discover the truth of the past, you had better read several books about it rather than one. But in those cases the likelihood that you would find one major, authoritative work was much greater. In social science that is not so common, and so the necessity of reading several works rather than one is much more urgent.

The rules of analytical reading are not in themselves applicable to the reading of several works on the same subject. They apply to each of the works that is read, of course, and if you want to read any of them well you have to observe them. But new rules of reading are required as we pass from the third level of reading (analytical reading), to the fourth (syntopical reading). We are now prepared to tackle that fourth level, having come to see, because of this character-istic of social science, the need for it.

Pointing this out makes it clear why we relegated the discussion of the social sciences to the last chapter in Part Three. It should now be clear why we organized the discussion in the way we did. We began with the reading of practical books, which are different from all others because of the special obligation to act that the reader is under if he agrees with and accepts what he is reading. We then treated fiction and poetry, which pose special problems that are un-like those of expository books. Finally, we dealt with three types of theoretical, expository writing—science and mathematics, philoso-phy, and social science. Social science came last because of the need to read it syntopically. Thus the present chapter serves as both the end of Part Three and an introduction to Part Four.

PART 4

The Ultimate Goals of Reading

20

The Fourth Level of Reading: Syntopical Reading

So far we have not said anything specific about how to read two or more books on the same subject. We have tried to suggest that when certain subjects are discussed, more than one book is relevant, and we have also from time to time mentioned, in a very informal way, certain related books and authors in various fields. Knowing that more than one book is relevant to a particular question is the first requirement in any project of syntopical reading. Knowing which books should be read, in a general way, is the second requirement. The second requirement is a great deal harder to satisfy than the first.

The difficulty becomes evident as soon as we examine the phrase "two or more books on the same subject." What do we mean by "same subject"? Perhaps this is clear enough when the subject is a single historical period or event, but in hardly any other sphere is there much clarity to be found. *Gone with the Wind* and *War and Peace* are both novels about a great war—but there, for the most part, the resemblance stops. Stendhal's *The Charterhouse of Parma* is "about" the same conflict—that is, the Napoleonic Wars—that Tolstoy's novel is "about." But of course neither is about the war, or indeed about war in general, as such. War provides the context or background of both stories—as it does for much of human life—but it is the stories on which the authors rivet our attention. We may learn something about the war—in fact, Tolstoy once said that he had learned much of what he knew about battles from Stendhal's account of the Battle of Waterloo—but we do not go to these novels or any others if our primary intention is to study war.

You could have anticipated that this situation would obtain in the case of fiction. It is inherent in the fact that the novelist does not communicate in the same way that an expository writer does. But the situation obtains in the case of expository works, as well.

Suppose, for example, that you are interested in reading about the idea of love. Since the literature of love is vast, you would have relatively little difficulty in creating a bibliography of books to read. Suppose that you have done that, by asking advisors, by searching through the card catalogue of a good library, and by examining the bibliography in a good scholarly treatise on the subject. And suppose in addition that you have confined yourself to expository works, despite the undoubted interest of novelists and poets in the subject. (We will explain why it would be advisable to do this later.) You now begin to examine the books in your bibliography. What do you find?

Even a cursory perusal reveals a very great range of reference. There is hardly a single human action that has not been called—in one way or another—an act of love. Nor is the range confined to the human sphere. If you proceed far enough in your reading, you will find that love has been attributed to almost everything in the universe; that is, everything that exists has been said by someone either to love or to be loved—or both.

Stones are said to love the center of the earth. The upward motion of fire is called a function of its love. The attraction of iron filings to a magnet is described as an effect of love. Tracts have been written on the love life of amoebae, paramecia, snails, and ants, to say nothing of most of the so-called higher animals, who are said to love their masters as well as one another. When we come to human beings, we discover that authors speak and write of their love for men, women, a woman, a man, children, themselves, mankind, money, art, domesticity, principles, a cause, an occupation or profession, adventure, security, ideas, a country life, loving itself, a beefsteak, or wine. In certain learned treatises, the motions of the heavenly bodies are said to be inspired by love; in others, angels and devils are differentiated by the quality of their love. And of course God is said to *be* Love.

Confronted with this enormous range of reference, how are we to state what the subject is that we are investigating? Can we even be sure that there is a single subject? When one person says "I love cheese," and another says "I love football," and a third says "I love mankind," are they all three using the word in any sense that is common? After all, one eats cheese but not football or mankind, one plays football but not cheese or mankind, and whatever "I love mankind" means, that meaning does not seem to be applicable to cheese or football. And yet all three do use the same word. Is there in fact some deep reason for that, some reason that is not immediately apparent on the surface? Difficult as that question is, can we say that we have identified the "same subject" until we have answered it?

Faced with this chaotic situation, you may decide to limit the enquiry to human love—to love between human beings, of the same sex or different sexes, of the same age or different ages, and so forth. That would rule out the three statements we have just discussed. But you would still find, even if you read only a small portion of the available books about the subject, a very great range of reference. You would find, for instance, that love is said by some writers to consist wholly in acquisitive desire, usually sexual desire; that is, love is merely a name for the attraction that almost all animals feel toward members of the opposite sex. But you would also find other authors who maintain that love, properly speaking, contains no acquisitive desire whatever, and consists in pure benevolence. Do acquisitive desire and benevolence have anything in common, considering that acquisitive desire always implies wanting some good *for oneself,* while benevolence implies wanting a good *for someone else?*

At least acquisitive desire and benevolence share a common note of tendency, of desire in some very abstract sense of the term. But your investigation of the literature of the subject would soon uncover writers who conceive of the essence of love as being cognitive rather than appetitive. Love, these writers maintain, is an intellectual act, not an emotional one. In other words, *knowing* that another person is *admirable* always precedes *desiring* him or her, in either of the two senses of desire. Such authors do not deny that desire enters into the picture, but they do deny that desire should be called love.

Let us suppose—in fact, we think it can be done—that you are able to identify some common meaning in these various conceptions of human love. Even then not all of your problems are solved. Consider the ways in which love manifests itself between and among human beings. Is the love that a man and woman have for each other the same when they are courting as when they are married, the same when they are in their twenties as when they are in their seventies? Is the love that a woman has for her husband the same as that she has for her children? Does a mother's love for her children change as they grow up? Is the love of a brother for his sister the same as his love for his father? Does a child's love for its parents change as he or she grows? Is the love that a man has for a woman, either his wife or some other, the same as the friendship he feels for another man, and does it make a difference what relationship he has with the man—such as one with whom he goes bowling, one with whom he works, and one whose intellectual company he enjoys? Does the fact that "love" and "friendship" are different words mean that the emotions they name (if that is in fact what they name) differ? Can two men of different ages be friends? Can they be friends if they are markedly different in some other respect, such as possession of wealth or degree of intelligence? Can women be friends at all? Can brothers and sisters be friends, or brother and brother, or sister and sister? Can you retain a friendship with someone you either borrow money from or lend it to? It not, why not? Can a boy love his teacher? Does it make a difference whether the teacher is male or female? If humanoid robots existed, could human beings love them? If we discovered intelligent beings on Mars or some other planet, could we love them? Can we love someone we have never met, like a movie star or the President? If we feel that we hate someone, is that really an expression of love?

These are just a few of the questions that would be raised by your reading of even a part of the standard expository literature of love. There are many other questions that could be asked. However, we think we have made the point. A curious paradox is involved in any project of syntopical reading. Although this level of reading is defined as the reading of two or more books on the same subject, which implies that the identification of the subject matter occurs before the reading begins, it is in a sense true that the identification of the subject matter must follow the reading, not precede it. In the case of love, you might have to read a dozen or a hundred works before you could decide what you were reading about. And when you had done that, you might have to conclude that half of the works you had read were not on the subject at all.

The Role of Inspection in Syntopical Reading

We have stated more than once that the levels of reading are cumulative, that a higher level includes all of those that precede or lie below it. It is now time to explain what that means in the case of syntopical reading.

You will recall that in explaining the relationship between inspectional reading and analytical reading, we pointed out that the two steps in inspectional reading—first, skimming; and second, superficial reading—anticipated the first two steps in analytical reading. Skimming helps to prepare you for the first step of analytical reading, in the course of which you identify the subject matter of whatever you are reading, state what kind of book it is, and outline its structure. Superficial reading, while it is also helpful in that first step of analytical reading, is primarily a preparation for the second step, when you are called upon to interpret a book's contents by coming to terms with the author, stating his propositions, and following his arguments.

In a somewhat analogous fashion, both inspectional and analytical reading can be considered as anticipations or preparations for syntopical reading. It is here, in fact, that inspectional reading comes into its own as a major tool or instrument for the reader.

Let us suppose once more that you have a bibliography of a hundred or so titles, all of which appear to be on the subject of love. If you read every one of them analytically, you would not only end up with a fairly clear idea of the subject that you were investigating—the "same subject" of the syntopical reading project—but you would also know which, if any, of the books you had read were not on that subject and thus irrelevant to your needs. But to read a hundred books analytically might well take you ten years. If you were able to devote full time to the project, it would still take many months. Some shortcut is obviously necessary, in the face of the paradox we have mentioned concerning syntopical reading.

That shortcut is provided by your skill in inspectional reading. The first thing to do when you have amassed your bibliography is to *inspect all of the books on your list*. You should not read any of them analytically before inspecting *all* of them. Inspectional reading will not acquaint you with all of the intricacies of the subject matter, or with all of the insights that your authors can provide, but it will perform two essential functions. First, it will give you a clear enough idea of your subject so that your subsequent analytical reading of *some* of the books on the list is productive. And second, it will allow you to cut down your bibliography to a more manageable size.

We can hardly think of any advice that would be more useful for students, especially graduate and research students, than this, if they would only heed it. In our experience, a certain number of students at those advanced levels of schooling have some capability of reading actively and analytically. There may not be enough of them, and they may be far from perfect readers, but they at least know how to get at the meat of a book, to make reasonably intelligible statements about it, and to fit it into a plot or plan of their subject matter. But their efforts are enormously wasteful because they do not understand *how to read some books faster than others.* They spend the same amount of time and effort on every book or article they read. As a result, they do not read those books that deserve a really good reading as well as they deserve, and they waste time on works that deserve less attention.

The skillful inspectional reader does more than classify a book in his mental card catalogue, and achieve a superficial knowledge of its contents. He also discovers, in the very short time it takes him to inspect it, *whether the book says something important about his subject or not.* He may not yet know what that something is precisely—that discovery will probably have to wait for another reading. But he has learned one of two things. Either the book is one to which he must return for light, or it is one that, no matter how enjoyable or informative, contains no enlightenment and therefore does not have to be read again.

There is a reason why this advice is often unheeded. In the case of analytical reading, we said that the skillful reader performs concurrently steps that the beginner must treat as separate. By analogy, it might seem that this kind of preparation for syntopical reading—the inspection of all of the books on your list before starting the analytical reading of any of them—could be done concurrently with analytical reading. But we do not believe that can be done by any reader, no matter how skillful. And this indeed is the mistake that so many younger researchers make. Thinking they can collapse these two steps into one, they end up reading everything at the same rate, which may be either too fast or too slow for a particular work, but in any event is wrong for most of the books they read.

Once you have identified, by inspection, the books that are relevant to your subject matter, you can then proceed to read them syntopically. Note that in the last sentence we did not say "proceed to read them analytically," as you might have expected. In a sense, of course, you do have to read each of the individual works that, together, constitute the literature of your subject, with those skills that you acquired by applying the rules of analytical reading. But it must never be forgotten that *the art of analytical reading applies to the read-*

ing of a single book, when understanding of that book is the aim in view. As we will see, the aim in syntopical reading is quite different.

The Five Steps in Syntopical Reading

We are now prepared to explain how to read syntopically. We will assume that, by your inspection of a number of books, you have a pretty good idea of the subject that at least some of them are about, and furthermore that this is the subject you want to investigate. What, then, do you do?

There are five steps in syntopical reading. We shall not call them rules, although we might, for if any of the steps is not taken, syntopical reading becomes much more difficult, perhaps impossible. We will discuss them roughly in the order in which they occur, although in a sense all of them have to take place for any of them to.

STEP 1 IN SYNTOPICAL READING: FINDING THE RELEVANT PASSAGES. Since we are of course assuming that you know how to read analytically, we are assuming that you could read each of the relevant books thoroughly if you wanted to. But that would be to place the individual books first in the order of your priorities, and your problem second. In fact, the order is reversed. *In syntopical reading, it is you and your concerns that are primarily to be served, not the books that you read.*

Hence the first step at this level of reading is another inspection of the whole works that you have identified as relevant. Your aim is to find the passages in the books that are most germane to your needs. It is unlikely that the whole of any of the books is directly on the subject you have chosen or that is troubling you. Even if this is so, as it very rarely is, you should read the book quickly. You do not want to lose sight of the fact that you are reading it for an ulterior purpose—namely, for the light it may throw on your own problem—not for its own sake.

It might seem that this step could be taken concurrently with the previously described inspection of the book, the purpose of which was to discover whether the book was at all relevant to your concerns. In many cases, that is so. But it is unwise to consider that this is always possible. Remember that one of the aims of your first inspection of the book was to zero in on the subject matter of your syntopical reading project. We have said that an adequate understanding of the problem is not always available until you have inspected many of the books on your original list. Therefore, to try to identify the *relevant passages* at the same time that you identify the *relevant books* is often perilous. Unless you are very skillful, or already quite familiar with your subject, you had better treat the two steps as separate.

What is important here is to recognize the difference between the first books that you read in the course of syntopical reading, and those that you come to after you have read many others on the subject. In the case of the later books, you probably already have a fairly clear idea of your problem, and in that case the two steps can coalesce. But at the beginning, they should be kept rigorously separated. Otherwise, you are likely to make serious mistakes in identifying the relevant passages, mistakes that will have to be corrected later with a consequent waste of time and effort.

Above all, remember that your task is not so much to achieve an overall understanding of the particular book before you as to find out how it can be useful to you *in a connection that may be very far from the author's own purpose in writing it.* That does not matter at this stage of the proceedings. The author can help you to solve your own problem without having intended to. In syntopical reading, as we have noted, the books that are read serve you, not the other way around. In this sense, syntopical reading is the most active reading you can do. Analytical reading is also active, of course. But when you read a book analytically, you put yourself in a relation to it of disciple to master. When you read syntopically, *you* must be the master of the situation.

Because this is so, you must go about the business of coming to terms with your authors in a somewhat different way than before.

STEP 2 IN SYNTOPICAL READING: BRINGING THE AUTHORS TO TERMS. In interpretive reading (the second stage of analytical reading) the first rule requires you to come to terms with the author, which means identifying his key words and discovering how he uses them. But now you are faced with a number of different authors, and it is unlikely that they will have all used the same words, or even the same terms. *Thus it is you who must establish the terms, and bring your authors to them rather than the other way around.*

This is probably the most difficult step in syntopical reading. What it really comes down to is forcing an author *to use your language, rather than using his.* All of our normal reading habits are opposed to this. As we have pointed out several times, we assume that the author of a book we want to read analytically is our better, and this is particularly true if the book is a great one. Our tendency is to accept the author's terms and his organization of the subject matter, no matter how active we may be in trying to understand him. In syntopical reading, however, we will very quickly be lost if we accept any one author's terminology. We may understand *his* book, but we will fail to understand the others, and we will find that not much light is shed on the subject in which we are interested.

Not only must we resolutely refuse to accept the terminology of *any one* author; we must also be willing to face the possibility that *no* author's terminology will be useful to us. In other words, we must accept the fact that coincidence of terminology between us and any of the authors on our list is merely accidental. Often, indeed, such coincidence will be inconvenient; for if we use one term or set of terms of an author, we may be tempted to use others among his terms, and these may get in the way rather than help.

Syntopical reading, in short, is to a large extent an exercise in translation. We do not have to translate from one natural language to another, as from French to English. But we do impose a common terminology on a number of authors who, whatever natural language they may have shared in common, may not have been specifically concerned with the problem we are trying to solve, and therefore may not have created the ideal terminology for dealing with it.

This means that as we proceed on our project of syntopical reading we must begin to build up a set of terms that first, helps us to understand all of our authors, not just one or a few of them, and second, helps us to solve our problem. That insight leads to the third step.

STEP 3 IN SYNTOPICAL READING: GETTING THE QUESTIONS CLEAR. The second rule of interpretive reading requires us to find the author's key sentences, and from them to develop an understanding of his propositions. Propositions are made up of terms, and of course we must do a similar job on the works we are reading syntopically. But since we ourselves are establishing the terminology in this case, *we are faced with the task of establishing a set of neutral propositions as well.* The best way to do this is to frame a set of questions that shed light on our problem, and to which each of our authors gives answers.

This, too, is difficult. The questions must be stated in such a way and in such an order that they help us to solve the problem we started with, but they also must be framed in such a way that all or most of our authors can be interpreted as giving answers to them. The difficulty is that the questions we want answered may not have been seen as questions by the authors. Their view of the subject may have been quite different from ours.

Sometimes, indeed, we have to accept the fact that an author gives *no* answer to one or more of our questions. In that case, we must record him as silent or indeterminate on the question. But even if he does not discuss the question explicitly, we can sometimes find an implicit answer in his book. *If* he had considered the question, we may conclude, he would *then* have answered it in such and such a way. Restraint is necessary here; we cannot put thoughts into our authors' minds, or words into their mouths. But we also cannot depend entirely on their explicit statements about the problem. If we could depend on any one of them in that way, we probably would have no problem to solve.

We have said that the questions must be put in an order that is helpful to us in our investigation. The order depends on the subject, of course, but some general directions can be suggested. The first questions usually have to do with *the existence or character of the phenomenon or idea we are investigating.* If an author says that the phenomenon exists or that the idea has a certain character, then we may ask further questions of his book. These may have to do with *how the phenomenon is known or how the idea manifests itself.* A final set of questions might have to do with *the consequences of the answers to the previous questions.*

We should not expect that all of our authors will answer our questions in the same way. If they did, we would once again have no problem to solve; it would have been solved by consensus. Since the authors will differ, we are faced with having to take the next step in syntopical reading.

STEP 4 IN SYNTOPICAL READING: DEFINING THE ISSUES. If a question is clear, and if we can be reasonably certain that authors answer it in different ways—perhaps pro and con—then an issue has been defined. It is the issue between the authors who answer the question in one way, and those who answer it in one or another opposing way.

When only two answers are given by all of the authors examined, the issue is a relatively simple one. Often, more than two alternative answers are given to a question. In that case, the opposing answers must be ordered in relation to one another, and the authors who adopt them classified according to their views.

An issue is truly joined when two authors who understand a question in the same way answer it in contrary or contradictory ways. But this does not happen as often as one might wish. Usually, differences in answers must be ascribed to *different conceptions of the question* as often as to *different views of the subject.* The task of the syntopical reader is to define the issues in such a way as to insure that they are joined as well as may be. Sometimes this forces him to frame the question in a way that is not explicitly employed by any author.

There may be many issues involved in the discussion of the problem we are dealing with, but it is likely that they will fall into groups. Questions about the character of the idea under consideration, for example, may generate a number of issues that are connected. A number of issues revolving around a closely connected set of questions may be termed the *controversy* about that aspect of the subject. Such a controversy may be very complicated, and it is the task of the syntopical reader to sort it out and arrange it in an orderly and perspicuous fashion, even if no author has managed to do that. This sorting and arranging of the controversies, as well as of the constituent issues, brings us to the final step in syntopical reading.

STEP 5 IN SYNTOPICAL READING: ANALYZING THE DISCUSSION. So far we have found the relevant passages in the works examined, created a neutral terminology that applies to all or most of the authors examined, framed and ordered a set of questions that most of them can be interpreted as answering, and defined and arranged the issues produced by differing answers to the questions. What then remains to be done?

The first four steps correspond to the first two groups of rules for analytical reading. Those rules, when followed and applied to any book, allowed us to answer the questions, What does it say? and How does it say it? In our syntopical reading project, we are similarly able at this point to answer the same questions about the discussion concerning our problem. In the case of the analytical reading of a single work, two further questions remained to be answered, namely, Is it true? and What of it? In the case of syntopical reading, we are now prepared to address ourselves to similar questions about the discussion.

Let us assume that the problem with which we began was not a simple one, but was rather one of those perennial problems with which thinkers have struggled for centuries, and about which good men have disagreed and can continue to disagree. We should recognize, on this assumption, that our task as syntopical readers is not merely to answer the questions ourselves—the questions that we have so carefully framed and ordered both to elucidate the discussion of the subject and the subject itself. The truth about a problem of this sort is not found so easily. In fact, we would probably be presumptuous to expect that the truth could be found in any one set of answers to the questions. Rather, it is to be found, if at all, in *the conflict of opposing answers,* many if not all of which may have persuasive evidence and convincing reasons to support them.

The truth, then, insofar as it can be found—the solution to the problem, insofar as that is available to us—consists rather in the *ordered discussion itself* than in any set of propositions or assertions about it. Thus, in order to present this truth to our minds—and to the minds of others—we have to do more than merely ask and answer the questions. We have to ask them in a certain order, and be able to defend that order; we must show how the questions are answered differently and try to say why; and we must be able to point to the texts in the books examined that support our classification of answers. Only when we have done all of this can we claim to have analyzed the discussion of our problem. And only then can we claim to have understood it.

We may, indeed, have done more than that. A thorough analysis of the discussion of a problem may provide the groundwork for further productive work on the problem by others. It can clear away the deadwood and prepare the way for an original thinker to make a breakthrough. Without the work of analysis, that might not have been possible, for the dimensions of the problem might not have been visible.

The Need for Objectivity

An adequate analysis of the discussion of a problem or subject matter identifies and reports the major issues, or basic intellectual oppositions, in that discussion. This does not imply that disagreement is always the dominant feature of every discussion. On the contrary, agreement in most cases accompanies disagreement; that is, on most issues, the opinions or views that present opposite sides of the dispute are shared by several authors, often by many. Seldom do we find a solitary exponent of a controversial position.

The agreement of human beings about the nature of things in any field of inquiry establishes some presumption of the truth of the opinions they commonly hold. But their disagreement establishes the counter-presumption—that *none* of the opinions in conflict, whether shared or not, may be wholly true. Among conflicting opinions, one may, of course, be wholly true and all the rest false; but it is also possible that each expresses *some portion of the whole truth;* and, except for flat and isolated contradictions (which are rare in any discussion of the kind of problems we are dealing with here), it is even possible that *all the conflicting opinions may be false,* just as it is possible for that opinion to be false on which all seem to agree. Some opinion as yet unexpressed may be the truth or nearer to it.

This is another way of saying that the aim of a project of syntopical reading is not final answers to the questions that are developed in the course of it, or the final solution of the problem with which the project began. This is particularly true of the report we might try to make of such syntopical reading. It would be dogmatic, not dialectical, if, on any of the important issues that it identified and analyzed, it asserted or tried to prove the truth or falsity of any view. If it did that, the syntopical analysis would cease to be syntopical; it would become simply one more voice in the discussion, thereby losing its detached and objective character.

The point is not that one more voice carries no weight in the forum of human discussion on important issues. The point is that a different type of contribution to the pursuit of understanding can and should be made. And this contribution consists in being resolutely objective and detached throughout. The special quality that a syntopical analysis tries to achieve can, indeed, be summarized in the two words "dialectical objectivity."

The syntopical reader, in short, tries to *look at all sides and to take no sides.* Of course, he will fail in this exacting ideal. Absolute objectivity is not humanly possible. He may succeed in taking no sides, presenting the issues without prejudice to any partisan point of view, and treating opposing views impartially. But it is easier to take no sides than to look at all sides. In this latter respect, the syntopical reader will undoubtedly fail. All possible sides of an issue cannot be exhaustively enumerated. Nevertheless, he must try.

Taking no sides is easier than looking at all sides, we say, but it remains difficult even so. The syntopical reader must resist certain temptations and know his own mind. Perfect dialectical objectivity is not guaranteed by avoiding *explicit* judgments on the truth of conflicting opinions. Partiality can intrude in a variety of subtle ways— by the manner in which arguments are summarized, by shades of emphasis and neglect, by the tone of a question or the color of a passing remark, and by the order in which the various different answers to key questions are presented.

In order to avoid some of these dangers, the conscientious syntopical reader may resort to one obvious device and use it as much as possible. That is, *he must constantly refer back to the actual text of his authors,* reading the relevant passages over and over; and, in presenting the results of his work to a wider audience, he must quote the opinion or argument of an author in the writer's own language. Although it may appear to do so, this does not contradict what we said earlier about the necessity of finding a neutral terminology in which to analyze the problem. That necessity remains, and when summaries of an author's argument are presented, they must be presented in that language and not the author's. But the author's own words, carefully quoted so as not to wrench them out of context, must accompany the summary, so that the reader can judge for himself whether the interpretation of the author is correct.

Only the syntopical reader's firm intention to avoid them can be relied on to prevent other sorts of departure from dialectical objectivity. That ideal demands a deliberate effort to balance question against question, to forgo any comment that might be prejudicial, to check any tendency toward overemphasis or underemphasis. In the last analysis, although a reader may be the judge of the effectiveness of a written report of a dialectical exposition, only the writer of it—only the syntopical reader himself—can know whether he has satisfied these requirements.

An Example of an Exercise in Syntopical Reading: The Idea of Progress

An example may be helpful to explain how syntopical reading works. Let us consider the idea of progress. We do not take this subject at random. We have done extensive research on it.* The example would not be so useful to you if that were not so.

The investigation of this important historical and philosophical idea occupied several years. The first task was to produce a list of works to be examined for relevant passages—to amass a bibliography (it finally ran to more than 450 items). This task was accomplished by a series of inspectional readings of several times that many books, articles, and other pieces. It is important to point out that in the case of the idea of progress, as would be true in the case of most other important ideas, many of the items finally judged to be relevant were found more or less by accident, or at least with the help of educated guesses. There were obvious places to start; many recent books contain the word "progress" in their titles. But others do not, and most of the older books, although relevant to the subject, do not even employ the term.

A few fictional and poetical works were read, but on the whole it was decided to concentrate on expository works. We have already

---

* The results of these researches were published as *The Idea of Progress,* New York: Praeger, 1967. The work was done under the auspices of the Institute for Philosophical Research, of which the authors are respectively Director and Associate Director.

observed that including novels, plays, and poems in a syntopical reading project is difficult, and this is so for several reasons. First of all, the backbone or essence of a story is its plot, not its positions on issues. Second, even the most talkative characters seldom take clear positions on an issue—they tend to talk, in the story, about other matters, mainly emotional relations. Third, even if a character does make such a speech—as, for example, Settembrini does about progress in Thomas Mann's *Magic Mountain*—we can never be sure that it is the *author's* view that is being represented. Is the author being ironic in allowing his character to go on about the subject? Is he intending you to see the foolishness of the position, rather than its wisdom? Generally speaking, an intensive effort of synthetic interpretation is required before a fictional work can be placed on one side or another of an issue. The effort is so great, and the results essentially so dubious, that usually it is prudent to abstain.

The discussion of progress in the many works that remained to be examined was, as is usually the case, apparently chaotic. Faced with this fact, the task was, as we have indicated, to develop a neutral terminology. This was a complex undertaking, but one example may help to explain what was done.

The word "progress" itself is used by authors in a number of different ways. Most of these different ways reflect no more than shades of meaning, and they can be handled in the analysis. But the word is used by *some* authors to denote a certain kind of movement forward in history that is not an improvement. Since *most* of the authors use the word to denote a historical change in the human condition that is for the better, and since betterment is of the essence of the conception, the same word could not be applied to both views. In this case, the majority gained the day, and the minority faction had to be referred to as authors who assert "non-meliorative advance" in history. The point is that when discussing the views of the minority faction, *we could not employ the word "progress," even though the authors involved had used it themselves.*

The third step in syntopical reading is, as we have noted, getting the questions clear. Our intuition about the primary question in the case of progress turned out to be correct upon examination. The first question to ask, the question to which authors can be interpreted as giving various answers, is, Does progress occur in history? Is it a fact that the general course of historical change is in the direction of improvement in man's condition? Basically, there are three different answers to this question put forth in the literature of the subject: (1) Yes, (2) No, and (3) We cannot know. However, there are a number of different ways of saying Yes, several different ways of saying No, and at least three different ways of saying that we cannot know whether human progress occurs or not.

The multifarious and interrelated answers to this primary question constitute what we decided to call the *general* controversy about progress. It is general in the sense that every author we studied who has anything significant to say about the subject takes sides on the various issues that can be identified within it. But there is also a *special* controversy about progress, which is made up of issues that are joined only by progress authors—authors who assert that progress occurs. These issues have to do with the nature or properties of the progress that they all, *being progress authors,* assert is a fact of history. There are only three issues here, although the discussion of each of them is complex. They can be stated as questions: (1) Is progress necessary, or is it contingent on other occurrences? (2) Will progress continue indefinitely, or will it eventually come to an end or "plateau out"? (3) Is there progress in human nature as well as in human institutions—in the human animal itself, or merely in the external conditions of human life?

Finally, there is a set of subordinate issues, as we called them, again only among progress authors, about the *respects* in which progress occurs. We identified six areas in which progress is said by some authors to occur, although other writers deny its occurrence in one or more of these areas—although never in all (since they are by definition authors who assert the occurrence of some kind of progress). The six are: (1) progress in knowledge, (2) technological progress,

(3) economic progress, (4) political progress, (5) moral progress, and (6) progress in the fine arts. The discussion of the last point raises special problems, since in our opinion no author genuinely *asserts* that such aesthetic progress occurs, although a number of writers *deny* that progress occurs in this respect.

The structure of the analysis of progress just described exemplifies our effort to define the issues within the discussion of this subject and to analyze the discussion itself—in other words, to take the fourth and fifth steps in syntopical reading. And something like this must always be done by a syntopical reader, although of course he does not always have to write a long book reporting his researches.*

The Syntopicon and How to Use It

If you read this chapter carefully, you will have noticed that, although we spent some time discussing it, we did not really solve what we called the paradox of syntopical reading. That paradox can be stated thus: Unless you know what books to read, you cannot read syntopically, but unless you can read syntopically, you do not know what to read. Another way to state it is in the form of what may be called the fundamental problem of syntopical reading, namely, that if you do not know where to start, you cannot read syntopically; and even if you have a rough idea of where to begin, the time required to find the relevant books and relevant passages in those books may exceed the time required to take all of the other steps combined.

Actually, of course, there is at least a theoretical resolution of the

---

* Now that such a book has been written and published, we hope that it will indeed make possible a breakthrough in thought such as we envisaged as the fruit of syntopical reading, and that the book on progress may facilitate further work in its field, as other books produced by the Institute for Philosophical Research on the ideas of freedom, happiness, justice, and love have done in theirs—work that was inordinately difficult before these books appeared.

paradox and solution of the problem. Theoretically, you could know the major literature of our tradition so thoroughly that you had a working notion of where every idea is discussed in it. But if you are such a person, you need no help from anybody, and we cannot tell you anything you do not know about syntopical reading.

On the other hand, even if you did not have this knowledge yourself, you might be able to apply to someone else who did. But you should recognize that if you were able to apply to such a person, his advice might turn out to be almost as much a hindrance as a help. If the subject was one on which he had himself done special research, it would be hard for him merely to tell you the relevant passages to read without telling you *how to read them*—and that might well get in your way. But if he had not done special research on the subject, he might not know a great deal more than yourself, although it might seem so both to him and to you.

What is needed, therefore, is a reference book that tells you where to go to find the relevant passages on a large number of subjects of interest, without at the same time saying how the passages should be read—without prejudging their meaning or significance. The Syntopicon is an example of such a work. Produced in the 1940s, it is a topical index to the set of books titled *Great Books of the Western World*. Under each of some 3,000 topics or subjects, it lists references to pages within the set where that subject is discussed. Some of the references are to passages covering many pages, others are to key paragraphs or even parts of paragraphs. No more time is required to find them than is needed to take down the indicated volume and flip through its pages.

The Syntopicon has one major defect, of course. It is an index of just one set of books (albeit a large one), and it gives only a very rough indication of where passages may be found in other books that are not included in the set. Nevertheless, it always provides you with at least a place to start on any syntopical reading project. And it is also true that the books included in the set are ones that you would almost always want to read anyway, in the course of any such project. Thus the Syntopicon should be able to save the mature scholar or reader who is beginning his research into a certain problem much of the preliminary labor of research, and advance him rapidly to the point where he can begin to think independently about it, because he knows what thinking has been done.

Useful as the Syntopicon is for that kind of reader, it is much more useful for the beginner. The Syntopicon can help such a reader in three ways: initiatively, suggestively, and instructively.

It works *initiatively* by overcoming the initial difficulty that anyone faces when confronted by the classical books of our tradition. These works are a little overpowering. We may wish that we had read them, but often we do not do so. We find ourselves advised from all sides to read them, and we are given reading programs, beginning with the easier works and proceeding to the more difficult ones. But all such programs require the reading of whole books or, at least, the integral reading of large parts of them. It is a matter of general experience that this kind of solution seldom achieves the desired result.

A syntopical reading of these major works with the aid of the Syntopicon provides a radically different solution. The Syntopicon initiates the reading of great books by enabling persons to read particular ones on the subjects in which they are interested; and on those subjects, to read relatively short passages from a large number of authors. It helps us to read *in* the great books before we have read *through* them.

Syntopical reading in the great books, with the help of the Syntopicon, may also work *suggestively*. Starting from the reader's existing interest in a particular subject, it may arouse or create other interests in related subjects. And once started on an author, it is hard not to explore the context. Before you know it, you have read a good portion of the book.

Finally, syntopical reading with the aid of the Syntopicon works *instructively,* in three distinct ways. This, in fact, is one of the major benefits of this level of reading.

First, the topic in connection with which the passage is being read serves to give direction to the reader in interpreting the passage.

But it does not tell him what the passage means, since the passage may be relevant to the topic in several or many different ways. Hence the reader is called upon to *discover precisely what relevance the passage has to the topic.* To learn to do this is to acquire a major skill in the art of reading.

Second, the collection of a number of passages on the same topic, but from different works and different authors, serves to *sharpen the reader's interpretation of each passage read.* Sometimes, when passages from the same book are read in sequence and in the context of one another, each becomes clearer. Sometimes the meaning of each of a series of contrasting or conflicting passages from different books is accentuated when they are read against one another. And sometimes the passages from one author, by amplifying or commenting on the passages from another, materially help the reader's understanding of the second author.

Third, if syntopical reading is done on a number of different subjects, the fact that the same passage will often be found cited in the Syntopicon under two or more subjects will have its instructive effect. The passage has an amplitude of meaning that the reader will come to perceive as he interprets it somewhat differently in relation to different topics. Such multiple interpretation not only is a basic exercise in the art of reading but also tends to make the mind habitually alert to the many strains of meaning that any rich or complex passage can contain.

Because we believe that the Syntopicon can be useful to any reader wishing to read in the manner described in this chapter, be he a beginner or a mature scholar and researcher, we have taken the liberty of adopting its name for this level of reading. We hope the reader will forgive us what may seem to be a small self-indulgence. In return for that forgiveness, we would like to point out an important fact. There is a considerable difference between syntopical reading, with a small "s," and Syntopical reading, where the latter phrase refers to reading the great books with the help of the Syntopicon. Syntopical reading, in the latter sense, can constitute a *part* of any syntopical reading project where the term is used in the former sense, and perhaps it would always be wise to start there. But syntopical reading with a small "s" is a term of much wider application than Syntopical reading.

On the Principles That Underlie Syntopical Reading

There are those who say that syntopical reading (in the broader sense just mentioned) is impossible. It is wrong, they say, to impose a terminology, even a "neutral" one (if there is any such thing), on an author. His own terminology must be treated as sacrosanct, because books should never be read "out of context," and besides, translation from one set of terms to another is always dangerous because words are not controllable like mathematical symbols. Further, the objectors maintain, syntopical reading involves reading authors widely separated in space and time, and differing radically in style and approach, as if they were members of the same universe of discourse, as if they were talking to one another—and this distorts the facts of the matter. Each author is a little universe in himself, and although connections can be made between different books written by the same author at different times (even here there are dangers, they warn), there are no clear connections relating one author to another. They maintain, finally, that the *subjects* that authors discuss, as such, are not as important as the *ways* in which they discuss them. The style, they say, is the man; and if we ignore *how* an author says something, in the process of trying to discover *what* he says, we will miss both kinds of understanding.

It should be apparent that we disagree with all of those charges, and therefore an answer to each of them is in order. Let us take them one at a time.

First, to the point about *terminology*. To deny that an idea can be expressed in more than one set of terms is similar to denying that translation is possible from one natural language to another. That denial is made, of course. Recently, for example, we read an introduction to a new translation of the Koran that began by saying that to translate the Koran is impossible. But since the author then proceeded to explain how he had done it, we could only assume that he meant that translation is particularly difficult in the case of a book held to be holy by large numbers of people. We would agree. But the difficult is not the impossible.

In fact, the view that an author's terms must be treated as sacrosanct is probably always merely another way of saying that it is difficult to translate from one terminology to another. We would agree to that, too. But again, the difficult is not the impossible.

Second, to the point about *the separateness and uniqueness of authors.* This comes down to saying that if Aristotle, for example, walked into our office, attired no doubt in robes and accompanied by an interpreter who knew both modern English and classical Greek, we would not be able to understand him or he us. We simply do not believe it. Doubtless Aristotle would be amazed at some of the things he saw, but we are quite confident that within ten minutes we could, if we wanted to, be engaged in a philosophical discussion of problems that we shared. There might be recurrent difficulties about certain conceptions, but as soon as we recognized them as such, we could resolve them.

If that is possible (and we do not really think anyone would deny it), then it is not impossible for one book to "talk" to another through the medium of an interpreter—namely, you, the syntopical reader. Care is required, of course, and you should know both "languages"—that is, both books—as well as you can. But the problem is not insuperable, and it is simply foolish to suggest that it is.

Finally, to the point about the *manner or style.* This is equivalent, we think, to saying that there is no rational communication among men, but that all men communicate at the emotional level, which is the same level at which they communicate with pets. If you say "I love you" to your dog in an angry tone of voice, he will cower; but he does not understand you. Can anyone seriously assert that there is *nothing more* than tone of voice or gesture in vocal communications between two human beings? Tone of voice is important, particularly when emotional relations are the primary content of the communication; and body language probably has things to tell us if we will only listen (look?). But there is something else, too, in human communication. If you ask someone how to reach the exit, and he tells you to follow Corridor B, it does not matter what tone of voice he employs. He is either right or wrong, lying or telling the truth, but the point is that you will soon find that out by following Corridor B. You have understood *what* he said as well as reacting, no doubt in all sorts of ways, to *how* he said it.

Believing, then, that translation is possible (because it is done all the time), that books can "talk" to one another (because human beings do so), and that there is an objective, rational content of communication between human beings when they are trying to be rational (because we can and do learn from each other), we believe that syntopical reading is possible.

Summary of Syntopical Reading

We have now completed our discussion of syntopical reading. Let us therefore display the various steps that must be taken at this level of reading in outline form.

As we have seen, there are two main stages of syntopical reading. One is preparatory, and the other is syntopical reading proper. Let us write out all of these steps for review.

I. SURVEYING THE FIELD PREPARATORY TO SYNTOPICAL READING

1. Create a tentative bibliography of your subject by recourse to library catalogues, advisors, and bibliographies in books.

2. Inspect *all* of the books on the tentative bibliography to ascertain which are germane to your subject, and also to acquire a clearer idea of the subject.

Note: These two steps are not, strictly speaking, chronologically distinct; that is, the two steps have an effect on each other, with the second, in particular, serving to modify the first.

II. SYNTOPICAL READING OF THE BIBLIOGRAPHY AMASSED IN STAGE I

1. Inspect the books already identified as relevant to your subject in Stage I in order to find the most relevant passages.

2. Bring the authors to terms by constructing a neutral terminology of the subject that all, or the great majority, of the authors can be interpreted as employing, whether they actually employ the words or not.

3. Establish a set of neutral propositions for all of the authors by framing a set of questions to which all or most of the authors can be interpreted as giving answers, whether they actually treat the questions explicitly or not.

4. Define the issues, both major and minor ones, by ranging the opposing answers of authors to the various questions on one side of an issue or another. You should remember that an issue does not always exist explicitly between or among authors, but that it sometimes has to be constructed by interpretation of the authors' views on matters that may not have been their primary concern.

5. Analyze the discussion by ordering the questions and issues in such a way as to throw maximum light on the subject. More general issues should precede less general ones, and relations among issues should be clearly indicated.

Note: Dialectical detachment or objectivity should, ideally, be maintained throughout. One way to insure this is always to accompany an interpretation of an author's views on an issue with an actual quotation from his text.

21

Reading and the Growth of the Mind

We have now completed the task that lay before us at the beginning of this book. We have shown that activity is the essence of good reading, and that the more active reading is, the better it is.

We have defined active reading as the asking of questions, and we have indicated what questions must be asked of any book, and how those questions must be answered in different ways for different kinds of books.

We have identified and discussed the four levels of reading, and shown how these are cumulative, earlier or lower levels being contained in later or higher ones. Consequent upon our stated intention, we have laid more stress upon the later and higher levels of reading than upon the earlier and lower ones, and we have therefore emphasized analytical and syntopical reading. Since analytical reading is probably the most unfamiliar kind for most readers, we have discussed it at greater length than any of the other levels, giving its rules and explaining them in the order in which they must be applied. But almost everything that was said of analytical reading also applies, with certain adaptations that were mentioned in the last chapter, to syntopical reading as well.

We have completed our task, but you may not have completed yours. We do not need to remind you that this is a practical book, nor that the reader of a practical book has a special obligation with respect to it. If, we said, the reader of a practical book accepts the ends it proposes and agrees that the means recommended are appropriate and effective, then he must act in the way proposed. You may not accept the primary aim we have endorsed—namely, that you should be able to read as well as possible—nor the means we have proposed to reach it— namely, the rules of inspectional, analytical, and syntopical reading. (In that case, however, you are not likely to be reading this page.) But if you do accept that aim and agree that the means are appropriate, then you must make the effort to read as you probably have never read before.

That is your task and your obligation. Can we help you in it in any way?

We think we can. The task falls mainly on you—it is you who, henceforth, must do all the work (and obtain all the benefits). But there are several things that remain to be said, about the end and the means. Let us discuss the latter first.

What Good Books Can Do for Us

"Means" can be interpreted in two ways. In the previous paragraph, we interpreted the term as referring to the rules of reading, that is, the *method* by which you become a better reader. But "means" can also be interpreted as referring to *the things you read*. Having a method without materials to which it can be applied is as useless as having the materials with no method to apply to them.

In the latter sense of the term, the means that will serve you in the further improvement of your reading are the books you will read. We have said that the method applies to anything you read, and that is true, if you understand by the statement any *kind* of book— whether fiction or nonfiction, imaginative or expository, practical or theoretical. But in fact, the method, at least as it is exemplified in our discussion of analytical and syntopical reading, *does not apply to every book*. The reason is that some books do not require it.

We have made this point before, but we want to make it now

again because of its relevance to the task that lies before you. *If you are reading in order to become a better reader, you cannot read just any book or article.* You will not improve as a reader if all you read are books that are well within your capacity. You must tackle books that are beyond you, or, as we have said, books that are over your head. Only books of that sort will make you stretch your mind. And unless you stretch, you will not learn.

Thus, it becomes of crucial importance for you not only to be able to read well but also to be able to identify those books that make the kinds of demands on you that improvement in reading ability requires. A book that can do no more than amuse or entertain you may be a pleasant diversion for an idle hour, but you must not expect to get anything but amusement from it. We are not against amusement in its own right, but we do want to stress that *improvement in reading skill does not accompany it.* The same goes for a book that merely informs you of facts that you did not know without adding to your understanding of those facts. Reading for information does not stretch your mind any more than reading for amusement. It may seem as though it does, but that is merely because your mind is fuller of facts than it was before you read the book. However, your mind is essentially in the same condition that it was before. There has been a quantitative change, but no improvement in your skill.

We have said many times that the good reader makes demands on himself when he reads. He reads actively, effortfully. Now we are saying something else. The books that you will want to practice your reading on, particularly your analytical reading, *must also make demands on you.* They must seem to you to be beyond your capacity. You need not fear that they really are, because there is no book that is completely out of your grasp if you apply the rules of reading to it that we have described. This does not mean, of course, that these rules will accomplish immediate miracles for you. There are certainly some books that will continue to extend you no matter how good a reader you are. Actually, those are the very books that you must seek out, because they are the ones that can best help you to become an ever more skillful reader.

Some readers make the mistake of supposing that such books—the ones that provide a constant and never-ending challenge to their skill—are always ones in relatively unfamiliar fields. In practice, this comes down to believing, in the case of most readers, that only scientific books, and perhaps philosophical ones, satisfy the criterion. But that is far from the case. We have already remarked that the great scientific books are in many ways easier to read than non-scientific ones, because of the care with which scientific authors help you to come to terms, identify the key propositions, and state the main arguments. These helps are absent from poetical works, and so in the long run they are quite likely to be the hardest, the most demanding, books that you can read. Homer, for example, is in many ways harder to read than Newton, despite the fact that you may get more out of Homer the first time through. The reason is that Homer deals with subjects that are harder to write well about.

The difficulties that we are talking about here are very different from the difficulties that are presented by a bad book. It is hard to read a bad book, too, for it defies your efforts to analyze it, slipping through your fingers whenever you think you have it pinned down. In fact, in the case of a bad book, there is really nothing *to* pin down. It is not worth the effort of trying. You receive no reward for your struggle.

A good book does reward you for trying to read it. The best books reward you most of all. The reward, of course, is of two kinds. First, there is the improvement in your reading skill that occurs when you successfully tackle a good, difficult work. Second—and this in the long run is much more important—a good book can teach you about the world and about yourself. You learn more than how to read better; you also learn more about life. You become wiser. Not just more knowledgeable—books that provide nothing but information can produce that result. But wiser, in the sense that you are more deeply aware of the great and enduring truths of human life.

There are some human problems, after all, that have no solution. There are some relationships, both among human beings and between human beings and the nonhuman world, about which no one can have the last word. This is true not only in such fields as science and philosophy, where it is obvious that final understanding about nature and its laws, and about being and becoming, has not been achieved by anyone and never will be; it is also true of such familiar and everyday matters as the relation between men and women, or parents and children, or man and God. These are matters about which you cannot think too much, or too well. The greatest books can help you to think better about them, because they were written by men and women who thought better than other people about them.

The Pyramid of Books

The great majority of the several million books that have been written in the Western tradition alone—more than 99 per cent of them—will not make sufficient demands on you for you to improve your skill in reading. This may seem like a distressing fact, and the percentages may seem an overestimate. But obviously, considering the numbers involved, it is true. These are the books that can be read only for amusement or information. The amusement may be of many kinds, and the information may be interesting in all sorts of ways. But you should not expect to learn anything of importance from them. In fact, you do not have to read them—analytically—at all. Skimming will do.

There is a second class of books from which you can learn—both how to read and how to live. Less than one out of every hundred books belongs in this class—probably it is more like one in a thousand, or even one in ten thousand. These are the good books, the ones that were carefully wrought by their authors, the ones that convey to the reader significant insights about subjects of enduring interest to human beings. There are in all probability no more than a few thousand such books. They make severe demands on the reader. They are worth reading analytically—once. If you are skillful, you will be able to get everything out of them that they can give in the course of one good reading. They are books that you read once and then put away on your shelf. You know that you will never have to read them again, although you may return to them to check certain points or to refresh your memory of certain ideas or episodes. (It is in the case of such books that the notes you make in the margin or elsewhere in the volume are particularly valuable.)

How do you know that you do not ever have to read such books again? You know it by your own mental reaction to the experience of reading them. Such a book stretches your mind and increases your understanding. But as your mind stretches and your understanding increases, you realize, by a process that is more or less mysterious, that you are not going to be changed any more in the future by this book. You realize that you have grasped the book in its entirety. You have milked it dry. You are grateful to it for what it has given you, but you know it has no more to give.

Of the few thousand such books there is a much smaller number—here the number is probably less than a hundred—that cannot be exhausted by even the very best reading you can manage. How do you recognize this? Again it is rather mysterious, but when you have closed the book after reading it analytically to the best of your ability, and place it back on the shelf, you have a sneaking suspicion that there is more there than you got. We say "suspicion" because that may be all it is at this stage. If you knew what it was that you had missed, your obligation as an analytical reader would take you back to the book immediately to seek it out. In fact, you cannot put your finger on it, but you know it is there. You find that you cannot forget the book, that you keep thinking about it and your reaction to it. Finally, you return to it. And then a very remarkable thing happens.

If the book belongs to the second class of books to which we referred before, you find, on returning to it, that there was *less there than you remembered*. The reason, of course, is that you yourself have grown in the meantime. Your mind is fuller, your understanding greater. The book has not changed, but you have. Such a return is inevitably disappointing.

But if the book belongs to the highest class—the very small number of inexhaustible books—you discover on returning that *the book seems to have grown with you*. You see new things in it—whole sets of new things—that you did not see before. Your previous understanding of the book is not invalidated (assuming that you read it well the first time); it is just as true as it ever was, and in the same ways that it was true before. But now it is true in still other ways, too.

How can a book grow as you grow? It is impossible, of course; a book, once it is written and published, does not change. But what you only now begin to realize is that the book was so far above you to begin with that it has remained above you, and probably always will remain so. Since it is a really good book—a great book, as we might say—it is accessible at different levels. Your impression of increased understanding on your previous reading was not false. The book truly lifted you then. But now, even though you have become wiser and more knowledgeable, it can lift you again. And it will go on doing this until you die.

There are obviously not many books that can do this for any of us. Our estimate was that the number is considerably less than a hundred. But the number is *even less than that for any given reader.* Human beings differ in many ways other than in the power of their minds. They have different tastes; different things appeal more to one person than to another. You may never feel about Newton the way you feel about Shakespeare, either because you may be able to read Newton so well that you do not have to read him again, or because mathematical systems of the world just do not have all that appeal to you. Or, if they do—Charles Darwin is an example of such a person—then Newton may be one of the handful of books that are great for you, and not Shakespeare.

We do not want to state authoritatively that any particular book or group of books must be great for you, in this sense, although in our first Appendix we do list those books that experience has shown are capable of having this kind of value for many readers. Our point, instead, is that *you should seek out the few books that can have this value for you.* They are the books that will teach you the most, both about reading and about life. They are the books to which you will want to return over and over. They are the books that will help you to grow.

The Life and Growth of the Mind

There is an old test—it was quite popular a generation ago—that was designed to tell you which books are the ones that can do this for you. Suppose, the test went, that you know in advance that you will be marooned on a desert island for the rest of your life, or at least for a long period. Suppose, too, that you have time to prepare for the experience. There are certain practical and useful articles that you would be sure to take with you. You will also be allowed ten books. Which ones would you select?

Trying to decide on a list is instructive, and not only because it may help you to identify the books that you would most like to read and reread. That, in fact, is probably of minor importance, compared with what you can learn about yourself when you imagine what life would be like if you were cut off from all the sources of amusement, information, and understanding that ordinarily surround you. Remember, there would be no radio or television on the island, and no lending library. There would be just you and ten books.

This imagined situation seems bizarre and unreal when you begin to think about it. But is it actually so unreal? We do not think so. We are all to some extent persons marooned on a desert island. We all face the same challenge that we would face if we really were there—the challenge of finding the resources within ourselves to live a good human life.

There is a strange fact about the human mind, a fact that differentiates the mind sharply from the body. The body is limited in ways that the mind is not. One sign of this is that the body does not continue indefinitely to grow in strength and develop in skill and grace. By the time most people are thirty years old, their bodies are as good as they will ever be; in fact, many persons' bodies have begun to deteriorate by that time. *But there is no limit to the amount of growth and development that the mind can sustain.* The mind does not stop growing at any particular age; only when the brain itself loses its vigor, in senescence, does the mind lose its power to increase in skill and understanding.

This is one of the most remarkable things about human beings, and it may actually be the major difference between *Homo sapiens* and the others animals, which do not seem to grow mentally beyond a certain stage in their development. But this great advantage that man possesses carries with it a great peril. *The mind can atrophy,* like the muscles, *if it is not used.* Atrophy of the mental muscles is the penalty that we pay for not taking mental exercise. And this is a terrible penalty, for there is evidence that atrophy of the mind is a mortal disease. There seems to be no other explanation for the fact that so many busy people die so soon after retirement. They were kept alive by the demands of their work upon their minds; they were propped up artificially, as it were, by external forces. But as soon as those demands cease, having no resources within themselves in the way of mental activity, they cease thinking altogether, and expire.

Television, radio, and all the sources of amusement and information that surround us in our daily lives are also artificial props. They can give us the impression that our minds are active, because we are required to react to stimuli from outside. But the power of those external stimuli to keep us going is limited. They are like drugs. We grow used to them, and we continuously need more and more of them. Eventually, they have little or no effect. Then, if we lack resources within ourselves, we cease to grow intellectually, morally, and spiritually. And when we cease to grow, we begin to die.

Reading well, which means reading actively, is thus not only a good in itself, nor is it merely a means to advancement in our work or career. It also serves to keep our minds alive and growing.

APPENDIX A

A RECOMMENDED READING LIST

On the following pages appears a list of books that it would be worth your while to read. We mean the phrase "worth your while" quite seriously. Although not all of the books listed are "great" in any of the commonly accepted meanings of the term, all of them will reward you for the effort you make to read them. All of these books are over most people's heads—sufficiently so, at any rate, to force most readers to stretch their minds to understand and appreciate them. And that, of course, is the kind of book you should seek out if you want to improve your reading skills, and at the same time discover the best that has been thought and said in our literary tradition.

Some of the books are great in the special sense of the term that we employed in the last chapter. On returning to them, you will always find something new, often many things. They are endlessly re-readable. Another way to say this is that some of the books—we will not say exactly how many, nor will we try to identify them, since to some extent this is an individual judgment—are over the heads of all readers, no matter how skillful. As we observed in the last chapter, these are the works that everyone should make a special effort to seek out. They are the truly great books; they are the books that anyone should choose to take with him to his own desert island.

The list is long, and it may seem a little overwhelming. We urge you not to allow yourself to be abashed by it. In the first place, you are likely to recognize the names of most of the authors. There is nothing here that is so recondite as to be esoteric. More important, we want to remind you that it is wise to begin with those books that interest you most, for whatever reason. As we have pointed out several times, the primary aim is to read well, not widely. You should not be disappointed if you read no more than a handful of the books in a year. The list is not something to be gotten through in any amount of time. It is not a challenge that you can meet only by finishing every item on it. Instead, it is an invitation that you can accept graciously by beginning wherever you feel at home.

The authors are listed chronologically, according to the known or supposed date of their birth. When several works of an author are listed, these too are arranged chronologically, where that is possible. Scholars do not always agree about the first publication of a book, but this need not concern you. The point to remember is that the list as a whole moves forward through time. That does not necessarily mean that you should read it chronologically, of course. You might even start with the end of the list and read backward to Homer and the Old Testament.

We have not listed all the works of every author. We have usually cited only the more important titles, selecting them, in the case of expository books, to show the diversity of an author's contribution to different fields of learning. In some instances, we have listed an author's works and specified, in brackets, those titles that are especially important or useful.

In drawing up a list of this kind, the greatest difficulty always arises with respect to the relatively contemporary items. The closer an author is to our own time, the harder it is to exercise a detached judgment about him. It is all very well to say that time will tell, but we may not want to wait. Thus, with regard to the more recent writers and books, there is much room for differences of opinion, and we would not claim for the later items on our list the degree of authority that we can claim for the earlier ones.

There may be differences of opinion about some of the earlier items too, and we may be charged with being prejudiced against some authors that we have not listed at all. We are willing to admit that this may be true, in some cases. This is our list, and it may differ in some respects from lists drawn up by others. But it will not differ very significantly if everyone concurs seriously in the aim of making up a reading program that is worth spending a lifetime on. Ultimately, of course, you should make up your own list, and then go to work on it. It is wise, however, to read a fair number of the books that have been unanimously acclaimed before you branch off on your own. This list is a place to begin.

We want to mention one omission that may strike some readers as unfortunate. The list contains only Western authors and books; there are no Chinese, Japanese, or Indian works. There are several reasons for this. One is that we are not particularly knowledgeable outside of the Western literary tradition, and our recommendations would carry little weight. Another is that there is in the East no single tradition, as there is in the West, and we would have to be learned in all Eastern traditions in order to do the job well. There are very few scholars who have this kind of acquaintance with all the works of the East. Third, there is something to be said for knowing your own tradition before trying to understand that of other parts of the world. Many persons who today attempt to read such books as the *I Ching* or the *Bhagavad-Gita* are baffled, not only because of the inherent difficulty of such works, but also because they have not learned to read well by practicing on the more accessible works—more accessible to them—of their own culture. And finally, the list is long enough as it is.

One other omission requires comment. The list, being one of books, includes the names of few persons known primarily as lyric poets. Some of the writers on the list wrote lyric poems, of course, but they are best known for other, longer works. This fact is not to be taken as reflecting a prejudice on our part against lyric poetry. But we would recommend starting with a good anthology of poetry rather than with the collected works of a single author. Palgrave's

The Golden Treasury and *The Oxford Book of English Verse* are excellent places to start. These older anthologies should be supplemented by more modern ones—for example, Selden Rodman's *One Hundred Modern Poems,* a collection widely available in paperback that extends the notion of a lyric poem in interesting ways. Since reading lyric poetry requires special skill, we would also recommend any of several available handbooks on the subject—for example, Mark Van Doren's *Introduction to Poetry,* an anthology that also contains short discussions of how to read many famous lyrics.

We have listed the books by author and title, but we have not attempted to indicate a publisher or a particular edition. Almost every work on the list is available in some form, and many are available in several editions, both paperback and hard cover. However, we have indicated which authors and titles are included in two sets that we ourselves have edited. *Titles* included in *Great Books of the Western World* are identified by a single asterisk; *authors* represented in *Gateway to the Great Books* are identified by a double asterisk.

1. Homer (9th century B.C.?)
   * *Iliad*
   * *Odyssey*
2. The Old Testament
3. Aeschylus (*c.* 525–456 B.C.)
   * Tragedies
4. Sophocles (*c.* 495–406 B.C.)
   * Tragedies
5. Herodotus (*c.* 484–425 B.C.)
   * *History* (of the Persian Wars)
6. Euripides (*c.* 485–406 B.C.)
   * Tragedies
   (esp. *Medea, Hippolytus, The Bacchae*)
7. Thucydides (*c.* 460–400 B.C.)
   * *History of the Peloponnesian War*

8. Hippocrates (*c.* 460–377? B.C.)
   * Medical writings
9. Aristophanes (*c.* 448–380 B.C.)
   * Comedies
   (esp. *The Clouds, The Birds, The Frogs*)
10. Plato (*c.* 427–347 B.C.)
    * Dialogues
    (esp. *The Republic, Symposium, Phaedo, Meno, Apology, Phaedrus, Protagoras, Gorgias, Sophist, Theaetetus*)
11. Aristotle (384–322 B.C.)
    * Works
    (esp. *Organon, Physics, Metaphysics, On the Soul, The Nichomachean Ethics, Politics, Rhetoric, Poetics*)
12. ** Epicurus (*c.* 341–270 B.C.)
    Letter to Herodotus
    Letter to Menoeceus
13. Euclid (*fl.c.* 300 B.C.)
    * *Elements (of Geometry)*
14. Archimedes (*c.* 287–212 B.C.)
    * Works
    (esp. *On the Equilibrium of Planes, On Floating Bodies, The Sand-Reckoner*)
15. Apollonius of Perga (*fl.c.* 240 B.C.)
    * *On Conic Sections*
16. ** Cicero (106–43 B.C.)
    Works
    (esp. *Orations, On Friendship, On Old Age*)
17. Lucretius (*c.* 95–55 B.C.)
    * *On the Nature of Things*
18. Virgil (70–19 B.C.)
    * Works
19. Horace (65–8 B.C.)
    Works
    (esp. Odes and Epodes, *The Art of Poetry*)

20. Livy (59 B.C.–A.D. 17)
    History of Rome
21. Ovid (43 B.C.–A.D. 17)
    Works
    (esp. *Metamorphoses*)
22. ** Plutarch (*c.* 45–120)
    * *Lives of the Noble Grecians and Romans Moralia*
23. ** Tacitus (*c.* 55–117)
    * *Histories*
    * *Annals*
    Agricola
    Germania
24. Nicomachus of Gerasa (*fl.c.* 100 A.D.)
    * *Introduction to Arithmetic*
25. ** Epictetus (*c.* 60–120)
    * *Discourses*
    Encheiridion (Handbook)
26. Ptolemy (*c.* 100–178; *fl.* 127–151)
    * *Almagest*
27. ** Lucian (*c.* 120–*c.* 190)
    Works
    (esp. *The Way to Write History, The True History, The Sale of Creeds*)
28. Marcus Aurelius (121–180)
    * *Meditations*
29. Galen (*c.* 130–200)
    * *On the Natural Faculties*
30. The New Testament
31. Plotinus (205–270)
    * *The Enneads*
32. St. Augustine (354–430)
    Works
    (esp. *On the Teacher,* * *Confessions,* * *The City of God,* * *Christian
    Doctrine*)

33. *The Song of Roland* (12th century?)
34. *The Nibelungenlied* (13th century)
    (The *Völsunga Saga* is the Scandinavian version of the same
       legend.)
35. *The Saga of Burnt Njal*
36. St. Thomas Aquinas (*c.* 1225–1274)
    * *Summa Theologica*
37. ** Dante Alighieri (1265–1321)
    Works
    (esp. *The New Life, On Monarchy,* * *The Divine Comedy*)
38. Geoffrey Chaucer (*c.* 1340–1400)
    Works
    esp. * *Troilus and Criseyde,* * *Canterbury Tales*)
39. Leonardo da Vinci (1452–1519)
    Notebooks
40. Niccolò Machiavelli (1469–1527)
    * *The Prince*
    Discourses on the First Ten Books of Livy
41. Desiderius Erasmus (*c.* 1469–1536)
    The Praise of Folly
42. Nicolaus Copernicus (1473–1543)
    * *On the Revolutions of the Heavenly Spheres*
43. Sir Thomas More (*c.* 1478–1535)
    Utopia
44. Martin Luther (1483–1546)
    Three Treatises
    Table-Talk
45. François Rabelais (*c.* 1495–1553)
    * *Gargantua and Pantagruel*
46. John Calvin (1509–1564)
    Institutes of the Christian Religion
47. Michel de Montaigne (1533–1592)
    * *Essays*

48. William Gilbert (1540–1603)
    * *On the Loadstone and Magnetic Bodies*
49. Miguel de Cervantes (1547–1616)
    * *Don Quixote*
50. Edmund Spenser (*c.* 1552–1599)
    Prothalamion
    The Faerie Queene
51. ** Francis Bacon (1561–1626)
    Essays
    * *Advancement of Learning*
    * *Novum Organum*
    * *New Atlantis*
52. William Shakespeare (1564–1616)
    * Works
53. ** Galileo Galilei (1564–1642)
    The Starry Messenger
    * *Dialogues Concerning Two New Sciences*
54. Johannes Kepler (1571–1630)
    * *Epitome of Copernican Astronomy*
    * *Concerning the Harmonies of the World*
55. William Harvey (1578–1657)
    * *On the Motion of the Heart and Blood in Animals*
    * *On the Circulation of the Blood*
    * *On the Generation of Animals*
56. Thomas Hobbes (1588–1679)
    * *The Leviathan*
57. René Descartes (1596–1650)
    * *Rules for the Direction of the Mind*
    * *Discourse on Method*
    * *Geometry*
    * *Meditations on First Philosophy*
58. John Milton (1608–1674)
    Works

(esp. * the minor poems, * *Areopagitica,* * *Paradise Lost,* * *Samson Agonistes*)

59. ** Molière (1622–1673)
Comedies
(esp. *The Miser, The School for Wives, The Misanthrope, The Doctor in Spite of Himself, Tartuffe*)

60. Blaise Pascal (1623–1662)
* *The Provincial Letters*
* *Pensées*
* Scientific treatises

61. Christiaan Huygens (1629–1695)
* *Treatise on Light*

62. Benedict de Spinoza (1632–1677)
* *Ethics*

63. John Locke (1632–1704)
* *Letter Concerning Toleration*
* "Of Civil Government" (second treatise in *Two Treatises on Government*)
* *Essay Concerning Human Understanding*
Some Thoughts Concerning Education

64. Jean Baptiste Racine (1639–1699)
Tragedies
(esp. *Andromache, Phaedra*)

65. Isaac Newton (1642–1727)
* *Mathematical Principles of Natural Philosophy*
* *Optics*

66. Gottfried Wilhelm von Leibniz (1646–1716)
Discourse on Metaphysics
New Essays Concerning Human Understanding
Monadology

67. ** Daniel Defoe (1660–1731)
Robinson Crusoe

68. ** Jonathan Swift (1667–1745)

A Tale of a Tub
Journal to Stella
* *Gulliver's Travels*
A Modest Proposal
69. William Congreve (1670–1729)
The Way of the World
70. George Berkeley (1685–1753)
* *Principles of Human Knowledge*
71. Alexander Pope (1688–1744)
Essay on Criticism
Rape of the Lock
Essay on Man
72. Charles de Secondat, Baron de Montesquieu (1689–1755)
Persian Letters
* *Spirit of Laws*
73. ** Voltaire (1694–1778)
Letters on the English
Candide
Philosophical Dictionary
74. Henry Fielding (1707–1754)
Joseph Andrews
* *Tom Jones*
75. ** Samuel Johnson (1709–1784)
The Vanity of Human Wishes
Dictionary
Rasselas
The Lives of the Poets
(esp. the essays on Milton and Pope)
76. ** David Hume (1711–1776)
Treatise of Human Nature
Essays Moral and Political
* *An Inquiry Concerning Human Understanding*
77. ** Jean Jacques Rousseau (1712–1778)
* *On the Origin of Inequality*

* *On Political Economy*

Emile

* *The Social Contract*

78. Laurence Sterne (1713–1768)

    * *Tristram Shandy*

    A Sentimental Journey Through France and Italy

79. Adam Smith (1723–1790)

    The Theory of Moral Sentiments

    * *Inquiry into the Nature and Causes of the Wealth of Nations*

80. ** Immanuel Kant (1724–1804)

    * *Critique of Pure Reason*

    ˣ *Fundamental Principles of the Metaphysics of Morals*

    * *Critique of Practical Reason*

    * *The Science of Right*

    * *Critique of Judgment*

    Perpetual Peace

81. Edward Gibbon (1737–1794)

    * *The Decline and Fall of the Roman Empire*

    Autobiography

82. James Boswell (1740–1795)

    Journal

    (esp. *London Journal*)

    * *Life of Samuel Johnson Ll.D.*

83. Antoine Laurent Lavoisier (1743–1794)

    * *Elements of Chemistry*

84. John Jay (1745–1829), James Madison (1751–1836), and Alexander Hamilton (1757–1804)

    * *Federalist Papers*

    (together with the * *Articles of Confederation,* the * *Constitution of the United States,* and the * *Declaration of Independence*)

85. Jeremy Bentham (1748–1832)

    Introduction to the Principles of Morals and Legislation

    Theory of Fictions

86. Johann Wolfgang von Goethe (1749–1832)

* *Faust*
   Poetry and Truth
87. Jean Baptiste Joseph Fourier (1768–1830)
    * *Analytical Theory of Heat*
88. Georg Wilhelm Friedrich Hegel (1770–1831)
    Phenomenology of Spirit
    * *Philosophy of Right*
    * *Lectures on the Philosophy of History*
89. William Wordsworth (1770–1850)
    Poems
    (esp. *Lyrical Ballads,* Lucy poems, sonnets; *The Prelude*)
90. Samuel Taylor Coleridge (1772–1834)
    Poems
    (esp. "Kubla Khan," *Rime of the Ancient Mariner*)
    Biographia Literaria
91. Jane Austen (1775–1817)
    Pride and Prejudice
    Emma
92. ** Karl von Clausewitz (1780–1831)
    On War
93. Stendhal (1783–1842)
    The Red and the Black
    The Charterhouse of Parma
    On Love
94. George Gordon, Lord Byron (1788–1824)
    Don Juan
95. ** Arthur Schopenhauer (1788–1860)
    Studies in Pessimism
96. ** Michael Faraday (1791–1867)
    Chemical History of a Candle
    * *Experimental Researches in Electricity*
97. ** Charles Lyell (1797–1875)
    Principles of Geology

98. Auguste Comte (1798–1857)
    The Positive Philosophy
99. ** Honoré de Balzac (1799–1850)
    Père Goriot
    Eugénie Grandet
100. ** Ralph Waldo Emerson (1803–1882)
    Representative Men
    Essays
    Journal
101. ** Nathaniel Hawthorne (1804–1864)
    The Scarlet Letter
102. ** Alexis de Tocqueville (1805–1859)
    Democracy in America
103. ** John Stuart Mill (1806–1873)
    A System of Logic
    * *On Liberty*
    * *Representative Government*
    * *Utilitarianism*
    The Subjection of Women
    Autobiography
104. ** Charles Darwin (1809–1882)
    * *The Origin of Species*
    * *The Descent of Man*
    Autobiography
105. ** Charles Dickens (1812–1870)
    Works
    (esp. *Pickwick Papers, David Copperfield, Hard Times*)
106. ** Claude Bernard (1813–1878)
    Introduction to the Study of Experimental Medicine
107. ** Henry David Thoreau (1817–1862)
    Civil Disobedience
    Walden
108. Karl Marx (1818–1883)

* *Capital*
(together with the * *Communist Manifesto*)
109. George Eliot (1819–1880)
Adam Bede
Middlemarch
110. ** Herman Melville (1819–1891)
* *Moby-Dick*
Billy Budd
111. ** Fyodor Dostoevsky (1821–1881)
Crime and Punishment
The Idiot
* *The Brothers Karamazov*
112. ** Gustave Flaubert (1821–1880)
Madame Bovary
Three Stories
113. ** Henrik Ibsen (1828–1906)
Plays
(esp. *Hedda Gabler, A Doll's House, The Wild Duck*)
114. ** Leo Tolstoy (1828–1910)
* *War and Peace*
Anna Karenina
What Is Art?
Twenty-three Tales
115. ** Mark Twain (1835–1910)
The Adventures of Huckleberry Finn
The Mysterious Stranger
116. ** William James (1842–1910)
* *The Principles of Psychology*
The Varieties of Religious Experience
Pragmatism
Essays in Radical Empiricism
117. ** Henry James (1843–1916)
The American
The Ambassadors

118. Friedrich Wilhelm Nietzsche (1844–1900)
     Thus Spoke Zarathustra
     Beyond Good and Evil
     The Genealogy of Morals
     The Will to Power
119. Jules Henri Poincaré (1854–1912)
     Science and Hypothesis
     Science and Method
120. Sigmund Freud (1856–1939)
     * *The Interpretation of Dreams*
     * *Introductory Lectures on Psychoanalysis*
     * *Civilization and Its Discontents*
     * *New Introductory Lectures on Psychoanalysis*
121. ** George Bernard Shaw (1856–1950)
     Plays (and Prefaces)
     (esp. *Man and Superman, Major Barbara, Caesar and Cleopatra,*
        Pygmalion, Saint Joan)
122. ** Max Planck (1858–1947)
     Origin and Development of the Quantum Theory
     Where Is Science Going?
     Scientific Autobiography
123. Henri Bergson (1859–1941)
     Time and Free Will
     Matter and Memory
     Creative Evolution
     The Two Sources of Morality and Religion
124. ** John Dewey (1859–1952)
     How We Think
     Democracy and Education
     Experience and Nature
     Logic, the Theory of Inquiry
125. ** Alfred North Whitehead (1861–1947)
     An Introduction to Mathematics
     Science and the Modern World

   The Aims of Education and Other Essays
   Adventures of Ideas
126. ** George Santayana (1863–1952)
   The Life of Reason
   Skepticism and Animal Faith
   Persons and Places
127. Nikolai Lenin (1870–1924)
   The State and Revolution
128. Marcel Proust (1871–1922)
   Remembrance of Things Past
129. ** Bertrand Russell (1872–1970)
   The Problems of Philosophy
   The Analysis of Mind
   An Inquiry into Meaning and Truth
   Human Knowledge; Its Scope and Limits
130. ** Thomas Mann (1875–1955)
   The Magic Mountain
   Joseph and His Brothers
131. ** Albert Einstein (1879–1955)
   The Meaning of Relativity
   On the Method of Theoretical Physics
   The Evolution of Physics (with L. Infeld)
132. ** James Joyce (1882–1941)
   "The Dead" in *Dubliners*
   Portrait of the Artist as a Young Man
   Ulysses
133. Jacques Maritain (1882–1973)
   Art and Scholasticism
   The Degrees of Knowledge
   The Rights of Man and Natural Law
   True Humanism
134. Franz Kafka (1883–1924)
   The Trial
   The Castle

135. Arnold Toynbee (1889–1975)
  A Study of History
  Civilization on Trial
136. Jean-Paul Sartre (1905–1980)
  Nausea
  No Exit
  Being and Nothingness
137. Aleksandr I. Solzhenitsyn (1918–2008)
  The First Circle
  Cancer Ward

APPENDIX B

EXERCISES AND TESTS AT THE
FOUR LEVELS OF READING

Introductory

This Appendix offers a highly abbreviated sample of what Reading Exercises for independent study or group study are like. Obviously the sample cannot provide a thorough or exhaustive set of exercises, such as one would expect to find in a manual or workbook. However, it can perhaps go a certain way toward suggesting what such exercises would be, and how to get the most out of them.

The Appendix contains brief exercises and test questions at each of the four levels of reading:

At the First Level of Reading—Elementary Reading—the texts used are biographical notes about two of the authors included in *Great Books of the Western World*, John Stuart Mill and Sir Isaac Newton.

At the Second Level of Reading—Inspectional Reading—the texts used are the tables of contents of two works included in *Great Books of the Western World*, Dante's *Divine Comedy* and Darwin's *The Origin of Species*.

At the Third Level of Reading—Analytical Reading—the text used is *How to Read a Book* itself.

At the Fourth Level of Reading—Syntopical Reading—the texts used are selected passages reprinted from two other works included in *Great Books of the Western World*, Aristotle's *Politics* and Rousseau's *The Social Contract*.

Appendix B: Exercises and Tests

The reader will probably find that the sample exercises at the first two levels of reading are more familiar and conventional than those at the last two levels. This Appendix, unlike a more elaborate manual, can do little more than reinforce and clarify the distinctions between the various levels of reading and the differences between the various kinds of books. It cannot attempt to provide a really comprehensive and intensive exercise workbook.

It has become commonplace to criticize reading exercises and test questions on the grounds that they are not scientifically standardized, that they are culturally discriminatory, that by themselves they are not reliably predictive of success in schooling or in subsequent career progress, that questions often permit of more than one appropriate or "correct" answer, and that for all these reasons, grading by tests is to a certain extent arbitrary.

Much of this and similar criticism of the tests is valid, particularly if major decisions about school standing or placement, or about employment opportunities, are based exclusively on results drawn from these tests. However, many of the tests do effectively distinguish or identify degrees of competence, and they will continue to be widely employed in making academic and career judgments about individuals. Even if there were no other reasons, this reason by itself makes it desirable that the reader have some familiarity with the mechanics of these exercises and test questions.

It is particularly to be noted that the texts used in most such reading exercises are selected primarily for the sake of the test questions that are based on them. Hence the texts themselves are for the most part unrelated; frequently they are fragments—bits and pieces of technical pedantry or mere trivia.

In this Appendix, merely exemplary though it be, the emphasis is quite otherwise. The texts used for practice and to provide material for testing are *themselves worth reading*. Indeed, they are indispensable reading for anyone who wishes to advance beyond the first levels of reading. The texts are selected and the questions based on them are designed as tools for learning how to read what is worth reading.

A word about the form of the questions used in the tests that appear in the following pages. It is customary in such tests to employ a number of different kinds of questions. There are essay questions and multiple-choice questions. An essay question, of course, requires the person being tested to respond to something he has read in an extended statement. Multiple-choice questions are in turn of many kinds; usually they are presented in homogeneous groups. Sometimes a series of statements follows the reading exercise, and the person being tested is asked to indicate which statement best expresses the main idea or ideas of the passage read. In other cases the reader may be offered a choice of statements about a detail in the text, only one of which is a valid interpretation of the text, or at least is more apt than the others; or it may be the other way around; one is an incorrect choice, and the others are correct. Or a verbatim quotation may be given from the text to discover whether the reader has taken note of it and remembered it. Sometimes, in a statement either quoted directly or simply drawn from the text the reader will find a blank indicating that one or more words that will make sense of the statement have been omitted. Then follows a list of choices, lettered or numbered, among which the person being tested is asked to choose the phrase that, when inserted in the blank, best completes the statement.

Most questions may be answered directly from the passage read. But some questions require the reader to go outside the text for material that it is assumed he knows, material required to answer the question correctly. Still other questions are inferential: that is, they draw certain inferences from the text. The person taking the test is asked to select from a group of possibilities the inferences that can reasonably be drawn from the text; or he may be expected to recognize and discard inferences that are spurious and have no foundation in the text.

If one is faced with the task of creating a standardized test to be used widely in critical academic and career situations, then the choice of the kinds of questions and the framing of the questions themselves become critical as well. Fortunately, we do not face that kind of task in this Appendix. Instead, we are merely suggesting some approaches that may be tried in a course of independent study aimed at improving one's own reading skills. We will employ in what follows most of the kinds of questions just described—not segregating the types in groups as is usually done—and some other kinds as well. Some are quite easy, others are very difficult; the difficult questions may be the most fun to try to answer.

Because some of the questions are very difficult, and because we have framed them with the intention as much of causing you to reflect on what you have read as to test you on what you have read, we have in many cases given more than the customary short and cryptic answers to the questions. This is particularly so in the case of the questions in the last part of this Appendix, the section dealing with syntopical reading. There, we have taken the liberty of leading the reader by the hand, as it were, framing the questions in such a way as to suggest an overall interpretation of the texts read, and answering the questions as much as possible as though we were present in person.

I. Exercises and Tests at the First Level of Reading: Elementary Reading

Two short biographical sketches appear in this section of the Appendix. One outlines the life of John Stuart Mill, the other that of Sir Isaac Newton. The Mill sketch appears first, although of course Newton predates Mill by nearly two centuries.

This biographical sketch of Mill is reprinted from Volume 43 of *Great Books of the Western World*. Besides the Declaration of Independence, the Articles of Confederation, the U.S. Constitution, and the *Federalist Papers* of Hamilton, Madison and Jay—the founding documents of America—that volume contains three complete works by Mill: *On Liberty, Representative Government* and *Utilitarianism*. These are three of Mill's greatest works, but they by no means exhaust his writings. *The Subjection of Women,* for example, is of great contemporary interest, not only because Mill was one of the first thinkers in Western history to advocate complete equality for women, but also because of the book's trenchant style and the many insights it expresses about the relations of men and women at any time and place.

At the first level of reading, speed is not of the essence. The sketch of Mill's life that follows is about 1,200 words long. We suggest that it be read at a comfortable speed—in perhaps six to ten minutes. We also suggest that you mark phrases and sentences in the text that especially interest you and perhaps also make a few notes. Then try to answer the questions we have appended.

JOHN STUART MILL
1806–1873

Mill, in his *Autobiography,* declared that his intellectual development was due primarily to the influence of two people: his father, James Mill, and his wife.

James Mill elaborated for his son a comprehensive educational program, modelled upon the theories of Helvétius and Bentham. It was encyclopedic in scope and equipped Mill by the time he was thirteen with the equivalent of a thorough university education. The father acted as the boy's tutor and constant companion, allowing Mill to work in the same room with him and even to interrupt him as he was writing his *History of India* or his articles for the *Encyclopedia Britannica.* Mill later described the result as one that "made me appear as a 'made' or manufactured man, having had a certain impress of opinion stamped upon me which I could only reproduce."

The education began with Greek and arithmetic at the age of three. By the time he was eight Mill had read through the whole of Herodotus, six dialogues of Plato and considerable history. Before he was twelve he had studied Euclid and algebra, the Greek and Latin poets, and some English poetry. His interest in history continued, and he even attempted writing an account of Roman government. At twelve he was introduced to logic in Aristotle's *Organon* and the Latin scholastic manuals on the subject. The last year under his father's direct supervision, his thirteenth, was devoted to political economy; the son's notes later served the elder Mill in his *Elements of Political Economy*. He furthered his education by a period of studies with his father's friends, reading law with Austin and economics with Ricardo, and completed it by himself with Bentham's treatise on legislation, which he felt gave him "a creed, a doctrine, a philosophy . . . a religion" and made a "different being of him."

Although Mill never actually severed relations with his father, he experienced, at the age of twenty, a "crisis" in his mental history. It occurred to him to pose the question: "Suppose that all your objects in life were realized; that all the changes in institutions and opinions which you are looking forward to, could be completely effected at this very instant: would this be a great joy and happiness to you?" He reported that "an irrepressible self-consciousness distinctly answered, 'No,' " and he was overcome by a depression which lasted for several years. The first break in his "gloom" came while reading Marmontel's *Mémoires:* "I . . . came to the passage which relates his father's death, the distressed position of the family, and the sudden inspiration by which he, then a mere boy, felt and made them feel that he would be everything to them—would supply the place of all that they had lost." He was moved to tears by the scene, and from this moment his "burden grew lighter."

From the time he was seventeen, Mill supported himself by working for the East India Company, where his father was an official. Although he began nominally as a clerk, he was soon promoted to assistant-examiner, and for twenty years, from his father's death in 1836, until the Company's activities were taken over by the British Government, he had charge of the relations with the Indian states, which gave him wide practical experience in the problems of government. In addition to his regular employment, he took part in many activities tending to prepare public opinion for legislative reform. He, his father, and their friends formed the group known as "philosophical radicals," which made a major contribution to the debates leading to the Reform Bill of 1832. Mill was active in exposing what he considered departures from sound principle in parliament and the courts of justice. He wrote often for the newspapers friendly to the "radical" cause, helped to found and edit the *Westminster Review* as a "radical" organ, and participated in several reading and debating societies, devoted to the discussion of the contemporary intellectual and social problems.

These activities did not prevent him from pursuing his own intellectual interests. He edited Bentham's *Rationale of Judicial Evidence.* He studied logic and science with the aim of reconciling syllogistic logic with the methods of inductive science, and published his *System of Logic* (1843). At the same time he pushed his inquiries in the field of economics. These first took the form of *Essays on Some Unsettled Questions in Political Economy* and were later given systematic treatment in the *Principles of Political Economy* (1848).

The development and productivity of these years he attributed to his relationship with Mrs. Harriet Taylor, who became his wife in 1851. Mill had known her for twenty years, since shortly after his "crisis," and he could never praise too highly her influence upon his work. Although he published less during the seven years of his married life than at any other period of his career, he thought out and partly wrote many of his important works, including the essay *On Liberty* (1859), the *Thoughts on Parliamentary Reform,* which later led to the *Representative Government* (1861), and *Utilitarianism* (1863). He attributed to her especially his understanding of the human side of the abstract reforms he advocated. After her death he stated: "Her memory is to me a religion, and her approbation the standard by which, summing up as it does all worthiness, I endeavour to regulate my life."

Mill devoted a large part of his last years directly to political activity. In addition to his writings, he was one of the founders of the first women's suffrage society and, in 1865, consented to become a member of Parliament. Voting with the radical wing of the Liberal Party, he took an active part in the debates on Disraeli's Reform Bill and promoted the measures which he had long advocated, such as the representation of women, the reform of London government, and the alteration of land tenure in Ireland. Largely because of his support of unpopular measures, he was defeated for re-election. He retired to his cottage in Avignon, which had been built so that he might be close to the grave of his wife, and died there May 8, 1873.

Note that the questions in these tests are not all of the same type: there are several kinds of multiple-choice questions and some essay questions as well. Some questions call for information not included in the passage you have read—the background information a capable reader brings to whatever he reads. Select *all* the answers which seem to you to be valid, whether they are stated or implied in the text, or simply seem to you true on the basis of logic or your background information.

Test A: *Questions about the biographical sketch of John Stuart Mill*

1. During the latter part of Mill's life, England was ruled by (a) George IV (b) William IV (c) Victoria (d) Edward VII.
2. Mill's early education was largely designed by (a) Jeremy Bentham (b) his father, James Mill (c) the *Encyclopaedia Britannica* for which his father wrote articles (d) Marmontel's *Mémoires*.

3. By the time he was eight years old, Mill had read (a) Herodotus (b) six dialogues of Plato (c) Lincoln's Gettysburg Address.

4. Mill went to work for the East India Company to support himself at the age of (a) 14 (b) 17 (c) 21 (d) 25.

5. At the age of twenty, Mill experienced a (a) quarrel with his father (b) crisis in his mental history (c) "crisis" in his mental history (d) love affair with a married woman.

6. Mill, his father, and their friends called themselves "philosophical radicals" because they believed (a) in the overthrow of the government by violence (b) that reforms should be made in Parliamentary representation (c) that the study of philosophy should be dropped from college curriculums.

7. Among the authors whom Mill read as a young man, and who probably influenced his thinking, were (a) Aristotle (b) Dewey (c) Ricardo (d) Bentham.

8. Which of these well known works of Mill is not mentioned in the text? (a) *On Liberty* (b) *Representative Government* (c) *Utilitarianism* (d) *The Subjection of Women.*

9. Were he alive today, is it likely or not likely that Mill would be

	LIKELY	NOT LIKELY
(a) a supporter of the women's liberation movement	____	____
(b) in favor of universal education	____	____
(c) an active segregationist	____	____
(d) a strong advocate of censorship of newspapers and other mass media	____	____

10. It can be inferred from the text that Mill considered his wife (the former Mrs. Harriet Taylor), both during their marriage and after her death, to be (a) his severest critic (b) his best friend (c) his greatest enemy (d) his muse.

Turn to p. 411 for the answers to Test A.

Sir Isaac Newton is of enormous interest to scholars and historians of science at the present day. There are two main reasons for this. The first is a commonplace. By combining analysis with experimentation—by combining theorizing with systematic observation of natural phenomena—men like Galileo and Newton launched an intellectual revolution and helped to usher in our modern age of science. Not only did they discover truths about the physical world that continue to be relevant and important, but they also developed new methods of studying nature that have proved to be of wide usefulness in many areas of study and research.

That, as we said, is a commonplace; that aspect of Newton's life and achievement has been known and discussed for centuries. More recently, Newton has become the center of a worldwide study of the character of genius. Scholars and students of science and literature endlessly rank scientists and authors as more or less great, or on a scale ranging from extraordinary to genius. There is a considerable body of learned opinion that maintains that Newton was the supreme genius—the greatest intellect of all time. Many efforts have been made to characterize and account for genius. Precocity, the ability to concentrate, acute intuitiveness, rigorous analytical capacity—by terms such as these genius is described. All these terms seem to apply to Isaac Newton.

The biographical sketch of Newton that follows is reprinted from Volume 34 of *Great Books of the Western World*. That volume contains the texts of Newton's *Mathematical Principles of Natural Philosophy* (often known as Newton's *Principia*) and of his *Optics*; it also contains the text of the *Treatise on Light* of the Dutch physicist Christiaan Huygens. The biography of Newton is somewhat longer than the one of Mill; therefore, take ten to twelve minutes to read it. As before, mark the most striking passages and make notes. Then try to answer the questions that follow.

SIR ISAAC NEWTON
1642–1727

Newton was born at Woolsthorpe, Lincolnshire, on Christmas Day, 1642. His father, a small farmer, died a few months before his birth, and when in 1645 his mother married the rector of North Witham, Newton was left with his maternal grandmother at Woolsthorpe. After having acquired the rudiments of education at small schools close by, Newton was sent at the age of twelve to the grammar school at Grantham, where he lived in the house of an apothecary. By his own account, Newton was at first an indifferent scholar until a successful fight with another boy aroused a spirit of emulation and led to his becoming first in the school. He displayed very early a taste and aptitude for mechanical contrivances; he made windmills, water clocks, kites, and sundials, and he is said to have invented a four-wheel carriage which was to be moved by the rider.

After the death of her second husband in 1656, Newton's mother returned to Woolsthorpe and removed her eldest son from school so that he might prepare himself to manage the farm. But it was soon evident that his interests were not in farming, and upon the advice of his uncle, the rector of Burton Coggles, he was sent to Trinity College, Cambridge, where he matriculated in 1661 as one of the boys who performed menial services in return for their expenses. Although there is no record of his formal progress as a student, Newton is known to have read widely in mathematics and mechanics. His first reading at Cambridge was in the optical works of Kepler. He turned to Euclid because he was bothered by his inability to comprehend certain diagrams in a book on astrology he had bought at a fair; finding its propositions self-evident, he put it aside as "a trifling book," until his teacher, Isaac Barrow, induced him to take up the book again. It appears to have been the study of Descartes' *Geometry* which inspired him to do original mathematical work. In a small commonplace book kept by Newton as an undergraduate, there are several articles on angular sections and the squaring of curves, several calculations about musical notes, geometrical problems from Vieta and Van Schooten, annotations out of Wallis' *Arithmetic of Infinities,* together with observations on refraction, on the grinding of spherical optic glasses, on the errors of lenses, and on the extraction of all kinds of roots. It was around the time of his taking the Bachelor's degree, in 1665, that Newton discovered the binomial theorem and made the first notes on his discovery of the "method of fluxions."

When the Great Plague spread from London to Cambridge in 1665, college was dismissed, and Newton retired to the farm in Lincolnshire, where he conducted experiments in optics and chemistry and continued his mathematical speculations. From this forced retirement in 1666 he dated his discovery of the gravitational theory: "In the same year I began to think of gravity extending to the orb of the Moon, . . . compared the force requisite to keep the Moon in her orb with the force of gravity at the surface of the earth and found them to answer pretty nearly." At about the same time his work on optics led to his explanation of the composition of white light. Of the work he accomplished in these years Newton later remarked: "All this was in the two years of 1665 and 1666, for in those years I was in the prime of my age for invention and minded Mathematics and Philosophy more than at any time since."

On the re-opening of Trinity College in 1667, Newton was elected a fellow, and two years later, a little before his twenty-seventh birthday, he was appointed Lucasian professor of mathematics, succeeding his friend and teacher, Dr. Barrow. Newton had already built a reflecting telescope in 1668; the second telescope of his making he presented to the Royal Society in December, 1671. Two months later, as a fellow of the Society, he communicated his discovery on light and thereby started a controversy which was to run for many years and to involve Hooke, Lucas, Linus, and others. Newton, who always found controversy distasteful, "blamed my own imprudence for parting with so substantial a blessing as my quiet to run after a shadow." His papers on optics, the most important of which were communicated to the Royal Society between 1672 and 1676, were collected in the *Optics* (1704).

It was not until 1684 that Newton began to think of making known his work on gravity. Hooke, Halley, and Sir Christopher Wren had independently come to some notion of the law of gravity but were not having any success in explaining the orbits of the planets. In that year Halley consulted Newton on the problem and was astonished to find that he had already solved it. Newton submitted to him four theorems and seven problems, which proved to be the nucleus of his major work. In some seventeen or eighteen months during 1685 and 1686 he wrote in Latin the *Mathematical Principles of Natural Philosophy*. Newton thought for some time of suppressing the third book, and it was only Halley's insistence that preserved it. Halley also took upon himself the cost of publishing the work in 1687 after the Royal Society proved unable to meet its cost. The book caused great excitement throughout Europe, and in 1689 Huygens, at that time the more famous scientist, came to England to make the personal acquaintance of Newton.

While working upon the *Principles*, Newton had begun to take a more prominent part in university affairs. For his opposition to the attempt of James II to repudiate the oath of allegiance and supremacy at the university, Newton was elected parliamentary member for Cambridge. On his return to the university, he suffered a serious illness which incapacitated him for most of 1692 and 1693 and caused considerable concern to his friends and fellow workers. After his recovery, he left the university to work for the government. Through his friends Locke, Wren, and Lord Halifax, Newton was made Warden of the Mint in 1695 and four years later, Master of the Mint, a position he held until his death.

For the last thirty years of his life Newton produced little original mathematical work. He kept his interest and his skill in the subject; in 1696 he solved overnight a problem offered by Bernoulli in a competition for which six months had been allowed, and again in 1716 he worked in a few hours a problem which Leibniz had proposed in order to "feel the pulse of the English analysts." He was much occupied, to his own distress, with two mathematical controversies, one regarding the astronomical observations of the astronomer royal, and the other with Leibniz regarding the invention of calculus. He also worked on revisions for a second edition of the *Principles,* which appeared in 1713.

Newton's scientific work brought him great fame. He was a popular visitor at the Court and was knighted in 1705. Many honors came to him from the continent; he was in correspondence with all the leading men of science, and visitors became so frequent as to prove a serious discomfort. Despite his fame, Newton maintained his modesty. Shortly before his death, he remarked: "I do not know what I may appear to the world, but to myself I seem to have been only like a boy playing on the seashore, and diverting myself in now and then finding a smoother pebble or a prettier shell than ordinary, whilst the great ocean of truth lay all undiscovered before me."

From an early period of his life Newton had been much interested in theological studies and before 1690 had begun to study the prophecies. In that year he wrote, in the form of a letter to Locke, an *Historical Account of Two Notable Corruptions of the Scriptures,* regarding two passages on the Trinity. He left in manuscript *Observations on the Prophecies of Daniel and the Apocalypse* and other works of exegesis.

After 1725 Newton's health was much impaired, and his duties at the Mint were discharged by a deputy. In February, 1727, he presided for the last time at the Royal Society, of which he had been president since 1703, and died on March 20, 1727, in his eighty-fifth year. He was buried in Westminster Abbey after lying in state in the Jerusalem Chamber.

Test B: Questions about the biography of Sir Isaac Newton

1. Before Newton gained admission to Trinity College, Cambridge, he took a special interest in (a) politics (b) theology (c) mechanical devices (d) science and mathematics.

2. Newton was knighted by (a) King Charles II (1660–1685) (b) King James II (1685–1688) (c) Queen Anne (1702–1714) (d) King George I (1714–1727).

3. When Trinity College was closed for two years from 1665 to 1667 as a consequence of the spreading of the Great Plague from London to Cambridge, Newton along with many other students took an extended holiday on the Continent. (True or False?)

4. Newton was elected to Parliament on the basis of (a) his handling of antiroyalist rioting among the students (b) his opposition to James II's attempt to repudiate the Oath of Allegiance and Supremacy (c) his handling of student and faculty panic in the face of the spread of the Great Plague from London to Cambridge.

5. During the latter part of his life, Newton was occupied and distressed by his involvement in controversies regarding (a) astronomical observations of the astronomer royal (b) the invention of the calculus (c) the prophecies of Daniel.

6. Newton originally wrote his *Mathematical Principles of Natural Philosophy* in (a) Greek (b) Latin (c) English.

7. Among other matters, the work explained (a) why apples fall (b) the orbits of the planets (c) how to square a circle (d) in what respects God is a geometrician.

8. Optics is (a) the general name given to the study of light, the

radiant energy that among other things by its action upon the organs of vision enables man to see (b) the general name for the study of the eye in man and other animals (c) the technology of the production of the lens and its use in telescopes.

9. Newton, in his *Optics,* (a) proved that light travels at 300,000 kilometers an hour (b) revealed the composition of white light (c) described how white light can be broken up by a prism into the colors of the spectrum (d) outlined some military uses of the telescope.

10. As an old man, Newton remarked: "I do not know what I may appear to the world, but to myself I seem to have been only like a boy playing on the seashore, and diverting myself in now and then finding a smoother pebble or a prettier shell than ordinary, whilst the great ocean of truth lay all undiscovered before me." Comment on this statement in 250 words.

Turn to p. 411 for the answers to Test B.

You have now completed the two-part reading exercise at the first level of reading. You will of course have noted that, as we reminded you they would, the questions draw not only on the texts read but also on historical and other information not explicitly included in the text. The capable reader, even at this first level, can bring useful information to bear on whatever he reads. In general, the better informed he is, the better he reads.

If you have done reasonably well in answering the test questions, it must be obvious to you that you are a pretty well-rounded reader and that you have reached and even exceeded the standards set for Elementary Reading. We hope you have also recognized that these exercises and tests were designed not only to improve your skill as a reader but also to help you learn something worth knowing, or to apply something you already know to what you read.

II. Exercises and Tests at the Second Level of Reading: Inspectional Reading

The tables of contents of two works included in *Great Books of the Western World* are used as texts for reading and testing in this section of Appendix B. In addition, short biographical sketches of their authors—Dante and Darwin—are also reprinted here, for the reader's information and also as material from which test questions are drawn.

The biography of Dante and the table of contents of his *Divine Comedy* are taken from Volume 21 of *Great Books of the Western World*. That volume contains only the *Divine Comedy*. But Dante wrote other works, in prose and verse, of great interest and beauty, although only his *Comedy* (the adjective "Divine" was added after his death) is widely read today.

You will recall, from Chapter 4, that there are two steps in Inspectional Reading. The first we called Pre-Reading or Skimming; the second, Superficial Reading. As we do not have the entire text of the *Divine Comedy* before us for this sample reading exercise, we will treat the table of contents of the work, given here in its entirety, as though it were a book in itself. That is, we suggest that you spend less than ten minutes (here, speed *is* of the essence) systematically skimming the whole table of contents, after which you can try answering some questions; and then we will ask you to read the table of contents over again superficially—that is, in about twenty minutes—and then answer some more questions.

The total reading time to be devoted to the table of contents of the *Divine Comedy* is therefore half an hour. Considering that scholars have devoted thirty years of their lives to the *Divine Comedy,* we dare say that thirty minutes of inspection is indeed superficial. At the same time, it is not presumptuous or vain. One can learn a lot about this great poem in half an hour. And as to those for whom Dante and the *Divine Comedy* are vague names at best, a careful inspection of the table of contents may induce them to inspect the whole work, or even lead them on to read the whole analytically, at the third level of reading.

Before giving the table of contents your first inspection—before either pre-reading or systematically skimming it—read the biographical note about Dante in a few minutes. It will help you understand what Dante is planning and doing in the *Divine Comedy*—and also help you to answer some of our questions.

DANTE ALIGHIERI
1265–1321

Dante Alighieri was born in Florence about the middle of May, 1265. The city, then under its first democratic constitution, was sharply divided between the Papal party of the Guelphs and the Imperial party of the Ghibellines. Dante's family were adherents of the Guelph faction, and when Dante was only a few months old, the Guelphs obtained decisive victory at the Battle of Benevento. Although of noble ancestry, the Alighieri family was neither wealthy nor particularly prominent.

It seems probable that Dante received his early education at the Franciscan school of Santa Croce. He evidently owed much to the influence of Brunetto Latini, the philosopher and scholar who figured largely in the councils of the Florentine commune. Before Dante was twenty, he began writing poetry and became associated with the Italian poets of the "sweet new style," who exalted their love and their ladies in philosophical verse. Dante's "lady," whom he celebrated with singular devotion, was a certain Beatrice. According to Boccaccio's life of Dante, she was Beatrice Portinari, daughter of a Florentine citizen, who married a wealthy banker and died when she was but twenty-four. Dante first sang of Beatrice in the *Vita Nuova* (1292), a sequence of poems with prose comment in which he recounts the story of his love, of the first meeting when they were both nine years of age, of the exchange of greetings which passed between them on May Day, 1283, and of Beatrice's death in 1290.

Upon turning thirty, Dante became actively involved in Florentine politics. The constitution of the city was based upon the guilds, and Dante, upon his enrollment in the guild of physicians and apothecaries, which also included book dealers, became eligible for office. He participated in the deliberations of the councils, served on a special embassy, and in 1300 was elected one of the six priors that governed the city. The former struggle between the Guelphs and Ghibellines had appeared in new form in the conflict between the Whites and the Blacks. As one of the priors, Dante seems to have been influential in the move to lessen factionalism by banishing from Florence the rival leaders, including among the Blacks his wife's relative, Corso Donati, and among the Whites his "first friend," the poet, Guido Cavalcanti. Despite the opposition of Dante and the White leaders to Papal interference in Florentine affairs, Pope Boniface VIII in 1301 invited Charles of Valois, brother of King Philip of France, to enter Florence to settle the differences between the two factions. Actually he assisted the Blacks to seize power, and more than six hundred Whites were condemned to exile. In 1302 Dante, with four others of the White party, was charged with corruption in office. He was condemned to pay a fine of five thousand florins within three days or lose his property, exiled for two years, and denied the right ever again to hold public office. Three months later, upon his refusal to pay the fine, Dante was condemned to be burned alive if he should come within the power of the republic.

"After it was the pleasure of the citizens of the most beautiful and most famous daughter of Rome, Florence, to chase me forth from her sweet bosom," Dante writes of his exile in the *Convivio,* "I have gone through almost every region to which this tongue of ours extends, showing against my will the wound of fortune." It is recorded that Dante attended a meeting at San Godenzo, where an alliance was formed between the Whites in exile and the Ghibellines, but he does not seem to have been present in 1304 when the combined forces were defeated at Lastra. Perhaps he had already separated himself from the "evil and foolish company" of his fellow-exiles, "formed a party by himself," and found his "first refuge and hostelry" at the court of the Della Scalas in Verona. Probably during the following years he spent time at Bologna and later at Padua, where Giotto is said to have entertained him. Toward the end of 1306 he was the guest of the Malaspinas in Lunigiana and acted as their ambassador in making peace with the Bishop of Luni. Some time after this date he may have visited Paris and attended the university there.

During the early years of his exile Dante appears to have studied in those subjects which gained him the title of philosopher and theologian as well as poet. In the *Convivio,* probably written between 1305 and 1308, he tells how, after the death of Beatrice, he turned to Cicero's *De Amicitia* and the *Consolatio Philosophiae* of Boethius, which awoke in him the love of philosophy. To sing its praises he began his *Convivio,* which he intended to be a kind of treasury of universal knowledge in the form of poems connected by lengthy prose commentaries. At the same time he worked upon the *De Vulgari Eloquentia,* a Latin treatise in which he defended the use of Italian as a literary language.

The election of Henry of Luxemburg as emperor in 1308 stirred Dante's political hopes. When Henry entered Italy in 1310 at the head of an army, Dante in an epistle to the princes and people of Italy hailed the coming of a deliverer. At Milan he paid personal homage to Henry as his sovereign. When Florence, in alliance with King Robert of Naples, prepared to resist the emperor, Dante in a second epistle denounced them for their obstinacy and prophesied their doom. In a third epistle he upbraided the Emperor himself for his delay and urged him on against Florence. It was probably during this period that he wrote his *De Monarchia,* an intellectual defense of the emperor as the sovereign of the temporal order. The death of Henry in 1313, after a year or so of ineffectual fighting, brought an end to the political aspirations of Dante and his party. The city of Florence in 1311 and again in 1315 renewed his condemnation.

After Henry's death, Dante passed the rest of his life under the protection of various lords of Lombardy, Tuscany, and the Romagna. According to one tradition, he retired for a time to the monastery of Santa Croce di Fonte Avellana in the Appenines, where he worked on the *Divine Comedy,* which may have been planned as early as 1292. He was almost certainly for a time at the court of Can Grande della Scala, to whom he dedicated the *Paradiso.* In 1315 Florence issued a general recall of exiles. Dante refused to pay the required fine and to "bear the brand of oblation," feeling that such a return would derogate from his fame and honor. To the end of his life he appears to have hoped that his *Comedy* would finally open the gates of the city to him.

The last few years of the poet's life were spent at Ravenna, under the patronage of Guido da Polenta, a nephew of Francesca da Rimini. Dante's daughter, Beatrice, was a nun in that city, and one of his sons held a benefice there; his wife seems to have resided in Florence throughout his exile. Dante was greatly esteemed at Ravenna and enjoyed a congenial circle of friends. Here he completed the *Divine Comedy* and wrote two eclogues in Latin which indicate that a certain contentment surrounded his closing days. Returning from a diplomatic mission to Venice on behalf of his patron, he caught a fever and died September 14, 1321. He was buried at Ravenna before the door of the principal church, with the highest honors, and "in the habit of a poet and a great philosopher."

Now spend about ten minutes pre-reading or skimming the following table of contents systematically. The text used here is that of the Charles Eliot Norton translation. Other translators would of course present the table of contents in somewhat different terms.

TABLE OF CONTENTS OF THE *DIVINE COMEDY*

HELL

CANTO I: Dante, astray in a wood, reaches the foot of a hill which he begins to ascend; he is hindered by three beasts; he turns back and is met by Virgil, who proposes to guide him into the eternal world.

CANTO II: Dante, doubtful of his own powers, is discouraged at the outset. Virgil cheers him by telling him that he has been sent to his aid by a blessed Spirit from Heaven, who revealed herself as Beatrice. Dante casts off fear, and the poets proceed.

CANTO III: The gate of Hell. Virgil leads Dante in. The punishment of those who had lived without infamy and without praise. Acheron, and the sinners on its bank. Charon. Earthquake. Dante swoons.

CANTO IV: The further side of Acheron. Virgil leads Dante into Limbo, the First Circle of Hell, containing the spirits of those who lived virtuously but without faith in Christ. Greeting of Virgil by his fellow poets. They enter a castle, where are the shades of ancient worthies. After seeing them Virgil and Dante depart.

CANTO V: The Second Circle, that of Carnal Sinners. Minos. Shades renowned of old. Francesca da Rimini.

CANTO VI: The Third Circle, that of the Gluttonous. Cerberus. Ciacco.

CANTO VII: The Fourth Circle, that of the Avaricious and the Prodigal. Pluto. Fortune. The Styx. The Fifth Circle, that of the Wrathful.

CANTO VIII: The Fifth Circle. Phlegyas and his boat. Passage of the Styx. Filippo Argenti. The City of Dis. The demons refuse entrance to the poets.

CANTO IX: The City of Dis. Erichtho. The Three Furies. The Heavenly Messenger. The Sixth Circle: that of the Heretics.

CANTO X: The Sixth Circle. Farinata degli Uberti. Cavalcante Cavalcanti. Frederick II.

CANTO XI: The Sixth Circle. Tomb of Pope Anastasius. Discourse of Virgil on the divisions of the lower Hell.

CANTO XII: The Seventh Circle, that of the Violent, first round: those who do violence to others. The Minotaur. The Centaurs. Chiron. Nessus. The River of boiling blood, and the sinners in it.

CANTO XIII: The Seventh Circle, second round: those who have done violence to themselves and to their goods. The Wood of Self-murderers. The Harpies. Pier dello Vigne. Lano of Siena and others.

CANTO XIV: The Seventh Circle, third round: those who have done violence to God. The Burning Sand. Capaneus. Figure of the Old Man in Crete. The rivers of Hell.

CANTO XV: The Seventh Circle, third round: those who have done violence to Nature. Brunetto Latini. Prophecies of misfortune to Dante.

CANTO XVI: The Seventh Circle, third round: those who have done violence to Nature. Guido Guerra, Tegghiaio Aldobrandi and Jacopo Rusticucci. The roar of Phlegethon as it pours downward. The cord thrown into the abyss.

CANTO XVII: The Seventh Circle, third round: those who have done violence to Art. Geryon. The Usurers. Descent to the Eighth Circle.

CANTO XVIII: The Eighth Circle: that of the fraudulent; first pouch: pandars and seducers. Venedico Caccianimico. Jason. Second pouch: false flatterers. Alessio Interminei. Thais.

CANTO XIX: The Eighth Circle: third pouch: simonists. Pope Nicholas III.

CANTO XX: The Eighth Circle: fourth pouch: diviners, soothsayers, and magicians. Amphiaraus. Tiresias. Aruns. Manto. Eurypylus. Michael Scott. Asdente.

CANTO XXI: The Eighth Circle: fifth pouch: barrators. A magistrate of Lucca. The Malebranche. Parley with them.

CANTO XXII: The Eighth Circle: fifth pouch: barrators. Ciampolo of Navarre. Fra Gomita. Michel Zanche. Fray of the Malebranche.

CANTO XXIII: The Eighth Circle. Escape from the fifth pouch. The sixth pouch: hypocrites, in cloaks of gilded lead. Jovial Friars. Caiaphas. Annas. Frate Catalano.

CANTO XXIV: The Eighth Circle: The poets climb from the sixth pouch. Seventh pouch, filled with serpents, by which thieves are tormented. Vanni Fucci. Prophecy of calamity to Dante.

CANTO XXV: The Eighth Circle: seventh pouch: fraudulent thieves. Cacus. Agnello Brunelleschi and others.

CANTO XXVI: The Eighth Circle: eighth pouch: fraudulent counsellors. Ulysses and Diomed.

CANTO XXVII: The Eighth Circle: eighth pouch: fraudulent counsellors. Guido da Montefeltro.

CANTO XXVIII: The Eighth Circle: ninth pouch: sowers of discord and schism. Mahomet and Ali. Fra Dolcino. Pier da Medicina. Curio. Mosca. Bertran de Born.

CANTO XXIX: The Eighth Circle: ninth pouch. Geri del Bello. Tenth pouch: falsifiers of all sorts. Alchemists. Griffolino of Arezzo. Capocchio.

CANTO XXX: The Eighth Circle: tenth pouch: false personators, false moneyers, and the false in words. Myrrha. Gianni Schicchi. Master Adam. Sinon of Troy.

CANTO XXXI: The Eighth Circle. Giants. Nimrod. Ephialtes. Antæus sets the Poets down in the Ninth Circle.

CANTO XXXII: The Ninth Circle: that of traitors; first ring: Caina. Counts of Mangona. Camicion de' Pazzi. Second ring: Antenora. Bocca degli Abati. Buoso da Duera. Count Ugolino.

CANTO XXXIII: The Ninth Circle: second ring: Antenora. Count Ugolino. Third ring: Ptolomea. Frate Alberigo. Branca d' Oria.

CANTO XXXIV: The Ninth Circle: fourth ring: Judecca. Lucifer. Judas, Brutus and Cassius. Centre of the Universe. Passage from Hell. Ascent to the surface of the Southern Hemisphere.

PURGATORY

CANTO I: The new theme. Invocation to the Muses. Dawn of Easter on the shore of Purgatory. The Four Stars. Cato. The cleansing of Dante's face from the stains of Hell.

CANTO II: Sunrise. The Poets on the shore. Coming of a boat, guided by an angel, bearing souls to Purgatory. Their landing. Casella and his song. Cato hurries the souls to the mountain.

CANTO III: Ante-Purgatory. Souls of those who have died in contumacy of the Church. Manfred.

CANTO IV: Ante-Purgatory. Ascent to a shelf of the mountain. The negligent, who postponed repentance to the last hour. Belacqua.

CANTO V: Ante-Purgatory. Spirits who had delayed repentance, and met with death by violence, but died repentant. Jacopo del Cassero. Buonconte da Montefeltro. Pia de' Tolomei.

CANTO VI: Ante-Purgatory. More spirits who had deferred repentance till they were overtaken by a violent death. Efficacy of prayer. Sordello. Apostrophe to Italy.

CANTO VII: Virgil makes himself known to Sordello. Sordello leads the Poets to the Valley of the Princes who had been negligent of salvation. He points them out by name.

CANTO VIII: Valley of the Princes. Two Guardian Angels. Nino Visconti. The Serpent. Corrado Malaspina.

CANTO IX: Slumber and Dream of Dante. The Eagle. Lucia. The Gate of Purgatory. The Angelic Gatekeeper. Seven P's inscribed on Dante's Forehead. Entrance to the First Ledge.

CANTO X: Purgatory proper. First Ledge: the Proud. Examples of Humility sculptured on the rock.

CANTO XI: First Ledge: the Proud. Prayer. Omberto Aldobrandeschi. Oderisi d' Agubbio. Provenzan Salvani.

CANTO XII: First Ledge: the Proud. Instances of the punishment of Pride graven on the pavement. Meeting with an Angel who removes one of the P's. Ascent to the Second Ledge.

CANTO XIII: Second Ledge: the Envious. Examples of Love. The Shades in haircloth, and with sealed eyes. Sapìa of Siena.

CANTO XIV: Second Ledge: the Envious. Guido del Duca. Rinieri de' Calboli. Instances of the punishment of Envy.

CANTO XV: Second Ledge: the Envious. An Angel removes the second P from Dante's forehead. Discourse concerning the Sharing of Good. Ascent to the Third Ledge: the Wrathful. Vision of Examples of Forbearance.

CANTO XVI: Third Ledge: the Wrathful. Marco Lombardo. His discourse on Free Will, and the corruption of the World.

CANTO XVII: Third Ledge: the Wrathful. Issue from the Smoke. Vision of Instances of the punishment of Anger. Ascent to the Fourth Ledge, where Sloth is purged. Second Nightfall in Purgatory. Virgil explains how Love is the root alike of Virtue and of Sin.

CANTO XVIII: Fourth Ledge: the Slothful. Discourse of Virgil on Love and Free Will. Throng of Spirits running in haste to redeem their Sin. Examples of Zeal. The Abbot of San Zeno. Instances of the punishment of Sloth. Dante falls asleep.

CANTO XIX: Fourth Ledge. Dante dreams of the Siren. The Angel of the Pass. Ascent to the Fifth Ledge: The Avaricious. Pope Adrian V.

CANTO XX: Fifth Ledge: the Avaricious. The Spirits celebrate examples of Poverty and Bounty. Hugh Capet. His discourse on his descendants. Instances of the punishment of Avarice. Trembling of the Mountain.

CANTO XXI: Fifth Ledge. The shade of Statius. Cause of the trembling of the Mountain. Statius does honor to Virgil

CANTO XXII: Ascent to the Sixth Ledge. Discourse of Statius and Virgil. Entrance to the Ledge: the Gluttonous. The Mystic Tree. Examples of Temperance.

CANTO XXIII: Sixth Ledge: the Gluttonous. Forese Donati. Nella. Rebuke of the women of Florence.

CANTO XXIV: Sixth Ledge: the Gluttonous. Forese Donati. Piccarda Donati. Bonagiunta of Lucca. Pope Martin IV. Ubaldin dalla Pila. Bonifazio. Messer Marchese. Prophecy of Bonagiunta concerning Gentucca, and of Forese concerning Corso de' Donati. Second Mystic Tree. Instances of the punishment of gluttony. The Angel of the Pass.

CANTO XXV: Ascent to the Seventh Ledge. Discourse of Statius on generation, the infusion of the Soul into the body, and the corporeal semblance of Souls after death. The Seventh Ledge: the Lustful. The mode of their Purification. Examples of Chastity.

CANTO XXVI: Seventh Ledge: the Lustful. Sinners in the fire, going in opposite directions. Instances of the punishment of Lust. Guido Guinicelli. Arnaut Daniel.

CANTO XXVII: Seventh Ledge: the Lustful. Passage through the Flames. Stairway in the rock. Night upon the stairs. Dream of Dante. Morning. Ascent to the Earthly Paradise. Last words of Virgil.

CANTO XXVIII: The Earthly Paradise. The Forest. A Lady gathering flowers on the bank of a little stream. Discourse with her concerning the nature of the place.

CANTO XXIX: The Earthly Paradise. Mystic Procession or Triumph of the Church.

CANTO XXX: The Earthly Paradise. Beatrice appears. Departure of Virgil. Reproof of Dante by Beatrice.

CANTO XXXI: The Earthly Paradise. Reproachful discourse

of Beatrice, and confession of Dante. Passage of Lethe. Appeal of the Virtues to Beatrice. Her Unveiling.

CANTO XXXII: The Earthly Paradise. Return of the Triumphal procession. The Chariot bound to the Mystic Tree. Sleep of Dante. His waking to find the Triumph departed. Transformation of the Chariot. The Harlot and the Giant.

CANTO XXXIII: The Earthly Paradise. Prophecy of Beatrice concerning one who shall restore the Empire. Her discourse with Dante. The river Eunoë. Dante drinks of it, and is fit to ascend to Heaven.

PARADISE

CANTO I: Proem. Invocation. Beatrice, and Dante transhumanized, ascend through the Sphere of Fire toward the Moon. Beatrice explains the cause of their ascent.

CANTO II: Proem. Ascent to the Moon. The cause of Spots on the Moon. Influence of the Heavens.

CANTO III: The Heaven of the Moon. Spirits whose vows had been broken. Piccarda Donati. The Empress Constance.

CANTO IV: Doubts of Dante, respecting the justice of Heaven and the abode of the blessed, solved by Beatrice. Question of Dante as to the possibility of reparation for broken vows.

CANTO V: The sanctity of vows, and the seriousness with which they are to be made or changed. Ascent to the Heaven of Mercury. The shade of Justinian.

CANTO VI: Justinian tells of his own life. The story of the Roman Eagle. Spirits in the planet Mercury. Romeo.

CANTO VII: Discourse of Beatrice. The Fall of Man. The scheme of his Redemption.

CANTO VIII: Ascent to the Heaven of Venus. Spirits of Lovers. Charles Martel. His discourse on the order and the varieties in mortal things.

CANTO IX: The planet Venus. Conversation of Dante with

Cunizza da Romano. With Folco of Marseilles. Rahab. Avarice of the Papal Court.

CANTO X: Ascent to the Sun. Spirits of the wise, and the learned in theology. St. Thomas Aquinas. He names to Dante those who surround him.

CANTO XI: The Vanity of worldly desires. St. Thomas Aquinas undertakes to solve two doubts perplexing Dante. He narrates the life of St. Francis of Assisi.

CANTO XII: Second circle of the spirits of wise religious men, doctors of the Church and teachers. St. Bonaventura narrates the life of St. Dominic, and tells the names of those who form the circle with him.

CANTO XIII: St. Thomas Aquinas speaks again, and explains the relation of the wisdom of Solomon to that of Adam and of Christ, and declares the vanity of human judgment.

CANTO XIV: At the prayer of Beatrice, Solomon tells of the glorified body of the blessed after the Last Judgment. Ascent to the Heaven of Mars. Spirits of the Soldiery of Christ in the form of a Cross with the figure of Christ thereon. Hymn of the Spirits.

CANTO XV: Dante is welcomed by his ancestor, Cacciaguida. Cacciaguida tells of his family, and of the simple life of Florence in the old days.

CANTO XVI: The boast of blood. Cacciaguida continues his discourse concerning the old and the new Florence.

CANTO XVII: Dante questions Cacciaguida as to his fortunes. Cacciaguida replies, foretelling the exile of Dante, and the renown of his Poem.

CANTO XVIII: The Spirits in the Cross of Mars. Ascent to the Heaven of Jupiter. Words shaped in light upon the planet by the Spirits. Denunciation of the avarice of the Popes.

CANTO XIX: The voice of the Eagle. It speaks of the mysteries of Divine justice; of the necessity of Faith for salvation; of the sins of certain kings.

CANTO XX: The song of the Just. Princes who have loved

righteousness, in the eye of the Eagle. Spirits, once Pagans, in bliss. Faith and Salvation. Predestination.

CANTO XXI: Ascent to the Heaven of Saturn. Spirits of those who had given themselves to devout contemplation. The Golden Stairway. St. Peter Damian. Predestination. The luxury of modern Prelates. Dante alarmed by a cry of the spirits.

CANTO XXII: Beatrice reassures Dante. St. Benedict appears. He tells of the founding of his Order, and of the falling away of its brethren. Beatrice and Dante ascend to the Starry Heaven. The constellation of the Twins. Sight of the Earth.

CANTO XXIII: The Triumph of Christ.

CANTO XXIV: St. Peter examines Dante concerning Faith, and approves his answer.

CANTO XXV: St. James examines Dante concerning Hope. St. John appears, with a brightness so dazzling as to deprive Dante, for the time, of sight.

CANTO XXVI: St. John examines Dante concerning Love. Dante's sight restored. Adam appears, and answers questions put to him by Dante.

CANTO XXVII: Denunciation by St. Peter of his degenerate successors. Dante gazes upon the Earth. Ascent of Beatrice and Dante to the Crystalline Heaven. Its nature. Beatrice rebukes the covetousness of mortals.

CANTO XXVIII: The Heavenly Hierarchy.

CANTO XXIX: Discourse of Beatrice concerning the creation and nature of the Angels. She reproves the presumption and foolishness of preachers.

CANTO XXX: Ascent to the Empyrean. The River of Light. The celestial Rose. The seat of Henry VII. The last words of Beatrice.

CANTO XXXI: The Rose of Paradise. St. Bernard. Prayer to Beatrice. The glory of the Blessed Virgin.

CANTO XXXII: St. Bernard describes the order of the Rose, and points out many of the Saints. The children in Paradise. The angelic festival. The patricians of the Court of Heaven.

CANTO XXXIII: Prayer to the Virgin. The Beatific Vision. The Ultimate Salvation.

Test C: First series of questions about the Divine Comedy *of Dante*

1. Dante divides his work into (a) three (b) four (c) six major parts.
2. The major parts are titled (a) Earth, Moon, Heaven, Angelic Circles (b) Hell, Purgatory, Paradise (c) Inferno, Purgatorio, Paradiso.
3. The major parts are subdivided into (a) cantos (b) chapters (c) sections.
4. The number of subdivisions in each of the major parts (a) are approximately equal (b) are either 33 or 34 (c) range between 23 and 44.
5. The total number of subdivisions in the work is (a) 99 (b) 100 (c) 101.
6. The main division of Hell seems to be into (a) circles (b) ledges (c) pouches.
7. The main division of Purgatory seems to be into (a) circles (b) ledges (c) pouches.
8. The main division of Paradise seems to be according to (a) the order of the virtues and vices (b) the order of the angelic hierarchy (c) the order of the planets of the solar system.
9. In Hell, the movement is (a) downwards (b) upwards. In Purgatory the movement is (a) downwards (b) upwards.
10. The Earthly Paradise is found by Dante (a) in the part of the poem titled Purgatory (b) in the part of the poem titled Paradise.

Turn to p. 411 for the answers to Test C.

Now, having skimmed the table of contents of the *Divine Comedy* and answered this first series of questions, take twenty minutes to read the table of contents superficially.

Test D: Further questions about Dante's Divine Comedy

1. Dante is guided through Hell by (a) Beatrice (b) Virgil (c) Lucifer.
2. Virgil is sent to help Dante by (a) Beatrice (b) God (c) St. Bernard.
3. Dante's main concern is to describe (a) life after death (b) the kinds of lives men live on earth.
4. The *Divine Comedy* is (a) essentially a comic poem (b) a poetic treatment of selected theses in moral theology (c) an imaginative construct of the entire universe.
5. On which of the following ideologies and teachings does the poem seem to be most dependent? (a) Humanistic (b) Greek and Latin (c) Christian.
6. The Slothful are punished on the Fourth Ledge of Purgatory. Is it significant that before leaving this ledge Dante falls asleep? (Yes or No?)
7. In Canto 34 of Hell Dante and Virgil reach the center of the universe. Why?
8. In Canto 9 of Purgatory seven P's are inscribed on Dante's forehead, and one of these P's is removed as Dante passes upward past each of the ledges of the Mountain of Purgatory. What is the significance of the P's?
9. Virgil accompanies Dante to the Earthly Paradise (Cantos 28–33 of Purgatory) but departs in Canto 30 and does not go with Dante to Paradise. Why?
10. In Cantos 11 and 12 of Paradise St. Thomas Aquinas narrates the life of St. Francis and St. Bonaventura narrates the life of St. Dominic. What is the significance of this?

The last five questions in Test D, which deal mainly with the symbolism of Dante's *Divine Comedy,* may be difficult or even impossible to answer on the basis of reading the table of contents alone.

For that reason, if for no other, we have provided quite full answers to these questions. The justification for asking such questions is twofold. First, we are not *certain* that they cannot be answered from the table of contents alone. Second, and more important, they are designed to suggest one of the major characteristics of Dante's great work: that is, that it is symbolic through and through. Almost every statement Dante makes, and almost every person and event he describes, has at least two meanings, and often three or four. We think that fact is probably clear from reading the table of contents alone, even if the details are not all spelled out. Hence it might be interesting to try to answer Questions 6–10 in this test without any outside help whatever even if you have never read Dante before or read about him. In other words, if you have to guess, how close are your guesses?

Turn to p. 412 for the answers to Test D.

The biography of Charles Darwin and the table of contents of his *The Origin of Species* that appear on the following pages are taken from Volume 49 of *Great Books of the Western World.* Besides *The Origin of Species,* that volume also contains *The Descent of Man,* in which Darwin applied his general theory, as expounded in the *Origin,* to the puzzling question of the evolution of the human species.

As in the case of Dante, read the biography of Darwin quickly— in five or six minutes—and then skim or pre-read the table of contents of *The Origin of Species,* devoting no more than ten minutes to the task.

CHARLES DARWIN
1809–1882

In evaluating the qualities that accounted for his "success as a man of science," Charles Darwin in his modest autobiography, written "because it might possibly interest my children," traces from his early youth "the strongest desire to understand and explain" whatever he observed. His childhood fantasies were concerned with fabulous discoveries in natural history; to his schoolmates he boasted that he could produce variously colored flowers of the same plant by watering them with certain colored fluids.

His father, a highly successful physician, was somewhat puzzled by the singular interest of his second son as well as by his undistinguished career in the classical curriculum of Dr. Butler's day school; he accordingly decided to send him to Edinburgh to study medicine. At Edinburgh Darwin collected animals in tidal pools, trawled for oysters with Newhaven fishermen to obtain specimens, and made two small discoveries which he incorporated in papers read before the Plinian Society. He put forth no very "strenuous effort" to learn medicine.

With some asperity, Dr. Darwin proposed the vocation of clergyman as an alternative. The life of a country clergyman appealed to young Darwin, and, after quieting his doubts concerning his belief in "all the dogmas of the Church," he began this new career at Cambridge. He proved unable, however, to repress his scientific interests and developed into an ardent entomologist, particularly devoted to collecting beetles; he had the satisfaction of seeing one of his rare specimens published in Stephen's *Illustrations of British Insects.* As at Edinburgh, he enjoyed many stimulating associations with men of science. It was a professor of botany at Cambridge, J. S. Henslow, who arranged for his appointment as naturalist on the government ship, H. M. S. *Beagle.*

From 1831 to 1836 the *Beagle* voyaged in Southern waters. Lyell's researches into the changes wrought by natural processes, set forth in *Principles of Geology,* gave direction to Darwin's own observations of the geological structure of the Cape Verde Islands. He also made extensive examinations of coral reefs and noted the relations of animals on the mainland to those of the adjacent islands, as well as the relation of living animals to the fossil remains of the same species.

Darwin described the voyage of the *Beagle* as "by far the most important event in my life." Besides making him one of the best qualified naturalists of his day, it developed in him the "habit of energetic industry and of concentrated attention." This new purposefulness on the part of his son was succinctly noted by Dr. Darwin, who remarked upon first seeing him after the voyage: "Why, the shape of his head is quite altered."

After his return, Darwin settled in London and began the task of organizing and recording his observations. He became a close friend of Lyell, the leading English geologist, and later of Hooker, an outstanding botanist. In 1839 he married his cousin, Emma Wedgwood, and toward the end of 1842, because of Darwin's chronic ill-health, the family moved to Down, where he lived in seclusion for the rest of his days. During the six years in London, he prepared his *Journal* from the notes of the voyage and published his carefully documented study of *Coral Reefs.*

The next eight years were spent in the laborious classification of barnacles for his four-volume work on that subject. "I have been struck," he wrote to Hooker, "with the variability of every part in some slight degree of every species." After this period of detailed work with a single species, Darwin felt prepared to attack the problem of the modification of species which he had been pondering for many years.

A number of facts had come to light during the voyage of the *Beagle* that Darwin felt "could only be explained on the supposition that species gradually become modified." Later, after his return to England, he had collected all the material he could find which "bore in any way on the variation of plants and animals under domestication." He soon perceived "that selection was the keystone of man's success. But how selection could be applied to organisms living in a state of nature remained for some time a mystery." One day, while reading Malthus on *Population,* it suddenly occurred to him how, in the struggle for existence, which he had everywhere observed, "favorable variations would tend to be preserved and unfavorable ones to be destroyed. The result would be the formation of a new species. Here then I had at last a theory by which to work."

He confided this theory to Hooker and Lyell, who urged him to write out his views for publication. But Darwin worked deliberately; he was only half through his projected book, when in the summer of 1858, he received an essay from A. R. Wallace at Ternate in the Moluccas, containing exactly the same theory as his own. Darwin submitted his dilemma to Hooker and Lyell, to whom he wrote: "Your words have come true with a vengeance—that I should be forestalled." It was their decision to publish an abstract of his theory from a letter of the previous year together with Wallace's essay, the joint work being entitled: *On the Tendency of Species to form Varieties and on the Perpetuation of Varieties and Species by Natural Means of Selection.*

A year later, on November 24, 1859, *The Origin of Species* appeared. The entire first edition of 1,250 copies was sold on the day of publication. A storm of controversy arose over the book, reaching its height at a meeting of the British Association at Oxford, where the celebrated verbal duel between T. H. Huxley and Bishop Wilberforce took place. Darwin, who could not sleep when he answered an antagonist harshly, took Lyell's advice and saved both "time and temper" by avoiding the fray.

In his work, however, he stayed close to his thesis. He expanded the material of the first chapter of the *Origin* into a book, *Variation of Plants and Animals under Domestication* (1868). In *The Descent of Man and Selection in Relation to Sex* (1871), Darwin fulfilled his statement in the *Origin* that "light would be thrown on the origin of man and his history." The *Expression of the Emotions* (1872) offered a natural explanation of phenomena which appeared to be a difficulty in the way of acceptance of evolution. His last works were concerned with the form, movement, and fertilization of plants.

Darwin's existence at Down was peculiarly adapted to preserve his energy and give direct order to his activity. Because of his continual ill-health, his wife took pains "to shield him from every avoidable annoyance." He observed the same routine for nearly forty years, his days being carefully parcelled into intervals of exercise and light reading in such proportions that he could utilize to his fullest capacity the four hours he devoted to work. His scientific reading and experimentation, as well, were organized with the most rigorous economy. Even the phases of his intellectual life non-essential to his work became, as he put it, "atrophied," a fact which he regretted as "a loss of happiness." Such non-scientific reading as he did was purely for relaxation, and he thought that "a law ought to be passed" against unhappy endings to novels.

With his wife and seven children his manner was so unusually "affectionate and delightful" that his son, Francis, marvelled that he could preserve it "with such an undemonstrative race as we are." When he died on April 19, 1882, his family wanted him to be buried at Down; public feeling decreed that he should be interred in Westminster Abbey, where he was laid beside Sir Isaac Newton.

TABLE OF CONTENTS OF *THE ORIGIN OF SPECIES*

AN HISTORICAL SKETCH
INTRODUCTION

Chapter I. Variation under Domestication
Causes of variability. Effects of habit and the use or disuse of parts. Correlated variation. Inheritance. Character of domestic varieties. Difficulty of distinguishing between varieties and species. Origin of domestic varieties from one or more species.

Domestic pigeons, their differences and origin. Principles of selection, anciently followed, their effects. Methodical and unconscious selection. Unknown origin of our domestic productions. Circumstances favourable to man's power of selection.

Chapter II. Variation under Nature

Variability. Individual differences. Doubtful species. Wide ranging, much diffused, and common species vary most. Species of the larger genera in each country vary more frequently than the species of the smaller genera. Many of the species of the larger genera resemble varieties in being very closely, but unequally, related to each other, and in having restricted ranges.

Chapter III. Struggle for Existence

Its bearing on natural selection. The term used in a wide sense. Geometrical ratio of increase. Rapid increase of naturalized animals and plants. Nature of the checks to increase. Competition universal. Effects of climate. Protection from the number of individuals. Complex relations of all animals and plants throughout nature. Struggle for life most severe between individuals and varieties of the same species: often severe between species of the same genus. The relation of organism to organism the most important of all relations.

Chapter IV. Natural Selection; or the Survival of the Fittest

Natural selection. Its power compared with man's selection. Its power on characters of trifling importance. Its power at all ages and on both sexes. Sexual selection. On the generality of intercrosses between individuals of the same species. Circumstances favourable and unfavourable to the results of Natural Selection, namely, intercrossing, isolation, number of individuals. Slow action. Extinction caused by natural selection. Divergence of character, related to the diversity of inhabitants of any small area, and to naturalisation. Action of natural selection, through divergence of character and extinction, on the descendants from a common parent. Explains the grouping of all organic beings. Advance in organisation. Low forms preserved. Convergence of character. Indefinite multiplication of species. Summary.

Chapter V. Laws of Variation

Effects of changed conditions. Use and disuse, combined with natural selection; organs of flight and of vision. Acclimatisation. Correlated variation. Compensation and economy of growth. False correlations. Multiple, rudimentary, and lowly organised structures variable. Parts developed in an unusual manner are highly variable; specific characters more variable than generic: secondary sexual characters variable. Species of the same genus vary in an analogous manner. Reversions to long-lost characters. Summary.

Chapter VI. Difficulties on Theory

Difficulties of the theory of descent with modification. Absence or rarity of transitional varieties. Transitions in habits of life. Diversified habits in the same species. Species with habits widely different from those of their allies. Organs of extreme perfection. Modes of transition. Cases of difficulty. *Natura non facit saltum.* Organs of small importance. Organs not in all cases absolutely perfect. The law of unity of type and of the conditions of existence embraced by the theory of natural selection.

Chapter VII. Miscellaneous Objections to the Theory of Natural Selection

Longevity. Modifications not necessarily simultaneous. Modifications apparently of no direct service. Progressive development. Characters of small functional importance, the most constant. Supposed incompetence of natural selection to account for the incipient stages of useful structures. Causes which interfere with the acquisition through natural selection of useful structures.

Graduations of structure with changed functions. Widely different organs in members of the same class, developed from one and the same source. Reasons for disbelieving in great and abrupt modifications.

Chapter VIII. Instinct

Instincts comparable with habits, but different in their origin. Instincts graduated. Aphides and ants. Instincts variable. Domestic instincts, their origin. Natural instincts of the cuckoo, molothrus, ostrich, and parasitic bees. Slavemaking ants. Hive-bee, its cell-making instinct. Changes of instinct and structure not necessarily simultaneous. Difficulties of the theory of the natural selection of instincts. Neuter or sterile insects. Summary.

Chapter IX. Hybridism

Distinction between the sterility of first crosses and of hybrids. Sterility various in degree, not universal, affected by close interbreeding, removed by domestication. Laws governing the sterility of hybrids. Sterility not a special endowment, but incidental on other differences, not accumulated by natural selection. Causes of the sterility of first crosses and of hybrids. Parallelism between the effects of changed conditions of life and of crossing. Dimorphism and trimorphism. Fertility of varieties when crossed and of their mongrel offspring not universal. Hybrids and mongrels compared independently of their fertility. Summary.

Chapter X. On the Imperfection of the Geological Record

On the absence of intermediate varieties at the present day. On the nature of extinct intermediate varieties; on their number. On the lapse of time, as inferred from the rate of denudation and of deposition. On the lapse of time as estimated by years. On the poorness of our palaeontological collections. On the intermittence of geological formations. On the denudation of granitic areas. On the absence of intermediate varieties in any one formation. On the sudden appearance of groups of species. On their sudden appearance in the lowest known fossiliferous strata. Antiquity of the habitable earth.

Chapter XI. On the Geological Succession of Organic Beings

On the slow and successive appearance of new species. On their different rates of change. Species once lost do not reappear. Groups of species follow the same general rules in their appearance and disappearance as do single species. On extinction. On simultaneous changes in the forms of life throughout the world. On the affinities of extinct species to each other and to living species. On the state of development of ancient forms. On the succession of the same types within the same areas. Summary of preceding and present chapters.

Chapter XII. Geographical Distribution

Present distribution cannot be accounted for by differences in physical conditions. Importance of barriers. Affinity of the productions of the same continent. Centres of creation. Means of dispersal by changes of climate and of the level of the land, and by occasional means. Dispersal during the glacial period. Alternate glacial periods in the north and south.

Chapter XIII. Geographical Distribution—continued

Distribution of fresh-water productions. On the inhabitants of oceanic islands. Absence of batrachians and of terrestrial mammals. On the relation of the inhabitants of islands to those of the nearest mainland. On colonisation from the nearest source with subsequent modification. Summary of the last and present chapters.

Chapter XIV. Mutual Affinities of Organic Beings, Morphology, Embryology, Rudimentary Organs

Classification, groups subordinate to groups. Natural system. Rules and difficulties in classification, explained on the theory of descent with modification. Classification of varieties. Descent always used in classification. Analogical or adaptive characters. Affinities, general, complex, and radiating. Extinction separates and defines groups. Morphology, between members of the same class, between parts of the same individual. Embryology, laws of, explained by variations not supervening at an early age, and being inherited at a corresponding age. Rudimentary organs: their origin explained. Summary.

Chapter XV. Recapitulation and Conclusion

Recapitulation of the objections to the theory of natural selection. Recapitulation of the general and special circumstances in its favour. Causes of the general belief in the immutability of species. How far the theory of natural selection may be extended. Effects of its adoption on the study of natural history. Concluding remarks.

Test E: *Questions about Darwin and about* The Origin of Species

1. In *The Origin of Species* Darwin undertakes to describe the origin and evolution of man. (True or False?)
2. The work is divided into (a) 12 (b) 15 (c) 19 chapters.
3. The book emphasizes the role of domestication in natural selection. (True or False?)
4. Darwin asserts that the struggle for life is (a) more severe (b) less severe between individuals of the same species than it is between individuals of different species.
5. Darwin takes no account of, and does not try to answer, difficulties of and objections against his theory. (True or False?)
6. Darwin was unable to complete *The Origin of Species,* and the book therefore lacks a chapter summing up his theory and his conclusions. (True or False?)
7. Darwin enjoyed taking part in the disputes that developed as a consequence of his work. (True or False?)

8. In the famous debate at Oxford between T. H. Huxley and Bishop Wilberforce, which man defended Darwin and his theory?

9. Darwin described as "by far the most important event in my life" (a) his reading of Malthus's *Essay on the Principle of Population* (b) his youthful study of medicine (c) his voyage on the *Beagle*.

10. Darwin thought that "a law ought to be passed" against (a) novels (b) pornographic novels (c) novels having scientists as their main characters (d) novels with unhappy endings.

Turn to p. 412 for the answers to Test E.

Those questions were all very easy ones. Now take another twenty minutes to read the table of contents of *The Origin of Species* (see p. 391) superficially, and then we will ask you to consider some more difficult questions.

Test F: *Further questions about Darwin and* The Origin of Species

1. Darwin, making extensive use of the geological record, considers it (a) complete and satisfactory (b) incomplete but an invaluable source of data on the origin of species.

2. *Species* refers to a group of animals or plants (a) lower (b) higher than a *genus*.

3. Members of a species share common characteristics, and can interbreed and reproduce their kinds. (True or False?)

4. Members of a genus share common characteristics, but are not necessarily able to interbreed and reproduce their kind. (True or False?)

5. Of the following factors, which ones play a major role and which a minor role in natural selection?

	MAJOR	MINOR
(a) The struggle for existence	____	____
(b) Variation of individuals	____	____
(c) Heritability of traits	____	____

6. Darwin compares the power of natural selection to that of man's selection. Which does he think is greater?

7. The Latin phrase *Natura non facit saltum* appears in the table of contents. Can you translate this phrase? Can you state the significance of the phrase for Darwin's theory?

8. What is the significance of geological dispersion and of natural barriers such as the oceans on the evolution of species?

9. In his Introduction to *The Origin of Species,* Darwin refers to the origin of species as "that mystery of mysteries, as it has been called by one of our greatest philosophers." Can you state fairly exactly the problem that his work sets out to solve? You might try to do this in no more than a sentence or two.

10. What is Darwin's theory—in a nutshell? Can you state it in no more than 100 words?

Turn to p. 413 for the answers to Test F.

You have now completed the two-part exercise at the second level of reading. As before, you will have noted that the questions draw not only on the texts read but also on historical and other information. Indeed, you may feel that some of the questions were eminently unfair. And so they would be, if any critical decision depended on your ability to answer them. That, of course, is not so. We hope that the questions you were unable to answer, or that you found it very difficult to answer, will not irritate you, but will instead lead you to search in the works that have been only superficially discussed here for better answers than the ones we have given. Better answers are available in the works themselves. And also answers to many more interesting questions that we have not had the time, the space, or the wit, to ask.

III. Exercises and Tests at the Third Level of Reading: Analytical Reading

The text used for the exercises in this part of the Appendix is this book itself. We would prefer it if this were not so. There are many books that it would be better and more fruitful to practice analytical reading on. But over against that preference there is one overriding consideration: this book is the only one that we can be sure that all persons taking this test have read. The only alternative would be to reprint another book along with this one, and that is out of the question.

You will recall that the analytical reader must always attempt to answer four questions about whatever book he is reading: (1) What is the book about as a whole? (2) What is being said in detail, and how? (3) Is the book true, in whole or part? (4) What of it? The fifteen rules of reading, as they are listed on pp. 161–62 and discussed at length in Part Two, are designed to help the analytical reader answer these questions. Can you answer them about this book?

You must be the judge of whether you can or not. There are no answers at the end of this Appendix to these four questions. The answers are in the book itself.

Not only is it true that we have done the best job we could of making these matters clear in writing the book. It is also true that in an important sense it would be inappropriate to try to help you any more than we already have. Not only is analytical reading work—it is lonely work. The reader is alone with the book he is reading. Basically, there is no resource to exploit except his own thought; there is no place to go for insight and understanding except into his own mind.

We have explained how the questions must be answered for, and the rules applied to, different kinds of books. But we cannot state how they are to be applied to any given work. The reader himself must be the one to do that.

There are, nevertheless, a few things that can be said without exceeding the proprieties. We have not concealed the fact that this is a practical book, so applying the first rule of structural analysis is easy enough. We think we have also made it pretty clear what the book is about as a whole, although now you should state this more briefly than we have done in any one place. We hope that our organization into four parts and twenty-one chapters is perspicuous. However, in outlining the book, it might be desirable to comment on the unequal treatment, in terms of numbers of pages, accorded the various levels of reading. The first level of reading—elementary reading—receives relatively short shrift in this book, although it is of undoubted importance. Why? The third level of reading—analytical reading—receives much more extensive and intensive coverage than any of the other levels. Again, why?

With regard to the fourth rule of structural analysis, we want to emphasize that the problem we set out to solve cannot be defined simply as teaching you to read. There is nothing in this book, for example, that would be of much help to a first- or second-grade teacher. We have concentrated instead on reading in a certain way, and with certain goals in mind. In applying the fourth rule of reading, that way and those goals should be described with precision.

Similarly with the second stage of analytical reading—interpretation. The first three rules at that stage must be applied by the reader without our help: the rules that require you to come to terms, to find the key propositions, and to construct the arguments. There would be no point in our trying to list what we think are the terms of this work—the important words that must be understood commonly by you and by us if the work as a whole is to communicate knowledge, or impart skill. Nor will we repeat the propositions that we have asserted, and that the reader, if he has read analytically, should be able to state in his own words. Nor will we repeat the arguments. To do so would be to write the book over again.

Something can be said, however, about the problems that we did and did not solve. We believe we did solve the main problem that faced us at the beginning—the problem that you must have identified in your application of the fourth rule of structural analysis. We do not believe that we solved all of the problems of reading that face students and adult readers today. For one thing, many of these problems involve individual differences between human beings. No book on a general subject can ever hope to solve such difficulties.

The criticism of a book as a communication of knowledge involves, as you will recall, the application of seven rules, three of which are general maxims of intellectual etiquette, and four of which are specific criteria for points of criticism. We have done what we could to recommend the maxims of intellectual etiquette (they are discussed in Chapter 10). With regard to the first three points of criticism, we can have nothing to say. But a few remarks about the last of the four criteria of criticism—to show wherein the analysis in the book is incomplete—are not inappropriate.

We would say that our analysis or account is incomplete in two respects. The first is in regard to the first level of reading. There is much more to be said about elementary reading, but we do want to emphasize that that was not our primary concern. Nor would we claim for our discussion of the subject any degree of finality. Elementary reading could be discussed, and has been discussed, in quite different ways.

The other respect in which our analysis is incomplete is much more important. We did not say all that could be said—perhaps not even all that we could say—about syntopical reading. There are two reasons for this.

First, syntopical reading is extraordinarily hard to describe and explain without having the texts of various authors in front of one. Fortunately, we will have the opportunity in the last part of this Appendix, which follows, of presenting an actual exercise in syntopical reading. But even there we will be confined to two short texts by only two authors. A full-scale exercise would involve many texts from many authors, and the examination of many complex questions. Space limitations prohibit that here.

Second, it is almost impossible to describe the intellectual excitement and satisfaction that come from syntopical reading without actually sharing the experience of doing it. Nor is the understanding that one finally arrives at attained in a day. Often, it takes months or years to unwind the twisted thread of the discussion of an important point, a thread that may have been in the process of becoming twisted over centuries. Many false starts are made, and many tentative analyses and organizations of the discussions must be proposed, before any real light is thrown on the subject. We have suffered through many of these problems, and we know how disheartening the business can be at times. As a result, however, we also know how wonderful it can be when one finally wins one's way through to a solution.

Are there other respects in which our analysis is incomplete? We can think of a few possibilities. For example, does the book fail to differentiate sufficiently between what might be called first-intentional reading (that is, reading a text) and second-intentional reading (that is, reading a commentary on that text)? Is enough said about reading heretical in contradistinction to canonical texts; or enough about the reading of texts that stand detached, above so-called canonical and heretical texts? Is enough attention paid to the problems raised by special vocabularies, especially in science and mathematics? (This aspect of the general problem of reading is mentioned in the chapter on reading social science.) Perhaps not enough space is devoted to the reading of lyric poetry. Beyond that, we are not sure that we know of anything that deserves criticism on this last count. But we would not be surprised to discover that some defects or failures that are not at all obvious to us are perfectly obvious to you.

IV. Exercises and Tests at the Fourth Level of Reading: Syntopical Reading

Two texts are used for the exercises in this fourth and last part of the Appendix. One consists of selected passages from the first two chapters of Book I of Aristotle's *Politics.* The other consists of selected passages from Book I of Rousseau's *The Social Contract*—a sentence from the Introduction to the book, and passages from Chapters 1, 2, 4, and 6.

Aristotle's *Politics* appears in Volume 9 of *Great Books of the Western World.* Volumes 8 and 9 of the set are devoted to the complete works of Aristotle; besides the *Politics,* Volume 9 includes the *Ethics,* the *Rhetoric,* and the *Poetics,* as well as a number of biological treatises. Rousseau's *Social Contract* appears in Volume 38 of the set, a volume that includes other works by Rousseau as well—the essay *On the Origin of Inequality,* and *On Political Economy*—together with another important eighteenth-century French political book, Montesquieu's *The Spirit of Laws.*

You will recall that there are two stages of syntopical reading. One is a preparatory step, the other is syntopical reading proper. For the purposes of this exercise we assume that the first or preparatory step has already been taken—that is, that we have decided on the subject we wish to consider and have also decided on the texts we want to read. The subject in this case may be defined as "The Nature and Origin of the State"—a subject of importance about which a great deal has been thought and said. The texts are as described above.

We must assume further, if this exercise is not to exceed the limits set by the space available to us, that we have narrowed the question to be considered here, with the help of these two texts, to a single inquiry, which can be stated as follows: Is the State a *natural* arrangement, with all that that implies of goodness and necessity—or is it merely a *conventional* or *artificial* arrangement?

That is our question. Now read the two texts carefully, taking as much time as you wish or need. Speed is never important in syntopical reading. Make notes if you want to, and underline or otherwise mark passages when that seems desirable. And return to the texts as often as you wish in considering the questions that follow.

FROM BOOK I OF ARISTOTLE'S *POLITICS*

From Chapter 1

Every state is a community of some kind, and every community is established with a view of some good; for mankind always act in order to obtain that which they think good. But, if all communities aim at some good, the state or political community, which is the highest of all, and which embraces all the rest, aims at good in a greater degree than any other, and at the highest good. . . .

From Chapter 2

The family is the association established by nature for the supply of men's everyday wants, and the members of it are called by Charondas 'companions of the cupboard,' and by Epimenides the Cretan, 'companions of the manger.' But when several families are united, and the association aims at something more than the supply of daily needs, the first society to be formed is the village. And the most natural form of the village appears to be that of a colony from the family, composed of the children and grandchildren, who are said to be 'suckled with the same milk.' And this is the reason why Hellenic states were originally governed by kings; because the Hellenes were under royal rule before they came together, as the barbarians still are. . . .

When several villages are united in a single complete community, large enough to be nearly or quite self-sufficing, the state comes into existence, originating in the bare needs of life, and continuing in existence for the sake of a good life. And therefore, if the earlier forms of society are natural, so is the state, for it is the end of them, and the nature of a thing is its end. For what each thing is when fully developed, we call its nature, whether we are speaking of a man, a horse, or a family. Besides, the final cause and end of a thing is the best, and to be self-sufficing is the end and the best.

Hence it is evident that the state is a creation of nature, and that man is by nature a political animal. . . .

Now, that man is more of a political animal than bees or any other gregarious animals is evident. Nature, as we often say, makes nothing in vain, and man is the only animal whom she has endowed with the gift of speech. And whereas mere voice is but an indication of pleasure or pain, and is therefore found in other animals (for their nature attains to the perception of pleasure and pain and the intimation of them to one another, and no further), the power of speech is intended to set forth the expedient and inexpedient, and therefore likewise the just and the unjust. And it is a characteristic of man that he alone has any sense of good and evil, of just and unjust, and the like, and the association of living beings who have this sense makes a family and a state.

Further, the state is by nature clearly prior to the family and to the individual, since the whole is of necessity prior to the part; for example, if the whole body be destroyed, there will be no foot or hand, except in an equivocal sense, as we might speak of a stone hand; for when destroyed the hand will be no better than that. But things are defined by their working and power; and we ought not to say that they are the same when they no longer have their proper quality, but only that they have the same name. The proof that the state is a creation of nature and prior to the individual is that the individual, when isolated, is not self-sufficing; and therefore he is like a part in relation to the whole. But he who is unable to live in society, or who has no need because he is sufficient for himself, must be either a beast or a god: he is no part of a state. A social instinct is implanted in all men by nature, and yet he who first founded the state was the greatest of benefactors. For man, when perfected, is the best of animals, but, when separated from law and justice, he is the worst of all.

From Book I of Rousseau's *The Social Contract*

I mean to inquire if, in the civil order, there can be any sure and legitimate rule of administration, men being taken as they are and laws as they might be. . . .

From Chapter 1. Subject of the First Book

Man is born free; and everywhere he is in chains. One thinks himself the master of others, and still remains a greater slave than they. How did this change come about? I do not know. What can make it legitimate? That question I think I can answer. . . .

From Chapter 2. The First Societies

The most ancient of all societies, and the only one that is natural, is the family: and even so the children remain attached to the father only so long as they need him for their preservation. As soon as this need ceases, the natural bond is dissolved. The children, released from the obedience they owed to the father, and the father, released from the care he owed his children, return equally to independence. If they remain united, they continue so no longer naturally, but voluntarily; and the family itself is then maintained only by convention. . . .

The family then may be called the first model of political societies: the ruler corresponds to the father, and the people to the children; and all, being born free and equal, alienate their liberty only for their own advantage. . . .

From Chapter 4. Slavery

Since no man has a natural authority over his fellow, and force creates no right, we must conclude that conventions form the basis of all legitimate authority among men. . . .

From Chapter 6. The Social Compact

I suppose men to have reached the point at which the obstacles in the way of their preservation in the state of nature show their power of resistance to be greater than the resources at the disposal of each individual for his maintenance in that state. That primitive condition can then subsist no longer; and the human race would perish unless it changed its manner of existence.

But, as men cannot engender new forces, but only unite and direct existing ones, they have no other means of preserving themselves than the formation, by aggregation, of a sum of forces great enough to overcome the resistance. These they have to bring into play by means of a single motive power, and cause to act in concert.

This sum of forces can arise only where several persons come together: but, as the force and liberty of each man are the chief instruments of his self-preservation, how can he pledge them without harming his own interests, and neglecting the care he owes to himself? This difficulty, in its bearing on my present subject, may be stated in the following terms:

"The problem is to find a form of association which will defend and protect with the whole common force the person and goods of each associate, and in which each, while uniting himself with all, may still obey himself alone, and remain as free as before." This is the fundamental problem of which the *Social Contract* provides the solution. . . .

If then we discard from the social compact what is not of its essence, we shall find that it reduces itself to the following terms:

"Each of us puts his person and all his power in common under the supreme direction of the general will, and, in our corporate capacity, we receive each member as an indivisible part of the whole."

At once, in place of the individual personality of each contracting party, this act of association creates a moral and collective body, composed of as many members as the assembly contains votes, and receiving from this act its unity, its common identity, its life and its will. This public person, so formed by the union of all other persons, formerly took the name of *city* (polis), and now takes that of *Republic* or *body politic;* it is called by its members *State* when passive, *Sovereign* when active, and *Power* when compared with others like itself. Those who are associated in it take collectively the name of *people,* and severally are called *citizens,* as sharing in the sovereign power, and *subjects,* as being under the laws of the State. But these terms are often confused and taken one for another: it is enough to know how to distinguish them when they are being used with precision.

We will ask you to entertain two sets of questions about these two texts, after which we will suggest some tentative conclusions that we believe can justifiably be drawn from the texts.

Test G: Here is the first set of questions about Aristotle and Rousseau

1. Aristotle identifies three different types of human association. What are they?
2. These three types of association have certain things in common and also differ in significant respects. What do they have in common and how do they differ?
3. The three types of association differ in regard to their inclusiveness. Can you order them on a scale going from less to more inclusive?
4. All three types of association aim at fulfilling some natural need—that is, they achieve some good. The good achieved by the family—that is, the security of its members and the perpetuation of the race—is also achieved by the village, but in a higher degree. Is the good aimed at or achieved by the

state merely the same good in an even higher degree, or is it a different good altogether?

5. Another way to get at this difference is by still another question. Given that, for Aristotle, all three types of association are natural, are they natural in the same way?

6. Before turning to some questions about Rousseau in this first set of questions, we must mention the one remark of Aristotle's that raises a difficulty. Aristotle praises highly the man who first founded the state. Would he speak similarly of the man who first founded the family or the village?

7. What is the main problem that Rousseau poses about the state?

8. Does Rousseau pose this same problem about the family?

9. What is the opposite of the *natural* for Rousseau?

10. What is the basic or founding convention that, for Rousseau, makes the state legitimate?

Turn to p. 414 for the answers to Test G.

After this first set of questions about the two texts, we appear to have arrived at an interpretation of the two texts that sees them in disagreement on the question we have been considering. That question is, as you will recall: Is the state natural, or is it conventional or artificial? Rousseau appears to say that the state is conventional or artificial; Aristotle appears to say that it is natural.

Now take a few moments to consider whether this interpretation is correct. Is there anything about the problematic remark of Aristotle's we mentioned that calls the interpretation in doubt? Is there anything that Rousseau says that we have not discussed and that also must cause us to doubt this interpretation?

If you see why this interpretation is not correct, you will probably already have anticipated the few remaining questions we want to ask.

Test H: Here is the second set of questions

1. For Rousseau, is the state natural as well as conventional?
2. Does Aristotle agree in this?
3. Can this basic agreement between Aristotle and Rousseau be extended to further points?
4. In the answer to the last question, we spoke of the "good" that the state achieves which cannot be achieved without it. Is this "good" the same for Rousseau as for Aristotle?
5. One final question. Does the agreement we have found on our primary question mean that these two texts, short as they are, are in agreement on all points?

Turn to p. 416 for the answers to Test H.

We said at the beginning of this exercise that there are certain conclusions that can justifiably be drawn from the careful reading of these two important political texts. Among them are these: First, it is a basic truth about man that he is a political animal—you may use some other adjective if you wish—as contradistinguished from other social or gregarious animals: that is, that man is a rational social animal who constitutes a society to serve other than merely biological ends. It follows from this that the state is both natural and conventional—that it is both more and less natural than the family; and it follows also that the state must be formally *constituted:* other societies are not true states. Second, we may reasonably conclude that the state is a means, not an end. The end is the common human good: a good life. Hence man is not made for the state, but the state for man.

These conclusions seem to us to be justified, and we also believe that the answers we have given to the questions are correct. But more than feeling or belief is required in a genuine project of syntopical reading. We noted, in our discussion of this level of reading, that it is always desirable to document one's answers and conclusions from the texts of the authors themselves. We have not done that here. You might want to try to do it for yourself. If you are puzzled by any of our answers, see if you can find the passage or passages in the text, either by Aristotle or Rousseau, that must have formed the basis of the answer we give. And if you disagree with any of our answers or conclusions, see if you can document your disagreement by means of the words of the authors themselves.

Answers to Questions

Test A (p. 362)

1. (c) 2. (b) If you said (a) and (b) you would not really be wrong.
3. (a) and (b) 4. (b) 5. (c) Is it pedantic to say that (b) is an incorrect answer? Would the situation be different if (c) were not available as an answer? 6. (b) 7. (a), (c), and (d) The text indicates that Bentham was the most influential. 8. (d) 9. (a) and (b) Likely; (c) and (d) Not Likely. 10. (a), (b), and (d)

Test B (p. 369)

1. (c) 2. (c) 3. False 4. (b) 5. (a) and (b) 6. (b) 7. (b) The first answer ("Why apples fall") might have been considered correct if it had been phrased "How apples fall," although of course there is no mention of apples in the *Principia*. The point is that the work describes gravity and expounds its operation, but it does not say *why* it operates. 8. (a) 9. (b) and (c) 10. This striking statement has impressed generations of Newton idolaters. In commenting on it, you probably discussed the modesty of its author. Did you also make any mention of the metaphor that Newton employs? It is a memorable one.

Test C (p. 385)

1. (a) 2. (b) Dante's own titles were the ones that appear in (c); if you gave that as your answer we would therefore have to count it as correct. 3. (a) 4. (a) and (b) 5. (b) This is no accident, of course. Each major division of the poem (called in Italian a *cantiche*) contains 33 cantos: the first canto of Hell introduces the whole work. 6.

(a) Only the Eighth Circle is divided into pouches. 7. (b) Circles (a) is not really wrong. 8. (c) But (b) would also be correct, as in Dante's cosmology the nine orders of angels correspond to the nine heavenly bodies. 9. (a); (b) 10. (a)

Test D (p. 386)
1. (b) 2. (a) Beatrice acts for God, so (b) is not incorrect. 3. (b) 4. (b) and (c) Dante had not read Aristotle's *Poetics,* though he had read a synopsis of it suggesting that Aristotle defined a comedy as any work that ends fortunately. Dante's poem ends in Heaven, hence fortunately, and therefore he titled it *The Comedy:* but of course it is not a comic work. 5. (c) The poem is dependent on all three, but the Christian themes are the most important. 6. Yes. Dante felt that sloth had been one of his main sins, and he here symbolizes this by falling asleep. 7. In Dante's cosmology, the earth is the center of the universe, and Hell is at the center of the earth. 8. The P's stand for the Latin word *peccata,* sins: there are seven P's because there are seven deadly sins, from each of which the souls are absolved in their ascent up the Mountain of Purgatory. 9. Virgil, in the poem, is the symbol of all human knowledge and virtue. But, as a pagan who died before the birth of Christ, he cannot accompany Dante into Paradise. 10. The Franciscans and the Dominicans were the two great monastic orders of the Middle Ages. The Franciscans were contemplatives, the Dominicans were scholars and teachers. Dante here symbolizes the heavenly resolution of all differences between the two orders by having St. Thomas, the greatest representative of the Dominicans, narrate the life of St. Francis, the founder of the Franciscans; while St. Bonaventura, the representative of the Franciscans, narrates the life of St. Dominic, the founder of the Dominicans.

Test E (p. 396)
1. False 2. (b) 3. False. In fact, the statement is meaningless. 4. (a) 5. False 6. False 7. False 8. Huxley defended Darwin. 9. (c) 10 (d) To lovers of Darwin, this is one of the most charming facts about the man.

Test F (p. 397)

1. (b) 2. (a) 3. True. In fact, this comes close to being the definition of a species. 4. True. Members of a genus can interbreed and reproduce their kind only if they are also members of the same species. 5. (a), (b), and (c) all play major roles in natural selection. 6. Natural selection. Would Darwin change his mind if he were alive today, in the face of the evidence of man's destructive effect on the environment? Perhaps. But he might still continue to insist that in the long run, nature is more powerful than man. And then, too, man is himself a part of nature. 7. The phrase can be translated "Nature makes no jumps"—that is, sudden, great and abrupt variations do not occur naturally, but only small and gradual ones. Even if you were not able to translate the Latin, was the sense of this statement clear from the table of contents? The idea is significant because Darwin, taking it as true, explains the fact that there is great differentiation between species by the hypothesis of gaps in the geological record—so-called missing links—instead of by the hypothesis of created differences between species. 8. According to Darwin, if two varieties of a single species are widely separated over a considerable period of time so that they are physically hindered from interbreeding, the varieties tend to become separate species—that is, become incapable of interbreeding. It was his discovery of quite distinct species of birds on the oceanic islands during his service on the *Beagle* that first led him to see this fundamental point. 9. There are probably many ways to state the problem, but one way to do it is to ask two apparently simple questions. First, why are there many kinds of living things, instead of just one or a few? Second, how does a species come into existence, and how does it pass away—which, Darwin and his contemporaries knew from the geological record, had happened many times? It may be necessary to think about these questions for a while to realize why they are so very difficult and so very mysterious—but they are well worth thinking about. 10. We are not sure that an adequate answer to this question can be arrived at on the basis of a mere perusal, however intensive, of the table of contents of *The Origin of Species*. If you

were able to state the theory in a hundred words without having read the book, you are an extraordinary reader. Indeed, the question is not easy to answer briefly even if one has read the book; you might refer to our attempt to summarize the theory in Chapter 7. In a short passage in his own Introduction to the work, Darwin may have done it himself, and we quote the passage in its entirety here for what it is worth:

> As many more individuals of each species are born than can possibly survive; and as, consequently, there is a frequently recurring struggle for existence, it follows that any being, if it vary however slightly in any manner profitably to itself, under the complex and sometimes varying conditions of life, will have a better chance of surviving, and thus be *naturally selected*. From the strong principle of inheritance, any selected variety will tend to propagate its new and modified form.

Test G (p. 408)
1. The family, the village, the state.
2. They have in common that they are all modes of human association and that they are all natural. Aristotle is clear on the latter point: "It is evident," he says, "that the state is a creation of nature." However, the differences between the types of association are important. If you have not yet identified these differences, as Aristotle describes them, some further questions may be of help.
3. The family is the least inclusive. The village includes several families and is therefore more inclusive than the family. The state is the most inclusive of all, for it comes into existence "when several villages are united in a single complete community."
4. Aristotle says the state originates in "the bare needs of life," but that it continues in existence "for the sake of a good life." A "good life" seems to be different in kind from mere "life." In

fact, this seems to be the main difference between the state and the other two types of human association.

5. Though the types of association are indeed natural, they are not natural in the same way. Aristotle observes that many animals as well as men live in families; and he notes that such animals as bees seem to have organizations that are analogous to the village. But man differs in that, while being *social* like many other animals, he is also *political*. In his discussion of man's unique possession of speech, Aristotle is saying that man alone is political. He is *naturally* a political animal, and so the state, which serves the needs of this aspect of his being, is natural. But *only* the state, among the types of association that he experiences, serves this particular need.

6. Apparently Aristotle would not praise highly the man who first founded the village or the family, as he does the man who first founded the state. And this remark causes a difficulty, for if the state was first founded by someone, then it can be said to have been invented, and if it was invented, then is it not artificial? But we have concluded that it is natural.

7. The main problem Rousseau poses about the state is its legitimacy. If the state were not legitimate, Rousseau asserts, then its laws would not have to be obeyed.

8. He does not pose the same problem about the family. He clearly says that the basis of the family is a natural need— the same natural need that Aristotle describes.

9. The conventional. For Rousseau, the state is conventional; for if the state were like the family, that fact would legitimize paternal rule—the rule of a benevolent despot, which is what the father is to his family. Force—which is what the father has—cannot make a state legitimate. Only an agreed-upon understanding—a convention—can do that.

10. The Social Contract is, for Rousseau, the founding convention, undertaken at a first moment when all members of the

state are unanimous in desiring and choosing it. It is this that legitimizes the institution of the state.

Test H (p. 410)

1. Yes! He clearly says that men by nature *need* the state, for the state comes into existence at a time when life in the condition of nature is no longer possible for men, and without the state they could no longer continue to exist. Therefore, we must conclude that, in the view of Rousseau, the state is *both* natural and conventional. It is natural in the sense that it serves a natural need; but it is legitimate only if it is based on a founding convention—the Social Contract.

2. Yes, Aristotle and Rousseau agree that the state is both natural and conventional.

3. Aristotle and Rousseau also agree that the naturalness of the state is not like that of animal societies. Its naturalness arises from need or necessity; it achieves a good that cannot be achieved without it. But though the state is natural—that is, necessary—as a means to a naturally sought end, it is also a work of reason and will. The key word to define or identify this further agreement between the two writers is "constitution." For Aristotle, he who first "constituted" a society "founded" a state. For Rousseau, men by entering into a convention of government or social contract "constitute" a state.

4. No, the "good" the state achieves is not the same for Rousseau as for Aristotle. The reasons are complex, and are not really documented in the passages reprinted here. But Aristotle's conception of the "good life," which is the end that the state serves, is different from Rousseau's conception of the "life of the citizen," which for him is the end that the state serves. Fully to understand this difference would require reading further in the *Politics* and *The Social Contract*.

5. Clearly the two works are not in full agreement throughout. Even in these short selections, each of the authors raises

points that the other does not discuss. For example, there is no mention in the Rousseau text of a notion that is certainly important to Aristotle—namely, that man is essentially a political, as well as a social, animal. Nor does the word "justice" appear in the Rousseau text, although it seems to be a key term for Aristotle. On the other hand, there is no mention in the Aristotle text of such key terms and basic ideas as the social compact, the liberty of the individual, the alienation of that liberty, the general will, and so forth, all of which seem to be central in Rousseau's treatment of the subject.

INDEX

Aeneid (Virgil), 217

Aeschylus, 220

Andromeda Strain, The, (Crichton),
  60

Animal Farm (Orwell), 212

Apollonius, 258

Apology (Plato), 280

Aquinas, Thomas, 86, 121, 156,
  242, 276–77

Archimedes, 258

Aristophanes, 219

Aristotle, 64, 71, 78, 80, 85, 86, 88,
  91,143, 144, 145, 156, 159,
  169, 183, 194, 202, 207, 235,
  242, 246, 264, 273, 275–76,
  278, 281, 286, 325, 403–5

Arithmetic of Infinities (Wallis), 366

Art of Fiction, The (Henry James),
  208

Articles of Confederation, 170, 358

As You Like It (Shakespeare), 37

Augustine, 64, 241

Autobiography (J. S. Mill), 359

Bacon, Francis, 19, 138

Barnett, Lincoln, 261, 262

Berkeley, George, 274

Bhagavad-Gita, 339

Bible, 218, 287, 288

Boethius, 374

Boswell, James, 239

Brave New World (Huxley), 212

Burke, Edmund, 192

Byron, George Gordon, Lord, 217

Capital (Marx), 68, 81, 144

Cervantes, Miguel de, 138

Charterhouse of Parma, The
  (Stendhal), 301

Chaucer, Geoffrey, 176

Cicero, Marcus Tullius, 274, 374

City of God, The (Augustine), 64

*Civil Government, Second Treatise
  on* (Locke), 68, 170

Clarke, Arthur C., 60

Closing Circle, The (Commoner),
  261

Collier, Jeremy, 79

Commoner, Barry, 261, 262

Communist Manifesto (Marx and
  Engles), 68, 144, 192

Compleat Angler, The (Walton), 240

Confessions (Augustine), 241
Confessions (Rousseau), 241
Consolatio Philosophiae (Boethius), 374
Convivio (Dante), 373, 374
Coral Reefs (Darwin), 389
Crime and Punishment (Dostoevsky), 79
Critique of Judgment (Kant), 282
Critique of Practical Reason (Kant), 67, 144
Critique of Pure Reason (Kant), 67, 85, 144, 282

Dante Alighieri, 201, 217, 246, 355, 379–86
Darwin, Charles, 61, 62, 71, 81, 92, 104, 129, 155, 249, 334, 355, 371, 387–97
De Amicitia (Cicero), 374
De Monarchia (Dante), 375
De Vulgari Eloquentia (Dante), 374
Declaration of Independence, 41, 42, 358
Decline and Fall of the Roman Empire (Gibbon), 41, 42, 358
Descartes, René, 64, 277, 365
Descent of Man, The (Darwin), 62, 387, 390
Dewey, John, 159
Divine Comedy (Dante), 201, 217, 355, 371, 375, 376–87
Don Juan (Byron), 217
Donne, John, 240
Dostoevsky, Fyodor, 79

Eddington, A. S., 101
Einstein, Albert, 63, 249
Elements of Chemistry (Lavoisier), 253–54

Elements of Geometry (Euclid), 63, 64, 159, 205, 255, 256, 258
Elements of Law (Hobbes), 157
Elements of Political Economy (J. S. Mill), 360
Eliot, T. S., 223
Emerson, Ralph Waldo, 212, 282
Encyclopaedia Britannica, 181, 362
Epictetus, 160
Essay Concerning Human Understanding, An (Locke), 68, 72, 73, 82
Essay on the Principle of Population (Malthus), 397
Essays (Montaigne), 241
Ethics, Nicomachean (Aristotle), 80, 88, 91, 144, 169, 275, 281, 403
Ethics (Spinoza), 69, 278
Euclid, 64, 103, 104, 106, 107, 121, 128, 133, 159, 205, 255, 256, 258, 277, 365
Euripides, 220
Evolution of Physics, The (Einstein and Infeld), 63
Expression of Emotions in Man and Animals, The (Darwin), 390

Faraday, Michael, 240
Faraday the Discoverer (Tyndall), 240
Faulkner, William, 60
Faust (Goethe), 241
Federalist Papers, 170, 358
Fielding, Henry, 79, 219
First Circle, The (Solzhenitsyn), 212
Foundations of Geometry (Hilbert), 64
Freud, Sigmund, 72, 287

Galileo Galilei, 71, 104, 128, 130, 249, 260, 273, 278, 364
Gateway to the Great Books, 340
Geometry (Descartes), 64, 365
Gibbon, Edward, 33, 62, 155
Gilbert, William, 260
Goethe, Johann Wolfgang von, 241
Golden Treasury, The, (Palgrave), 340
Gone with the Wind (Mitchell), 60, 301
Grapes of Wrath, The (Steinbeck), 60
Great Books of the Western World, 321, 340, 355, 358, 364, 371, 387, 403

Hamlet (Shakespeare), 37, 93, 215, 218, 219
Harvey, William, 131, 260
Heartbreak House (Shaw), 220
Heinlein, Robert A., 60
Herbert, George, 240
Herodotus, 80, 359
Hilbert, David, 64
Hippocrates, 260
Historical Account of Two Notable Corruptions of the Scriptures (Newton), 368
History of India (James Mill), 359
Hobbes, Thomas, 64, 127, 157, 164, 194
Holy Bible, 218, 287, 288
Homer, 78, 176, 217, 241, 331, 338
How We Think (Dewey), 159
Hume, David, 155
Huxley, Aldous, 212
Huxley, T. H., 390
Huygens, Christiaan, 364, 367

I Ching, 339
Idea of Progress (C. Van Doren), 317
Iliad (Homer), 176, 217
Illustrations of British Insects (Stephen), 388
Infeld, Leopold, 63
Introduction to Mathematics (Whitehead), 261, 262
Introduction to Poetry (M. Van Doren), 340

James, Henry, 208
James, William, 63, 72
Jefferson, Thomas, 42
Journal (Darwin), 389
Joyce, James, 79
Julius Caesar (Shakespeare), 37

Kant, Immanuel, 67, 85, 144, 275, 276, 278, 279, 281–82
Kepler, Johannes, 273, 365
Koran, 287, 325

Latini, Brunetto, 372
Lavoisier, Antoine Laurent, 253, 254
Leaves of Grass (Whitman), 242
Leviathan (Hobbes), 64, 194
Life of Johnson (Boswell), 239
Lives (Walton), 240
Lives of the Noble Grecians and Romans (Plutarch), 240, 241
Locke, John, 68, 72, 73, 82, 127, 133, 170, 367, 368
Lucretius, 279
Lyell, Charles, 388, 389, 390

Machiavelli, Niccolò, 117, 118, 127, 157, 194
MacLeish, Archibald, 227

Magic Mountain, The (Mann), 318
Main Street (Lewis), 60
Malthus, Thomas Robert, 390
Mann, Horace, 22
Mann, Thomas, 318
Mao Tse-tung, 287
Marcus Aurelius, 160
Marvell, Andrew, 226, 227
Marx, Karl, 68, 81, 144, 192, 287
*Mathematical Principles of Natural
    Philosophy* [*Principia*]
    (Newton), 71, 251, 364, 367,
    369
Mémoires (Marmontel), 360
Mendel, Gregor Johann, 155
Metaphysics (Aristotle), 275
Middletown (Lynd), 60
Mill, James, 359
Mill, John Stuart, 355, 358–62
Milton, John, 33, 217, 241
Molière (Jean-Baptiste Poquelin),
    220
Montaigne, Michel de, 11, 127,
    241, 242, 247, 268
Montesquieu, Charles de
    Secondat, Baron de, 170

Naked Lunch (Burroughs), 60
Nature of the Physical World, The
    (Eddington), 101
Newton, Isaac, 71, 73, 104, 128,
    249, 251, 254, 258, 259, 273,
    331, 334, 355, 364–69
Nicomachean Ethics (Aristotle), 80,
    88, 91, 144, 169, 275, 281,
    403
Nicomachus, 258
Nietzsche, Friedrich, 278
1984 (Orwell), 212
Norton, Charles Eliot, 376

*Observations on the Prophecies of
    Daniel and the Apocalypse*
    (Newton), 368
Odyssey (Homer), 78, 176, 217
Oedipus Rex (Sophocles), 221
On Liberty (J. S. Mill), 358, 361
On the Motion of the Heart
    (Harvey), 131
On the Nature of Things
    (Lucretius), 279
On the Origin of Inequality
    (Rousseau), 403
On Political Economy (Rousseau),
    403
On the Soul (Aristotle), 275
*On the Tendency of Species to
    form Varieties and on the
    Perpetuation of Varieties and
    Spheres by Natural Means
    of Selection* (Darwin and
    Wallace), 390
One Hundred Modern Poems
    (Rodman), 340
O'Neill, Eugene, 221
Optics (Newton), 71, 259, 364, 367
Oresteia (Aeschylus), 221
Organon (Aristotle), 281, 360
Origin of Species, The (Darwin), 62,
    71, 81, 92, 129, 155, 355, 387,
    390–96
Orwell, George, 212
Othello (Shakespeare), 203
Oxford Book of English Verse, 340
Oxford English Dictionary, 176

Palgrave, Francis Turner, 339
Paradise Lost (Milton), 33, 217,
    241
Pensées (Pascal), 278
Physics (Aristotle), 71, 275, 281

Plato, 79, 144, 145, 241, 242, 260, 270, 274, 275, 276, 278, 280, 281
Pliny, 179
Plutarch, 240, 241
Poetics (Aristotle), 78, 143, 275, 403
Politics (Aristotle), 64, 159, 194, 275, 355, 403, 404–6
Pope, Alexander, 11
Portnoy's Complaint (Roth), 60
Prelude, The (Wordsworth), 217
Prince, The (Machiavelli), 117, 157, 194
Principia [Mathematical Principles of Natural Philosophy] (Newton), 71, 73, 258, 264, 367, 368
Principles of Geology, The (Lyell), 388
Principles of Political Economy (J. S. Mill), 361
Principles of Psychology (James), 63, 72
Protagoras (Plato), 280–81
Proust, Marcel, 127

Racine, Jean, 221
Rationale of Judicial Evidence (Bentham), 361
Reader's Digest, 247
Representative Government (J. S. Mill), 358, 361
Republic (Plato), 241, 282
Rhetoric (Aristotle), 403
Rodman, Selden, 340
Rousseau, Jean-Jacques, 64, 170, 241, 403, 406–8

Science, 261
Scientific American, 261
Scott, Walter, 138

Selection in Relation to Sex (Darwin), 390
Seventeenth Century Background, The (Willey), 245
Seventh Letter (Plato), 280
Shakespeare, William, 37, 85, 93, 176, 215, 219, 220, 224, 225, 246, 334
Shaw, George Bernard, 220, 250
Short View of the Immorality and Profaneness of the English Stage, together with the Sense of Antiquity upon this Argument (Collier), 79
Smith, Adam, 38, 64, 81, 104, 144
Social Contract, The (Rousseau), 64, 170, 355, 403, 406–8
Solzhenitsyn, Alexander, 212
Sophocles, 220, 221
Spinoza, Baruch, 69, 155, 156, 277, 278
Spirit of Laws, The (Montesquieu), 170, 403
Stendhal (Marie Henri Beyle), 301, 302
Subjection of Women, The (J. S. Mill), 359
Summa Theologica (Aquinas), 121, 242, 276, 277
Symposium (Plato), 144
System of Logic, A (J. S. Mill), 361

Theory of Moral Sentiments, The (Adam Smith), 144
Thomas, Dylan, 223
Thoughts on Parliamentary Reform (J. S. Mill), 361
Thucydides, 234, 235, 236, 243
Thus Spake Zarathustra (Nietzsche), 278

Index

"To His Coy Mistress" (Marvell), 226

Tolstoy, Leo, 127, 174, 214, 215, 233, 301

Tom Jones (Fielding), 79, 219

Treatise on Light (Huygens), 364

Two New Sciences (Galileo), 71, 130–31, 260

Tyndall, John, 240

Ulysses (Joyce), 79

U.S. Constitution, 86, 87, 88, 89, 170, 358

Universe and Dr. Einstein, The, (Barnett), 60, 261, 262

Utilitarianism (J. S. Mill), 358, 361

Van Doren, Mark, 201

Variation of Plants and Animals under Domestication, The (Darwin), 390

Virgil, 217

Vita Nuova, La (Dante), 372

Wallace, A. R., 390

Walton, Izaak, 240

War and Peace (Tolstoy), 213, 214, 215, 301

Wealth of Nations (Adam Smith), 38, 64, 81, 144

Westminster Review, 361

What Men Live By (Tolstoy), 174

White, E. B., 212

Whitehead, Alfred North, 261, 262, 274

Whitman, Walt, 242

Willey, Basil, 245, 280

Wordsworth, William, 217

Wren, Christopher, 367

"You, Andrew Marvell" (MacLeish), 227

DR. MORTIMER J. ADLER

(December 28, 1902–June 28, 2001)

Chairman and cofounder with Max Weismann of the Center for the Study of the Great Ideas and editor in chief of its journal *Philosophy is Everybody's Business,* founder and director of the Institute for Philosophical Research, chairman of the board of editors of *Encyclopædia Britannica,* editor in chief of the *Great Books of the Western World* and *The Syntopicon: An Index to the Great Ideas,* editor of *The Great Ideas Today* (all published by Encyclopædia Britannica), cofounder and honorary trustee of the Aspen Institute, past instructor at Columbia University, professor emeritus at the University of Chicago (1930–52).

Ongoing programs started or developed by Dr. Adler include: the Great Books Foundation (with Robert Hutchins), the Basic Program of Liberal Education for Adults at the University of Chicago (with Robert Hutchins), the executive seminars of the Aspen Institute, the Paideia Project (a plan for major reform of public school education), and the Great Ideas seminars at the Center for the Study of the Great Ideas—all promoting liberal education through an understanding of great works of philosophy, literature, history, science, and religion.

Dr. Adler was a highly productive author, educator, philosopher, and lecturer. As an author, Dr. Adler wrote more than fifty books and two hundred articles.

DR. CHARLES VAN DOREN

(1926–)

Dr. Van Doren earned his B.A. at St. John's College. He has advanced degrees in both literature and mathematics from Columbia University. Dr. Van Doren taught English at Columbia University and was the assistant director of the Institute for Philosophical Research where he worked with Dr. Adler beginning in 1961. He has written and edited more than a score of books, many of them in the field of history. Most recently Dr. Van Doren is a professor of English at the University of Connecticut.